World Cities and Nation States

World Cities and Nation States

Greg Clark
Chairman,
The Business of Cities, London

Tim Moonen
Director of Intelligence,
The Business of Cities, London

WILEY Blackwell

This edition first published 2017
© 2017 by John Wiley & Sons, Ltd

Registered Office
John Wiley & Sons, Ltd, The Atrium, Southern Gate, Chichester, West Sussex, PO19 8SQ,
United Kingdom.

Editorial Offices
9600 Garsington Road, Oxford, OX4 2DQ, United Kingdom.
The Atrium, Southern Gate, Chichester, West Sussex, PO19 8SQ, United Kingdom.

For details of our global editorial offices, for customer services and for information about how
to apply for permission to reuse the copyright material in this book please see our website at
www.wiley.com/wiley-blackwell.

The right of the author to be identified as the author of this work has been asserted in
accordance with the UK Copyright, Designs and Patents Act 1988.

Library of Congress Cataloging-in-Publication data applied for

ISBN: 9781119216421

A catalogue record for this book is available from the British Library.

Wiley also publishes its books in a variety of electronic formats. Some content that appears in
print may not be available in electronic books.

Cover image: 123ArtistImages/Gettyimages

Set in 9.5/12pt Trump Mediaeval by SPi Global, Pondicherry, India
Printed and bound in Malaysia by Vivar Printing Sdn Bhd

10 9 8 7 6 5 4 3 2 1

For Julia and Lucy

Contents

Foreword

This book begins with a simple premise: if the 20th century was defined by the nation state, our current century will be one driven by global cities. Beneath this observation, however, lies a complex web of implications for leaders across the world and across levels of government and society. In this insightful book, the authors show how adaptive nation states, in partnership with dynamic world cities, point the way towards a shared global future.

In response to the rising role of cities, we need to rethink the traditional arrangements of power between nations and regions. As responsibility shifts downwards, we need to reimagine the roles of legacy institutions that were intended to mediate between countries and invent new institutions that connect and empower cities. And as these global cities expand, we need to ensure that prosperity does not come at the expense of sustainability and equity.

Accelerating urbanisation is a natural response to trends in the global economy. International trade encourages specialisation, which, in turn, rewards agglomeration. By clustering skilled workers and similar types of industrial activity, cities and regions become more innovative and more productive. And despite predictions to the contrary, the benefits of proximity in both manufacturing and services have only increased from new technologies, thanks to everything from shortened product cycles and rapid prototyping to increased demand for customisation.

Still, these very forces of concentration, globalisation and connectivity that are causing the emergence of global cities are also creating challenges within them. Their rise in prosperity can also often come at the expense of secondary cities, increasing inequality across places. As economic hubs, they become magnets for migration, leading to challenges around settlement and integration. And cities that grow too fast or whose growth is too ungoverned often can develop in inefficient and unsustainable ways.

In many parts of the world, governance at the city level is showing it can innovate much more quickly than national governments, and these innovations are being shared and adapted by agile networks of global cities. But the message of this book is that global cities and nation states share a mutual interest in inventing solutions to the problems of our new urban century, and giving cities the tools to implement them at scale. Nation states therefore still have a pivotal role to play. There are a number of areas – national defense, international trade and the social safety net – where national governments must continue to set the rules and provide a stable environment. They also remain the most important source of long-term and large-scale investments in basic research, setting the platform for an innovative economy. But within a host of other policy areas, the best role for national governments is to be a partner – allowing their global cities the flexibility to customise solutions to their distinct challenges.

The rise of world cities in the global economy is not disappearing anytime soon. This reality demands a re-evaluation of how cities relate to their respective nations and to each other. These pages offer that valuable analysis – including both a look at the current variation of government systems across the world and a perspective on what cities need moving forward.

Bruce Katz,
Centennial Scholar, Brookings Institution
June 2016

Preface

This book has grown out of an initial study that was prepared for the Moscow Urban Forum in 2014. We wanted to inform the global discussion about the ways in which nation states were adjusting to the globalisation of major cities. The debate within nations about the role of their largest and most globally oriented cities varies hugely from one country to another. In some countries this is almost a national obsession, with continuous argument about whether having a global city is a net advantage or disadvantage. In some other countries the debate is almost totally absent, with either complete invisibility or complete acceptance of the global roles of major cities.

For the original study we consulted numerous books and academic journal articles to capture the latest insight into how the rise of world cities is changing government structures in nation states, and how both city and national governments are adapting to the new balance of power. We reviewed prominent contemporary books written in Europe, Asia and North America, and drew from the most recent findings of the World Bank, OECD and relevant international financial institutions.

For this book we identified 12 major world cities that reflected a range of geographic locations, constitutional structures, city statuses and development stages. Together these 12 cities' GDP exceeds $7 trillion, accounting for roughly a tenth of global GDP. We gradually built up 12 case studies, drawing on recently published books, academic journals, independent media, international benchmarks and local studies and reports.

The ideas and arguments for this book evolved through extensive consultation with current and former senior members of city governments, and with national officials with responsibility for urban policy. Our research also engaged with political science and urban development experts in each of the 12 cities, as well as with business leadership organisations in many of the 12 cities.

We are very grateful to the following individuals who gave us their time and wisdom:

- Uma Adusumilli, Chief of Planning Division, MMRDA, Mumbai, India.
- Bruce Berg, Associate Professor of Political Science, Fordham University, New York, US.
- Claudio Bernardes, President, Ingai Incorporadora S/A, São Paulo, Brazil.
- Professor Neil Bradford, Associate Professor of Political Science, Huron University College, University of Western Ontario, Canada.
- Professor Miguel Bucalem, Director, USP Cidades, São Paulo, Brazil.
- Dr Xiangming Chen, Director of Trinity College, Hartford Center for Urban and Global Studies, Connecticut, US.

- Rt Hon Greg Clark MP, former Minister for Universities, Science and Cities, UK. (Now UK Secretary of State for Business, Energy and Industrial Strategy).
- Professor Alistair Cole, Professor of Politics, Cardiff University, UK.
- John Dickie, Director of Strategy and Policy, London First.
- Fernando de Mello Franco, Municipal Secretary of Urban Development, São Paulo, Brazil.
- Professor Meric Gertler, President of the University of Toronto, Canada.
- Dr Vincent Gollain, Director, Department of Economy and Local Development, IAU IDF, Paris, France.
- Professor Hiroo Ichikawa, Executive Director of The Mori Memorial Foundation; Dean, Professional Graduate School, Meiji University, Japan.
- Dr Yeong-Hee Jang, former Senior Research Fellow, Seoul Institute, South Korea.
- Bruce Katz, Centennial Scholar, Brookings Institution
- Paul Lecroart, Senior Urban Planner at IAU (Institut D'Amenagement et D'Urbanisme) Île de France (IDF), France.
- Professor Christian Lefèvre, Directeur de l'Institut Français d'Urbanisme, France.
- Sir Edward Lister, former Chief of Staff and Deputy Mayor, Policy and Planning, GLA, London, UK.
- Professor Hideo Nakazawa, Faculty of Law, Chuo University, Japan.
- Narinder Nayar, Chairman of Mumbai First, Mumbai, India.
- Dr Karima Nigmatulina, Director at the Institute of Master Planning, Moscow, Russia.
- David O'Rear, Chief Economist, Hong Kong General Chamber of Commerce, Hong Kong (until 2015).
- Dr Abhay Pethe, Vibhooti Shukla Chair Unit in Urban Economics and Regional Development, University of Mumbai, India.
- Professor Nirmala Rao OBE, Pro-Director, SOAS, London, UK.
- Dr Xuefei Ren, Associate Professor of Sociology and Global Urban Studies, Michigan State University, US.
- Anacláudia Rossbach, Regional Advisor for Latin America and the Caribbean, Cities Alliance; Director President of Rede Interação São Paulo, Brazil.
- Professor Andrei Sharonov, Dean, Skolkovo Management School, Moscow, Russia.
- Professor Enid Slack, Director, Institute on Municipal Finance and Governance, Munk School of Global Affairs, University of Toronto, Canada.
- Andrew Stevens, Senior Researcher, Japan Local Government Centre
- Professor Tony Travers, Department of Government, LSE; Director of LSE London, London, UK.
- Professor Aleksandr Vysokovsky, Dean of the Graduate School of Urban Studies and Planning, Higher School of Economics, Moscow, Russia.
- Professor David Wolfe, Department of Political Science, Centre for International Studies, University of Toronto, Canada.
- Professor Fulong Wu, Bartlett Professor of Planning at the Bartlett School of Planning, University College London, UK.

- Kathryn Wylde, President and CEO, Partnership for New York City, US.
- Norio Yamato, Assistant Manager, Corporate Planning Office, Mori Building, Japan.
- Professor Robert Yaro, Former President, Regional Plan Association, New York.
- Professor Natalia Zubarevich, Director, Regional Programme, Independent Institute for Social Policy, Moscow, Russia.

With special thanks to Emily Moir for her support in preparing the text and in enabling us to complete the project. With thanks also to Jonathan Couturier, Steve Howard and Dr Patrick Kilkelly for their invaluable research, insight and editing support. Responsibility for any errors is entirely our own.

Section I   Introducing world cities and nation states

1

Introduction: Clash of the centuries?

The emergence of 'world cities', urban areas that are becoming global in character and orientation, is one of the most important phenomena of our time. World cities[1] are where much of the money, the knowledge and the decisions that shape the 21st century are generated. Their influence has propelled humanity beyond the inflection point from the 'age of the nation state' and into the 'age of cities'. And yet this new age inherits all the identities, institutions and organising principles of the nation state system. The tensions, trade-offs and opportunities that arise out of this unstable equilibrium are the subject of this book.

World cities confront nation states with a historic opportunity and challenge. These dynamic agglomerations of people, industries and infrastructure have the

---

[1] In this book, a world city is defined as one that not only participates in national and regional networks, but also influences and directs global flows of trade, investment and population. World cities host high concentrations of industries whose value chains are globally integrated, such as banking, electronics, ICT, telecoms, cars and tourism. They serve as national, regional and global headquarters for globally trading firms. Their employment and productivity advantages are magnets for domestic and overseas migrants, and their political and cultural importance makes them popular visitor gateways and aviation hubs. World cities also tend to assemble major institutions of knowledge, culture and recreation. They are not always national capitals, not least because several federal nations have deliberately created alternative capital cities.

There is debate in the literature as to whether 'global city' and 'world city' should be used synonymously. We follow Christof Parnreiter in viewing the differences to be too small to demand a sharp separation in an overview of this nature. Cf. Parnreiter (2013).

World Cities and Nation States, First Edition. Greg Clark and Tim Moonen.
© 2017 John Wiley & Sons, Ltd. Published 2017 by John Wiley & Sons, Ltd.

potential to help a national economy be more globally connected and productive, and to spread multiple benefits across national systems of cities through connectivity, economic specialisation and co-operation. Their activities might increase the connection of their national economy to global systems of trade, investment and talent. They also provide entry points to international markets, and are the spur for entrepreneurship and clustering activity for globally trading firms and sectors. In an increasingly urbanised global economy, world cities help to build the 'business brands' of nations and provide them with reputational advantages.

But world cities also depend on nation states and national governments in order to manage the effects of their global integration. Rapid population growth and diversification, urban restructuring and a surge in international investment can lead to multiple challenges. Inflation, congestion, stretched housing and labour markets, exposed infrastructure deficits, land-use dilemmas, ill-equipped city systems, sensitive environmental weaknesses and social divisions can all be 'side effects' of becoming a world city.

At the same time, national governments want to pay attention to the performance of other cities, towns and rural areas, and many look to address the impact the world city has on how other cities and regions within the nation develop. The world city may be understood in theory to offer competitive advantages and major contributions to fiscal resources, but the most visible effects may be de-population or de-clustering of other cities, or extreme concentrations of business, jobs and investment in one place. These challenges lie at the heart of the relationships and friction between nation states and their world cities, and lead to concerns about whether the 'world city model' is always a good one to adopt. Such apprehensions were very visible during the debate in the UK as to whether to leave the European Union and the subsequent fallout of 'Brexit', but they are also becoming increasingly influential in many other world cities and nation states.

In the current period, some world cities and national governments are beginning to embark upon a range of different forms of negotiation and collaboration around these issues that have major implications for the futures of both. These emerging dialogues and co-operation aim to address the understanding of the world city model and its needs, enhance the complementary roles of multiple cities within a national system, increase or improve governance and investment in the world cities, or develop national policies and platforms that can support different kinds of cities with specific tools and interventions. In this book we explore this new ground by examining the different ways in which world cities and nation states are contributing to each other's shared goals.

Each city's organisational and legal framework is different and complex, and the range of institutional dynamics in the world's major cities has not been compared in this way before. The book draws on the latest practical experience of 12 cities around the world – in Asia, Europe, Latin America and North America – to identify the trends and innovations in relations between central governments, state or provincial governments and their main international gateway city. Drawing upon a mix of local and governmental insight and global expertise, we identify recent innovations and reforms in governance, communication, investment and planning between different tiers of government. The book pinpoints the potential for nation states to leverage their world city to achieve mutually beneficial national outcomes, but it also raises challenges to the world city model that should be the focus of concerted attention.

Urbanisation and globalisation: The age of world cities

History shows that cities tend to embrace international opportunities in waves and cycles (Clark and Moonen, 2013). Which cities take part in a given wave may depend on major geopolitical events, key industries, new technologies, connective infrastructures or the whims of city, mercantile and/or national leaders. What is clear is that today, more cities than ever are participants in the cycle of globalisation that began after 2008–9. Many of them have no prior global experience, while others draw on a legacy of earlier phases of outward-facing trade and engagement; as new sectors emerge and integrate, and as some countries increase or resume their global orientation, new world cities are emerging all the time.

One upshot of 21st century globalisation is that more countries have seen their leading city or group of cities become international commercial and corporate management hubs and visitor destinations, serving large customer and client markets in their wider regions beyond national borders. National policymakers find that these cities fundamentally alter the migration patterns of workers, set new business and service standards and have a major impact on the number and kind of international firms, capital and visitors that a nation attracts.

The previous cycles, in which world cities such as London, New York and Tokyo thrived, hinged on cities playing hub roles in finance, business, media, leisure tourism and commodities. In the current cycle, science, medicine, ICT, cleantech, traded urban services, higher education, design and real estate are now prominent activities for globalising cities. World cities have also become complex visitor economies – not just attracting holidaymakers but also students, researchers, events and congresses. Established and emerging world cities all compete for investors, entrepreneurs and start-ups by focusing on liveability, culture and urban regeneration.

This new cycle of world cities is shaped by a clearer grasp of the mistakes of the past and concerns for the future. The 2008–9 financial crisis exposed the weaknesses of city development approaches that had become over-dependent on one sector – be it financial services, real estate, IT or tourism. Its fall-out has also highlighted the fragile investment profile of many cities as they seek to update and renew their own systems – housing, education and infrastructure. It has also focused attention on cities' environmental and spatial resilience, and how to avoid becoming 'locked in' to an undesirable development path.

This current cycle has also homed in on the growing inequalities within and between cities, which has prompted a tide of pessimistic opinion in many countries opposed to the perceived impacts of the 'world city model'. In many cases, national leadership and public discourse have become more equivocal about whether and how to support major urban centres on their globalisation journey. This cycle of globalisation is therefore unusual because the growing international economic roles of world cities are coinciding with a rise in nationalism, separatism and hostility to immigration (Dowling, 2014; Hashi, 2014; Seib, 2014). These are difficult tensions to resolve.

The future imperatives for world cities

World cities face a number of similar or overlapping challenges that require facilitation and support from national governments. They have little choice but to adapt to increased competition for mobile firms, jobs, people, goods, capital and services (Herrschel, 2014). They face demands to address the externalities that accompany intense demand, such as housing supply constraints, income inequalities and over-burdened infrastructure. Most have to operate in a context of constrained public investment and cuts to intergovernmental transfers and grants. Sub-national public investment declined by up to a fifth within the OECD in the five years after the financial crisis, and evidence from non-OECD countries indicates this drop is even more stark (Allain-Dupre, 2015). Because even world cities have to achieve 'more with less', they have to appeal to alternative sources of international investment, which usually demands that they present a simple and consistent strategy, and assemble a clear pipeline of competitive projects for development. Given these combined imperatives, the leadership of world cities is by no means straightforward.

The distinctive elements of this new cycle of world cities – wide-ranging competition, new industry trends, strategic awareness and conflict between the 'winners' and 'losers' of globalisation – all demand a fresh set of relationships and partnerships with leaders and agencies in national government. Nation states are only just getting to grips with this new terrain. As this book demonstrates, the agenda for the future is now coming into view.

Nation states in the urban age

The 20th century is now, in retrospect, widely regarded as the century of the nation state (Waltz, 1999). The global economy experienced a sustained surge in growth and trade after 1945, and it is easy to forget that during those decades national governments deliberately tried to prevent industrial and office development becoming over-concentrated in their major cities. Subsidies, regulations, financial instruments and the relocation of business parks and public sector jobs were used to de-centralise economic activity and spread growth more evenly. Policies were also put in place to curb population concentration. This approach was evident in cities as varied as London, Paris, Seoul and Tokyo. Brazil went one step further and relocated its capital city from Rio de Janeiro to inland Brasília partly in order to de-centralise industrial activities and reduce growth in its large southern cities.

Not all national governments were proactive or successful in these efforts. Some tried to mitigate the externalities of their world city but succeeded only in disrupting cluster agglomeration and damaging overall competitiveness. Others failed to provide a consistent legal and regulatory framework or delivery mechanism to allow world cities to thrive. Many have now abandoned the hope of homogeneity on a national scale and are devising new approaches for their nation and world city (Bunnell, 2002; World Bank, 2009).

This book is about the transition that has since taken place from the age of the nation state to the age of cities. It explores how nation states are responding to the largely unanticipated urbanisation of the global economy with new policies, reforms and methods of joint working. It analyses whether, why and how nation states really have become more place-specific in their approach to their cities, and what the implications are for city competitiveness and national cohesion (Hill and Fujita, 2011).

The twin processes of urbanisation and globalisation have required nation states to re-think traditional approaches. Not only do they face the rise of world cities, they also have to recognise three other essential trends that are explained and explored in this book:

1. Metropolitanisation;
2. Systems of cities;
3. Internationalisation of multiple cities.

The first trend that nation states have to take seriously is the emergence of city regions and metropolitan areas. As cities grow they expand beyond their set borders and boundaries, and their economic and social 'footprint' becomes ever larger. If national and state governments fail to respond to this phenomenon, what follows are large and expensive co-ordination failures between neighbouring municipalities that are politically independent of each other and yet are functionally inter-dependent, sharing a common business community, labour market, infrastructure platform and housing system. National and state governments can adjust to the growth in city regions by changing the boundaries of cities, by creating additional co-ordination vehicles, by reforming city governance or by incentivising co-operation in other ways (Arretche, 2013).

Nation states have to adapt to a second trend – the need to accommodate 'systems of cities' with complementary roles (World Bank, 2009). Within and across national borders, networks of cities often form a complementary system of different functions and specialisations. This often demands new national approaches. In China, for example, since the mid-2000s the national urban policy has begun to plan its huge scale of urbanisation by identifying large regional city clusters as strongholds of future sustainable development. The Pearl River Delta, Yangtze River Delta and the Beijing–Tianjin–Hebei regions have all become the subject of regional plans, with the aim of accelerating development, bridging regional divides and restructuring the economy.

The third trend to which nation states have to respond is the emerging capacity of multiple cities in the same nation to acquire international roles. As new waves of globalisation occur, new economic sectors internationalise and integrate, and a larger range of cities has the potential to enter the global system of trade and exchange. This can lead to nations having more than one 'world city'. While this is already common in larger nations (for example, in the United States New York, San Francisco, Los Angeles and Chicago might all be seen as world cities, and in China Hong Kong, Beijing and Shanghai all have global reach and roles), this can also occur in much smaller nations. In Switzerland, both Zurich and Geneva are world cities. Elsewhere in Europe, Barcelona and Madrid, and Munich, Berlin and Frankfurt, are all examples of more than one city developing clear international roles within the same country. We find similar phenomena in

South Africa (Cape Town and Johannesburg), Australia (Sydney, Melbourne and now Brisbane) and Canada (Toronto, Vancouver and Montreal). In many other countries, from the UK and France to Russia and Japan, a second city has a clear aspiration to become the second world city to complement their more established world city sibling.

Having learnt some painful lessons from the past, nation states are beginning to identify the opportunities as well as the threats of globalisation and the rise of world cities. National governments can leverage world cities to achieve development goals that are otherwise hard to achieve. They have also become more willing to endorse urbanisation processes because to do otherwise would weaken their attraction as a place for capital or for talent (Herrschel, 2014). This book shows that territorial approaches adopted by national governments are at different points along a continuum between 'old-style' development policies and 'new-style' approaches. The agility with which countries adapt their ways of working shapes not only how effective they are in pursuing their development objectives, but also has implications for the fortunes of their most globally oriented cities.

In this book we evaluate how far world cities are moving forward to secure mutually productive relationships with their nation states and compatriot cities, and how much farther there is to go. We argue that there are many dimensions to this challenge that make it rather more complex than simply a question of growth and productive agglomeration. In the current cycle of globalisation, world cities have to develop the tools and the leadership to plan and guide their own success, but they also need national partners to help them achieve their competitive and citizen aspirations. Equally, world cities have to contribute actively to the health and vitality of the wider national economy, not just through redistributive fiscal mechanisms but also by acting as an interface for engaging with global markets and knowledge, and as a driver of complementary development and dispersed value chains. This also places responsibility on higher tiers of government to ensure that disparities do not become too great and to create viable strategies for balanced and complementary growth. This matrix of shared imperatives is displayed in Figure 1.1.

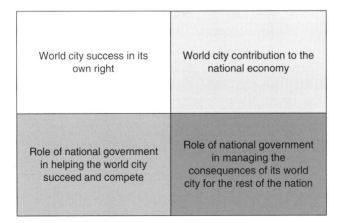

Figure 1.1: The four dimensions of successful national government and world city relationships.

Different models and starting points

The relationships between national governments and world cities are important and far-reaching in all cases, and the message from this book is that their character varies widely. As we show, the mega-trends of continental integration, globalisation and de-centralisation do not play out in the same way for all world cities. Each city inherits a different set of organisations, state structures and path dependencies (see Table 1.1). As such, when it comes to finding a new path conducive to the global urban age, they have a different set of constraints and needs.

Arguably the most decisive factor that shapes the relationship between world cities and nation states is the national system of government. There are essentially four basic types of political arrangement that set the terms for the responsibilities of national government and for the nature of the dialogue between a world city and its national government:

- Centralised unitary systems;
- Federal systems;
- Specially empowered cities;
- Independent city-states.

This typology is the basis for the following sections of the book which compare and contrast the intergovernmental relationships within these distinct models.

Centralised unitary systems

In centralised government systems, the central government controls most public spending and almost all macro policy on economic competition, taxation, infrastructure planning and immigration. These countries' world cities are usually the capital city and centre of state power, which offers the competitive advantage that

Table 1.1: Government systems and city designations in the 12 world cities

	National government system	Higher tiers of govt	Metropolitan government	Special designated city
Hong Kong	Unitary	1	No	Yes
London	Unitary	1	Yes	No
Moscow	Federal	1	Yes	Yes
Mumbai	Federal	2	No	No
New York	Federal	2	No	No
Paris	Unitary	1	Yes	No
São Paulo	Federal	2	No	No
Shanghai	Federal	1	Yes	Yes
Singapore	City-State	0	—	—
Seoul	Unitary	1	Yes	Yes
Tokyo	Unitary	1	Yes	Yes
Toronto	Federal	2	No	No

Note: Under Hong Kong's 'one country two systems model', the city has a high degree of legal and fiscal autonomy akin to a city-state, but within a Chinese national framework that controls security, defence, and foreign relations, and exercises influence more broadly.

national politicians are automatically aware of many of the city's obvious needs. In these nations the tensions between serving the needs of the world city and looking to the effects upon, and needs of, the second tier of cities and a wider set of regions, is often most acute. National leaders, therefore, tend to pay close attention to city policy and major city projects, and most large infrastructure projects depend on at least some national-level capital investment. National policies may also designate key clusters and business districts and set the standard of social housing and public services. Examples include New Zealand, the Republic of Ireland, the United Kingdom, the majority of African countries and, to a lesser extent, France and Japan.

Federal systems with a strong tier of state government

In many federal systems it is the state or provincial governments that are *de facto* world city managers. This 'middle' tier usually has the authority to decide all the policies that shape how the world city develops: governance, fiscal policy, infrastructure planning and the allocation of resources to urban development or elsewhere. Even though the world city is always by far the largest in the state, the electoral balance in state governments is often tilted towards rural areas or smaller cities. This means that state-level decisions rarely favour a pro-urban or pro-world city agenda.

Most world cities that operate under these arrangements are not national capital cities. Their relationship with the federal government is more remote, often mediated via a state or provincial government. Formally, these world cities are just one of several thousand municipalities vying for federal attention. This makes a customised relationship difficult, and puts the onus on city governments to be proactive and on the metropolitan area to self-organise. Sometimes, the regional expansion of a world city may even spill over the borders of more than one state or province – as with New York City and Brussels – giving rise to obvious co-ordination issues.

National governments in federal systems may issue directives, provide advisory support and fund programmes, but they do not become directly involved in urban governance, and the ministerial focus on the world city may be less sustained. With central grants typically comprising only 5–20% of city revenues, the government's main roles lie elsewhere: their control of economic, population and immigration policies; their ownership of strategic public land; their management of railways, ports and airports; their research and infrastructure investment programmes; their welfare and poverty initiatives; and their national urban and economic development frameworks. Examples of this model include Australia, Brazil, Canada, India and the United States.

Specially empowered cities

A number of world cities enjoy a high degree of autonomy despite being ruled in full or in part by a sovereign national government and/or operating within a federal system. These federal systems are effectively hybrids, where most of the territory operates through a states and provinces system, but larger and important cities may attain an equivalent status to a state or province and manage their own affairs more directly. Moscow and Shanghai are examples of cities that are directly recognised by their federal governments and have gained a high level of self-governing powers and fiscal resources. Hong Kong is a rather different and unique case, possessing a high degree of autonomy within the 'one country, two systems' approach. Abu Dhabi and Dubai constitute another model of highly empowered emirate cities within a broader confederation.

Independent city-states

A very small number of cities have a fully independent or autonomous structure that means they are not administered as a part of any national government, and have their own diplomatic and military apparatus. These function as unified metropolitan areas with a highly centralised, unitary government and a single parliamentary chamber. The city-state system assigns local bodies formal advisory and management roles, and so they do not form an empowered 'lower tier' of government that is found in cities such as London and Tokyo. Unlike other world cities, being a small city-state demands constant attention to resource management (water, energy). Singapore fits the city-state model more closely than any other major city. Cities such as Berlin and Hamburg are also sometimes described as city-states because of their high degree of self-government, but within this typology they belong among the specially empowered cities because they, of course, are subject to German federal legislation.

Other inherited factors

This book highlights three other important factors which shape the character of city-state relationships in the modern age:

- Size and scale;
- Political polarisation;
- The national system of cities.

First, world cities emerge in their own spatial context and evolve to have rather different population sizes and geographical scales (see Table 1.2 and Figure 1.2). Size alone is no determinant of the degree of global orientation or world city status. Dubai, for example, has rapidly emerged as a world city despite having a population of less than three million, whereas Mexico City and Cairo have only very limited functions of a world city despite their huge populations. Size and scale not only affect how world cities compete, but also affect their ability to thrive in inherited institutional frameworks. Land-limited cities such as Singapore have not spilled over into a manufacturing hinterland, whereas Hong Kong has been able to through its relationship with the Pearl River Delta. But, for many emerging world cities, the major challenge is dealing with scale and getting

Table 1.2:   Size and scale of world cities and world city regions

City	City population/m.	City size/ km²	Region	Regional population/m	Region size/km²
Hong Kong	7.3	1100	Greater Pearl River Delta	65	55,000
London	8.8	1500	Greater South East	24	39,700
Moscow	12.2	2500	Moscow and Moscow Region	19	47,000
Mumbai	12.6	440	Mumbai Metropolitan Region	21.5	4350
New York	8.5	1100	Tri-state region	23	34,000
Paris	2.2	105	Île-de-France	12	12,000
São Paulo	12	1500	São Paulo Metropolitan Region	21	8000
Shanghai	24.2	6200	Yangtze River Delta	100	100,000
Singapore	5.5	720	—	—	—
Seoul	9.8	605	National Capital Region	26	12,000
Tokyo	13.5	2200	Tokyo Metropolis	36	14,000
Toronto	2.9	630	Greater Toronto Area	6.7	14,000

Sources: Census and Statistics Department, The Government of the Hong Kong Special Administrative Region, 2015; Greater London Authority Datastore, 2015; INSEE, 2016a, 2016b; Russian Federation Federal Statistics Service, 2014; Municipal Corporation of Greater Mumbai, 2015; IBGE, 2015; National Bureau of Statistics of China, 2015; Department of Statistics Singapore, 2015; Seoul Metropolitan Government, 2015; Tokyo Metropolitan Government, 2014; Ontario Ministry of Finance, 2014; Statistics Bureau of Guangdong Province, 2015; Office for National Statistics (UK), 2014; United Nations Department of Economic and Social Affairs, 2014; United States Census Bureau, 2014; EMPLASA, 2016; Statistics Korea, 2016; Geographical Information Authority of Japan, 2014; OECD Stat., 2016.

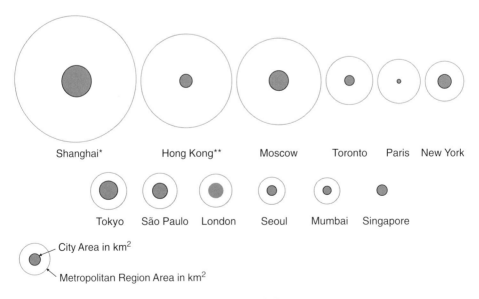

* Metro area = Area of Yangtze River Delta Economic Zone
** Metro area = Area of Pearl River Delta Economic Zone

Figure 1.2:   Comparative size of world cities and their metropolitan regions.

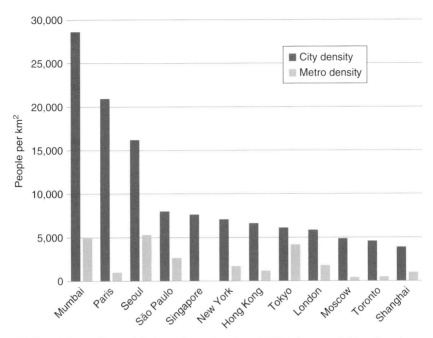

NB: Population and area data for metro regions from OECD where available, otherwise based on independent sources. Wider city-regional data used for Hong Kong and Shanghai.

Figure 1.3:   Comparative density of 12 world city government units and their metropolitan regions.

the national system to adapt to realities of massive urbanisation (Figure 1.3). Weak growth management resulting from underpowered city government and/or weak alignment between institutional and functional geography, often results in congestion, low productivity, inequality and inflation.

Given the different models of governance described above and the different patterns of 'shared authority' implicit in all of the models, it is clear that a high degree of negotiated collaboration between world cities and nation states is desirable. However, negotiated working is not always easy to achieve because of a second factor: intergovernmental conflict. Division along party political lines often influences the speed of progress for world cities. This is especially true in cities that are deeply polarised politically and ideologically, which, from this book's case studies, include São Paulo, Toronto and Paris, but also include cities such as Milan, Madrid, Brussels and Buenos Aires. In federal systems, the incumbent state government is often ruled by a different party to the city government. Inter-party rivalry can result in deadlock and tension, and brief periods of political alignment represent an important opportunity to build trust, deliver reform and push through projects.

A third factor is the national system of cities within which world cities sit. Capitals such as London, Moscow, Paris and Seoul have historically always been much larger than their national counterparts due to their lead roles in industrialisation, commerce, trade, institution hosting, diplomatic and media functions,

Table 1.3: Size of world cities' metropolitan areas compared to their nation state

	% of national population	% of national GDP
Singapore	100	100
Seoul	50	46
Tokyo	28	32
Paris	19	31
London	19	28
Toronto	17	17
São Paulo	10	18
Moscow	8	30
New York	5	8
Shanghai	2	4
Mumbai	1.5	7.5
Hong Kong	0.5	4

decision-making and even empire. The urban system may have evolved over time, but their position at the top of the hierarchy is absolutely unchallenged. This means that these cities dominate the political, economic and cultural life of their nations, and central governments are usually vigilant about their impact on national affairs. World cities that tower above the rest of their country's urban system have great advantages of agglomeration and political influence. However, sometimes they must also manage political grievances that emerge when disparities are perceived to grow too large.

In other city systems, world cities have developed in a context where some compatriot cities are as large, if not larger, than them and where they are not the automatic gateway for investors and decision-makers. At certain points in the last 50 years, Mumbai, Shanghai and Toronto have all been less favoured by their national governments compared to other large cities (Delhi, Beijing and Montreal, respectively), and each operates in a more evenly balanced system with three to six other major population and corporate centres. To a lesser extent, a diffuse national system is also visible in the cases of New York and São Paulo, where competitive or antagonistic relations with other big cities are much less common (Table 1.3). In this book we argue that the character of the national system of cities is important if world cities are to manage some of the negative externalities that accompany their own growth and success.

Overview of the book

This book is divided into five sections. Section I sets the scene for substantive case studies and analysis later on. In Chapter 2, we put the current dilemmas between world cities and nation states in historic context and review the existing literature that addresses this specific question. The status of the nation state amid the rise of world cities has been neglected and under-estimated. The chapter examines the new wave of optimism about cities' capacity to shape their own policies and destinies. It urges caution about this optimism and proposes a more comparative international perspective. Recent work on a wider mix of world cities and changing national governance is highlighted, which lays the groundwork for the approach taken in the rest of the book.

Sections II, III and IV examine the changing world city/nation state relationships on a city-by-city basis. Each section addresses different types of government systems which provide many of the initial conditions for how multi-level governance can unfold and evolve.

Section II examines 'unitary' systems, nation states whose sovereignty is concentrated within a single centralised government. This system remains the most popular in the world, adopted in more than three-quarters of nation states. There are several reasons why unitary systems were established. Frequently, they evolved from systems of monarchical rule where authority was enforced from a core power base. They were also a popular solution for countries that, when founded, were relatively ethnically and linguistically homogeneous. In this system, the spectrum of powers and autonomy that sub-national units such as cities or regions can exercise may vary, but always depends on decisions made by central government. In unitary systems, the largest and most globally oriented city is nearly always the capital city, which brings distinctive tensions in how the city itself is governed. Indeed, there are many examples where central governments have been known to abolish city or metropolitan governments altogether. The proximity of national politicians to the city itself, however, does ensure that the world cities featured in this section are always uppermost in public and political debate.

Chapter 3 picks up the story of London, a historically independent and assertive city in a highly centralised unitary government arrangement. London, in many respects, epitomises the challenges currently facing world cities, especially in terms of growth management, investment, national inequalities and political hostility. This chapter reviews the important cycles of improvement in city governance over the past 30 years and the role of actively engaged ministries and units within central government. Despite success with eye-catching co-funded projects, the city is now confronting the implications of a highly centralised public finance system and the unusually weak recent economic performance of the UK's large secondary cities. Despite the risks to London presented by the UK's decision to leave the European Union in 2016, the institutional development in and with cities since 2010 promises a new era of more negotiated intergovernmentalism and a more empowered system of metropolitan governments and combined authorities across the UK.

In Chapter 4 we review the other leading world city in Europe, Paris. As the capital of an archetypal centralised state, Paris has experienced a great deal of institutional re-shuffling in recent years amid the push to build a metropolitan approach to innovation, housing and social cohesion. This chapter describes the renewed engagement of senior national officials in the Grand Paris project, which has coincided with the ongoing fragmentation of the whole capital region into numerous spheres of authority. It assesses whether the latest cycle of reforms has the practical effect of enhancing Paris's capacity to deliver change at the pace and scale that is needed to address existing gaps. The Paris experience offers lessons about effective and ineffective state interventions in an institutionally overcrowded metropolis.

With a capital region of nearly half the national population, the city of Seoul plays a fundamental role in shaping the Korean economy and society. In Chapter 5, the role of the national government in supporting Seoul's transition into an upper-income world city is explored. As a designated 'special city' with its own metropolitan government and directly elected mayor, Seoul is emerging out of a long history of centralised rule. The city and nation state now have to negotiate the externalities of the capital's growth, including its under-managed regional scale of development and the limited attractiveness of Korea's second-tier cities. The chapter underlines the importance of national governments adopting different approaches to their world cities in new cycles of development.

The case of Tokyo, explained in Chapter 6, reveals the challenges of governing the world's most populated urban area in the context of persistent low economic growth and deflation. Tokyo is still the only city in Japan governed as a metropolitan prefecture, and has special fiscal and political autonomy that give it unusually wide tax-raising and service delivery capability. Policy co-operation between the city and the national government has been essential to revitalise the urban fabric and make Tokyo more open to investment, but the limits of its world city model are now being reached. The chapter provides perspective on the constraints that a national government can come up against in seeking to make reforms in the interests of the competitiveness of its world city.

Section III examines the challenges for world cities that exist in federal states where political power is more dispersed and when attention on leading cities is more inconsistent. Many of the largest and most diverse and influential countries have a federal character. In federal systems, state and provincial government units share sovereignty with the national government, which prohibits unilateral changes or reforms from the national level. In many cases, it is the states and provinces themselves which are unitary and have the authority to amalgamate or empower local municipalities. Different federal systems organise distinctive powers and responsibilities in governmental tiers, and so the relationship between the world cities and the national governments varies among the four systems outlined in this section.

Chapter 7 turns to India to explore the challenges of Mumbai, as a megacity and national financial hub, in negotiating support and reform from above. Mumbai is an example of a world city whose higher tier of government has failed to create the institutions or the planning and co-ordination mechanisms required to govern the metropolitan space. This chapter describes the mixed effects of past reforms and investments and explains how the Government of India policy has not created the conditions for the state government to overcome short-term political imperatives and act in the long-term interest of its major city. The current national government has been a cause for optimism around smarter and more business-friendly growth, but the chapter reflects on the urgency to make a step change that will allow Mumbai to avoid becoming permanently locked in to an unsustainable and unequal growth model.

New York City, the subject of Chapter 8, today has arguably the most remote relationship with its national government of any of the cities featured in this book. The lack of attention paid by the federal government to its main business hub in the past 20 years is contributing to unmanaged regional growth, underinvestment, an affordability crisis and environmental vulnerability. This chapter shows how federal support for New York City now tends to manifest in the form of crisis response. It highlights the risks that are even posed to world-class cities if national governments disinvest, apply rigidly prescriptive policies and become polarised along ideological lines.

Located 1000 kilometres south of the capital Brasilia, São Paulo's attempts to engage its federal government in recognising its position as Brazil's world city are the focus of Chapter 9. The city has still not come to terms with its earlier 50-year surge in in-migration and continues to face a substantial infrastructure deficit and major investment needs which require help from higher tiers of government. The chapter illustrates how fruitful relationships between federal and world city governments in emerging economies require committed leadership, especially in a context where large metropolitan areas lack recognition in national public life. São Paulo has worked hard to show it can be more than simply a tax resource for poorer regions and needs to be supported through fiscal reforms, funding disbursements and changes to regulation.

Chapter 10 returns to North America to explore Toronto's changing relationship with higher tiers of government. As Canada's first world city, the city shares responsibility and resources with the provincial government and the federal Government of Canada for different dimensions of urban development. The chapter highlights how strong government alignment and partnership was critical to Toronto's earlier emergence as a high quality 'city that works', but more recently fragmented financing and co-ordination have resulted in congestion, housing shortages and weak clustering. The failure of Canadian federalism to devise a focused and integrated approach to the distinctive needs and opportunities of its five major cities is analysed, as is the role of business and civic alliances in building bridges with Ontario and Ottawa.

The rich and complex history of some world cities is such that they have developed unusual arrangements that grant them a special degree of autonomy. These cities are the subject of Section IV. Some have attained semi-autonomous or autonomous capacity as a result of historic colonial relationships. Others have been nominated as 'special' cities, nominated or designated by national governments to be granted self-government rights and privileges. In this section we highlight how, for these 'special' cities, autonomy and empowerment can work as a double-edged sword. Increased independence brings well-known and well-understood benefits but also places burdens and expectations on cities, and can present trade-offs in terms of how they compete and position their economies in global markets.

In Chapter 11 we review the special autonomous region of Hong Kong, whose relationship with mainland China has been the subject of major scrutiny and debate since the British handover in 1997. In the two decades since, Hong Kong has received careful and timely support from the Chinese central government which has enabled it to open up a vast market as an economic hinterland and to retain its own policies on immigration, currency and media. The chapter emphasises Hong Kong and China's inter-dependence as they pursue their development goals, in spite of the controversy over Beijing's desire to retain its role as gatekeeper to the city's leadership. Hong Kong is well placed to benefit from further approved integration with the Pearl River Delta, support for its global renminbi trading status and license from central government to play the role of laboratory for Chinese and Asian urbanism.

Moscow is a federal city of Russia and has far-reaching budgetary and strategic capacity compared to nearly all other Russian cities. In Chapter 12 we focus on the role of the federal government in enabling Moscow to attract international capital and traded sectors, but also in managing (or not) the asymmetric patterns of development in Russia that threaten to overload demand on the capital city. Moscow's powerful city government maintains a close, complex and largely positive relationship with the federal government, and the latter has offered support for high-profile projects such as metro modernisation, Moscow River upgrades and the 2018 World Cup. This chapter witnesses the process of centralisation and concentration underway in Russia and the importance of consistency and coherence in national policy to prevent and mitigate negative side effects.

As a city with the powers of a province, Shanghai also has a distinct relationship with Beijing in the Chinese government system. In Chapter 13 we trace how the city's 30-year period of growth has been navigated and negotiated with central government. In particular, Shanghai stands out for its pragmatic and opportunist leadership that is prepared to take risks and draw on personal connections with national leaders to pursue ambitions for the city. Equally, Shanghai's success is an important element of the legitimacy of the Chinese Communist Party. Despite occasional scandals, central government support for Shanghai has been remarkably successful but new tactics will be required to achieve a more sustainable and regional model of urbanisation.

The final case study in Chapter 14 of this book belongs fittingly to Singapore, the only world city that is a fully independent city-state. For more than 50 years the island nation has not had to negotiate intergovernmental relationships in the same way as other cities. This chapter reflects on the handicaps as well as the advantages of not having a nation state above and around the city, and the role these have played in fostering openness to global investment and expertise. The dividends of a highly integrated government with minimal co-ordination failures are discussed to show Singapore has avoided many of the critical mistakes or problems that afflict other established world cities. The chapter concludes by underscoring the incomplete model of the city-state's success, and the potential to incorporate non-governmental sources of leadership to help address deficits in the next cycle.

Together these 12 case studies reveal a great deal about the changing intergovernmental nexus world cities have to navigate. In Section V we summarise and evaluate the findings across these dozen cities. In Chapter 15 we focus on the putative needs of the world cities themselves, and how national governments have been reacting to new imperatives. But the needs of the world city are only one half of the story. In Chapter 16 we turn the tables to evaluate how world cities are responding to the unintended consequences that globalisation has had on national development patterns, and, in particular, the spatial imbalances that have appeared as agglomeration in globalised urban areas has intensified.

"Over the long run and at a distance, cities and states have proved indispensable to each other," wrote Charles Tilly in his 1990 classic *Coercion, Capital, and European States, AD 990–1990*. This book's essential contribution is to show why this mutual inter-dependence is not set to evaporate in the so-called urban age, with all its talk of the 'rise of city-states'. Instead, a spirit of partnership between them will be essential to their survival, sustainability and success.

2

Cities and nation states: The story so far

For most of the 6000 years since written records began, sovereign states have been the exception, and empires, tribes, kin groups and theocracies the norm. Throughout these six millennia, fully fledged cities have risen, thrived and fallen, across Mesopotamia, the Indus Valley, Egypt, Afghanistan, China, Europe, North America and elsewhere. Up until the last 500 years, the idea of a system of national states was unfamiliar to nearly all of these cities. Today, in 2016, the world's territory is divided up into nearly 200 independent states, each of which recognises and accepts each other's sovereignty. If we take a long view, the co-existence of cities and nation states is still a recent phenomenon.

In this chapter we examine the ways in which cities and nation state relationships have evolved and how they have been explained in recent academic and policy literature. In particular, we focus on how the twinned phenomena of urbanisation and globalisation in the last 40 years have prompted a great deal of speculation on the demise of nation states. Conjecture of this kind has tended to fall into two camps: either pessimism about the rise of cities in thrall to neoliberal dogma, or optimism that cities can prevail over national dysfunction through their own independent initiative and invention. We propose an alternative approach that traces the empirical activity of city decision-makers in tandem and partnership with higher-tier government officials and departments. This alternate perspective has the advantage that it can account for the rich diversity of values, systems and institutions currently at play in the global system. It also offers a more curious and more modest take on the

World Cities and Nation States, First Edition. Greg Clark and Tim Moonen.
© 2017 John Wiley & Sons, Ltd. Published 2017 by John Wiley & Sons, Ltd.

changing character of the city–state relations, identifying change amid continuity rather than radical disjuncture often posited elsewhere.

The rise of the nation state and the implications for cities

The roots of what we now call the nation state began in the late Middle Ages, at a
time when cities themselves were thriving (McNeely, 1995). Cities such as
Baghdad, Damascus and Samarkand were advanced intellectual and production
centres. Other places along the Silk Road, such as Merv in modern-day
Turkmenistan, Bukhara in modern-day Uzbekistan and Rayy in Persia, were
viewed as beautiful trading cities (Frankopan, 2015). In 13th and 14th century
Europe, the biggest concentrations of power and control over trade routes were
found in cities. Dozens of dense urban centres in modern-day Italy, Germany,
Switzerland and France became autonomous from aristocratic rule, and many
acquired budgets larger than any neighbouring kingdom. Sovereign kings and
princes often granted rights and privileges to towns in order to protect urban residents from lords. Some of the first town councils were established at this time, and
the recognition of free towns allowed cities in the Hanseatic League to grow in size
and influence. In countries where the sovereign lacked full authority, such as in
Italy and Switzerland, cities became independent republics whereby the nobility
came to live in the city itself. In others, cities were never fully independent but had
certain tax benefits and gained representation in national assemblies. Many cities
in Europe also became sanctuaries for people and capital because they were more
secure and protected. Europe was connected to the Middle East and to Asia through
its highly interconnected cities (Smith, 1776; Lachmann, 2002, 2010).

In the centuries that followed, almost every city with independent military
power gradually came under the control of states (Lachmann, 2002). The early
Italian wars between 1494 and 1530, at a time when the Mediterranean was
Europe's richest region, saw the leading Italian city-states unable to withstand
the might of state armies. Artillery had begun to make it possible to besiege large
cities successfully. From the 16th century onwards in Europe, rural interests
began to persuade or compel city elites to abandon their independence and enter
into institutionalised nationwide networks. Political power moved north-west
in Europe, and after the Treaty of Westphalia in 1648, at the end of Europe's 30
Years War, the nation state quickly became the dominant form of territorial
organisation. Cities grew politically dependent upon them.[1] A process of consolidation of political power unfolded, as up to 500 city-states and state-like authorities eventually were reduced to fewer than 30 states. Nascent industry moved
out of cities and into the countryside. By 1700, city-states and urban leagues had
all but disappeared (Tilly, 1990; Coatsworth *et al.*, 2015). Cities still thrived and
many maintained their previous growth, but they now tended to operate within
empires, as with the Mughal cities of Lahore and Delhi, the Ottoman cities of

---

[1] One of the immediate effects of the Treaty was the obstruction of overseas shipping traffic to
Antwerp, which ended its brief stay as the most dynamic commercial city in Europe.

Istanbul and Aleppo, and the Russian imperial city of St Petersburg, or within consolidated states such as Amsterdam and Leiden in the Dutch Republic.

The reasons for the rise of the nation state are much debated. One thing which is clear is that nation states operated a more efficient model than city-states and other forms of authority. In particular, their control of larger populations generated more tax revenue and military resources just as conflict and border defence became more expensive. Nation states were not designed or pre-planned, but through constant processes of trial and error, they became very effective at collecting resources, managing distribution and providing services and security (Poggi, 2004). Many scholars also argue for the impact of the early modern military revolution, the rise of international trade and the implications of imperialism and slavery, all of which favoured the rise of large, professional, bureaucratic nation states at the expense of self-governing cities. But it is important to remember this transformation did not wholly uproot the geographies of commerce. In *The Wealth of Nations*, Adam Smith (1776: 336) noted that political capitals were rarely centres of trade and industry beyond what was necessary for local consumption. He highlighted only London, Lisbon and Copenhagen as cities that were home both to parliaments and to international trading functions, because business conditions are often unfavourable in political centres. In fact, cities such as Lyon, Guangzhou and Boston played key trading roles despite limited political powers. Although nation states were in the ascendancy, "cities remained the driving forces" and their states "had to come to terms with them and tolerate them" (Braudel, 1991: 341).

Competitive nation states cemented their foothold through mercantilist tactics and policies in the 17th and 18th centuries. Trade tariffs, restrictions and monopolistic practices were all introduced as states, notably Holland, France and England, competed for commercial dominance. Mercantilism was a catalyst for European nation states to grow long-distance trade, to build empires and to embed national homeland identities. Although mercantilism ultimately helped trigger rapid urbanisation and industrialisation, this occurred in tandem with political centralisation and the rise of nationalism. For Peter Taylor (1995), this period began the high watermark of 'mutuality' between cities and nation states, as national policies were generally well aligned with the economic development imperatives of large, productive cities. Tacit partnerships between nation states such as the Netherlands, the United Kingdom and the United States, and their fast-changing cities (in modern-day 'Randstad', the North of England and the Rust Belt) were a hallmark of the late 18th and 19th centuries. Agglomeration processes intensified in the 19th century and urbanists of the time predicted a future of uneven growth in favour of the big industrial cities (Weber, 1899).

The two world wars ultimately eroded some of the imperial hierarchies. As the aspiration and the struggle for self-determination gained momentum throughout Africa, Asia and Latin America, many political organisations and ethnic groups adopted the national territorial model for organising a society and a political system. In the post-war decades, the nation state became globally established as the dominant unit for political organisation and economic regulation, with the support and guidance of supra-national organisations. Under the moral and political aegis of the United Nations, the nation state was ratified and sustained as a sovereign institutional platform that had the final say on the trade of goods,

Table 2.1:   Differences between traditional and new development policies (developed from OECD)

	Traditional development policies: 'Regional planning' 1950s to 1990s	New development policies: 'Territorial development' 1990s to present
Objectives	Balance national economies by compensating for disparities Narrow economic focus	Increase regional development performance across the whole nation Integrate economic with spatial, environmental and social development measures
Strategies	Sectoral approach	Integrated development programmes and projects
Geographical focus	Political regions	Metropolitan regions and economic regions
Target	Lagging regions	All regions – Metropolitan regions – connections between regions and across national borders
Context	National economy	International economy and local economies
Tools	Subsidies, incentives, State aid and regulations	Assets, drivers of growth/productivity, soft and hard infrastructures, skills and entrepreneurship, collaboration incentives, development agencies, co-operative governance, financial intermediation, investment incentives
Actors	National governments and sometimes regional governments	Multiple levels of government, private and civic actors, implementation agencies, collaborative governance. A major role for business and civic institutions

the attraction and investment of capital and on the negotiation of trade agreements and strategic alliances. National-level policies supported processes of mass production and consumption to manage demand, and national political cultures fundamentally shaped the character of their leading cities.

In nearly all countries, and especially in advanced industrial democracies, the big cities in the post-war era were rarely more than the administrative 'tool' for policies devised by national or state government decision-makers (Giersig, 2008). 'Regional' policies were widely introduced to balance national economies and integrate lagging regions through subsidies, incentives and regulations (Table 2.1). National governments in centralised states frequently tried to limit the influence of larger city governments that did not follow instructions. Organisations such as the District de la Région Parisienne and the Government Office for London were established as branches of central government operating at the regional level, reporting directly to the state. In London's case, the defiant city government was abolished altogether in 1986.

Nation states and the 'world cities' literature

Since the 1980s, many analysts of global economics and politics have tended to give less analytical priority to the nation state and much more to the transnational networks that connect and are constituted by global cities. The contention that newly labelled 'world cities' would begin to detach from their wider national economy and society was, in hindsight, somewhat over-stated. It is arguable that this approach tended to exaggerate the effect of short-term changes in international finance and under-estimate longer-term changes in the domestic market and domestic economy (Gordon, 1999). Nevertheless, the framing of global cities in a world of declining nation state power has been widespread and influential and deserves to be analysed in more detail.

As national leaders and governments came to power with new economic solutions and ideas, a wave of liberalisation began in the global economy that saw flows of capital, goods, information and labour accelerate faster than political structures could adjust. Cities that had been in a spiral of decline and de-population as a result of de-industrialisation and disinvestment suddenly appeared more flexible than their national governments at taking advantage of the new order; some rapidly became switchboards for key corporate decision-making and negotiations between national and international representatives in government and business alike. Analysts and commentators searched for new conceptual tools to grasp this change.

The emergence of a new way of thinking about cities coincided with a wave of optimism and prophecy about the future of global society, as the Berlin Wall came down, the Soviet Union collapsed and regional economic integration accelerated. Francis Fukuyama's (1989) 'The End of History' thesis famously declared the triumph of Western liberal democracy and the inevitable supremacy of global capitalism; this had an echo in the 'end of the nation state' foreseen by management and economics analyst Kenichi Ohmae (1995). Ohmae viewed nation states as inefficient and bureaucratic obstacles to globalised economic growth. As businesses increasingly operated in transnational spaces, he argued, the nation state was becoming obsolete. This reflected a widely shared view that the shared goals of economic policy after 1945 (full employment, stable prices and a steady balance of payments) had reached an impasse and were no longer deliverable via the nation state. Economic and political change led many to argue that other levels of government were now more relevant than the nation state (Horsman and Marshall, 1994; Jessop, 1997).

It was in the context of this new consensus that the notion of the 'world city' really took off. It had already gained currency through the influential work of John Friedmann (1986) in his article, 'The world city hypothesis'. The world city, according to Friedmann, is a node within a global economic system that locates its production and markets in certain key sites, and where connections between them form a network of world cities. Drawing on a neo-Marxist explanatory framework, a hierarchy could be drawn of world cities, divided into 'core' and 'semi-peripheral' countries and, within these, into primary and secondary cities. The core primary cities were considered to be Tokyo, Los Angeles, Toronto, London and Paris. These cities have 'global control functions' for corporate headquarters, international finance, global transport, communications and business services, and they facilitate the flow of capital and talent among them.

Friedmann's work gave rise to a series of studies investigating the 'world city hypothesis' (Therborn, 2011: 272). World cities are, in this hypothesis, those which concentrate financial services activity and associated support services. The leading cities were designated 'command centres' thanks to their role as nodal points in globalised business and world financial markets (Sassen, 1999; Therborn, 2011). A 1995 collection entitled *World Cities in a World System* updated and developed the hypothesis (Knox and Taylor, 1995). One important principle of the paradigm is that the mutuality between cities and states has declined as a result of trans-state capitalist processes first set in train by the United States in the post-war era, which has resulted in the unprecedented influence of the global economy on domestic economies (Taylor, 1995).

Many studies identified erosion in the authority of central banks and state regulation. European states were seen as increasingly powerless in governing the market institutions that operate from their jurisdictions, and a similar toothlessness was observed of the US Federal Reserve (Germain, 1997; Dyson *et al.*, 1998). As the effectiveness of monetary and exchange rate policy instruments and credit controls declined, nation states were viewed as impotent in controlling global business in major cities. The central banking institutions of any single state were thought to be unable to significantly control world credit practices. Some proponents argued that the notion of a national economy was obsolete, that London may no longer need Britain, and New York could dispense with the United States, given the global networks and priorities of each (Langley, 2002).

For a previous generation of sociologists, such as Immanuel Wallerstein, nation states had been the key agents in the global system. For this new wave of 'world cities' scholars, leading cities are the drivers of change, with the capacity to shape, coerce, exploit and co-operate. In *The Global City: New York, London, Tokyo*, Saskia Sassen (1991) identified the differentiation of businesses' activities in the global marketplace, which leads to much greater complexity in their management functions. Business outsourcing to specialised firms that operate internationally strengthens the city-to-city networks and creates a tightly linked web of cities all hosting globalised businesses and services (Sassen, 2005). For Sassen, "the economic fortunes of these cities become increasingly disconnected from their broader hinterlands or even their national economies" and much more indexed to global demand (ibid: p. 30).

This view is a response to the increasingly specialised economic roles world cities play in their national system of cities and the global system. Financial services have indeed been a key driver of world cities' global orientation in recent cycles. Most world cities have a disproportionately large financial and business services cluster compared to the rest of their nation states (see Table 2.2). In terms of gross output, Hong Kong's finance and business cluster is 12 times as large as its share of the Chinese population, for example, and Moscow's concentration is nearly five times. At the opposite end of the spectrum, relative concentrations in Seoul and Tokyo are much lower (1.3–1.5 times) because of their more diversified roles in technology, R&D, chemicals and other sectors which are also traded globally.

On the other hand, world cities are at different stages in cycles of industrialisation and de-industrialisation. Hong Kong, New York, Seoul and London all have a lower share of manufacturing relative to their population size, having made a

Table 2.2:　World cities' share of national economic output in financial services
and manufacturing

	% of national share of business/ financial services sector	Sector size compared to share of population (average = 1)	% of national share of manufacturing sector	Sector size compared to share of population (national = 1)
Hong Kong	6.3	11.99	0.1	0.26
London	44.3	2.02	15.9	0.73
Moscow	38	4.78	13.8	1.73
Mumbai	5.7	3.4	3.5	2.06
New York	11.4	1.91	3.0	0.50
Paris	40.4	2.15	19.1	1.02
São Paulo	27.1	2.76	21.2	2.16
Seoul	67	1.39	31.9	0.66
Shanghai	6.1	3.47	4.5	2.55
Singapore	100	1	100	1
Tokyo	43.9	1.47	24.2	0.81
Toronto	27.6	1.65	19.2	1.15

Source: Istrate and Nadeau (2012).

full transition into a more diversified services economy. But not all established world cities have shed their manufacturing capability. Paris, Toronto and Sydney retain a *larger* share of the manufacturing economy relative to their population size. Meanwhile, Shanghai and São Paulo are still industrial powerhouses for their national and continental economies.

The impact of the 'world cities' paradigm on urban and political research was significant and wide-ranging. In particular, it triggered a new programme of investigation into the changing scales of government and governance. Analysts highlighted three trends: (i) the 'hollowing out' and redistribution of state capacity 'upwards' to supra-national levels and 'downwards' to sub-national and local levels; (ii) the integration of new, non-government partners into the project of governing; and (iii) a more strategic and international focus to policy that focuses on ability to innovate and compete globally (Jessop, 1997).

What the paradigm often neglected, however, was the ways in which nation states still played important facilitating roles in the new cycle of globalisation. New national policies began to focus on supply-side factors to achieve competitiveness. Even in more centralised countries, central governments no longer directly allocate production, capital, land and labour to different parts of the country. In one notable example, in 1994 China enacted a revolutionary fiscal reform to de-centralise its system and encourage city governments to lease state-owned land for revenue. In the case of Seoul and Tokyo, their respective national governments have shifted from their policies of de-concentration from their capital cities in favour of improving urban quality in them. Since the 1980s, nations have become more *place-specific* in their approach to economic development. Some nation states have clearly recognised the fact that flows of capital and content increasingly take place between cities, and that policy design and implementation can often be more effective and accountable in cities (Hill and Fujita, 2003; Amen *et al.*, 2011).

A return to city-states?

Alongside this economic divergence of world cities and nation states, commentators in this period also identified a resurgent *political* tension between leading cities and their national governments. An early example of this friction was visible in New York – mayoral candidate Norman Mailer proposed to secede in 1969, and President Gerald R. Ford later refused to bail out the City in the midst of its fiscal crisis in 1975. This was followed by the failure of President Jimmy Carter's urban plan in 1978 (Smith, 2002). London also witnessed its fair share of political friction in the 1980s and central government eventually abolished the Greater London Council. Later, the OECD (2005: 124) highlighted many other cases where the efforts of city governments to seek opportunities at the global level and to acquire more fiscal and legislative flexibility led to conflict with higher-tier governments who were unconvinced of the "positive-sum gains in de-centralisation."

The rise of intergovernmental antagonism has stimulated a recent second wave of studies that has sharpened the analysis of how world cities and nation states now interact. Within the discipline of international relations, scholars have begun to recognise the central significance of large cities to the more globalised political order (Curtis, 2014, 2016). World cities are viewed as holding more potential to address transnational challenges (for example, climate change and terrorism) than hierarchical and centralised state structures. Given the paradigm shift from (national) government to (international) governance in the 21st century, world cities are understood as key actors within this new framework (Acuto, 2013). Scholars have also highlighted the way in which high-speed rail links, air-traffic routes and digital infrastructure between major cities challenge the presumption of territorial sovereignty that has predominated for the last 200 years. The hegemony of nation states has, on this view, already been partially displaced by the fluid networks of world cities and will be radically disrupted in the next few decades. The OECD (2016) captures this zeitgeist when it asks rhetorically, "are cities the new countries?" These narratives recognise that these city-led processes are nascent, although from a global perspective there is a risk of exaggerating or pre-empting the extent to which major cities are yet able to "bypass traditional hierarchical and state dominated channels" (Curtis, 2014).

One of the most advanced contributions to this debate has occurred in the distinct context of the post-crisis United States. Urban experts and policy advisers there have hailed a recent 'metropolitan revolution' in which the traditional relation of federal and republic is being inverted (Katz and Bradley, 2013). From this perspective, the federal centre has come to be viewed as bureaucratic, compartmentalised, reactive, short-sighted and overly legalistic. In contrast, cities are innovative, integrated, flexible, long-sighted and outcome-directed. In some ways this binary view is the latest in a long historical literature which understands cities as embodying capitalism and freedom and states as embodying coercion and feudalism (Pirenne, 1925; Tilly, 1990; Braudel, 1991). At the same time, Benjamin Barber and others have proposed, with only some rhetorical exaggeration, that cities should 'rule the world' (Barber, 2013). Barber cites New York's former mayor Michael Bloomberg, who once declared, "I have my own army in the NYPD, my own state department," and, when asked what would happen if Washington did not like it, responded, "well, I don't listen to Washington very much" (ibid: 6). In the same vein, it is now common for analysts to describe London, New York and Paris as 'city-states' whose characteristics make them "heirs to Athens" (Mount, 2015). From the perspective of some proponents of this new world order, national political control over cities is on the wane and opportunities to reduce it further should be pursued.

Reasons for caution

The two waves of the 'world cities' literature we have highlighted here by no means share everything in common. There are empirical and conceptual disagreements about the extent to which cities (individually and collectively) can shape their own destiny, and ideological differences about the extent to which the rise of world cities should be endorsed or resisted. But they do share, even if implicitly, a conviction that cities have the capacity to supplant nation states and transform the political order in the not-so-distant future. Yet the literature asserting the economic and political ascendance of world cities has also been criticised from different angles as speculative, parochial.

First, some commentators have voiced concerns about the limited empirical evidence for the world city paradigm. Its analysis of world history is often described as abstract, speculative, too caught up in meta-narratives and ultimately unverifiable. The lack of attention paid to the relations between world cities and the less globalised national system of cities is also a barrier to a more comprehensive perspective of urbanisation (Polese, 2005; Beaverstock, 2011; Parnreiter, 2013).

Second, there is also sustained criticism of the Western-centric character of the world city literature. A Euro-American bias, it has been argued, implicitly sets up world cities such as London and New York as a benchmark against which other globalising cities might be judged. This leaves cities in the global South 'off the map'. The world city narrative risks overlooking the connection between and significance of hundreds of cities and millions of people to the world economy (Robinson, 2002; Massey, 2007; Watson, 2013). Furthermore, even among the largest and most globalised cities, the examples and models tend to be drawn from familiar Western cases rather than wider illustrations such as Tokyo, Seoul and Shanghai which became global within developmental states, and which operate in very different national systems and regional alliances. These alternative perspectives make clear that national governments are especially crucial in emerging world cities that are still growing in population, scale and prosperity. Until very recently there has been almost no attempt to explore the range of ways in which nation state and city actors behave and the different competitive and institutional constraints they face (Hill and Kim, 2000; Rohlen, 2002; Hill and Fujita, 2003; Hill, 2004; Zhang, 2014; Bunnell, 2015).

There is, thirdly, concern that the world cities paradigm over-emphasises the economic significance of world cities and removes nation states too quickly from economic analysis. Markets are embedded in wider social and political relations and reflect decisions made by state authorities. States create and reform the legal and financial instruments necessary for global interaction, and world cities are often critically reliant on states to bail them out in times of financial or environmental crisis (Smith *et al.*, 1999; Therborn, 2011).

Recent literature on the intergovernmental tensions that arise in the current cycle of globalisation and urbanisation has belatedly started to highlight the multiple Western and especially non-Western approaches to these dilemmas. These are valuable as they illustrate the rich variety of world city/nation state relationships and the hybrid forms of adjustment and negotiation that are emerging. It highlights the imperative to look more closely at international experience, as we do throughout the rest of this book. Following Ardalan (2004: 218), we argue that "in order to understand how national governments respond to globalization one needs to understand what goes on inside the nation state."

The ongoing relevance of the nation state

Despite the prevailing optimism that exists about the capacity of large cities to catalyse global change and to win major reforms that can enable them to take the lead over their own development, there are several reasons to think it may be premature.

The first and most obvious problem is the hyperbole of the claim that nation states do not matter any longer. In many or even most cases, nation states are not just 'bulwarks' against openness, or against the threat of ceding power to world cities and global forces. Nation states also continue to play a critical enabling role and, of course, underpin city activities by providing regulation, security and a powerful source of territorial identity. Around the world, many have even tried to reassert their functional importance in governing an urbanising economy. Globalisation also offers opportunities for national governments to achieve development goals that were otherwise impossible. Some analysts note, for example, that states now tend to endorse urbanisation processes because to do otherwise would weaken their attraction as a place for capital or for talent (Ardalan, 2004; Herrschel, 2014).

The relevance of nation states to world cities is immediately visible in their overall territorial policies, which have evolved at different paces and scales over time. In the post-war era, most states developed *regional* policies, which traditionally sought to constrain growth in the most developed regions and incentivise growth in other regions. Meanwhile, urban policies between the 1960s and 1990s traditionally focused on ameliorating urban problems rather than recognising the economic potential of cities and systems of cities. Neither of these traditional regional or urban policies fitted well with the globalisation

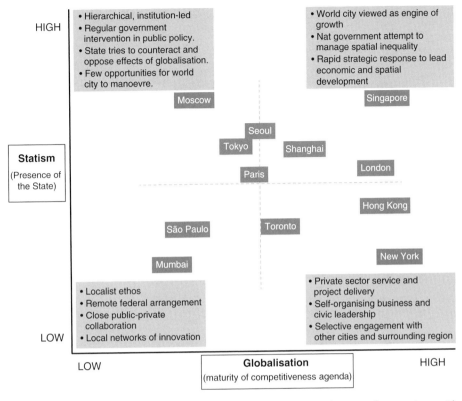

Figure 2.1: Typology of world cities and nation state traditions of engaging with globalisation.

of cities and city-regions, where the dynamics have been more about capturing internationally contested opportunities. But around the world, the tools used for effective spatial development are quickly changing. Globalisation places new stresses on how national and sub-national economies perform, and is influencing the ways in which national development policies are designed and executed. These are summarised in Table 2.2.

The range of regional and urban policies adopted in the past highlights how cities have become world cities in very different ways, because they are immersed in different economic and political traditions that shape the character of their engagement with international affairs and opportunities (Xu and Yeh, 2011). Drawing on a model developed by Herrschel (2014), we may see cities falling into one of four quadrants that reflect their national government's level of involvement and commitment to globalisation (see Figure 2.1):

1. World cities in an interventionist and relatively mono-cultural state that has been reluctant to proceed with liberalisation and other openness reforms. Often, their national governments have tried to 'balance' development and build the domestic assets to be competitive, but often agglomeration builds up around the main city. Examples include Moscow and Seoul.

2. World cities that operate in a bureaucratic and professionalised state structure that is, for historic and size reasons, tactically committed to internationalism. These cities look to integrate a pro-global approach across nearly all areas of government policy and delivery. The classic example here is Singapore, and we may also place Abu Dhabi and Dubai in this category.
3. World cities in a market-oriented economy that receive minimal support from the national government. They tend to exist in a 'low-investment, low-return equilibrium' that encourages experimentation to finance and initiate large projects. As a result, these cities tend to have high-quality local leadership and engaged business communities that closely monitor strategic needs. An obvious example would be New York.
4. World cities in a fragmented government system that have a distant or antagonistic relationship with national/federal government, especially in relation to fiscal needs. They tend to have a shorter history of global engagement and rely on strong local institutions and commercial expertise to provide direction and responsiveness to international competition. Examples include São Paulo and Mumbai.

   Of course only some cities fit squarely in one of these quadrants – many others may be considered 'hybrids' in that they possess characteristics from more than one quadrant. This model complements but is distinct from the organising typology of political systems featured in this book – unitary, federal and special status cities. It highlights the fact that some federal systems have allowed their world cities to be highly open to global opportunities (for example, US/New York) while others have been rarely or sporadically global in their economic development agenda (India/Mumbai, Brazil/São Paulo). Similarly, unitary nation states can be positive (UK/London) or more ambivalent (Russia/Moscow) towards global influences and the effects of globalisation for long stretches at a time. These default political and cultural stances to globalisation are often quite deeply bound up with the self-identity of nation states. Although they do change over time, they may be hard to shift quickly and political leaders have to work within established parameters.

   Whichever end of the spectrum world cities find themselves in, the incentive structure built into national frameworks fundamentally shapes outcomes of urban growth and development. There is growing evidence, for example, that the character of a fiscal system can incentivise unwanted sprawl and destructive competition between municipalities, unless there is judicious reform at the national level (Tompson, 2015). States often also hold the key in terms of how efficient and how specialised the use of inner city land is, and how well integrated new migrants are. For these reasons, the World Bank (2009: 3) argues that "urbanization is too important to be left to cities alone" and requires sustained national dedication. Findings from the OECD (2013) also indicate that growth, sustainability and inclusiveness policies in cities are more effective when there is close partnership with national policy-makers. States may face the choice of whether to retreat from responsibilities for urban and metropolitan issues, or to rebuild their capacity to engage effectively with economic change in their leading cities (Xu and Yeh, 2011: 8).

What is clear, however, is that world cities have had to adapt to nation states whose governmental institutions are sometimes slow to react, or where effective laws take too long to come into force. This is already very visible with issues such as air and water quality, business and investment climate, and climate change. With the latter, prominent city governments take action on global warming despite the absence of national policies, through local regulations, programme administration, procurement policies and property management (OECD, 2010). Contributors to the World Bank's Sustainable Cities agenda have argued that "national governments can easily step up to the plate" by removing policy barriers for world cities to act on climate change, and improving communication between levels of government (Comstock, 2012).

National governments have begun to respond to the needs of world cities, recognising their importance to the national economy (OECD, 2006). Some realise that world cities are different to other cities, whether in terms of size, density, financial needs, administrative strength and/or the complexity of their challenges (Slack and Côté, 2014).

As we shall see, there are examples of national governments that accelerate funding for transportation infrastructure into and within world cities, to enable them to function as gateways and serve as markets for production centres across the country. Reforms led by higher tiers of government have also devised improved governance models for cities, while improving financial systems is also widely regarded as essential to the long-term success of cities and nations (World Bank Institute, 2014). One study found that seven of fourteen nations had developed special compensatory measures to help world cities manage the unique costs of hosting political functions, and the associated infrastructural and security strains of being a high-demand city (Young, 2008). There are also examples where states increase capacity and incentives for smaller municipalities in world cities through training and shared services (Kübler and Rochat, 2013).

The imperatives for national governments do not just apply to established and high-income countries. After a cycle of extraordinarily dynamic growth, world cities in emerging economies are entering a new period of challenges that will rely critically on their national governments. Countries such as Brazil, Russia and China have begun to experience slower growth and job creation as their export-driven models suffer. These countries are witnessing the limits of their respective macroeconomic approaches, whether they have hinged on a credit-fuelled consumer boom (Brazil), on commodities (Russia) or on high corporate and sovereign debt levels (China). The ability of emerging world cities to come through economic headwinds like those experienced in 2015–16 may depend on the resolve of their national governments to enact structural reforms to reduce bureaucracy, enhance the role of the private sector and, in some cases, to increase national fiscal spending of their own. National partners are also responsible for working effectively and intensively with the major international investment banks (for example, the Asia Infrastructure Investment Bank and the World Bank) in order to ensure delivery of key infrastructure projects in major cities. And new dilemmas have arisen as to how to channel national resources to cities in ways that can encourage ambition, innovation and partnerships with civic and private sector organisations.

Summary

Claims about the demise of sovereign national governments in a globalised and highly urbanised world have proven exaggerated. National governments certainly no longer have absolute authority and tend to negotiate and experiment with regional and city partners. This process is very visible in cities such as Paris, where political relationships between the different tiers have improved over time and a more multipolar system has evolved. But even when nation states no longer dictate policy, they continue to play critical roles. Their ability to manage and control migration into, and often across, their territories affects the talent strategies and population management planning of world cities. Their choices about where to locate national military, trade, research or scientific facilities can have big impacts on agglomeration. Their planning policies and regimes can enable or constrain the local governments in world cities as they try to adapt to infrastructure demand, reverse urban sprawl and make developments more attractive to international capital. The way they lobby for intergovernmental rules, treaties and regulations has big implications for their leading cities' reach and competitiveness. Their response to key industries during economic downturns, whether through economic stimulus, grants or tax, tariff and regulatory adjustments, can inject momentum for a new cycle of growth in a sector, or can stop it in its tracks. And their redistribution of revenues can be critical to national cohesion (Singapore Ministry of Finance, 2009; Turok and Parnell, 2009; NYC Mayor's Office of Operations, 2010; Chase, 2013). Unfortunately, however, these national-level interventions are not always successful and often create unintended consequences and path dependencies for both world cities and for the wider nation that are difficult or costly to escape.

In 2016, world cities "sit at the confluence" of the commercial push for competitiveness and efficiency, and the agenda of the state political structure (Herrschel, 2014: 3). In the modern history of nation states, the relationships between major cities and their national governments has been one of tension, trade-offs and diplomacy. For some, there is "no way to fully resolve these tensions" simply because citizen needs will inevitably clash with the policies and priorities of national government (Young, 2008). But there are signs that a new phase of dialogue and reform has begun, one that acknowledges the mutual requirements and responsibilities of cities and national governments, and which recognises their inter-dependence. The next three sections of this book explore the latest progress in different kinds of world city.

Section II World cities in tight nations: Unitary systems in transition

London: From centralism to negotiated growth management

Daniel Chapma (2014), licensed under CC BY 2.0

World Cities and Nation States, First Edition. Greg Clark and Tim Moonen.
© 2017 John Wiley & Sons, Ltd. Published 2017 by John Wiley & Sons, Ltd.

London is the capital and 'front door' of a densely settled, medium-sized island nation which is also the world's fifth largest economy. As Europe's leading gateway for companies, capital and talent, London is just over half way through a 60-year cycle of rapid population growth, from 6.5 million to 11 million. It now has more people living within the city limits than ever before as well as a substantial commuter catchment across the Greater South East (Table 3.1). The city has a unique global reach in its DNA as a result of centuries of trade, empire, openness and diversity, and has recently applied these strengths to become a world leader in financial and business services, creative and media production, design and higher education.

London's recent success and growth brings major redevelopment, investment and growth management challenges. The city anticipates generating 1.3 million extra jobs in the next two generations but has to achieve the space, accessibility and affordability to accommodate this growth. As by far the United Kingdom's largest, most productive and competitive city, it also faces significant national political obstacles to gaining a consensus to support its global city growth agenda, encapsulated in the national referendum decision to leave the European Union in June 2016. Across the nation there is a perception that London is now a 'remote, elitist, unaffordable and decadent centre of globalisation', and that it has benefited unfairly from central government investment over the past two decades (Brown, 2016: 5). The political repercussions of 'Brexit' threaten to partially erode the framework that provided so much success for London in the last 25 years (for example, if the UK leaves the European Single Market in financial services) and to delay the next cycle of projects on which London relies.

At the same time, any comparative analysis of London's relationship with national government cannot escape the fact that the city exists in one of the world's most centralised government systems. Central government controls over 90% of public spending and borrowing, and all macro policy on economic competition, taxation and immigration. The city is unique in the UK in having a metropolitan government with an elected mayor (although others are about to follow), but London Mayoral powers are limited compared to other world cities, and local government roles are shared with 33 London boroughs that deliver the majority of local services.

This chapter emphasises how London's governance has gone through several important cycles in the past 30 years: from the abolition of the citywide government, the creation of the Government Office for London in the 1990s, the increasing self-organisation of the London business community, and finally the

Table 3.1:   London's metropolitan area: size and economic performance

% of national population	% of national GDP	GVA per capita vs national average (1)	City global competitiveness rank	Country global competitiveness rank	Annualised employment growth 2000–14	Annualised GDP growth 2000–14	% of national employment
19%	28%	1.44	2	10	1.1%	1.3%	20%

Source: Parilla et al., 2015; OECD Stat., 2014; World Economic Forum, 2015; EIU, 2012.

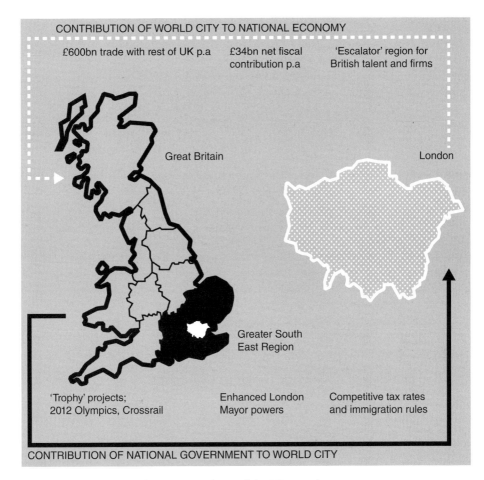

Figure 3.1: Reciprocity between London and the UK central government.

creation of a new two-tier metropolitan system shared between the 33 boroughs, the Mayor and Greater London Authority (GLA). London's 21st century framework has been supported by actively engaged ministries of central government and the Prime Minister's Office, and the Mayor's powers have incrementally grown. London now has its third mayor, and both previous mayors achieved considerable impact through influence, networking and diplomacy with central government. As a result, London is perceived to have improved the management of its transport challenges and its international promotion (Figure 3.1). However, the relationship between the Mayor, the London Assembly and the boroughs has not always been well articulated and this has been an ongoing source of dissatisfaction.

This chapter also highlights the limitations of the UK's centralised finance system, whereby London has had to 'bid' for financial support from central government for large 'trophy' projects (for example, the Jubilee Line, Millennium projects, the Olympic Games, Crossrail 1, Crossrail 2). The city's very success in advocating for this investment has exposed limitations in an arrangement whereby projects can only be mounted one at a time, each requiring extensive case making, protracted negotiation, promotional and lobbying effort. The emphasis on eye-catching projects eclipses London's more systemic investment needs, and the city has responded by developing long-term infrastructure plans to explain the investment gaps, priorities and costs to central government.

London's transformation as a world city now gives rise to widespread political concern that the capital's contribution to national economic growth (net fiscal contribution, access to world-class expertise, innovation spin-offs, professional development) no longer outweighs the negative effects of its tendency to 'suck in' talent, jobs and investment from the rest of the UK. This perception is heightened by the unusually weak economic performance of the UK's large secondary cities. London is an example of the way in which a world city can become increasingly divergent from its nation state, economically, culturally, demographically and politically, and of the political risks if gaps widen between those who benefit from a city's global status and those (within and outside it) who feel they do not. London's experience illustrates the importance for world cities and nation states to strike new deals and arrangements that adequately respond to these changing realities.

London's historic relationship with central government

London's history of maritime discovery, trade, navigation, banking, insurance, asylum, freedom of speech and association and openness to minorities all date back to its founding purpose as a Roman trading post. London has a rich tradition of local government going back to 1185 when the City of London was founded to express the mercantilist ethic of local businesses. The City first received a self-governing charter in 1067 and ever since it has played a dual role as a trading centre and a fiercely independent government that has resisted reform or assimilation.

The UK national government has wielded centralised power over London's investment and policy goals for several centuries. The country's small size, history of unifying separate kingdoms, parliamentary tradition and intensity of industrialisation, trade and empire led to an unusual concentration of the national population in London and economic activity in the City of London. Central governments have therefore long been concerned about the city's impact on national affairs, and vigilant about the risk of London self-government. Fragmentation within London's self-government has also been an issue.

London's pre-eminence is an enduring feature of the British urban system that has not always been popular across the nation. King James I (1603–1625) despaired of the unconstrained growth of the capital: "Soon London will be all England". In 1722, writer Daniel Defoe remarked that London "sucks the vitals of trade in this island to itself". A century later, journalist William Cobbett described London as "the Great Wen of all" – an overcrowded city which drained the life from the rest of the UK (cited in Travers, 2004). This view can still be heard in popular discourse.

As London expanded and became an imperial capital, its needs were periodically met by a responsive central government. Parliament introduced a

Metropolitan Board of Works in 1855 to oversee infrastructure development, and later created a London County Council, which gave the city a directly elected authority for the first time. Meanwhile, the larger northern cities had considerable autonomy and throughout the late 19th century were led by philanthropically minded Victorian industrialists and reformists. This constituted a so-called golden age of city leadership in the UK that ushered in new civic institutions and built a legacy of high-quality infrastructure. As such, neither London nor other British cities were subject to excessive centralisation until the mid-20th century and the establishment of the welfare state.

In 1944, the national framework for London's future development was set out in the Abercrombie Plan. The Plan's recommendations included the creation of a Green Belt and eight 'New Towns' beyond London; the plans were enthusiastically pursued from the 1950s onwards. The containment of growth by the new Green Belt encouraged 'leapfrog' development into distant towns in the 'Home Counties', which absorbed much of London's functional population over the subsequent half century. With the Home Counties evolving into a new suburbia and a market supply region for an expanding London economy, academics and business leaders in the capital had begun lobbying central government to create an institution to govern the built-up area of London and to set up a commission into the future of the capital's governance. This eventually resulted in a Royal Commission which proposed a Greater London Council (GLC) in 1960 – agreed to by Parliament in 1962. Under the new system, the Council was assigned few strategic responsibilities while the new and enlarged boroughs were given more powers (Travers, 2015).

In the post-war decades, London began to experience the effects of de-industrialisation, and this process coincided with a national policy to equalise and de-concentrate growth. The lack of new investment in the northern cities and then the Midlands had also left these regions struggling with industrial decline. National government identified London's primacy as 'the regional problem' and responded with several regional balancing policies to shift economic activity from the capital (Massey, 1979). Supported by the London government of the time, these policies saw London lose more than one million people to the surrounding Greater South East, and fall to its own 100-year population low of 6.7 million by 1985.

Together, the post-imperial years, the excessive damage and de-population after World War 2 and then the successive waves of de-industrialisation hit London very hard. How that de-industrialisation was both contested and managed, and how London was encouraged to shift rapidly into advanced traded services, explains why and how it took a path to world city status in the 1990s and 2000s. Initially, London became the UK's guinea pig for post-industrial development in the 1980s. Central government established a new kind of urban development corporation in London that could bypass local authorities' planning and investment powers in order to activate economic growth in derelict brownfield areas. The London Docklands Development Corporation was the pioneer, overseeing the regeneration of the Isle of Dogs into a new financial centre – now Canary Wharf. Around the same time it became apparent that many of London's post-war housing developments had been poorly designed and constructed. Over the past 40 years they have required sustained intervention and investment from central government, in partnership with local boroughs, in order to remodel and renew them.

Central government's relations with the London city government and several 'New Left' borough councils reached an all-time low in the mid-1980s. Amid open political hostility, the GLC leadership defied many national initiatives that were intended to improve competitiveness and inspire an outward-looking agenda in other UK cities. Central government responded in 1986, coincidentally the year of London's Big Bang in financial services, by abolishing what it saw as a bureaucratic and anti-business GLC. In a new, more centralised framework, the London councils had to 'bid' for central government funds for regeneration projects, and a number of 'quangos' – taxpayer-funded organisations – gained remits over specific city functions.

A hiatus in London government therefore appeared just as the city began to take on new global business roles. In the years after 1986, London's future was managed by four main actors: the boroughs, the City of London Corporation representing the historic commercial centre, central government departments and the Government Office for London, a small central government body with a budget of just £1 billion that was not equipped to play the role of a metropolitan authority. The lack of citywide direction was compounded by the nationalisation of the business rate in 1990, which reduced incentives for the local boroughs to attract investment.

The abolition of a citywide government saw working relationships begin to flourish between national leadership and a new London growth coalition. Positive, pragmatic and less ideologically politicised partnerships between London boroughs and businesses created a recipe that the central government was prepared to support. A Cabinet Sub-Committee for London was created in 1992, chaired by the Secretary of State for the Environment. In 1993, central government supported the creation of the London First Centre, which promoted London internationally for the first time. When the new Labour Government was elected in 1997, the momentum grew towards the re-establishment of a capital city government. A new era began for London with the election of the first Mayor and the creation of the Greater London Authority (GLA) in 2000.

London entered into a pattern of bidding for financial support from central government and other agencies such as lottery funds for large 'trophy' projects. This process began with the Docklands regeneration and Channel Tunnel Rail Link, and expanded with the Jubilee Line extension, South Bank development and Millennium projects (for example, the London Eye, the Millennium Dome, the Tate Modern and the Millennium Bridge) in the 1990s. This stimulated confidence in London's capacity to implement regeneration and waterfront projects successfully with national financial backing.

The return to city government and changes in city powers since 2000

Since 2000, the innovation of London's mayoral system and citywide government has been a major anomaly in British governance. Power in London has, in effect, been shared between the central government and its agencies, the citywide government (the GLA) and the 32 local boroughs (some of which are also called cities) and the ancient City of London. Well over three-quarters of the money spent both by the Mayor and by the boroughs comes via central government grants and programmes, rather than locally generated and managed funds. Each year the Mayor negotiates with the Government over the size of the GLA's grant, and must constantly lobby to achieve strategic goals or to pay for new items of infrastructure. The first two London Mayors, Ken Livingstone and Boris Johnson, were very effective at using their profile to advocate for modest concessions for London.

The Greater London Authority Act that set up the new mayoral system left many opportunities for central government to intervene in city government activity (for example, to impose a minimum budget for police or for transport). Central government also gave only modest funding to the London Development Agency (now closed down) and the surrounding Regional Development Agencies. But it did also create legislation allowing the city to introduce a Congestion Charge scheme and agree a ten-year transport investment plan to pay for major rail and bus improvements.

In the past decade the UK government has decided to manage the stresses of London's world city growth path rather than intervene to change the formula for success. It has focused on promoting London as an international city and sought to manage the growth it brings by improving public service delivery, high-capacity transport, social inclusion and quality of life. The Prime Minister's 2004 Strategy Unit expressed the prevailing attitude, namely that "London's challenge is to resolve tensions arising from its intensity". In return, London did not challenge the growing net fiscal outflows (in the region of £15 billion +/– £5 billion in most years since 1990) to the rest of the UK that resulted from its success.

The post-2000 citywide government system has fostered an increase in innovation in the way major projects are financed. Although the new transport authority (TfL) has received central government grants, it has also been authorised to borrow without the consent of central government (but within 'prudential', official rules), and has been able to use the city's Congestion Charge to generate net revenue of over £1 billion. A new funding structure was agreed for the £15 billion cost of Crossrail – one-third central government grant, 30% from London business rates and an infrastructure levy, and almost all the rest from the city government (GLA) and TfL. Even the £9 billion public sector funding for the London Olympics was only two-thirds provided by central government, with the city government and National Lottery paying the rest. Increasingly, London infrastructure has become more dependent on 'value capture financing' that leverages the value created in surrounding commercial and residential development, rather than relying on central government grants (Rogers and Blight, 2012; Crossrail, 2016; Transport for London, 2016).

Revisions to the GLA's powers in 2007 and 2011 have given more powers to the Mayor of London on climate change policy, planning and housing. The central Government Office for London was abolished, and the Mayor and GLA have taken on incremental additional powers. They have gained land acquisition and social housing powers from the national Homes and Communities Agency, which means London receives grants from central government for housing purposes. Mayoral Development Corporations have been created for specified areas, while London has a single Enterprise Panel, with working groups to manage and advise on future infrastructure, skills and employment, future sectors (digital, creative, etc.) and small businesses. London has been able to prepare the most convincing and far-reaching set of strategic plans of any British city – from economic development to spatial to environmental and cultural strategies. The city has shown the national level that city governments and local authorities in the UK do have the capabilities and enthusiasm to assume new responsibilities.

Central government was undoubtedly vigilant in its support of London's financial services sector needs after the 2008–9 financial crisis, despite the public backlash against the banking industry. It successfully resisted European regulation, reduced the top rate of tax to 45%, cut the bank levy and supported initiatives for London to become a leader in Islamic and yuan-denominated finance. UK government has continued to support a competitive and stable corporate tax regime, and to defend the City of London against new rules that have threatened to raise costs and legal barriers to London's foreign exchange trading. Support for the City of London post-Brexit is a priority for central government, not least because of the proportion of UK tax take its activities generate.

In 2016 central government is still very much a key player in London. It has final authority over public spending, economic competition, taxation and immigration levels and vital public infrastructure decisions. Its approach to public finances fundamentally shapes the capacity for London's boroughs to plan and develop the city's neighbourhoods. It treats the activity of governing London as a shared endeavour with the GLA and the boroughs and there is substantial and active co-operation between them and the national ministries. These include, in particular, the Prime Minister's Office and the Treasury, but also the Department for Communities and Local Government, the Department of Transport, the Home Office and the Foreign and Commonwealth Office. The role of the Mayor is still very much linked to the ability to use influence, network and publicity to raise awareness of London's needs to these departments. As Mayor Boris Johnson explained in 2013, "that is part of the pitch I have to make to government. If you want London, the motor of the economy, to keep roaring, then you must make sure that you invest in infrastructure, housing and transport" (Johnson, cited in Pickford, 2013).

In summarising the first 16 years of the new governance system in London, the national Communities and Local Government Committee (2016: 42) simply states that, "Devolution to London…has been a success." That notwithstanding, London's governance arrangements still have some major issues to address in the future. These include:

- What is the right level of fiscal autonomy for London and other UK cities? Do the current set of growth deals and settlements with the larger cities go far enough and will they be implemented effectively?
- What is the right number of boroughs and competences for the local tier of government in London? Is 33 boroughs (32 plus the City) the right number and can they work well together in larger units and with the citywide GLA and Mayor?

- Does the role of the London Assembly within the GLA need to be refined and recast? At present it is largely a scrutiny body for the Mayor. Is that the right role?
- How can the Greater South East, London and its city region be best organised? Does it need more co-ordination?

These questions are all regularly debated in London's ever-open and vibrant governance discourse, and have taken on even more pertinence since the UK referendum decision to leave the European Union.

The national system of cities: London and the UK

London's globalisation and metropolitanisation have had a profound impact on cities all over the UK. The large provincial British cities – Manchester, Birmingham, Leeds, Bristol, Glasgow, Edinburgh and Cardiff – all depend on London for some element of economic success. London also has strong corridor links with regional cities such as Bournemouth, Brighton, Oxford, Reading, Swindon, Cambridge and Peterborough, as well as small cities just beyond the Greater London border (Taylor *et al.*, 2009).

In the last 30 years, London has functioned as an 'escalator region' that attracts and hones the best and most ambitious talent from other British cities, before many members of the professional workforce then return to other regions with enhanced skills in later life. This, combined with the influx of well-qualified foreign workers and dramatic improvement in its own school education, has seen London's labour force become much more educated over the past two decades. But in recent years concerns have been raised that the 'escalator effect' is diminishing and talent that is honed in London no longer re-locates as frequently to other UK regions to increase productivity there (Champion, 2008).

Central government has become more alert to the performance gap between London and the rest of the UK. During the boom from 1997 to 2006, London and the south-east was responsible for 37% of the UK's growth in output. Since 2007, the share has soared to 48%. London and its wider region makes a larger per capita contribution to national finances, as its high-paid and profitable sectors generate much more income tax, corporation tax and business rates. London also concentrates the major share of new job growth (Chakrabortty, 2013; London Finance Commission, 2013).

The controversy about the London–UK disparity has been fuelled by a perception that the capital has unduly benefited from central government investment decisions since 2000. A 2015 report argued that planned public infrastructure investment allocated to London amounted to over £5300 per capita, compared to just £400–£1900 per capita in other UK regions (Sheffield Political Economy Research Institute, 2015). One reason why London secures more capital investment is because of the way it has combined different sources of financing to make projects viable, as it has been able to exploit its high land values for private investment. The investment gap is made starker by the under-performance of England's secondary ('core') cities. Only one of the eight core cities (Bristol) has a per capita output above the national average, a situation that is almost unique among developed nations.

Meanwhile, London's directly elected mayoral system, with a very visible figurehead, has become an attractive model for some other large British cities. Those cities that have chosen elected mayors – such as Bristol and Liverpool – have gained a clearer voice in dialogue with central government. They also have a mandate to implement strategic decisions and a window of tenure security through electoral cycles. However, an alternative governance model has also become very popular for some other major UK cities. The Combined Authority, first developed by Greater Manchester and now pursued by several other city regions is a means to achieve combined governance without creating an additional elected tier, while Greater Manchester will adopt a directly elected mayoral model from 2017. Local governments in these locations agree to form a combined government for certain services, and local politicians then play both local and city-regional roles as leaders of the combined authority as well as their local roles. This reduces the perceived problem in the London arrangements where boroughs, the Assembly and the Mayor each operate as part of different structures.

The austerity era and devolution to city regions

One of the impacts of the financial crisis in the UK was the push towards public spending austerity that saw the central government look for new ways to streamline government. In 2010 the new national coalition government established a new ministerial position, the Minister for Cities and The Constitution. From 2013 to 2015 the ministerial post was located in the Cabinet Office supported by a Cities Policy Unit as well as officials in the Department for Business, Innovation and Skills (BIS), the Department for Communities and Local Government (DCLG), the Department of Transport and HM Treasury. This period illustrated the role of the Cabinet Office in developing the government's coordinating role around infrastructure and national policy priorities, while partnering closely with cities to identify individually negotiated local and metropolitan solutions.

During the course of the 2010–2015 government, the Minister for Cities oversaw an important shift in central government's allocation of new powers to England's larger cities in the form of 'City Deals.' These are negotiated packages of reform and devolution, agreed with the national government's Cities Policy Unit. They give England's second cities more control over local public spending and growth decisions. Each Deal is different: Manchester can 'earn back' money generated from local investment in transport infrastructure; Bristol can pool business rate income; and Leeds can raise funding for apprenticeships. A Local Growth Committee, operating as a sub-committee of the UK Cabinet, provided inter-ministerial co-ordination and oversaw the first programme of City Deals. Since 2015, the Cabinet Office, DCLG and BIS collectively oversee a Cities and Local Growth Agenda.

Nearly a decade on from the financial crisis, local governments in the UK continue to feel the effects of deficit reduction. Local budgets were cut by £18 billion in real terms between 2010 and 2015, with a further £10 billion forecast up until 2020. This is in addition to savings made to 'unprotected' areas of national spending, and the relatively flat level of capital investment as a share of national GDP. However, the process of fiscal devolution that is underway amid this long-term pressure on public spending creates a precedent for the future transfer of more responsibilities from central government to London and other English city regions. The public debate about the future of Scotland, and the enhanced fiscal autonomy of Scotland and Wales, has raised the profile of city devolution and provided an opportunity for London to lead the debate about which tier of government is most effective in managing public spending. There is now widespread consensus, for example, that central government has failed in its management of national IT projects and in its procurement processes (Gainsbury and Neville, 2015). The alliance between London and the secondary 'core cities' has played a significant role in London's effort to communicate the collective benefits of growth to central government and the British public.

As part of the devolutionary impulse, in autumn 2015 central government announced a plan to let councils in England keep 100% of business rates from 2020. This represented a historic opportunity for local governments in cities. The national revenue support grant is being phased out, and the existing system of top-ups and tariffs extended. Safety nets to protect less business-friendly city authorities against big drops in revenue will remain, but the current levy on disproportionate gains is ending. Cities that create combined authorities with directly elected citywide mayors – as Manchester and Sheffield have done – are now able to increase rates for certain infrastructure projects by up to 2%. For London, business rates revenue – which is currently split approximately 60%–40% in favour of the boroughs – will increase the predictability of the funding stream and give a stronger platform for large infrastructure projects.

As the debate about devolution has unfolded, North–South asymmetries in England have gradually become one of the most high-profile issues in national political conversation. A 2014 poll found that a majority of non-Londoners regarded London as a net positive contributor to the British economy, but only three in ten thought their local city was helped by London's success (*The Economist*, 2016). In the same year, Chancellor George Osborne announced a major plan to rebalance the UK economy, noting that "London dominates more and more. And that's not healthy for our economy" (HM Treasury, 2014). Nicknamed the Northern Powerhouse, the plan aimed to leverage northern cities' science and technology sector potential, improved transport infrastructure and devolved political powers to increase agglomeration in the large city regions in the north of England and give them 'borrowed scale'. Since 2015, cities have been able to apply for control over strategy and spending in areas such as housing, transport and skills, provided that they agree to an elected mayor. After the surprise outright Conservative election victory in 2015, the national government identified the Northern Powerhouse as an opportunity to accelerate the pace of change, as well as to grow party political support in a part of the country where it has not been successful. The Northern Powerhouse became a defining moniker for the project of economic re-balancing, but its future direction is uncertain in the post-EU referendum UK government administration. If visible progress is made on the catalytic infrastructure such as High Speed 2 and High Speed 3, and the ongoing devolution deals with cities and city-regions, it has the potential to transform England's spatial economy and reduce some of the wide disparities between London and the UK's largest secondary cities.

Ongoing challenges where London needs help from national government

London's governance and investment model has been fairly successful at achieving key infrastructure and policy outcomes since 2000. But as the capital has inter-nationalised its workforce and economy, its economic, cultural and political divergence from most of the rest of the UK has come to present significant barriers to a shared national strategy for urban growth; barriers which may continue to grow in the aftermath of Brexit. Thirty-nine per cent of Londoners are born outside of the UK, compared to 13% in the rest of the UK, and as the national referendum on EU membership confirmed, Londoners are generally more pro-Europe, pro-diversity and pro-globalisation than the UK population as a whole. Support for the anti-immigration political party UKIP has also been less than half as widespread in London compared to the rest of the nation. The acrimony of the Brexit decision has even led to a minority of London residents supporting full independence from the UK (ONS, 2013; Freedland, 2014; Blinder, 2015; YouGov, 2016).

The decision to leave the EU presents new risks to London's economy and its status as one of the world's three or four leading financial centres. The import and export of financial and business services with Europe has been an important part of the city's growth in the last 25 years, while its labour market has been supported by recruitment of a large EU workforce in banking, construction, design, health, higher education, hospitality, law, tourism and other sectors. London is also the European headquarters for nearly 200 of the Fortune 500 firms. At the time of writing, in August 2016, the UK's negotiating position had yet to be set out, but London's access to the European Single Market through 'passporting' for financial services is now in question, unless the UK subsequently joins the European Economic Area (EEA), which appears unlikely given the political environment. Other European financial centres, including Amsterdam, Dublin, Frankfurt, Luxembourg and Paris, are seeking to absorb some of London's functions and euro-denominated business (PwC, 2016).

There are other short- and long-term risks for London and its ability to generate the tax revenues that support the rest of the UK. Corporate investment decisions will be delayed due to the uncertainty over future trade arrangements (London Assembly, 2016). The likely loss of European Structural and Investment Funds, and EU infrastructure investment via the European Investment Bank, may have a significant impact on the ability of London and especially other UK cities to bring forward the next wave of transport, energy, economic development and research projects (Metro Dynamics, 2016). And more broadly, the Brexit decision sends negative messages to international firms, investors, students and workers as to how welcome they may be in the UK, potentially undermining London's reputation for openness and tolerance. All of these factors mean that London's leaders now have to be galvanised to retain and leverage the city's comparative advantages, including its infrastructure, legal system and breadth and depth of skills.

Despite the turmoil unleashed by the Brexit decision, many of London's underlying growth needs remain regardless of the vote. These principally relate to London's growing population (regardless of EU migration), affordable housing, air quality, transport demand and infrastructure investment. Although London's own leadership can focus on issuing reassurance that London is open for business, investment and visitors and using the city's 'soft power' through its cultural assets, many of London's most urgent issue areas demand central government attention. The problem, however, is that they often demand policies that are potentially unpopular with the British electorate, not least because of a sense that London has benefited unfairly in the past. These imperatives include:

1. Successful Brexit negotiations and assurances;
2. Enhancements to fiscal autonomy;
3. Innovation to support more sustainable housing market;
4. Clarity over future air capacity;
5. Regional growth management in the Greater South East.

Successful Brexit negotiations and assurances

It is a critical medium-term imperative for the UK central government to ensure that the coming years of Brexit diplomacy do not hamper (or distract from) London's essential competitiveness framework. This means that the government has to provide as much certainty and predictability as possible, and ensure London's 'hard' and 'soft' assets are protected.

There are many dimensions to this imperative. First, central government will need to manage carefully any regulatory reform to support the City of London while also ensuring it can retain European Single Market access. Alternatively, national negotiations may also shape London's ability to become more of an offshore centre for renminbi trading, private banking and fintech (Agnew and Jenkins, 2016). Secondly, given the risks of talent flight from London to other cities in Europe – among both domestic and European workers – central government can support London by clarifying and guaranteeing the status of existing EU-born residents, and perhaps developing a clear immigration policy for high-skilled workers. Creative solutions to London's workforce requirements, such as a London-specific work permit in certain sectors, may be one option to be considered. At the same time, central government needs to dedicate sufficient parliamentary time to the large infrastructure projects that London will depend on in the next 10–20 years, and the potentially new financing models required to deliver them. All of these elements will have to be underpinned by a clear vision of the UK's (and its cities') roles in the future global economy.

The success which central government has in its exit negotiations with the European Union will fundamentally affect how London's relationship with the

UK unfolds over the coming decades. Failure to agree terms that protect London's global roles and competitiveness may result in London leaders seeking special terms with the EU and increasingly advocating for much more radical devolution models, including variations of the so-called 'city-state' solution.

Enhancements to fiscal autonomy

London's strong, consistent population and economic growth demands significant ongoing investment in transport, schools, housing, energy systems and technology. But the city has structural problems with financing infrastructure, because it exists in one of the most fiscally and financially centralised nation states in the world. Only around 7% of tax raised in London is spent by local or city representatives. Although the governance system has proven effective at extracting or 'winning' resources from central governments for individual projects – such as the Northern Line underground extension to Battersea – existing funding models for schools, housing and key infrastructure systems are not capable of managing predicted growth. As Deputy Mayor Sir Edward Lister has argued, "when we are operating on penny packets of money from Government and in relatively short timelines, we can never assemble the kind of cash that we are going to need in order to grow the city" (cited in Communities and Local Government Committee, 2016: 43).

London's security and transport investment remains vulnerable to cuts in central government grants, and there are many constraints to borrowing and tax increment financing for both the GLA and the boroughs. Central government is still the only authority with the capacity and resources to promote large projects, including guaranteeing project finance and using legislative power to ensure effective planning.

In 2012 and 2013 the London Finance Commission in 2013 examined potential new sources of revenue for the GLA, offset by a reduction in central government grants. It proposed that property taxation – including 100% of business rates, council tax, capital gains tax and stamp duty – be fully devolved to the GLA. One effect would be for London to develop areas in an 'Enterprise Zone' style. The Commission's findings were later endorsed by the Communities and Local Government Committee (2014):

> "Fiscal devolution in England is an idea whose time has come. The long shadows cast by the fiscal turmoil of the 1980s and 2000s – failed reform of local government finance, financial irresponsibility in parts of local government, inflexible, formulaic equalisation of local authorities' needs and resources and, above all, firm control by central Government – have started to recede."

Subsequently, the government considered the London Growth Deal in which these proposals were made. London won an extra £294 m in funding in two tranches, specifically dedicated to supporting housing, skills and infrastructure, from a newly established national Local Growth Fund. In terms of substantive fiscal devolution, however, gains have so far been very limited.

The Chancellor announced an important concession in 2015, whereby local authorities in England would be entitled to keep 100% of their business rates by the end of the 2015–2020 parliament, with some leeway to raise or lower them. This reform provides welcome incentives for London governments to grow commercial floorspace (but not their employment base or productivity, which may be more pertinent given London's shift towards the innovation economy). Beyond this, however, bigger concessions have not yet been forthcoming.

For Professor Tony Travers, the Commission's Chairman, "[t]he single biggest obstacle to reform is the fear within the Treasury and service departments that they will lose control of spending levels and provision which can only be run effectively by them." The Commission has become a template for British cities to build a pragmatic and evidence-based case for greater fiscal autonomy, but London may need bolder reforms if it is to meet unprecedented demands. After Brexit, Mayor Sadiq Khan reconvened the Commission to bring forward a stronger set of devolution plans. The challenge in this second phase is to propose a system where London governments not only have more control over their own finances, but have incentives to grow the tax base in a way that meets London's wider development aspirations, without appearing to negate London's responsibilities to the national finances (Communities and Local Government Committee, 2014; HM Government, 2014, 2015; BBC, 2015; LEP, 2016; McGough, 2016).

Innovation to support more sustainable housing market

Like other world cities, London has seen rapid rises in house prices since the early 1990s, and global demand has detached the city from the national market. These have had knock-on effects on labour costs and on the ability to attract skilled workers and key workers in the health and education sectors to the region. The supply of affordable housing has not been helped by falling central government housing investment since the mid-2000s, and a recent national cap on social rent has had distorting effects.

London now has a regional housing fund allocated by central government, and some central government incentives have been introduced to support large-scale private rented housing schemes, as well as to promote home ownership. But more changes are needed to address the housing gap, especially given that the existing pace of construction is threatened by the impact of Brexit on investor confidence. One role government can play is to invest more public money. A small step was taken in early 2016 when Whitehall announced it would directly commission 13,000 new homes around the country, including across key sites in London. Whether this marks the beginning of a wider policy shift towards public intervention in the housing market seems unlikely, and private developers will continue to generate the lion's share of future affordable housing via planning agreements (BBC, 2016). Many analysts are doubtful that the government's most recent Housing & Planning Bill will ultimately add more overall delivery capacity for new homes (Hopkirk, 2016).

The government can also give institutional investors more assurances to invest in scale, yield and quality by simplifying planning rules and helping to assemble large land parcels. It has recently taken important steps to assist in the re-use of public sector brownfield land. A London Land Commission was established in 2015 to identify key public brownfield sites to ensure all are developed by 2025. In January 2016, the Commission identified enough under-used land for 130,000 homes, with the final figure likely to be higher (GLA, 2015; Sullivan, 2016).

There are a number of actions central government could also take to improve the rate of supply in London. First, it is in a position to make borough targets binding and free boroughs up to use balance sheets prudentially. Second, it can restructure and devolve GLA powers to enable a more strategic approach to the way land is brought forward and changes in use are managed. Third, it can increase the enforceability of compulsory purchase powers. Fourth, it can help reform development finance to make it more London friendly. All of these policies require a step change in attitude whereby central government becomes substantially committed to devolution and intensive partnership with the GLA and the boroughs (Holman *et al.*, 2015).

Clarity over future air capacity

London's plans for more airport capacity have been repeatedly delayed by national governments. A decision on how to expand airport capacity was initially delayed until the Davies Commission reported after the 2015 General Election, partly due to existing pledges by national political parties. The decision was put back a further six months until after the 2016 London Mayoral elections. The lack of certainty and high airport taxes have seen the city begin to lose out to other western European gateways (Paris, Amsterdam) and the emerging centres of Dubai and Istanbul.

The regional airport system requires multiple new sources of capacity to come online before it becomes full by the 2030s. Heathrow Airport – the main hub for the south east of England – is already operating at 98% of its capacity, and Gatwick at 85%. London's leading European gateway position may be damaged if a firm central government decision is not taken and then followed up with a clear path to deliver the extra capacity promptly (CAA, 2014; Airports Commission, 2015). On this issue, central government has tended to place national electoral imperatives above the strategic needs of its globally facing world city.

Regional growth management in the Greater South East

London lacks effective tools to plan for growth across its functional economic region – including the whole 'Greater South East' of England. Currently, the planning process for the region involves more than 100 authorities plus transport and utility providers (AECOM, 2015). Currently, what regional thinking there is depends on central government rather than the existing regional players. A fully empowered regional government would be unacceptable to national government, but the national tier could still do a lot more to incentivise sub-regional collaboration, create shared approaches and boost understanding of regional inter-dependencies (Gordon and Travers, 2010). This would speed up alternative development options such as new towns, suburban intensification and 'garden cities'.

There are already examples where central government has shown support for integrated approaches to systems that extend beyond London boundaries. In 2016, transport secretary Patrick McLoughlin approved plans for Transport for London to take over operational control of suburban commuter services from regional rail companies. By taking over parts of the regional network when franchises are renewed, TfL would be able to integrate fares and provide more regular services on lines that are often subject to commuter criticism. There is a perception that central government has to provide more timely support to these initiatives and endorse solutions to boost stretched operational budgets (Topham, 2016).

Key actors and mechanisms that enable London to make progress with UK central government

In London the Mayor himself is critically important for making the case to central government. The Mayor has a unique platform to speak for the entire city, and until the election of Sadiq Khan in 2016, he has been in alignment with the political party in power at the national level. As the late Sir Peter Hall remarked, the London Mayor "has proved to be brilliantly effective in three ways: promoting London internationally, co-ordinating activities within London and making the case for London to central government" (quoted in Clark, 2015). But the agenda for London is incomplete: the escalating problems of housing and house prices, transport infrastructure and, above all, airport policy need urgent attention.

On key political issues such as the role of the Mayor, the Crossrail development schemes, housing supply and the addition of airport capacity in the region, business interest groups engage directly and successfully in the policy development process. The highly professional business leadership organisation London First has good channels of communication with central government, often working in tandem with the city government. It urges the national tier to be bold and decisive on major infrastructure projects (for example, Crossrail 2 and airport expansion) and to ensure that the business climate is kept attractive even during more turbulent periods for the economy.

London has found that forward-thinking and planning that leads to bold advocacy documents can help national governments observe the need for reform. For example, in 2015 London's Mayor, boroughs and the London Enterprise Panel (LEP) developed a long-term infrastructure plan to 2050 to set out likely needs and costs of investment. This Plan brought attention to the gaps in available funding. London is also tackling the national economic divide head-on, taking a lead in solving national challenges rather than hiding from the issue. An economic action plan prepared by the London Enterprise Panel in 2015 explicitly addressed London's relationships with the UK as a whole and with the Greater South East.

Conclusion

London is a world city that has benefited from successive cycles of adjustment in its relationship with central government, including the recent phase of policy and institutional development in and with cities since 2010. The result of the recent cycle of bespoke reforms for major cities is that the UK's highly central-ised governance system is evolving into a more 'negotiated' system. This system consists of a strong central state, substantially 'devolved' nations, a more empow-ered metropolitan government in London and combined authorities in city-regions (for example, Manchester and Sheffield) where the mayor is a 'first among equals' scrutinised by constituent councils. The national government has made positive steps to support national ministerial co-ordination on the cities agenda, as well as inter-city initiatives that strengthen the system of cities. The system of 'City Deals' set the ball rolling for stronger individual city-regional govern-ance frameworks and the momentum for further devolution into the 2020s appears unstoppable.

London has shown how important it is to work constructively with a second tier of cities to call for changes to central government policies and finance formulas. The optimism that now surrounds the future of Greater Manchester, the West Midlands and other city regions creates a more favourable political environment for London to extract genuine reforms for its own growth needs. However, the extent and complexity of its housing and transport infrastructure challenges are such that the capital depends on faster national decision-making and enhanced leadership capacity if it is to avoid reaching 'Peak London'.

One key disadvantage for London compared to other peer cities is the very limited national dialogue or perspective on how the wider city-region of London and the Greater South East of England should be organised and optimised. The conversation about London as a world city still tends to refer to its built-up area within the M25, and ignores the functional commuter region, even though it houses four of the region's six airports, two of the region's four leading global universities and significant parts of the region's growth clusters in life sciences, digital media, ICT and cleantech. These new growth sectors have a more com-plex regional geography than do finance and business services, and require their own opportunity framework. As part of the ongoing adjustment to London as a world city region, national policy will also need to undertake a full review of the future of the Green Belt, regional infrastructure and institutions in order to manage London's real economy and quality of life in an integrated way.

In the aftermath of Brexit, London now presents one of the clearest examples of a world city where the economic, cultural and demographic gulfs between it and the rest of the nation have begun to incur political reactions that threaten to rein in its global roles. In the coming years London will rely heavily on its central government to protect and re-affirm its hub status for global firms, talent and capital. At the same time, there is increased momentum for London to gain more independence and build a distinctive relationship with Europe, perhaps developing its own version of the 'one country, two systems' model. As the political fall-out continues, London's future relationships with Edinburgh,

Dublin and other leading European cities, as well as with global cities outside the EU, may take on new dimensions. Given what is at stake for London, and indeed the rest of the UK, it is likely that in the next stage of the relationship between world city and nation state, London leaders (and those in other UK cities and metropolitan areas) will have to make their voices heard much more loudly in national debates and negotiations.

4

Paris: Manufacturing a metropolis amid institutional complexity

Carlos Delgado (2012), licensed under CC BY 2.0

World Cities and Nation States, First Edition. Greg Clark and Tim Moonen.
© 2017 John Wiley & Sons, Ltd. Published 2017 by John Wiley & Sons, Ltd.

The Paris city region is continental Europe's main business gateway and a diversified global centre for tourism, science, high technology, creative industries and decision-making (Table 4.1). The iconic capital of the world's sixth largest economy, Paris remains an extraordinary brand phenomenon, beloved because of its architecture, cuisine and its historic role as the so-called 'birthplace of the Enlightenment' (Lehrer, 2015). The city functions as a major destination for foreign direct investment and public and private R&D investment, much of which is very well integrated with outstanding higher education institutions. Among its many celebrated modern-day strengths include world-class social and transport infrastructure, much of which is concentrated in the central zone.

Despite Paris's success, by the standards of other world cities its recent development path has been far from smooth. National taxation and regulatory frameworks have militated against growth in international financial services, and the city has achieved relatively modest rates of innovation and investment in recent years. Although gross added value has increased at a respectable rate since the turn of the century, job growth has been much lower. Housing shortages and relative unaffordability have made it less attractive for families, and social divisions between the wealthier west and the poorer east are entrenched. The city has witnessed a great deal of recent institutional reform that is designed to make it a more coherent and integrated city, of which the creation of Grand Paris is just one prominent example. Like other cities, it is now implementing a major new metro system and preparing new institutional and funding arrangements to meet its strategic development challenges.

France, in some ways, has been an archetypal centralised nation state dominated by a primate city. It is typical for the Prime Minister and President to take a very active role in formulating policy for the capital region. Although France is less fiscally centralised than countries such as the UK, public investment is managed through a system of grants and tax-sharing with local governments. State capital investment has always been critical to enabling Paris's large infrastructure projects and national legislation upholds a commitment to social housing and high-quality public services in the city. National policies, combined with the actions of regional and local authorities, are designed to attract investment in business districts and cultural projects, as well as sponsoring designated clusters. The character and reform of Paris's governance is also keenly debated at the National Assembly.

However, French politics has been evolving under the impact of internal and external pressures for change. The hierarchical model of a Paris Region

Table 4.1: Paris–Île-de-France's metropolitan area: key statistics

% of national population	% of national GDP	GVA per capita vs national average (1)	City global competitiveness rank	Country global competitiveness rank	Annualised employment growth 2000–14	Annualised GDP growth 2000–14	% of national employment
19%	31%	1.41	4	22	0.3%	0.7%	20%

Source: Parilla *et al.*, 2015; OECD Stat., 2014; World Economic Forum, 2015; EIU, 2012.

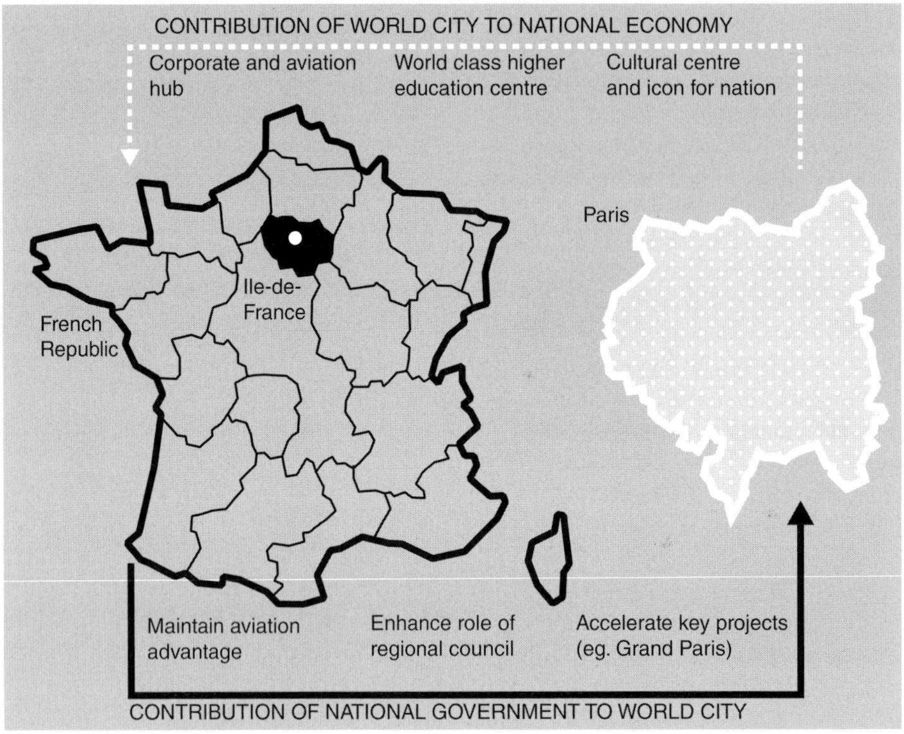

Figure 4.1:   Reciprocity between Paris and the French central government.

administered by the State has given way to a more self-organising metropolis based on multi-level governance and co-operation. The Paris region is in charge of regional transport, planning and land use, and shares responsibility with local governments for economic development and environmental issues. Meanwhile, over 100 inter-municipal *communautés* with fiscal powers have been established to deliver services and foster development. De-centralisation has fed fragmentation, which has created the impetus for the latest cycle of national intervention into Paris's future.

   This chapter highlights the response of national government in supporting a sequence of important metropolitan transport, housing and governance projects since 2010, which aim to help reduce Paris's spatial division and create a more integrated economic and social fabric (Figure 4.1). The Grand Paris Express transport project is reversing decades of transport under-investment and integrating the business districts of La Defense, Val-de-Seine, Plaine Saint-Denis and Paris-Saclay. Meanwhile, a new metropolitan government (La Métropole du Grand Paris) system has been in place since 2016 and aims, over time, to address the governance deficit and incorporate the three surrounding départements into the métropole of Greater Paris. This chapter also explores the national policy changes that have increased the role of the Île-de-France regional council to stimulate business growth and co-ordinate internationalisation, and the recent national law to grant metropolitan status to other French cities. Paris is in the process of adjusting to a great deal of change. What remains to be seen is whether the latest cycle of reforms has the practical effect of increasing Paris's capacity to deliver change more strategically and decisively than in the past.

History of Paris's relationship with national government

French nation state control of Paris has always been very important. Paris is the centre of state power, and for over 300 years from 1650 onwards it was vulnerable to successive revolutionary movements and attempts to overthrow the post-Napoleonic monarchy. In the 19th century, the government centralised administration and control over the army to a greater degree than any other European nation. Because of the prestige and centralisation of Paris, the city was a regular target for opponents seeking more say in the decision-making process (House, 2014). Governments viewed it as essential to prevent the rise of political opposition, which meant that for nearly the whole period from 1790 to the late 1970s, the city of Paris did not have a mayor (Subra and Newman, 2008).

In the decades after 1945, French national governments developed a carrot-and-stick policy to prevent industrial and office development becoming over-concentrated in the city of Paris. French firms that located in the wider region outside Paris benefited from subsidies, causing a de-centralisation of economic activity until the 1970s. Many public-service jobs were moved out of the capital. Financial instruments were created to reorient the pattern of urban development, so as to relocate manufacturing farther afield, and relocate the business functions across the Paris region (Crouch and Le Galès, 2012). The national government sought to limit the influence of local left-leaning politicians operating in the council of the Seine, the administrative area for Paris that had become a kind of metropolitan authority. Under President Charles de Gaulle, a new District de la Région Parisienne was established to define a regional strategy that could manage the anticipated influx of population. It resulted in the 1965 regional master plan which identified key projects such as the creation of La Defense business district and an RER train system to connect new towns to the centre. The District was directed by senior officials and reported directly to the State, with other land and urban agencies also fully controlled by the national level.

Political relationships between the State and local councillors only began to improve in the late 1970s, under new President Valery Giscard d'Estaing. A highly centralised system began to move towards a more multipolar one where the State was one (powerful) actor among many. A directly elected mayor for the central city was introduced in Paris in 1977, namely future President Jacques Chirac, who occupied the role for nearly two decades. In the special case of Paris, the State retained control of regional strategic planning and transport management until the end of the 1990s, within a framework of negotiation with the Regional Council whereby the State no longer prevailed on key projects (Cole, 2014).

As Paris spilled over way beyond its historic boundaries, the wider Île de France region became the logical unit to manage its metropolitan growth.

After the District experiment had struggled due to a lack of co-operation between communes and départements, the Paris Region was created in 1976 and re-named the Île-de-France. The entity was managed by a regional council, with one-third representation from local MPs. The regional council was set up to co-ordinate development, land use, transport and the economy, and gained full executive powers over a territory with the whole urbanised area inside its boundaries.

Over time, and with each administrative layer, Paris has acquired one of the most complex governance arrangements of any world city. The central municipal département of Paris is small, at just 105 km². It is home to less than 20% of what is now 12 million people living in the capital Île-de-France region (called the 'Paris Region'), and has a budget of just €8 billion. The Île-de-France itself, at more than 12,000 km², is composed of seven other départements in addition to Paris and encompasses the entire urban and functional area. With its own budget nearer €5 billion, it is one of 12 administrative regions in mainland France, yet generates nearly a third of national GDP. The Île-de-France regional council takes the lead on regional master planning and public transport and, since 2015, has also administered European Structural Funds.

Paris as an established world city

Since 2000, relations between Paris and its surrounding municipalities have improved significantly. The Mayor of Paris had previously been widely mistrusted by leaders outside the central municipality, but the decision in 2003 to launch a metropolitan conference (which began in 2006) in recognition of Paris's regional inter-dependence initiated a new phase of discussion about metropolitan collaboration. At the same time, new laws in 1999, 2004 and 2010 reinforced the process of inter-municipal co-operation. In Paris, this mainly took place among groups of municipalities *outside* the core city, without any mechanism for their full collaboration. Nevertheless, Paris has become a world leader in fostering collaborative activity among clusters of municipalities.

The Paris métropole forum – designating an area of 10 million people – deliberated on housing, transport, economic and tax policies. It developed its own budget and although it lacked formal powers, it began a process that was picked up by President Nicolas Sarkozy and accelerated with the support of his national Secretary of State for the capital region, Christian Blanc. The input of the State ultimately resulted in a geographically smaller métropole institution being proposed to overhaul the system of local authorities, joint inter-communal bodies and quangos that currently presides.

Central government has consistently backed a new role for Paris on the world stage, continuing into the Sarkozy and Hollande governments. Over the last 20 years, the priority has been to attract investment to business districts such as La Défense, and to prestigious cultural projects, IT and research clusters. Governments have invested large sums to improve Charles de Gaulle Airport and its connections to La Défense and Paris Orsay. The Government also backed bids to host the Olympics, up until 2005 when it surprisingly lost the bid to London for the 2012 Games. Its global perspective was, to some extent, balanced by a commitment to affordability: a 'Law for Solidarity and Urban Renewal' makes it compulsory for communes to have 20–25% of social housing in the housing stock by 2020, while the State now offers public subsidies to lower the price of land for housing delivery.

In 2008 an important shift occurred when central government appointed a Minister for Le Grand Paris to help a larger Paris "be a decisive national asset in the competition of the twenty-first century", according to the official mandate (Lefevre, 2012). The Minister oversaw a new €25 billion Grand Paris transportation plan which eventually was approved after a long period of disagreement with the regional government in charge of transport planning. The ministerial position was disbanded but the funding envelope for the 200-kilometre, 68-station metro system is now tightly linked to future planned development. Clusters of municipalities served by the Grand Paris metro are invited to participate in Territorial Development Contracts that ensure housing delivery and urban development around railway stations. These are jointly defined by the State and local actors in pursuit of housing and economic development objectives along the new metro route. They are, in part, a vehicle to negotiate the respective involvement of all actors. By March 2016, 19 have been signed and approved, although many faced local resistance and a slow approval process (Béhar, 2013; IAU île-de-France, 2015).

At the same time, national public policy has spurred research and innovation in the capital. On the one hand, the national government sponsors competitiveness clusters across the Paris region (for example, nanotechnology, aerospace and medicine) in order to provide them with the technology, talent and space needed to gain global reach. Recently, Paris has also benefited significantly from a shift in public investment, with projects labelled as *Opérations d'Intérêt National* (OIN) implemented by jointly developed agencies in which the four levels of local and regional government are represented.

One such project is the Paris Saclay centre for innovation, 20 kilometres south west of central Paris, which has received disbursements of public money for infrastructure and technology transfers to support leading French firms in the region. With €2 billion invested in Paris Saclay, the area is set to become a gateway for international researchers, students and start-ups. Central government has been an active player in encouraging the 18 higher education establishments, three communautés d'agglomération and 27 communes to co-operate. It has created a Public Delivery Agency for the area, with three central government representatives, ten local figures and another seven directly chosen by the Prime Minister. It is being financed through a national *Investments for the Future* programme, managed from the Prime Minister's Office, which covers most of the funds. The project is being delivered through two territorial contracts that embody the shared vision of the State and local authorities. It is symbolic of the strong role the State continues to play in a fragmented region when it comes to projects of national importance (Floc'h, 2015; Mérot, 2015; EPAPS, 2016; République Française, 2016).

From 2016, the new métropole entity covering the city of Paris and three surrounding departments, is gradually gaining its own taxation powers and powers

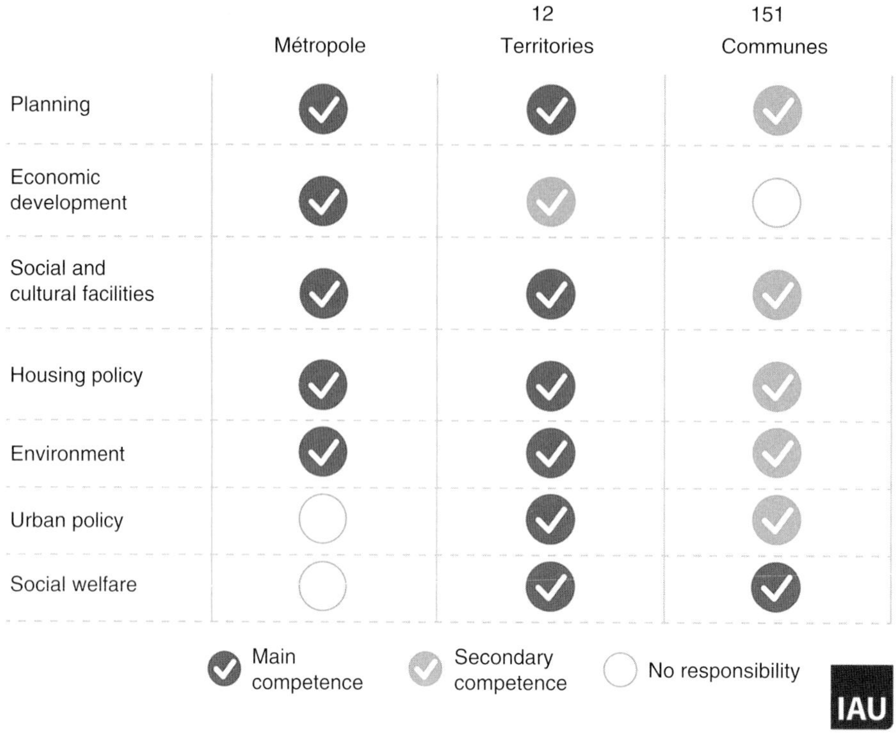

	12	151
	Métropole	Territories	Communes
Planning	✓ (main)	✓ (main)	✓ (secondary)
Economic development	✓ (main)	✓ (secondary)	○
Social and cultural facilities	✓ (main)	✓ (main)	✓ (secondary)
Housing policy	✓ (main)	✓ (main)	✓ (secondary)
Environment	✓ (main)	✓ (main)	✓ (secondary)
Urban policy	○	✓ (main)	✓ (secondary)
Social welfare	○	✓ (main)	✓ (main)

✓ Main competence   ✓ Secondary competence   ○ No responsibility

IAU

Figure 4.2:   Division of responsibilities within the new Grand Paris arrangement.

for planning, land use, social housing and economic development, while the départements will still deliver social services (Figure 4.2). The new institution raises awareness among the Paris public about urgent metropolitan-wide problems, but it remains to be seen if it will be more proactive in co-ordinating regional investment and using financial instruments to steer development wisely (Bowie, 2013a, 2013b). Another step in the de-centralisation process is the approval of the regional council's new regional master plan, which has integrated the Grand Paris project into its framework.

The political alignment between national and city level is an important prerequisite to building trust between city/metropolitan and national tiers. After the election of François Hollande in 2012, the party in power at the national level became aligned to the ruling party in many of France's largest cities. This promised to accelerate the transfer of competencies to the local and regional levels, but territorial interests often outweigh political affiliation in French politics. Today, central government plays a key role, alongside the Region, in funding strategic development projects, and intervenes in Paris's future partly because of its capital status and partly because it does not trust local authorities to act decisively. Central government intervention remains a double-edged sword in Paris, and is usually accompanied by bottom-up processes to complement the top-down intervention.

The national system of cities: Paris and France

Paris has always been much larger than other French cities. The French urban hierarchy stretches back as far as the Roman Empire, but evolved during the rapid re-urbanisation that took place between 1950 and 1980 (Pumain, 1997). The capital, more than six times larger than the next largest city, Lyon, exercises a great deal of influence over French economic and cultural life. Foreign firm headquarters are very rarely located outside of Paris, although some large domestic firms are based in cities such as Lyon and Strasbourg.

Over the past 30 years, French secondary cities have faced their own distinct challenges. Unlike British cities, French cities' problems were not linked primarily with industrial decline or with the 'hollowing out' of the inner city. They have, instead, often been associated with the lack of access to economic opportunity for ethnic minority groups in the city suburbs. Cities far from Paris – Strasbourg, Marseille, Nantes, Toulouse – have certainly gained population over the past 25 years and have developed cultural strength and the ability to pursue their own strategies. Nevertheless, inequality has grown within many of France's medium-sized cities and productivity performance has been low.

In the mid-2000s, the national government launched a series of measures to prepare French cities for European and global competition. In 2005 it identified 17 metropolitan regions that needed to co-operate for success, although a lack of funding has meant progress in this area has been slow. In 2006, its delegation on regional planning introduced a new suite of industrial policies, aiming to support clusters across France. These are designed to be centres of excellence that can attract investment and drive exports. Only 4 of the 17 clusters were located in the Paris Region.

The State has become more active at resolving urban fragmentation within French regions, including Paris, ever since the passing of legislation in 1999 to extend the concept of urban communities. In many cities, the State has effectively broken the governance deadlock with its new proposals. The 2014 Maptam law grants a special statute to the three largest cities (Paris, Lyon and Marseille) and also grants métropole status to nine other cities (Bordeaux, Grenoble, Lille, Nantes, Nice, Rennes, Rouen, Strasbourg and Toulouse).

With most metropolitan areas becoming functional in 2015 and 2016, Lyon and Marseille join Paris in exercising stronger economic development and planning powers within their boundaries. They combine the powers of local communes, co-operative inter-communal structures and the départements in an attempt to reduce local governance fragmentation. The other métropoles exercise similar rights although with less autonomy over spatial and economic planning. Even though the law applies slightly differently to each city, it does effectively acknowledge the metropolitan dimension of their challenges, and ensures that Paris is not treated with undue favouritism when it comes to resolving urban challenges at the national scale (Gittus, 2015; Mission Interministérielle pour le projet Métropolitan Aix-Marseille-Provence, 2015; Mouvement Métropole, 2015). These métropoles will require the state government to continue to support building implementational capacity. It is not yet clear if the métropole systems will, over the long run, help simplify the complex system of relations between central government and French cities. Although it brings together stakeholders, how well it will be mobilised politically remains to be seen. There are also arguments that the State should encourage non-institutional stakeholders (firms, civic groups and residents) to become involved with planning agencies to make the new metropolitan structures more resilient (Deraëvea, 2014).

Ongoing challenges where Paris needs help from national government

Despite the institutional progress under way, it is still apparent that Paris's overcrowded and underregulated governance system slows down long-term strategic planning decisions. The governance shortfall impacts on all the areas where Paris has imperatives as a world city in a competitive framework. It is exacerbated by the reliance on central government financial and political support to deliver transport projects and redevelopment schemes.

Clarity and confidence over future rationalised governance framework

The process of creating the new Paris Métropole system has been politically sensitive, as different interests continue to offer divergent proposals for what the metropolitan system should look like. In the years up to 2016, the French government faced the choice between two competing visions: a new metropolitan council with strong power, which concentrates most resources within the four central départements, or a more federal system with more power and resources remaining in the hands of sub-metropolitan authorities. At stake is where the balance of power should lie between the central government, the new métropole and the surrounding départements.

Rather than overhaul the existing structure, the new Grand Paris effectively adds a fifth tier of government in the region, and begins with a small budget of just €65 million. The protracted debate and modest initial outcome led one commentator to describe the process as "a mountain giving birth to a mouse." (Gilli, quoted in Delourme, 2015). An assembly of 209 councillors has jurisdiction on environmental and economic policy over the urbanised area of 7 million people. The new arrangement divides the outer suburbs into 12 territories that will replace the inter-communal system. The métropole is set to acquire powers over housing and urban planning, as well as presidential leadership and a physical headquarters, but the terms of political integration are a long way from being finalised.

Over the next 15 years, the organisation is likely to absorb taxation powers incrementally from the municipalities. Its success as a metropolitan body depends critically on the goodwill of future French national leaders in supporting and activating these incremental additions of power and capacity. A clear roadmap towards an empowered metropolitan entity will enable Paris to address some of its social and economic imbalances and provide confidence for public and private investors in housing and infrastructure.

Increased housing supply to create mixed-income communities

Although Paris has recently improved local planning tools and joint development agencies, housing shortages and unaffordability remains a critical challenge,
especially for younger people. Lower- and middle-income groups have been
largely pushed out of the inner city, although the local authorities have tried
to invest to make the suburban 'red belt' a more acceptable living location for
professionals.

The French Prime Minister has expressed determination to meet the ambitious
target of 70,000 units a year, a figure far in excess of those proposed in London and
New York. The Mobilisation Plan for Development and Housing intends to support communities that innovate to raise the housing rate. The State is also running
a New Programme for Urban Renewal at the national level, which has already
identified or provided support to 119 housing development and urban upgrade projects in the Paris Region. In addition to co-financing, it helps mobilise local actors
around social and development objectives. It forms part of a broader co-operation
mechanism entitled 'State-Region Contracts', which set out a joint budgetary and
planning vision between regions and central government. The contract for the
Paris Region saw its budget increase by 34% to €7.3 billion in the 2015–20 round,
in support of wider development objectives including housing. This increase is an
encouraging sign for future housing potential in the region, but is nonetheless
enmeshed in a complex overlap of initiatives that fragment policy formulation
(Île-de-France, 2015).

Other important recent tools created by the State to accelerate development
are Operations of National Interest (OINs) and Contracts of National Interest
(CINs). The first give the Government enhanced planning powers in a handful
of key sites, while the second allow fragmented local delivery partners to
formally join forces. The replacement of the region's Property and Public Works
Agency with a dedicated Grand Paris Planning body also signals intent to
simplify the delivery regime. The State also mandated the fusion of previously
separate publicly run property developers into one regional body, EFP Île-de-
France, to streamline regional bodies involved in land assembly (République
Française, 2014, 2015; ANRU, 2016).

Local governments all agree on the need to increase the construction rate, but
many in practice oppose house building in order to keep down the population.
The national government often disagrees with the municipalities on the necessary share of social housing (Bowie, 2013a, 2013b). It also has not provided a clear
system for taxing or capturing land value. Paris needs its national-tier government
to ensure the new Territorial Development Contracts function properly and do
not conflict with a planned regional housing authority (AOL).

A more empowered framework for the Paris region

Although a step forward for integration beyond the core city of Paris, the new
métropole does not cover the outer belt of urbanised Paris, called the 'Grande
Couronne', and therefore does not solve all the problems of inter-municipal

competition, duplication and tax allocation. The Île-de-France Region, and especially those départements left out of the project, now has an ambivalent role in relation to Paris.

One step forward in this area is new regulations and legislation to support the role of regions, including the Île-de-France regional council, in leading economic development. In mid-2015, the NOTRe bill came into force and granted regional institutions, including Paris, more exclusive sectoral power. For example, the council's capabilities to direct local economic development actors have been explicitly improved by a transfer of activities from the State. Its regional economic development plans have been granted a wider remit over business support and internationalisation. Some national civil servants have also been asked to work in the regional council. The intention is to give power and money to the regional council to support business growth and to reduce the number of bodies engaged in the process.

To anticipate its new role, the regional council has initiated several actions, with the Paris Region Economic Development Agency (PREDA) merging with the Centre Francilien de l'Innovation (Innovation Agency) in July 2014 to create Paris Regional Enterprises. As a result, the region's new strategy for economic development and innovation simplifies the process by which businesses can engage with the public sector and link up all agencies via a leadership board (Gonguet, 2014; Gittus, 2015; Vie Publique, 2015).

Regional reforms have also seen some transfer of power from départements to regions, and increased the minimum size of inter-communal communities to reduce the number of administrative layers between the region and the communes. What remains unclear is the relationship between the region's new powers and the prerogatives of the new Paris Métropole, as the latter will retain powers over economic and spatial planning within its jurisdiction. In the meantime, communes and the region itself will be able to delegate powers to the Métropole if they see fit, while the region itself is legally bound to develop its economic and spatial plans in co-operation with the métropole and its communes (Gittus, 2015; Husson, 2015; Jerome, 2015; Vie Publique, 2015).

Effective delivery of extended and enhanced public transport network

Despite a strong functioning system, Paris lacks links between suburbs, which is being addressed by the Grand Paris Express metro system, at a projected cost of more than €25 billion (Figure 4.3). The lack of mobility has been viewed as a major barrier to competitiveness and job creation, and the forthcoming network is an important catalyst to improve the efficiency of the region. Work has already begun on the extensions to lines 4, 14 and 15 (Jerome, 2014; Société du Grand Paris, 2014, 2015; Les Echos, 2016).

The public delivery agency for the project, Société du Grand Paris, is under the joint supervision of ministers such as the Minister for Economic Affairs, the Minister for Transport and the Minister responsible for Town Planning. The Government has raised taxes – such as housing, parking and business taxes – for collection by the Regional Council, in order to fund the Société's work. Paris requires national government co-operation to ensure the project is not unduly

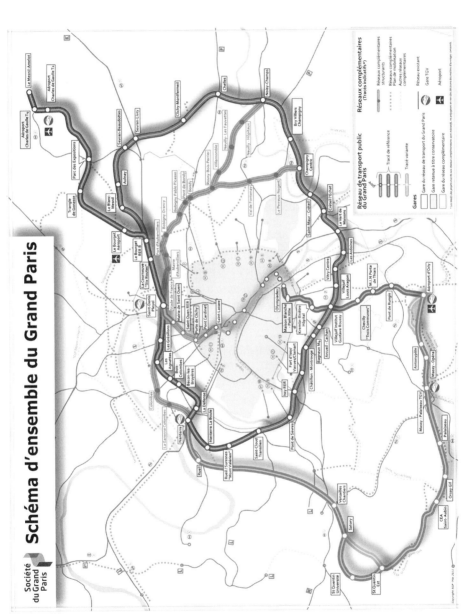

Figure 4.3: Map of the Grand Paris Express lines.

delayed by financing issues or changes to institutional leadership, such as occurred with the CEO of *Société du Grand Paris* in 2014. The most recent State announcement commits to a new €1.4 billion contribution for the 2015–2020 period, but consensus on further tax hikes to increase the investment rate is unlikely.

The State's role will also be crucial in financing and preparing the work for a proposed Charles-de-Gaulle Airport express train service. The Prime Minister announced in late 2015 that a public delivery agency would begin initial feasibility studies. The ambition is to connect the airport to the centre within 20 minutes to relieve local RER and road networks (MobiliCities, 2015; République Française, 2015).

Key actors and mechanisms that enable Paris to make progress with the nation state

Paris's major development challenges are often highlighted and addressed by individuals and agencies within the central Paris city government. The metropolitanisation (métropole) process was partly spurred by former Paris Mayor Bertrand Delanoë appointing a deputy mayor with responsibility for relations with the wider region. The city government then put forward a proposal for a 'metropolitan pole' which kick-started the governance debate.

Actors within the State itself have been key to mobilising its institutions. When faced with the region's proposed master plan in 2008, the then government thought it was not commensurate with what a global city region such as Paris could achieve. This continued in 2012 with the new Prime Minister, Manuel Valls, taking a personal involvement in the project with the support of his representative in the region, the prefect Jean François Carenco. Both have been key in making the State an arbitrator in the often tense negotiations between regional and local players over what shape the new Grand Paris should take, both in terms of the route of new metro lines and the governance structure of the métropole. Valls played a key role in pushing through the Maptam bill, which inaugurated metropolitan cities in France, embedding it within a broader structure of regional reform and rationalisation (Métropole du Grand Paris – Mission de Préfiguration, 2015; Wiel, 2015). The State's orchestrating role has also been embodied by its use of Contracts for Territorial Development and OINs. Dialogue between State, regions and communes has also been facilitated by forums for local representatives and urban professionals, including the Paris Métropole Mixed Syndicate and the International Workshop for Greater Paris (ibid).

At the same time, the Île-de-France Regional Council is the key negotiating partner with central government on the future development of the region. In December 2013, after a wide sub-regional consultation and difficult negotiation with the national government, the Regional Council approved the Île-de-France 2030 Regional Master plan, setting the ambitious housing goal of 70,000 units a year.

Economic governance in Paris has been largely shaped by government intervention and is rather corporatist and territorial. A number of bodies and agencies collectively debate policy, consult experts and advise national government. Most prominent is IAU-îdF, the planning agency for the Paris Region and an internationally recognised organisation which provides analysis and strategies for the region and other players. Others also play a role. These include APUR, the influential Paris Urban Planning Agency that convenes geographers, architects and planners and, to a lesser extent, AERF, an association of elected councillors which actively supports territorial reform.

Until recently, there had been no clear representation of the major private players in Paris, unlike in London or New York. The public and private sectors have often disagreed publicly on their vision for the future of the Île-de-France, and whether the focus should be social equality, environmental protection or economic development (Lefevre, 2012). Chambers of Commerce have tended to operate on their own rather than as part of an effective collaborative, and the private sector has only had an advisory role in strategic processes as part of a committee of partners. The regional elections of 2015, however, saw a new leadership team take over the Paris Region which has already set up a Strategic Council for Attractiveness and Employment. It will bring together the leading private sector stakeholders of the region to advise on economic policy – although its effectiveness remains to be seen (Île-de-France, 2016).

The fragmentation of leadership for economic development is expected to improve as the Île-de-France regional council becomes empowered to assemble assorted players to discuss a unified economic agenda. The Charles de Gaulle Airport Authority has also set an example by successfully creating a public–private non-profit association that works to attract international investors. This informal governance model is expected to be adopted by the regional council.

Conclusion

France is a highly centralised national polity in transition. Senior national politicians play a critical role in terms of the profile and the delivery of major projects and initiatives in the Paris Region, more so than in the other cities and regions in France. Yet the top-down hierarchy has evolved into a complex system of multi-level governance, where clustered collaboration between municipalities is more advanced than in almost any other world city. The potential game-changer is the new metropolitan government. In principle, the reform promises to increase the pace and scale of change in Paris. As in London, the new framework may help the city to manage its growth more deliberately and avoid experiencing the most iniquitous effects of social and economic exclusion. However, the risk is that the legislation will add yet another institutional layer to an already crowded system.

The new national policy changes to enhance the role of the Île-de-France regional council can catalyse necessary economic rebalancing in the Paris Region. The integration and empowerment of regional capabilities provides an important message to businesses and international investors as Paris seeks to grow its global city functions.

As Paris enters into a new cycle of potentially dynamic growth, it will become more important that other French métropoles also have the political consensus and implementation tools to make progress. Paris will likely need clearer channels to collaborate effectively with other French cities, and a more focused national urban policy will offer a welcome source of confidence and direction.

5

Seoul: Lessons from de-centralisation and de-concentration

Gusttawo OL (2015), licensed under CC BY 2.0

World Cities and Nation States, First Edition. Greg Clark and Tim Moonen.
© 2017 John Wiley & Sons, Ltd. Published 2017 by John Wiley & Sons, Ltd.

Seoul is one of eastern Asia's leading world cities and the national platform for the global operations of Korean multinational companies. It is one of the first, and to date only, major cities to have made a transition from low income to upper income status inside 50 years. As the capital of a developmental state, it has achieved an extremely rapid rate of technological innovation and production, combined with very large infrastructure investment and subsequent regeneration. It is also the junction box for an economy which has become one of the world's largest shipbuilders, steel producers and construction contractors. Seoul's distinctive government and business model has become an inspiration to other Asian cities, and to others elsewhere, showing how to climb global value chains while continually managing the adverse consequences of rapid growth and preparing the city and its citizens for new cycles of development.

Korea has a long history of centralised rule and until recently the central government was the decisive actor in Seoul's development. This chapter highlights how, in a small and densely populated unitary country, the national urban development and public investment strategy was phenomenally successful in the first phases of industrial growth. Seoul achieved a remarkable evolution through successive cycles as a result of massive infrastructure investment, rapid technological innovation, high public services spending and sound environmental management.

The example of Seoul offers a valuable window into the unexpected side effects that can accompany national policies to regulate growth and redistribute agglomeration. Sustained efforts from Korea's leadership over more than 30 years to de-concentrate away from the capital were inefficient and have since been abandoned. Korea's centralised political and fiscal system has also had to adjust to the distinctive needs of its most globalised city. This chapter shows how, since the mid-1990s, more local autonomy has gradually been introduced to cope with Seoul's challenges of transport, environment, housing, infrastructure and welfare. But, like London, these incremental adjustments have not been accompanied by significant fiscal devolution. At the same time, Seoul's development has spilled over beyond its borders and spread across a three-province, 26-million-person 'Capital Region' that comprises around half of the national population (Table 5.1).

Now the capital of a rich and maturing democracy, Seoul has entered a sustained period of slower growth and needs to finance the upgrade of aging infrastructure and adjust to an aging society. Over the next two decades it faces challenges that are familiar to more established world cities in the West: how to

Table 5.1:   Seoul's capital region: key statistics

% of national population	% of national GDP	GDP per capita vs national average (1)	City global competitiveness rank	Country global competitiveness rank	Annualised employment growth 2000–14	Annualised GDP growth 2000–14	% of national employment
49.5%	46%	0.97	20	26	1.9%	3.1%	47.7%

Source: Parilla *et al.*, 2015; OECD Stat., 2014; World Economic Forum, 2015; EIU, 2012.

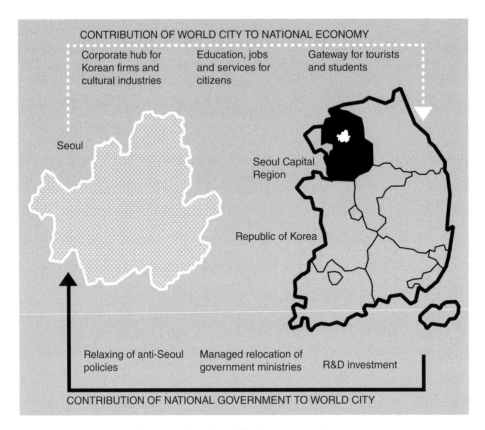

CONTRIBUTION OF WORLD CITY TO NATIONAL ECONOMY

Corporate hub for
Korean firms and
cultural industries

Education, jobs
and services for
citizens

Gateway for tourists
and students

Seoul

Seoul Capital
Region

Republic of Korea

Relaxing of anti-Seoul
policies

Managed relocation of
government ministries

R&D investment

CONTRIBUTION OF NATIONAL GOVERNMENT TO WORLD CITY

Figure 5.1:   Reciprocity between Seoul and the Korean central government.

build a more distinctive identity and urban fabric, improve housing affordability, respond effectively to climate change risks and co-ordinate with other actors to address imbalances and inefficiencies in the wider region. These challenges are of a different order to those it has had to face so far and will likely require new tools and new deals to be struck with national government (Figure 5.1). As with other world cities, as circumstances change, the equilibrium that Seoul strikes with its nation state has to be flexible and capable of recalibration if it is to remain a cohesive metropolis.

History of Seoul's relationship with central government

Koreans have long referred to the Seoul region as the Seoul Republic because of its dominance over all other national regions. For over 600 years it has held a status of prominence that puts it apart from all upper-tier governments in Korea. The only exception to this privilege was during the Japanese occupation of 1910 to 1945 when Seoul was put under the authority of Gyeonggi Province. Even during the occupation there was significant collaboration between the colonial administration and Korean capital (Mun, 2008), and Seoul was re-established as Korea's undisputed growth engine during the country's administration by the United States (1945 to 1948) and Ee Seung-man's unstable presidency of 1948 to 1960. Since then, nearly all central government agencies have (until very recently) been located in Seoul, and so major business headquarters clustered nearby to be close to political decision-making and gain exposure to international markets. The capital hosts an overwhelming share of Korea's foreign embassies, foreign consulates, stock brokerages, foreign bank offices, global media outlets and satellite networks. It even dominates in terms of international hotels, trading and telecommunications firms. Unsurprisingly, a clear majority of Korea's senior executives, researchers and innovators also operate in the city (Hill and Kim, 2000).

In the space of just 75 years, Seoul grew from a city of one million people to a megacity of more than 10 million, and its economic structure transformed from a rural, agrarian system to a labour-intensive export hub, and then to an advanced industrial and post-industrial economy. The authoritarian regime of Bak Jeong-hee (1961–1979) introduced *Gukgajohabjuui* – 'state corporatism' – a process of explicit collusion between Bak's administration and Korean industrial monopolies (Shin, 2008). Large companies were invited to invest in particular industry sectors and were given access to cheap credit, facilitated by foreign aid and a large reparation repayment from Japan after the normalisation of diplomatic relations in 1965. In this period, companies like Samsung (electronics) and Hyundai (vehicle and ship manufacturing) grew explosively. The family-run *jaebeol* corporation structure was well suited to prosper in the decades after the overthrow of the Second Republic in 1961, as it was able to respond quickly to market conditions. With the city under the authority of the Prime Minister's Office, the central government's firm economic and land development policies in the 1960s and 1970s helped Seoul (and Busan and Ulsan) develop new infrastructure and human capital. Most *jaebeol* activity was centred in Seoul, but other cities also became company hubs – Hyundai's shipbuilding operation dominated the south-eastern city of Ulsan and Pohang Steel is still based in Pohang. This model was essential to Korea's growth – in the three decades from 1960, Korea's GDP grew by an average of 9% each year, and GDP per capita increased more than six-fold to more than $8000 (Lee, 2014).

Seoul had begun to suck in population from about 1960, but its rapid growth was deliberately slowed by national urban policies that tried to reassign growth to other regions. The national perspective was that Seoul was overcrowded, overpriced and an impediment to growth elsewhere. In a deeply centralised system, the city was unable to respond to these policies with incentives or deregulation that could attract re-investment. This affected Seoul's economic dominance – its GDP per capita was around twice that of Korea in 1960, but this gap shrank and by 1990 it was roughly equal (Hill and Kim, 2000). On the other hand, government efforts since the 1960s aimed at reducing concentration in the capital area have backfired. Attempts at regulating – as opposed to managing – the use of space have achieved little in slowing down agglomeration in the region, and have produced a complex regulatory landscape (Korea Research Institute for Human Settlements, 2013).

Seoul gradually began to make the transition into a global city in the late 1980s as Korea democratised. Although the capital had built international connections since the 1960s' export-led industrial economic strategy, reform was catalysed by the 1988 Summer Olympics. The Seoul Olympics marked a watershed for Korean culture, business and politics; the first free democratic elections had taken place the year before. Just prior to the event, Seoul was granted significant autonomy (25.05.1988 law) as a 'special city'.

The city's leading family-owned conglomerates – *jaebol* – began to internationalise and relocate their branch plants to low-wage economies across eastern and south-eastern Asia. The capital region attracted a surge of jobs in knowledge and high-technology firms, and in 1988 it surpassed the combined population of all other provinces beyond the second region of Busan-Gyeongnam (Douglass, 2000). That year it was granted the legal status of 'special city' which marked it out from other metropolitan cities. Soon afterwards, US and European firms moved quickly to acquire more of Seoul's successful conglomerates. This incremental liberalisation was embedded in the second Seoul Metropolitan Readjustment Plan (1997), which recognised the region's role as South Korea's globally competitive hub (Korea Research Institute for Human Settlements, 2013).

Until the 1990s, Seoul was really just an appendage of central government, with central policy deciding local policy. Investment for the 1988 Olympics was allocated by central government principally as a means to promote Korea globally rather than to trigger a new cycle of strategic development in Seoul (Ryder, 2015). The government had always appointed the Mayor of Seoul itself until municipal self-government legislation in 1991. This act, which retained the 'special treatment' towards Seoul's metropolitan administration, featured many instances where Seoul's city leadership would have to consult the Prime Minister, for example if it wished to float bonds or reform the way it managed its balance sheet (OECD, 2005).

The capital's first directly elected mayor entered office in 1995, with enhanced responsibilities for education, crime, welfare and infrastructure systems in the core city, overseeing 25 smaller autonomous districts (*gu*) within what was still a compact 605 km^2 area. Under the new arrangements, Seoul was able to make progress with large-scale regeneration projects, most notably in Cheonggyecheon district, which has been redeveloped to support the city's transition towards creative and service industries. The metropolitan government has been able to dedicate the attention of senior officials to creating a joined-up approach across sectors – economic development, road management, civil engineering, urban planning and welfare – and increase citizen participation in decisions about urban change.

At the same time, national government began to promote Seoul as a world city within north-east Asia. This was part of an official policy of *segyehwa*, introduced in the mid-1990s to express open-mindedness and liberalisation towards international trade, exchange and investment. Since then, national policies to encourage inter-city competition for foreign investment have benefited Seoul. Between 1990 and 1999, foreign investment soared from $1 billion to $15 billion, a significant proportion of which was accounted for by corporate acquisitions. A free economic zone in nearby Incheon helped drive specialisation in business and financial services, nevertheless, international competitiveness in strategic industries such as fashion, IT and business services was largely achieved without central government support.

Adaptation in Seoul's global age

The 1997–8 Asian economic crisis exposed serious weaknesses in Korea's banking and business sectors, and led to many conglomerate bankruptcies and a currency depreciation (Tait, 2005). After an IMF bailout, Seoul's capital and real estate markets were opened to foreign investment, mergers and acquisitions. Korean businesses moved into IT development. In the aftermath of the crisis, the Seoul Metropolitan Government (SMG) implemented a series of transparency reforms under the leadership of Mayor Go Geon which were taken up and replicated by other city governments as well as the central government.

Central government has retained considerable oversight over Seoul's metropolitan government. Some argue that its attempts to empower the lower-level *gu* have constrained the city government's power to act (Ryder, 2015). Despite the city's lack of concrete policy competences, successive mayors have been ambitious in devising development aims to help Seoul modernise, become more transparent and transition to a higher-value economy. The Cheonggyecheon River regeneration was a high-profile example of the city government's intention to manage its own redevelopment projects. City Hall has also tried to overcome some of the bureaucratic and financial inflexibilities which prevent a more can-do governance system. Since the election of Mayor Bak Won-sun in 2011, the city has expanded attempts to engage citizens and grow the social economy as a means to grow channels of collaboration and communication at the local level. Strong and visible leadership has added momentum and credibility for reform of a centralised government apparatus (Symons, 2015).

In recent years the national government has taken a more hands-off approach and has looked to manage the wider framework conditions for Seoul. Jung Eun-bo, Korea's deputy finance minister, explained in 2014 that "[p]roject leadership will shift from the central government to the local governments. The government will provide support packages, including financing and deregulation" (Yoon, 2014). Meanwhile, Seoul's metropolitan leadership has recognised that city and national government capacity to solve the challenges of an aging society by themselves is limited, and has launched a new governance committee to give civic groups representation. Citizens' organisations, commercial bodies and sources of independent expertise will all be given scope to participate, while citizens also have a greater say over budget spending priorities as part of a new phase of public engagement in Seoul (Seoul Metropolitan Authority, 2015, 2016a; KBS News, 2016).

National government has been instrumental in ensuring R&D investment levels are some of the highest in the world. It has provided 50% of the financing for research grants to SMEs to encourage firms and universities to collaborate on technology projects. It has also reinforced innovation networks in the capital region, and encouraged more transport-oriented development to make clusters more effective and competitive. As a result, by 2009 Seoul had the highest share of national patents (nearly 70%) of any OECD city (OECD, 2012). The largest domestic firms such as Samsung and Hyundai have been able to compete and innovate in the global market because they have been able to establish their own science R&D capacity. In 2016, however, there are concerns that Seoul SMEs lack the resources to invest in R&D or access to university networks.

Seoul's world city model is not dissimilar to Tokyo's. It is principally a national platform for the global operations of Korean multinational companies, rather than a global hub for the operations of mobile global firms. It retains a very significant manufacturing sector, and has growing regional roles in film, fashion and music, without having witnessed extensive foreign immigration. It is also less socially and spatially polarised than many world cities. It is clear that Korea's greater embrace of free trade has benefited Seoul's competitiveness. Trade agreements with the EU and the US are in effect, which have opened up Seoul's industries to competition and investment, with likely impacts on productivity. The toleration of a stronger currency and commitment to domestic industrial policy reforms has put exporting Korean firms at an advantage in comparison to some Japanese counterparts (Yoon, 2014).

Unlike other rapidly expanding global centres, the population in the city itself is falling and is set to slip below 10 million in 2017, while it continues to grow rapidly in the wider region (Kwaak, 2014). The city is also aging rapidly; the median age recently surpassed 40 and is set to rise to 47 by 2030 (Chosun Ilbo, 2016). This has required a new leadership approach, especially under Mayor Bak Won-sun, a charismatic figure who is viewed by some commentators as a future presidential candidate. Tensions between the city and national government have occasionally increased over issues of regulation and financing of core public services such as hospitals, social care and childcare (An, 2016).

The central government has long espoused de-centralisation reform that relocates government ministries and other quasi-governmental bodies away from Seoul in order to achieve more balanced development. These have only been partially and fitfully enacted. Some of these relocation decisions were motivated by electoral reasons rather than strategic ones. Nevertheless, the government complex in downtown Seoul will stay home to many government offices, including foreign and justice ministries.

The national system of cities: Seoul and Korea

South Korea is a unitary republic with three main tiers of government:

1. The central state;
2. Eight provinces, six metropolitan cities and the Seoul Capital Region;
3. Smaller cities and municipalities.

The Korean state – and in particular its Economic Planning Board – has guided urban development for the last half century through its power to choose industrial locations. It has addressed Seoul's development in four broad phases (Korea Research Institute for Human Settlements, 2013). In the first phase in the 1960s and 1970s, partly for political reasons, it chose to discourage permits for new manufacturing firms in Seoul. This was intended to balance rapid urbanisation and relocate high-polluting sectors away from the capital. It also tried to cap students and introduced a green belt to curb growth.

From the 1980s onwards, as the problem of concentration worsened, it formalised and intensified its efforts at de-concentration by introducing new regulatory measures such as tax incentives, surcharges and stringent zoning laws to control urbanisation. These policies did not succeed in deterring R&D investment and the technology thrust of Seoul's metropolitan economy, and industrial innovation continued to occur in the region. Nor did a green belt policy deter explosive population growth, with many migrant construction and service workers settling in squatter areas on the city outskirts, or exploiting gaps in the green belt to the point where it progressively became redundant and was accused of distorting metropolitan growth. The region's share of Korea's population grew from 30% in 1970 to nearly 50% by the turn of the century (OECD, 2005).

In a third phase, from the 1990s, the central government sought to leverage Seoul's pre-eminence to make it South Korea's gateway into globalisation, while continuing de-concentration strategies. And in a fourth phase starting in the mid-2000s, central government acknowledged that its regulatory approach to spatial management had not succeeded in preventing concentration. As a result, it has slowly adopted a more deliberate planning mentality, seeking to ease regulatory burdens within the metropolitan area – although this has had knock-on effects on other Korean regions, worried that deregulation may concentrate activity even more in the capital region. At the same time, central government continues to seek more proactive, as opposed to reactive, means of affecting spatial concentration, while building on Seoul's role as a powerhouse in north-east Asia.

In the 1990s, central government established a specialised distribution of city roles whereby Seoul would focus on business and finance, Incheon would be a logistics and R&D supplier to Seoul, and Gyeonggi a manufacturing base. Public investments included a high-speed train between Seoul and second city Busan that more than halved travel time, and a new international airport that would support 24-hour operations. The establishment of Free Economic Zones led to fierce competition among cities and regions to be designated (Lee, 2014). Laws to encourage construction in teleports, convention centres and business parks have helped support Seoul's role for events and technology. But some commentators note that the creation of secondary 'innovation cities' and 'enterprise cities' was a short-term attempt to relieve political discontent rather than a long-term vision for the success of Korea's city system (Park, 2013).

Korea's second cities – such as Daegu and Busan – continue to face brain drain, population decline, low economic diversification and struggling city centres. The population share of Busan, Daegu and Gwangju regions has fallen relative to the Seoul region since 1985. At the same time, Korea is still very culturally divided by region with strong regional identities. In 2005, the OECD urged Seoul to widen public debate about how to build more balanced national growth and to enhance nationwide university co-operation. Although there is no widespread public discontent with the extent to which Seoul dominates the Korean political and economic landscape, there are concerns that the *jaebeol* influence on the Korean economy – most of which are headquartered in Seoul – is no longer fit for purpose. Some question whether their corporate governance is suited to the city's competitiveness model (Bak, 2015; Song, 2015).

Limited efforts at de-centralisation have been attempted. The 2003 and 2009 National Land Planning and Utilisation Acts sought to transfer urban planning authority to local authorities, to maximise local ownership – with the intention to encourage productive competition between cities (ibid). In 2015, mayors of Korea's larger second-tier cities called for the establishment of a three-tier system that would give their cities more autonomy and improve their competitiveness. An increase in the local consumption tax from 11% to nearer 20% has been requested in order to cope with an increased social welfare burden (Im, 2015).

As part of a shift to deregulation, the central government has approved commercial development in restricted 'green belt' areas of second cities to catalyse much-needed investment. The government also plans to provide better incentives for businesses to move or invest in the regions, such as tax cuts and exemptions from some regulations.

Central government also introduced a new three-layer urban and regional development structure to better manage territorial development and balance its system of cities. Its first layer, supra-economic regions, considers city-regions as the most productive unit of spatial organisation. They are designed to be treated as single economic entities through which economies of scale can be achieved. The second tier, consisting of seven mega-economic regional zones, seeks to foster greater competitiveness by furthering co-operation between different metropolitan areas. Each zone has an Economic Regional Development Plan to co-ordinate the process. The third tier – so-called 'Daily Living Spheres' – includes the spaces of everyday life, with a particular focus on improving conditions in neglected secondary or tertiary urban centres (OECD, 2012).

Seoul is nearly a decade into a long-term national project to relocate government ministries and semi-public bodies away from the capital to Sejong City in order to achieve more balanced development. These relocation decisions, which were initially controversial, extend a long line of de-centralisation policies, and are an attempt to try a different approach. More than 20 ministries have been headquartered there so far, although key defence functions and the President's Office are to stay in Seoul. The relocation is viewed by some as creating inefficiencies in the relationships between national and city government and business representatives. Beyond this move, there is currently little political momentum for a broader programme of de-centralisation and regionalisation. The National Assembly continues to defend centralised power, having turned down a bill for comprehensive transfer of State affairs to local governments (Oh, 2014).

Ongoing challenges where Seoul needs help from national government

The national government is now engaged in a more co-operative partnership with city governments such as Seoul. There is a widespread perspective that it has to take a leadership role in strengthening governance and updating Korea's legal and political institutions (Kim, 2015). The key areas where joint working is necessary include international investment, industry modernisation and fiscal reform.

A more competitive framework for external investment

Most analysts indicate that Seoul requires government regulation, tariffs and taxes and labour legislation that will encourage investors (Davis, 2015). The central government has moved incrementally to improve flexibility, and is in regular dialogue with foreign investors about their needs. A new fund to encourage foreign investor participation in start-up companies is modelled on Israel's success, but national government can do more to invest in marketing and positioning to find markets for SMEs, and to help the private sector make independent decisions on location and clustering. Support for entrepreneurship and opposition to monopolies will be a key part of the agenda to make the Seoul and Korean economy more competitive.

Vision to target key sectors to become more globally competitive

Seoul has unrealised potential in a number of important sectors – international higher education, fashion, digital cultural content (for example, animation, gaming and cartoons) and high-tech R&D. One way of boosting innovation is the attraction of foreign researchers and scientists, which relies on national government legislation on immigration to guarantee long-term stays and financial backing. Seoul's ambitions as an Asian cultural and creative centre may be predicated on a more deliberate strategy to become more pluralist and diverse, supported by central government reform.

Momentum for substantive fiscal devolution

Seoul operates within a system of highly centralised revenue collection, although it does have special fiscal rights. Property taxes are the main source of income for local authorities – including Seoul. Although national tax guidelines are relatively flexible for Seoul, which has more room for manoeuvre than other Korean cities, its autonomy only applies to a narrow range of taxes, and has been declining since the Asian financial crisis. As a result, Seoul's 2016 city budget of 24 trillion Won ($19 billion), although rising steadily over the previous four years, is still less than half of Tokyo's on a per capita basis – see Table 5.2 (Seoul Metropolitan Authority, 2016b).

Seoul is more than 80% budget independent, but national tax revenue outweighs local tax by a factor of 4 to 1 and the central government indicates how most money should be spent. In order to meet future challenges such as aging infrastructure and social services for an aging population, Seoul will require

Table 5.2:   Change in Seoul Metropolitan Government's budgetary spending, 2012–2016

	2016	Change since 2012
Social Welfare	KRW 8.3tn ($7bn)	+62%
Education	KRW 2.8tn ($2.4bn)	+15%
Roads/Transport	KRW 2.7tn ($2.3bn)	+56%
Public Spaces/Environment	KRW 1.8tn ($1.6bn)	+2%
Security/Policing	KRW 1.6tn ($1.3bn)	+26%
Culture and Tourism	KRW 631bn ($540m)	+40%
City Safety/Flood Defences	KRW 1.1tn ($950m)	+50%
Financing Activities	KRW 880bn ($800m)	−56%
General Administration	KRW 480bn ($410m)	+61%
Industrial Economy	KRW 480bn ($410m)	−4%
Urban Planning and Housing Management	KRW 329bn ($280m)	−6%
Contingencies	KRW 178bn ($150m)	−21%

national government to shift at least part of income and consumption taxes to the city. For Gim Yung-bong, Professor at Sejong University, "[i]t is time for market principles, not politics, to guide urban development in order to boost the self-sufficiency of our cities" (Park, 2013). However, because Seoul represents such a large portion of nationally collected taxes, any changes must be made bearing in mind the potential disadvantages faced by secondary cities (OECD, 2005).

Decentralisation of powers to the metropolitan government

Centralised rule is a product of perceived failures of local democracy in the aftermath of the Korean War, but for the last 25 years there have been consistent calls for more local autonomy to cope with the challenges of transportation, environment, housing, infrastructure, welfare and other public service delivery. The metropolitan government has become a more transparent and responsive institution thanks to ongoing reforms. It now works much more effectively to respond to local concerns and lower-tier municipal needs (Snyder *et al.*, 2012).

Seoul's new strategic 2030 plan aims to strengthen and connect growth around the three specialised urban centres – Seoul (culture), Gangnam (business) and Yeongdeungpo (finance). Its success as a long-term planning guideline depends on firm institutional alignment and central government strengthening of governance in the Capital Region.

In 2014, Mayor Bak Won-sun called for further de-centralisation of powers. The organisational reshuffle of the Ministry of Security and Public Administration, which oversees regional autonomy, represents an opportunity to renegotiate the transfer of duties to local governments in Seoul and other Korean cities.

Support and incentives for regional co-operation

Seoul has needed to make the case to central government of the benefits of broader regional co-operation – reduced transaction costs, greater efficiency and economic returns. Shared associations, committees, corporations and funds have boosted co-operation across jurisdictions, but a broader programme of co-ordinated development will be important if Seoul is to avoid a situation where remote suburbs are locked out from new sources of employment (Kim, 2006).

Key actors and mechanisms that enable Seoul to make progress with the nation state

Seoul's Metropolitan Mayor is a key actor in advocating for greater fiscal and political autonomy as the city looks to transition to a greener and more public-transport-oriented growth model. Organisational reform of the Ministry of Security and Public Administration, which oversees regional autonomy, presents an opportunity to recalibrate the transfer of powers to local governments in Seoul and other Korean cities. Seoul's leaders are making the case to central government of the cost benefits of a regional approach. In 2014, central government endorsed Seoul's role as a leader of other Korean municipalities, in terms of addressing regulation that may impede private investment and consumption.

The Mayor is also the highest profile spokesperson for Seoul's interests with national government. In recent years, Mayor Bak Won-sun has publicly requested central government support for childcare costs, small business protection, redevelopment compensation, engagement with North Korea and subway system upgrades (Kyunghyang Shinmun, 2012; Kim and Winkler, 2013). The Mayor does not have a regular or formal relationship with many departments – there was an eight-year gap between the Mayor's last two meetings with the national finance minister (Yeonhap News, 2014).

Seoul's city advocates cannot always make headway with central government because of the fragmented administrative mandates across central government departments. A siloed approach has stifled the emergence of an integrated approach to urban development at the national level. While the Presidential Committee for Regional Development, set up in 2008, seeks to address these issues, it lacks the implementation powers to resolve them (OECD, 2012).

Conclusion

Seoul has been an extraordinary example of a world city in a developmental state that has moved through multiple income brackets. It is now an established global centre comparing favourably to some of the 20th century's elite cities. In 2016, as a new Asia-Pacific system comes into view, Seoul is now in a new context of greater regional competition and specialisation. It has an economy that is highly dependent on a small number of companies and specialisms, modest productivity growth, skills mismatches and a fast-aging population. Seoul will need to lead Korea's shift to advanced manufacturing, a deeper domestic innovation system and to a new approach to international talent, and national government will play an instrumental role in all three areas.

Seoul's future will be influenced in part by the success of Korea's six other metropolitan cities – led by Daegu and Busan. Many of them struggle with population decline, a narrow economic base and unappealing city centres, and their governments express resistance against any moves towards deregulation that might lead to further concentration in Seoul. Seoul's own programmes of collaboration with these cities lack financial support, but central government is now pursuing a more negotiated relationship with them. The approval of commercial development in restricted 'green belt' areas of the secondary cities is one step to catalyse much-needed investment and regeneration, but a more compelling vision for the Korean 'system of cities' is needed if Seoul is to manage its own growth sustainably.

6

Tokyo: Shared global aspirations and blunted reforms

Yodalica (2014), licensed by CC BY 2.0

World Cities and Nation States, First Edition. Greg Clark and Tim Moonen.
© 2017 John Wiley & Sons, Ltd. Published 2017 by John Wiley & Sons, Ltd.

Tokyo is the world's most populated urban area and its largest functional economic unit with over $1.6 trillion in yearly output. One of Asia's first cities to globalise and achieve affluence in the 20th century, the city stands as a testament to urban management, logistics and re-invention. Its metropolitan area accounts for nearly a third of Japan's GDP and outperforms the rest of the country in most dimensions (Table 6.1). The sheer size of its customer and client market ensures it remains one of the 'Big Six' command and control centres of the global economy, and compared to many of its peers it maintains prodigious technological, transport and quality of life advantages.

As Japan's low economic growth and deflation persist into a third decade, Tokyo has had to face up to the legacies of the past, re-evaluate its strategic priorities and pursue a more balanced and sustainable growth model. The city's long-term priorities are to open and re-energise its economy to prepare for and finance a rapidly aging society. Higher value sectors, from financial services, robotics, life sciences and business tourism, are at the heart of the effort to stimulate growth. In the long-term aftermath of Fukushima, the city also aims to diversify its energy sector. Its vision focuses on becoming 'the world's best city' and an international model of sustainable development. Tokyo's leaders argue that Japan's future prosperity rests on the success of this strategy, for "if Tokyo is defeated in the global competition between cities, the entire country will decline" (Tokyo Metropolitan Government, 2015a).

Japan is a centralised unitary nation state, but Tokyo's metropolitan government was one of the first anywhere to acquire special fiscal and political autonomy and does not receive tax allocations from central government. Compared to other case studies in this book, central and Tokyo governments have tended to share objectives and communicate both formally and informally (Figure 6.1). The Prime Minister's Office and central ministries' main responsibilities to Japan's cities are to disburse powers, to invest in national infrastructure (such as high-speed rail, inter-city motorways and airports) and to manage framework conditions. This chapter highlights the growing policy co-operation between Tokyo's metropolitan leadership and the national government over the past 15 years, especially in supporting urban regeneration and investment readiness. But the Tokyo case also highlights the tensions of a world city in a relatively mono-ethnic country, and the resulting dilemmas around macroeconomic policy and government regulation. Entrenched vested interests continue to resist the sorts of transformative reform in Tokyo that would sustain its competitiveness across multiple sectors. Tokyo is now

Table 6.1: Tokyo's metropolitan area: key statistics

% of national population	% of national GDP	GDP per capita vs national average (1)	City global competitiveness rank	Country global competitiveness rank	Annualised employment growth 2000–14	Annualised GDP growth 2000–14	% of national employment
28%	32%	1.17	6	6	0.5%	0.6%	29%

Source: Parilla *et al.*, 2015; OECD Stat., 2014; World Economic Forum, 2015; EIU, 2012.

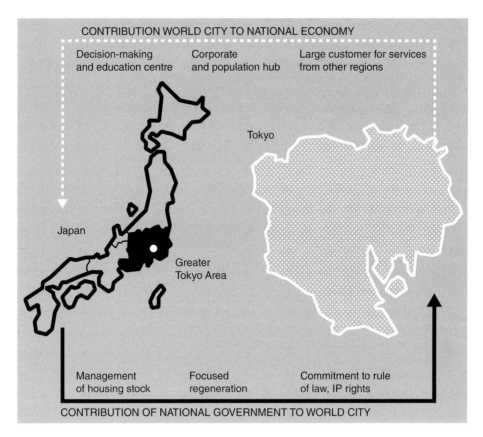

Figure 6.1: Reciprocity between Tokyo and the Japanese central government.

reaching the limits of its world city model and will depend on more agile and ambitious collaboration with central government if it is to make timely adjustments.

History of Tokyo's relationship with central government

Tokyo has been the centre of Japanese political and military power for over a century. The Meiji era (1868–1912) radically transformed the country's urban structure as feudalism was dismantled, social and physical mobility increased and industrialisation took off. Coastal cities, and Tokyo in particular, benefited from a booming export sector and their position along trade routes.

Japan's process of industrialisation was deliberately State-driven, as the central government was anxious to shore up the country's capacity to resist Western economic and military might. As a result, firms that could be trusted – that is, with close links to government – were privileged, assisted and protected. In a pattern that was common elsewhere in the 20th century, militarisation in the 1930s concentrated economic power even further around the political institutions in

Tokyo. Compared to most countries, the State played an indispensable strategic role in the economic development of its most globally oriented city, and this trend continued after the Second World War. Tokyo sat within a highly central-ised political system that promoted the capital as Japan's engine for growth, and the vehicle for national development goals and nationalistic ideals (Child Hill and Fujita, 1993; Kakiuchi, 2013; Pham, 2015).

In 1943, Tokyo's wards were placed under the control of the Tokyo Metropolitan Government (TMG). The merging of the City of Tokyo with Tokyo *fu* or urban prefectures created the modern-day Tokyo Metropolis in 1947. This was a unique arrangement in Japan that gave Tokyo relative freedom from the Ministry of Home Affairs (now Internal Affairs and Communication) which oversaw local authorities. The Local Autonomy Law (1947) and later amendments instigated a process of de-centralisation. Soon, 70% of Tokyo's revenue was derived from local taxes (as opposed to 30% elsewhere), signalling a relative independence from the central government purse. By 1989, 78% of TMG funds were metro-politan taxes (rising to 84% today) (Child Hill and Fujita, 1993; Kakiuchi, 2013; Pham, 2015; Tokyo Metropolitan Government, 2015b).

Tokyo led Japan's rapid industrialisation process between 1950 and 1990, while national policy sought to redistribute growth to the regions. The 1962 national Comprehensive Development Plan laid out national policy on balanced urbanisation and identified Tokyo as over-populated. But despite efforts at de-concentration, including new remote industrial towns, central government support for domestic manufacturers ultimately helped consolidate Tokyo as a major industrial, urban and political hub. Access to the national political insti-tutions in Tokyo continued to motivate corporations and companies to cluster nearby. Repeated attempts at legislation to de-centralise patterns of growth in Japan have been in tension with the economic and political pull that Tokyo generates (Hill and Kim, 2000; Saito, 2003; Sorensen, 2003; Waley, 2007).

As the metropolitan government gradually gained more experience and capac-ity, it took more of a lead on issues such as pollution, small business support and research and development, enacting policies that were only later endorsed by the centre. Under the administration of Governor Minobe (1967–1979), the TMG campaigned against national policy on pollution, and in favour of more local decision-making and autonomy. The TMG has continued to act as a first-mover on key issue areas, including the growing challenge of power generation. Its ambitions to be the source of policy leadership in certain cases have often been popular with the city electorate.

In the 1980s, Tokyo took on expanded hi-tech, finance and service roles as the State sought to transform it into a global city as part of a broader national economic shift. Its model was based on being the headquarters platform for Japan's own successful exporting corporations. Greater fiscal autonomy did not change the fact that Tokyo's growth coalition throughout this period continued as a close, semi-hierarchical relationship between the State and the capital. The new roles Tokyo took on merely reflected the new ambitions the State set out for its capital city, clearly laid out in the 1987 National Comprehensive Land Development Plan (Child Hill and Fujita, 1993; Hill and Kim, 2000; Kakiuchi, 2013).

The State also actively shaped the character of urban development in Tokyo, setting the objectives and relying on the TMG to implement them. Its involvement in waterfront development projects in the 1980s highlighted both its ambitions for its capital city and the extent of its influence. In the process, the State's relationship with the private sector remained particularly close (due to the strong convergence of political and economic elites in a developmental state). Local economic interests in Tokyo typically lobbied the central government, rather than the TMG, which was perceived as unapproachable and aloof when it came to dealing with the private sector (Saito, date unknown; Saito, 2003; Waley, 2007; Fujita, 2011).

Following Japan's economic crisis of 1989, the State partially liberalised the economy, relaxing urban land-use regulations and gradually accepting Tokyo's primacy. The TMG lobbied strongly for these changes as part of an increasingly assertive two-way relationship between the central government and the capital. The TMG was keen to use urban redevelopment projects as a way out of the crisis, but needed more flexible planning and regulatory frameworks to unlock private investment, and managed to convince the State to deliver these. The TMG also sought to respond to local demands for quality of life investments, as opposed to merely economic development projects. This lobbying resulted in substantial national reforms by the turn of the century which granted greater local autonomy to all Japanese cities, but without fully resolving the tension between the State's primacy and Tokyo's growing role as a world city (Saito, date unknown, 2012; Fujita, 2011).

Changes in city powers since 2000: What problems have been solved?

Amid the globalisation of finance, the transition to global city status was far from smooth in Tokyo due to a rise in property prices, unpopular development against the wishes of local municipalities, growing inequalities across the nation and an economic crash that stalled reform in the 1990s. The city began to lose its *de facto* status as Asia's transport gateway to Singapore, Hong Kong and Seoul. A 1998 political de-centralisation reform allowed the TMG to become a real regional government by handing off responsibility for local-level services, but further financial de-centralisation was not forthcoming (Waley, 2007; Tsukamoto, 2013).

Under the Koizumi administration (2001–2006), Japan finally and unambiguously accepted Tokyo's national pre-eminence and began to apply market principles to encourage specialisation, devolution and privatisation. The central government supported further deregulation of planning through its 2002 Urban Regeneration Law, and gave the private sector more latitude to lead on urban regeneration. Reforms to the National Planning Act in 2005 also granted greater leeway to all regions, including Tokyo, to develop their own local development plans based on government guidelines and objectives. Although rapid deregulation caused local political tensions, it also allowed local authorities to use a greater share of their tax base, instead of ceding it to the national level, and this change has yielded more revenue for Tokyo (Waley, 2007; Saito, 2012; Tsukamoto, 2013).

In the last decade, the national government has come to adopt a less top-down approach that is more conducive to competitiveness, and allowed Japanese cities to pursue development that is focused on liveability, in light of widespread frustration with State-mandated economic goals. In 2007, the State reduced financial transfers to the regions to foster independence, but this did not substantially alter the centralised character of fiscal arrangements in Japan. Central funding for public works has fallen away since the late 1990s, partly in response to fiscal pressures and partly as a way to encourage regional innovation in economic, spatial and fiscal management. The upshot was that Tokyo became the only jurisdiction to witness an increase in total local revenue. In addition, in 2009 the new ruling Democratic Party of Japan emphasised local accountability and competitiveness in an attempt to create innovation in local policies. Urban revitalisation is now a cornerstone of national policy.

In 2011, Tokyo launched a Special Zones initiative under the direction of the centrist national Democratic Party leadership. This represented the first time that Tokyo sought to attract foreign companies to dedicated zones. Initially, this strategy was designed to form clusters of Asian operational headquarters and R&D centres by offering tax benefits, deregulation and financial support to foreign firms setting up in five districts of the city. In 2012, the conservative Liberal Democratic Party returned to power and the Zone policy was expanded through the National Strategic Special Zones Initiative. The intention was to build international business hubs that attract international finance, talent and companies by making it much easier to conduct business in nine wards in Tokyo as well as in Kanagawa and Chiba's Narita. Other cities nominated include the Kansai Area (including Osaka), Niigata and Fukuoka. Among the most pertinent features of the policy are an attempt to build at higher densities to provide housing for those displaced by Fukushima, and to make more innovative use of public space to attract tourists and entrepreneurship. Relaxation of rules surrounding medical practitioners, school ownership, floor area ratios and heritage buildings has been deployed by the central government and the TMG in tandem, in anticipation of a step change of overseas interest in the lead up to the 2020 Olympics.

The reduction in central transfers in Japan has increased Tokyo's advantages relative to the rest of the country. The TMG has a significant budget at its disposal, reaching $115 billion in the 2015 fiscal year, of which nearly a sixth is allocated to investments. The overwhelming majority of these funds (84%) are locally raised – up from 70% three decades ago. In comparison, the Japanese average is roughly 50%, which in itself is a significant increase from its earlier levels of 30% (Tokyo Metropolitan Government, 2015b). Tokyo benefits from two local corporate taxes which provide a third of its revenue. Property taxes account for a further 23% and local consumption taxes another 13%.

Over recent decades, Tokyo has maintained a far healthier fiscal position than its central government, which, in part, has enabled it to sustain its relative financial independence. The TMG managed to reduce its debt burden from Y14 trillion to Y10 trillion between 2001 and 2013. As a result, its reliance on bond issues is relatively low (6.5% compared to a central government figure of nearly 40%) (ibid). Tokyo's sound fiscal position allows it to make substantial capital expenditures each year to urban redevelopment (Y290 million in 2015), waterfront area development (Y185 million), urban rapid transit railway projects (Y757 million) and water systems (Y1.1 billion). It also runs a reserve fund for investments in the forthcoming Olympics, which currently stands at nearly Y411 billion.

Despite this progressive devolution, the national government has retained a strong presence in Tokyo – it remains central as its global gateway and to national development policies, hence the national focus on Tokyo's 'renewal' since the 2000s. This relationship has been embodied by the delivery of the 2020 Olympics. As the Games are to be organised jointly by the IOC, the central government and the TMG, it has crystallised further the closeness of the world city and its nation state. Surprisingly, the central government share of spending has increased significantly since 2008, while the metropolitan government share has been on the decline, in relative terms, since the early 1990s (Waley, 2007; Tsukamoto, 2013;Tokyo Metropolitan Government, 2015b).

In recent years the Prime Minister's Office has maintained a close interest in Tokyo's execution of its programmes for national renewal. It runs an Urban Renaissance HQ, which helps co-ordinate TMG and central government policies on Tokyo. Such co-ordination means that when, for example, national government land and buildings are vacated or de-centralised from Tokyo, they are passed on to the TMG, which actively redevelops in favour of a more attractive mixed-use model (Fujita and Child Hill, 2005; Pham, 2015). The national Ministry of Land, Infrastructure, Transport and Tourism (MLIT) retains prerogatives over local urban planning, especially over urban renewal regulations and railway networks. It also oversees the Urban Renaissance Agency – a quango that manages real estate and urban development projects, and has major stakes in Tokyo regeneration schemes, such as the Otemachi district, Minato Mirai 21 and Yokohama (Pham, 2015).

The PM's Office is influential in setting the investment and business promotion agenda for Tokyo. It sets general goals and targets (for example, increasing foreign direct investment by Y35 trillion by 2020) and runs FDI promotion projects, such as *Invest Japan* and the National Strategic Special Zone initiatives, both of which have a strong bearing on Tokyo. Meanwhile, the Ministry of Economy, Trade and Industry and its sub-agencies issue binding guidelines on energy policy and public R&D investment to promote smart cities. Tokyo has little option but to comply with these national economic and environmental policy directives.

Japan's distinctive national development model has clearly helped Tokyo to manage some challenges that other world cities struggle with. It has helped manage its housing supply and affordability over the last decades, overseeing a steady rise in the stock of housing through a combination of zoning deregulation and top-down master-planning. The central government now fully recognises Tokyo's role as Japan's world city and is prepared to support its regeneration and repositioning in order to drive the national economy. Japan also positions Tokyo and other Japanese cities as pioneers of smart urban development, which attracts a great deal of interest from other national governments. Japanese smart city concepts (such as Kashiwa-no-ha, transit-oriented development and urban area management) are welcomed by the national ministries, and are demonstrated to other countries in eastern and southern Asia for how cities can embed disaster prevention, health innovation and new cluster incubation (Kashiwa-No-Ha Smart City, 2015).

The national system of cities: Tokyo and Japan

Today, Tokyo is the only city in Japan governed as a metropolitan prefecture, and is one of 47 prefectures in Japan. The TMG has a powerful governor and metropolitan assembly that preside over 23 Wards (population 9 million), each with its own mayor and local government, and 26 suburban cities to the west (population 4 million). The prefecture is home to one in ten Japanese but generates 20% of national GDP. It forms the dense core of a very large (13,000 km²) three-prefecture conurbation with a combined population of 36 million that has come to dominate the Japanese economy.

Many in Japan believe there is a 'Tokyo problem'. Its share of the command and control functions and its income advantages over secondary cities are viewed by other cities and rural areas as disproportionate. Osaka residents, in particular, widely feel that Tokyo drains their economic vitality, and the capital has to counter a widespread view in Japan that it has an over-concentration of functions and activities, rendered all the more acute as Osaka used to be the economic engine of Japan. Attempts by the central government to disperse economic clusters have largely been ineffective, although redistributive policies did manage to contain severe income inequalities (Child Hill and Fujita, 1993; Sorensen, 2002; Hill and Fujita, 2009; OECD, 2011; Chan and Boland, 2012; Kakiuchi, 2013; Moore, 2014).

Many others, however, argue that the clustering of economic activity benefits the country as a whole, as it raises productivity and allows secondary cities to support Tokyo in the supply chain (Sorensen, 2002). But the importance of supporting other cities and regions is an electoral imperative. Upon his re-election in 2012, Prime Minister Shinzo Abe re-stated his intention "to revitalize the regions and to halt the trend toward the rapid decline and extreme aging of the population" (The Prime Minister of Japan and his Cabinet, 2014).

In terms of Japan's spatial economy, Tokyo is integrated into a virtually seamless urban corridor running between Yokohama–Nagoya–Kyoto–Osaka–Kobe. Because of dense road and rail connections, Japan's secondary cities are not isolated but active participants in a system where Tokyo is the main node. Most are granted varying degrees of autonomy based on their size (as core, special or designated cities). The Decentralisation Promotion Law (1995), which came into force in 1998, redefined the blurred boundaries between local and national governments, and overhauled the system whereby local Governors were effectively just subcontractors for the national tier (Sorensen, 2002; Oshugi, 2011; Stevens, 2013).

Steps have since been taken to engage cities in the national decision-making process. In 2011, a Forum for Consultations between national and regional governments was created, which has begun to bargain with national government for distribution of funds and resources. This Forum acts as a consultative body to include the views of local government in the parliamentary process. The

Association of Mayors and Designated Cities also circulates its shared views on fiscal devolution and the need to recognise individual traits of cities and tailor policy accordingly (Stevens, 2013).

Tokyo is one of the first world cities to recognise that it has to take a lead in bridging the divide with the rest of the nation state. It has opted to invest elsewhere in Japan, using its renewable energy fund to finance a wood biomass power-generation plant in Sanjo City, Niigata. In 2015 it also launched a programme to invite foreign journalists to experience tourist routes between Tokyo and the Tohoku region. The TMG has devised a strategy that features urban–rural initiatives to be jointly enacted with other local governments. For Governor Masuzoe, these efforts "will clearly demonstrate the TMG's stance of coexisting and co-prospering with the rest of Japan" (Tokyo Metropolitan Government, 2015c).

Tokyo's superior fiscal flexibility and its ongoing ability to outperform other cities in terms of economic growth have prompted leaders of Japan's secondary cities to raise the agenda for greater devolution. Several are applying to change their designated status in order to achieve greater autonomy. Osaka has consistently asked for metropolitan status (*'to'*) on the same level as Tokyo, and interest has also been expressed in Nagoya. Osaka's demand, in particular, for local power stems from concerns in its regionalist movement that it has become relatively less desirable compared to Tokyo and has lost population. Although approved in principle in the 2012 Metropolitan Ward Law, greater autonomy is contingent on the agreement of all layers of urban government, referendums and the vagaries of domestic politics. Many observers have been doubtful that metropolitan status would be realised in the near future, and in 2015 Osaka Mayor Toru Hashimoto's referendum gamble to turn the city into a metropolitan government failed. This narrow defeat constituted a blow to Shinzo Abe's wider legislative agenda, but attempts to revive the Metro Osaka plan and ultimately create a second pole beyond Tokyo were underway in 2016 (Stevens, 2013; The Economist, 2014; The Mainichi, 2015). Osaka's ongoing efforts to merge its Prefecture and City to achieve greater autonomy and address region-wide infrastructure have also raised its competitive ambitions. The city's leaders have sought to position it as an alternative and complementary city to Tokyo, through eye-catching initiatives such as privatising the subway train operator in an IPO to attract private investment (Sato and Urabe, 2014).

Tokyo's larger inner city wards are growing strongly, with some rapidly approaching one million residents. The lack of autonomy for the Ward mayors to raise or set taxes to cope with increased pressure on schools and other social infrastructure, especially when compared to the relative autonomy of rural and de-populating prefectures, is becoming more of a political issue in Tokyo.

The future agenda for collaboration with national government

Tokyo is seeking to re-establish itself among the leading five or six cities in the world, and faces a range of challenges in the coming decades for which national investment or regulatory support is important. It is beginning a new phase of co-operation with the national government in the lead up to 2020 and the Olympic Games, which promises to be a catalyst for new agreements and institutional innovation.

Optimisation of National Strategic Special Zones

The central government's Zones policy has been in operation for more than three years, and involves reforms to relax regulations to make it more attractive to start up new businesses and test innovation across Japanese cities. The idea behind the Zones was to cut through vested interests and bureaucratic rigidities to bring forward commercial proposals that leverage Japan's technological advantages and which, if successful, could then be rolled out across the country.

The Zones policy has its own Minister of State, Shigeru Ishiba. It follows previous Zone initiatives – including a Zone for Asian headquarters – that have not reached their targets because of stringent tax conditions and vested industries that have erected barriers to new markets. The first roundtable about how such a Zone would be applied in Tokyo was held in October 2014 between national government, the concerned prefectural governments, experts and major companies, but only a few breakthroughs have materialised. The planning rules have, at least, enabled progress on a large underground bus terminal with links to Tokyo's international airports and regional cities, and a high-end residential project in the Atago district to attract foreign talent. For the new Zones to really harness Tokyo and Japan's innovation potential, the governments need to reach agreement on more specific projects, spaces and participating companies. Central government leadership has to show that it is also capable of making changes to big barriers such as the worker accreditation system (Foster, 2015; Tokyo Metropolitan Government, 2015c).

A long-term solution to fiscal re-distribution

Central government has pushed ahead with taxation reform to redistribute a higher proportion of local taxes raised by cities to less-populated areas, despite TMG opposition. From Tokyo's perspective, these measures are more of a regressive stopgap than a long-term solution. As part of this reform, some of Tokyo's own corporate inhabitant tax has been turned into a national tax, which has affected city revenues to the tune of more than $2 billion. The central government is also proposing further reforms to corporate tax allocations. Diplomatic and public relations skills will be critical to Tokyo finding alternative solutions. In 2014, Yasushi Aoyama, former Tokyo vice governor, predicted that "Governor Masuzoe will have to pick a fight (with the central government) sooner or later when it comes to the issue of tax revenue resources" (Tateno, 2014). All local governments in Tokyo are beginning to mobilise to make the case for an expansion of local tax revenue sources.

Agreements over financing of Olympic infrastructure to help re-introduce Tokyo to global audiences

The 2020 Olympic and Paralympic Games have highlighted Tokyo's need for ongoing infrastructure investment, and the TMG has actively used them to lobby for greater funding. To deliver the Games, Tokyo will require an upgrade of its urban fabric, with the help of national-tier bodies such as the Japan Sports Council, and via collaboration with neighbouring cities and prefectures. Its links to Haneda Airport and the quality of the metropolitan expressways also need improvement (Tabuchi, 2013; Masuzoe, 2014).

The central government is actively supporting the project, as the Olympics will not only showcase its vision for Tokyo and Japan as global leaders, but are seen as an opportunity to reverse the stagnation of the past two decades. The strong alignment between the State's vision, the city's needs and the private sector's potential are already helping to unlock public and private investment in green technology such as hydrogen fuel cells and generation systems, as well as a new financial centre in Toranomoninto. Tensions remain over operational details, however, with some planning aspects causing friction between the central government and the TMG (Inagaki, 2015; Pham, 2015; The Japan Times, 2016).

The budget for Olympic projects is not as large as some cities, but the high level of indebtedness of the central government means it will be a challenge to keep costs (construction and labour) under control and ensure on-time delivery of sustainable projects that can be showcased as something of a model for urban renewal (Inagaki, 2015).

Credible macro reforms to enhance the business climate

Many companies continue to prefer Singapore or Hong Kong's business environment, and some have even relocated from Tokyo in the last decade. There is a growing advocacy for a cut in local and national rates of corporate tax and an upgrade of financial infrastructure and legal regimes to enable Tokyo to compete in pharmaceuticals, hydrogen energy and other green technologies. Tokyo's plans to relax labour regulations in a planned special district to make it easier for foreigners to live and work, and in particular to designate the area from Otemachi to Kabutocho as the core of the city's future financial hub, will require central government approval (Masuzoe, 2014; Nikkei, 2014). Tokyo and central government have participated in meetings of a Tokyo Global Financial Center Promotion Council to improve corporate governance and transparency and encourage foreign investment, but progress will ultimately be judged on concrete results.

Overall economic success in Tokyo hinges on the success of macroeconomic policy. Long-term attractiveness and business loyalty also depend on the government's commitment to infrastructure, rule of law, democracy, intellectual property rights protection, a safe living environment, sound geopolitical relations with China and manageable levels of public debt.

Investment in resilience to natural disasters

Tokyo needs the central government to continue investing in the retrofitting of buildings to withstand earthquakes, to progress with a more diversified energy policy following the Fukushima disaster and upgrade national infrastructure to support emergency relief. The TMG is acutely aware that it can only deliver greater resilience through co-operation with national and regional authorities (Masuzoe, 2014).

Sharing the costs of an aging population

Tokyo's very low fertility rate (1.09), a declining national population and a lack of compensating foreign immigration, all contribute to a gradually worsening shortage of skilled workers. The TMG strives to improve its child and elderly care facilities, but it requires national help to adapt social security and economic systems to prepare for the new demographic situation and ensure Tokyo does not drain the rest of Japan's workforce. These adjustments will shape the city's future productivity and capacity for innovation (especially in service sectors) and will have big implications for its fiscal stability (Bertumen, 2014; Masuda; 2014; Masuzoe, 2014; Obe, 2014).

The aging population has also increased the number of empty and abandoned houses, even in the capital region. It is estimated that up to a quarter of Japan's housing stock could become vacant within the next 20 years, posing severe public service funding issues. Central government will have to decide whether and how to keep funding services in the most de-populated neighbourhoods as their tax base shrinks. Current policies aimed at removing the disincentives to demolition (such as private owners bearing the costs and high taxes on vacant land) are currently piecemeal. A more radical rethink from central government, such as greater re-use and a more flexible real estate policy, may be necessary if it is to contain the infrastructure costs of aging (Soble, 2015).

Key actors and mechanisms that enable Tokyo to make progress with the nation state

Most of Tokyo's day-to-day governance operates independently from national government. However, the TMG does negotiate, and sometimes dispute, policy with national Ministries in Kasumigaseki. Yasuo Tatsuta, Senior Director of the TMG, is a visible leader in negotiations to raise Tokyo's profile and needs. Tokyo's new Governor, Yoichi Masuzoe, is a powerful advocate for the city comparable to Mayor Johnson in London or Mayor Bloomberg in New York. His co-operative working relationship with Prime Minister Abe, his willingness to reach out to neighbouring cities as well as to global peers such as Beijing and Paris, indicate a new level of proactive city leadership (McDearman, Clark and Parilla, 2013; Tasker, 2014). Masuzoe participates at meetings of the National Governors' Association to argue for a rethinking of national policies and a less zero-sum perspective towards urban and rural development (Tokyo Metropolitan Government, 2015c). In 2014, he stated:

> "In order to protect and vitalise this centre of Japan, we will join forces with the central government. I will also fully leverage the experiences and personal ties I have cultivated during my time in national politics."

Tokyo does not have an organised system of business leadership comparable to London or New York, but groups of finance and technology firms have become active participants in the conversation about Tokyo's future as a world city. They have voiced the importance of competitiveness, and the need for Tokyo to showcase its technological strength up to and in 2020 in order to harness a new cycle of investment and exports. The Japan Center for Economic Research, the Daiwa Institute of Research and the Mizuho Research Institute are all advocates of more competitive financial centres (Tabuchi, 2013; Nikkei, 2014).

The Association of Mayors and Designated Cities makes collective demands for devolution in Japan. Up to 2016 it has not achieved many of its aims because of a lack of bargaining power and a lack of leadership to galvanise the municipalities. In 2014, Governor Masuzoe took steps to mend relations with the eight other surrounding prefectures that make up the National Capital Region, and which view the metropolitan government with suspicion. Previous Tokyo Governors Naoki Inose and Shintaro Ishihara did not attend the annual meeting but Masuzoe did choose to in 2014. Tokyo is taking the lead on sharing policy expertise and devising common solutions (Masuzoe, 2014; The Association of Mayors and Designated Cities, 2016).

One new development is the establishment of a 'Forum for Consultations Between National and Regional Governments'. This joint body provides for consultation around proposed national reforms (such as subsidy cuts and new city-level responsibilities). This Forum meets every six months in the presence of the Japanese Prime Minister, and although its discussions are non-binding, it has helped cities begin to feel recognised in recent social welfare and tax reforms.

Conclusion

With almost three-quarters of a century as an empowered metropolitan government, Tokyo's relationship with its nation state has evolved over several cycles of growth and development. It is clear that policy co-operation has increased over the past 15 years amid the shared recognition that Tokyo needs more investment in its city centre, better airport connections and more international links. The government framework has also helped Tokyo manage its housing supply and affordability better than many other world cities.

There is a broad consensus that macroeconomic policy and government regulation have held back Tokyo's progress as an international business location since the early 1990s, and now put the city's place among the world elite at risk. Tokyo's attractiveness and global competitiveness have become more of a priority in national policy, but the main levers to make the city more conducive to investment and talent have not yet proven very effective. The rigidities of Japan's tax and regulatory framework, and the entrenched interests of established industries and companies, have so far proven insurmountable.

Tokyo's big opportunity for catalytic change is the Olympic Games in 2020, and events of this scale often bring a governance dividend for host cities. The 2020 timetable has accelerated the agenda to revive financial services and is supported by current Prime Minister Abe and the Chief Cabinet Secretary. The Games provide momentum for deregulation reforms and education initiatives that make Tokyo more attractive and accessible to the private sector. If Tokyo can upgrade its financial infrastructure and legal regimes, and install the right mix of incentives, it will be much better placed to compete in the sectors in which it has excellence.

Japan is still sharply divided on the question of whether Tokyo ought to be supported or reined in. The capital's more empowered government and disproportionate share of corporate activity and human capital was tolerated while Japan's second cities still thrived, but the stagnation of Osaka, Nagoya and others has prompted many to call for a change of approach. Much will rest on the success of ongoing efforts to achieve greater integration and devolution for the metropolitan area of Osaka, and subsequently Nagoya. But central government reforms to redistribute more tax revenue to rural areas may have the effect of damaging Tokyo's capacity to shape its own productive growth and ultimately to create revenue in the future. In the new cycle, Tokyo's leadership has shown a welcome willingness to engage boldly and creatively with other cities and rural areas to build a shared agenda and raise awareness of their inter-dependence. This task of national diplomacy will likely become even more urgent as Tokyo tries to keep its place at the global top table.

Section III Working remotely: World cities in federal systems

7

Mumbai: The opportunity costs of leadership and co-ordination failure

A. Savin, licensed under CC BY 2.0

World Cities and Nation States, First Edition. Greg Clark and Tim Moonen.
© 2017 John Wiley & Sons, Ltd. Published 2017 by John Wiley & Sons, Ltd.

Mumbai is by far the most globalised city in southern Asia, and a regional centre of finance, decision-making, film and entertainment. Since the late 1980s, it has made a rapid economic transition from trade to services, and has become India's major corporate headquarters hub and main destination for foreign investment and joint ventures. Although it is not India's capital, it boasts the airport with the most international passengers, the busiest port system and the two largest stock exchanges in southern Asia (Clark and Moonen, 2014). Mumbai is also home to the region's biggest cultural export, in Bollywood, and is a dynamic centre for small trading businesses in the design, fashion, tourism and jewellery sectors. These multiple drivers have seen the city's population more than treble in 40 years, to the extent it is now one of the world's largest and most high-profile megacities (Table 7.1).

Mumbai is now a 23 million person metropolitan region, comprised of Greater Mumbai (440 km², 12 million people), seven other municipal corporations and nine smaller municipal councils. The 4350 km² region is part of a 110 million person state (Maharashtra) whose population is mainly rural, and whose system of government reflects this balance. Greater Mumbai has just six of the state's 48 MPs in a national parliament of 543 representatives. The federal structure of 29 states means that the Maharashtra state government, rather than the Government of India, is the higher-tier authority that has more regular and systematic interaction with the city. Maharashtra has discretion to decide urban governance and fiscal policy, and its urban agenda is only slowly becoming more visible. However, although central government is not directly active in Mumbai's governance, it is a key actor in the city region; its agencies control critical security, rail and trade infrastructure; it has active institutions 'on the ground' that use and rent land; it wields key financial powers and investment programmes and it shapes economic planning (Figure 7.1).

Mumbai has become a symbol of the challenges facing large cities in the global South. Its dynamic economy and capacity to create new jobs co-exist with extreme inequality and informality. Weak growth management has resulted in congestion, low productivity and severe asymmetries in the city's labour and property markets. Mumbai is a striking example of an emerging world city whose higher tiers of government have failed to create the institutions or the planning and co-ordination mechanisms to govern the metropolitan space. This chapter explains how Mumbai's relationship with its higher tiers of government has evolved and what past reforms, investments and interventions have and have not accomplished.

Table 7.1:   Mumbai metropolitan region's size and economic performance

% of national population	% of national GDP	GDP per capita vs national average (1)	City global competitiveness rank	Country global competitiveness rank	Annualised employment growth 2000–14	Annualised GDP growth 2000–14	% of national employment
1.5%	7.5%	1.2	70	55	2.3%	6.2%	1.7%

Source: Parilla *et al.*, 2015; World Bank, 2014; World Economic Forum, 2015; EIU, 2012.

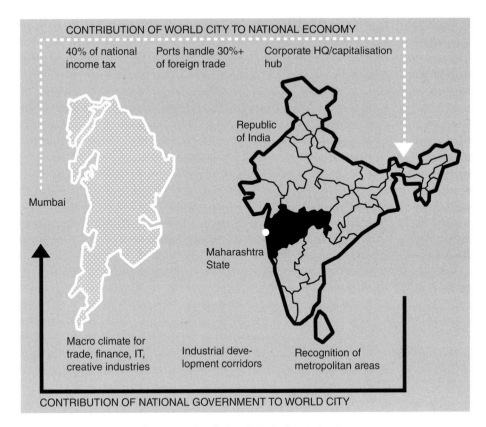

CONTRIBUTION OF WORLD CITY TO NATIONAL ECONOMY

40% of national income tax

Ports handle 30%+ of foreign trade

Corporate HQ/capitalisation hub

Republic of India

Mumbai

Maharashtra State

Macro climate for trade, finance, IT, creative industries

Industrial development corridors

Recognition of metropolitan areas

CONTRIBUTION OF NATIONAL GOVERNMENT TO WORLD CITY

Figure 7.1: Reciprocity between Mumbai and the Indian federal government.

History of Mumbai's relationship with higher tiers of government

Formerly known as Bombay, Mumbai's trajectory has been fundamentally shaped by the 1960 decision to split Mumbai State along linguistic lines and absorb the city into the much larger entity of Maharashtra. Although the Congress Party's High Command recommended to the Government of India in 1957 that Mumbai be made a city-state on account of its unique cosmopolitanism, the political repercussions saw the Government ultimately concede the right for Mumbai to be absorbed into the Marathi-dominated state (Guha, 2003).

Since independence, India's government has often treated Mumbai's urban challenges as welfare problems rather than as priorities for national strategic attention. National government plays much less of a role in Mumbai than in the capital Delhi, and its role has mostly been to issue directives, provide advisory support and fund programmes. Its primary relationship is with the state government and it interacts minimally with the municipal corporations or the metropolitan authority. The centre does nevertheless have jurisdiction over most of Mumbai's railway, port and airport assets, and requires city agencies to observe poverty alleviation and environmental programmes. Short-term contracts for ministerial commissioners, and the politicisation of appointments, have limited the scope for a sustained approach to Mumbai's governance from the national tier.

Mumbai's governance deficit has been apparent for more than 50 years when development first began to spill rapidly over pre-existing borders. Ninety per cent of the metropolitan population was concentrated within Greater Mumbai in 1961, but this had dropped to 60% by 2011. A positive regional approach only appeared in the 1970s, when the Mumbai Metropolitan Regional Development Authority (MMRDA) was created by the state government. The MMRDA was only a partial solution to the regional governance deficit because it lacked significant investment powers or control over key systems and did not benefit from clear divisions of responsibility between it and the Municipal Corporation of Greater Mumbai (MCGM) (Zérah, 2014).

Efforts to strengthen local government and leadership in Mumbai have not suited its urban model. State and national ministers in charge of urban development have rarely possessed a strong professional specialism, and Mumbai has been unable to grow a city leadership capacity to match its growth. Compared to the central–local government system that exists in unitary states such as the UK, Mumbai has to cope with a vastly more complex system involving partnerships between federal government and the states (Rao, 2015).

A 1992 constitutional amendment tried unsuccessfully to devolve powers to municipal governments such as Mumbai's. Although the reforms boosted the resources of some agencies, the distribution of power between the Maharashtra government and institutions in the metropolitan area was not fundamentally altered. However, central policy changes did invite the private sector to enter urban service delivery and project management, and companies entered into Mumbai PPPs in IT and construction (Rao, 2015). The idea of a Metropolitan Planning Committee was also introduced in the reforms, but has never been implemented anywhere across India (except Kolkata), partly because state governments have been reluctant to transfer power (Zérah, 2014).

Tensions between the state of Maharashtra and the MCGM have been exacerbated by the latter's own fragmented governance structure. The Mayor of the MCGM must share power with a Commissioner, who is largely viewed as a representative of the state. When the two clash, or one perceives overreach by the other, co-ordination is severely impeded and acts as a brake on decision-making (Zérah, 2014).

Amid the leadership and co-ordination dysfunction, there have been occasions when the Government of India has helped Mumbai prepare positively for globalisation, although there has been no sustained commitment to support its global city aspirations. The central government's macroeconomic framework changes allowed the city's finance and service sectors to begin to internationalise, and the Reserve Bank of India has provided financing support for the development of Bandra Kurla. The Indian State also granted official 'industry' status to the film sector in 1998 in order to end bad accounting and financing practices found extensively in film production, as a prerequisite to becoming a globally traded industry (Pethe, Tandel and Gandhi, 2012).

Incomplete initiatives and aborted reforms in the 21st century

In the early 2000s, the central government led the initiative to establish what steps were needed for Mumbai to become an international centre of finance. The Prime Minister's Office designated a contact point in New Delhi to support and monitor the Mumbai transformation project. When political alignment occurred with the election of the Congress in 2004, a new programme of financial assistance was offered for urban infrastructure. A *High-Powered Expert Committee* in the Finance Ministry examined the feasibility of making Mumbai a financial hub. But clarity about the meaning of becoming a global finance centre was missing. Progress in the sector was also held back by State and local government reluctance to address land-use regulation reform in Mumbai during the period of economic growth up to 2008 (Gómez-Ibáñez and Masood, 2007; Chattaraj, 2012a).

Central-government-sponsored schemes have made small steps towards improving housing policy in Mumbai. Greater resources have been allocated to Maharashtra state government, and national schemes (initiated by the Ministry of Housing and Urban Poverty Alleviation and the Ministry of Urban Development) have established the role of government as a facilitator and provider of affordable housing. In 2011, the state government decided to reform development controls and grant additional density to projects in Mumbai's suburbs to lower the price of housing and generate revenue for the state government and the MCGM. However, many commentators believe that the Maharashtra government's approach to charging developers for additional construction rights for housing projects may render smaller redevelopment projects unviable, and potentially may raise house prices in Mumbai's suburbs (Babar, 2015a).

Inter-party and intergovernmental conflict often shapes what is possible for Mumbai's urban policy. Up until 2014, the Congress Party was the incumbent state government for nearly all of the last 50 years, but at the national level it has been much less dominant since 1996. Inter-party rivalry has often resulted in deadlock and tension in approaches to Mumbai. Central government has occasionally subverted the state government's authority over urban development, and more commonly state governments ignore, delay or recast national initiatives. As Xuefei Ren and Liza Weinstein conclude, "[d]espite efforts made by the Indian central government to devolve power to the metropolitan scale, the authority and resources required for urban development remain at the middle rung of India's three-tiered federalist structure". The result is that the resources needed to plan and implement an urban vision for the city do not assemble at the metropolitan level, and many projects are not completed. Without political alignment, urban agendas in Mumbai have rarely been executed (Ren and Weinstein, 2013). It remains to be seen if the current Bharatiya Janata Party alignment across the state and national levels can translate into concerted action.

The lack of city government capacity to build and sustain long-term plans in Mumbai was highlighted in 2015 when the Greater Mumbai Development Plan up to 2034 was withdrawn. Concerns and objections were raised over its proposed densification measures, encroachment on remaining open spaces and a lack of provision for affordable housing. One of the Plan's flagship initiatives was to increase Floor Area Ratios, up from a current general limit of 1.33 to 8 in the densest areas and 5–6 in public transport hubs. If pursued in the new iteration, this may help bring safer, higher-quality and more spacious housing to millions of slum dwellers who have the financial means to live better but are trapped by an inadequate housing policy which precludes dense new developments. Higher tiers of government will play a role in helping the plan to be delivered with a coherent spatial approach that improves access to green space and transport links (Babar, 2015b; Nagpal, 2015; Nair, 2015; Yglesias, 2015; Desai, 2016).

As Mumbai seeks capital investment for the next cycle of long-awaited infrastructure projects, the MCGM relies on support from the state government's Chief Minister not just to fund projects but also to help the city tap the municipal bond market. The national market regulator, the Securities and Exchange Board of India, has highlighted the opportunities for cities such as Mumbai to mobilise taxable bonds, tax-free bonds and pooled financing and attract a new cadre of investors seeking alternative opportunities. The MCGM has been cautious because a successful bond issue depends on a sound credit rating.

The national system of cities: Mumbai and India

As the Mumbai case makes apparent, India's federal system leaves most urban responsibilities to state rather than national governments. Policy and planning for urban development are functions of the state governments. Grants from central government only account for 5% of city revenues in India, while grants and devolution from state governments make up a third. Property tax and other city revenues are by far the biggest revenue source, but these revenues are still low by international standards. There are also large inefficiencies in revenue collection, as only 37% of property taxes were collected across Maharashtra's urban areas in 2014, and only 46% of water charges. Fiscal imbalances between the centre and states have been partly addressed by Finance Commissions, but what actually is implemented depends mostly on the Maharashtra state government Commissions (Gumber, 2014; Mohanty, 2014).

As Maharashtra state is one of the most urbanised in India and rapidly approaching 50% urbanisation, the fiscal imbalances within the state are becoming more acute. The number of residents in urban areas in Maharashtra will soon surpass 60 million and may reach 80 million by 2030. A quarter of these residents will live in Greater Mumbai alone, not to mention those living in settlements across the metropolitan area. The MCGM absorbs the lion's share of urban funding in the state, with a little over R18,000 crore in revenue. Per capita, this translates into nearly R14,000 spent per person in Greater Mumbai, compared to less than R4000 in the rest of the state. These asymmetries accentuate the gulf between poorly defined urban boundaries in the Mumbai region and Mumbai itself (Gumber, 2014).

The Jawaharlal Nehru National Urban Renewal Mission (JNNURM) was introduced in 2005 as India adopted a demand-driven approach to cities for the first time. A meeting between Prime Minister Manmohan Singh, Maharashtra state officials and Bombay First resulted in the central government using part of this envelope of funding for Mumbai's own transformation project (Chattaraj, 2012a). Previous national urban policy had tried to foster equal development across cities, with federal urban development programmes focused on small tier 2 and tier 3 centres. As in other nations, this policy did not have entirely effective results, and urban policy has become more oriented towards the larger engines of growth. The 2005–2014 programme of funds released large sums of investment for urban projects – infrastructure, sanitation, housing and sustainability – subject to cities producing City Development Plans. It consolidated the trend towards Indian cities creating markets for investment in land, services and debt (Chattaraj, 2012a; Birkinshaw, 2014).

The JNNURM was not, however, a coherent national framework for urban growth, based as it was on ad hoc grants. Total investment in urban infrastructure is still under 1% of GDP, compared to nearly 3% of GDP in China, while urban governments account for only 3% of total public expenditure – compared to 20–35% in China – underlining the lack of investment autonomy and resources. In addition, fewer than half of the JNNURM initiatives in Maharashtra were completed, even though 97% of funds had been spent – highlighting severe project management inefficiencies. India continues to lack a clear spatial strategy, partly because its large size and federal structure make policy creation and co-operation challenging. The need for huge capital investment in India's cities means that the federal government may need to give cities and regions themselves more powers to institutionalise co-operation (Fraser, date unknown; Planning Commission, 2011; Gumber, 2014; Saldanha, 2016).

Since 2014 the new national government has prioritised urbanisation and infrastructure investment in high-growth centres such as Mumbai. Its new mission, replacing JNNURM, focuses on smarter GIS-based planning and waste management. The ministries of urban development and housing and urban poverty alleviation are rolling out key programmes such as the Smart City Mission, the Atal Mission for Rejuvenation and Urban Transformation (AMRUT), Swachh Bharat Mission and Pradhan Mantri Awas Yojana (Urban). The challenge for these initiatives is to ensure that these are effectively implemented by state governments such as Maharashtra, and the various urban local bodies in the cities. In most cases these schemes do not bring additional funding from the centre and rely on states deploying their own resources. (Sharma, 2016).

Even though central government may not directly fund many projects in Maharashtra, Prime Minister Modi's national infrastructure agenda is behind a recent upturn in capital investment across the state and India as a whole. He has helped to mobilise private finance and encourage states to complement national infrastructure efforts with their own plans. As a result, (public) capital spending in India rose by 50% between 2014–15 and 2015–16. A National Investment and Infrastructure Fund (a fund of funds and soon a direct investor) has also been set up to intensify capital investments, inviting private finance from global partners as well as state funding. The Prime Minister has also been active in the *Make in India* week staged in Mumbai in 2016, to showcase both the city as a global gateway and India's potential – while preparations for the event have themselves invited more infrastructure funding. Since 2015, central government has also put pressure on the Maharashtra state government to consider the 'odd/even' car rule that restricts vehicles to travelling every other day, a policy that has been implemented in Delhi (Business Insider India, 2015; Dhoot, 2015; Nair, 2015; Sikarwar, 2015; Singh, 2015; The Financial Express, 2015; Business Standard, 2016).

Central government is also encouraging the monetisation of land assets, similar to the Chinese model, to raise funds for urban development – although this must be handled carefully to limit speculation and unaffordability. Transit Oriented Development is also being encouraged by the central government, with the forthcoming Mumbai Metro's two new lines and other initiatives across India as flagship schemes. Mumbai's metro extensions are to be half financed by the state of Maharashtra, with the remaining capital supplied by international financial institutions (for example, the Asian Development Bank) and potentially Japanese government assistance. Central government assistance is currently not on the table, but could come later in the construction phase. The centre has also taken steps to tackle the housing market, by partially phasing out rent controls. These have long been associated with a stagnant housing market with a low investment and maintenance rate and low supply level. The new bill to be enacted by the states (Maharashtra included) is, however, contentious as it makes middle class tenants vulnerable to price increases, while the strengths of safeguards for poorer families are unclear (Nair, 2015; Phadke, 2015a, 2015b; Bonislawski, 2016; Lewis, 2016; The Indian Express, 2016).

The success of central government's interventions in India's urban areas will have global repercussions. India's urban population growth will account for a fifth of the global total up to 2030. How its cities handle this growth will affect international human development indicators and shape perceptions of urbanisation's benefits and potential. It is therefore crucial that India's new urban agenda is coherently articulated by a wider national policy that features mechanisms for implementation by the states (Nair, 2015; Bonislawski, 2016).

Ongoing challenges where Mumbai needs help from national government

Mumbai's most urgent or difficult challenges are not immediately solvable at the national level alone. The city requires a more empowered metropolitan governance structure, where agency responsibilities are more clearly differentiated, long-term plans made binding and an enhanced leadership model introduced. Many of these changes require state government co-operation first and foremost. Nevertheless, the current national government promises changes to the way in which cities and metropolitan areas are governed and managed. These may draw inspiration from successful models internationally and recognise explicitly the role played by India's largest cities in national economic performance. Attention to a number of policy areas will be important to Mumbai's development in the next two cycles.

Leveraging ownership of strategic railway and port infrastructure and land

The State-owned Indian Railways is in charge of plans and budgets for large railway lands, and central government must approve any development in Mumbai that crosses over suburban railways. The new government is exploring a comprehensive overhaul of the railway system. There is scope for much stronger co-ordination between the central railway authorities, MMRDA and the state government, based on an integrated selection and management of projects. The metro rail system has shown that the MMRDA and state governments can take the investment lead in such projects. Joint responsibilities for long-distance rail corridors have the potential to open up land and provide affordable housing beyond the city and suburban district.

The centrally owned Mumbai Port Trust also owns significant port land and is now committed to opening it up to develop the seafront. Stringent national Coastal Regulation Zone norms set by the Union Ministry of Environment and Forests have so far restricted development despite land scarcity. The relaxation of these norms may allow land reclamation and the unlocking of development potential, especially for tourism.

Complementing smart cities with smart governance agenda

The Prime Minister of India, Narendra Modi, has initiated serious thinking about smart cities as he looks to boost smaller satellite cities and kick start inland industrial growth. The scheme promises to deliver public money in private sector partnerships to deliver water supply, modern sewerage systems, solid waste management and infrastructure, if city bodies are able to execute them effectively (The Times of India, 2014).

The attention directed at smart cities is welcome in incentivising better standards, but is just the start of a deeper process of reform. For these projects to translate into a broader agenda for Mumbai and India's larger cities, attention towards smart governance is needed in order to tackle co-ordination failures. Improving co-ordination would increase the rate of investment, which McKinsey Global Institute has identified as the biggest priority for India's leading cities if they are to drive national economic growth in the way that China's largest cities have done (Sankhe *et al.*, 2010).

Constitutional changes to strengthen metropolitan leadership and resources of local governments

Mumbai has an extraordinarily fragmented governance system comprising seven municipal corporations, nine municipal councils and over 20 parastatal agencies. The quality of local governance has come under scrutiny in recent years, with Mumbai registering low scores (below 5/10) on a national survey for its level of staffing, resources and coherent planning. That nearly half of urban revenue in Maharashtra's cities is spent on salaries underlines the inefficiencies of the current system which inhibit investment capacity (Saldanha, 2016).

Many commentators argue that Mumbai should be more independent from central government party politics, and should be allowed to create a metropolitan authority with some executive power. This would require constitutional amendments to recognise metropolitan areas and determine the role of state agencies and municipal agencies within them (Slack, 2014; Rao, 2015; Saldanha, 2016).

The investment capacity and professional experience of urban local bodies is critical to the improvement of service delivery in big cities such as Mumbai. Local agencies bear most of the burden of urban service provision with little support from state and central governments. Mumbai needs central government firstly to build technical and managerial depth at the local government level. It then needs it to lead on a rewrite of intergovernmental fiscal rules that will empower urban local bodies and allow them to participate in capital markets, as well as to monetise land assets (as the MMRDA already does), introduce user charges, retain GST revenues or pursue PPPs in more sectors. The centre also has to recognise and work with a wider range of institutions in the region beyond only the state government. Collaboration with the private sector will be an important element of these devolutionary processes (Gumber, 2014; Sharma, 2014; Rao, 2015).

Optimise the opportunity around development corridors

The Indian government has more scope to intervene in inter-urban development than on development *within* cities. It is a co-sponsor of the Delhi Mumbai Industrial Corridor (DMIC), along with the Japanese government. It also supports the Mumbai Bangalore economic corridor initiative that has Japanese and British support. These corridors portend a future Indian urban policy that may attend to the country's spatial economy, designating smarter urban growth along industrial routes and raising their profile. The government can maximise the opportunity by creating legislation for fast-track planning and incentivising collaboration across the participating 'corridor' states.

In 2015 a major breakthrough occurred as the national cabinet approved a $15 billion deal for Japan to build a high-speed train line between Mumbai and Ahmedabad. This 500-kilometre line would reduce the journey time by around 75% to just two hours. Under the terms of the agreement, Japan will lend half the project funds at very low long-term interest rates. The line promises to improve access to regional markets and optimise agglomeration forces in Mumbai and other major cities (Shukla *et al.*, 2015).

Reforms to promote internationalisation of the financial sector

After a decade of inaction, new proposals involving Bombay First and the Reserve Bank of India aim to clarify Mumbai's ambitions in the financial sector. Central government can provide the essential 'nuts and bolts' policy reforms that will attract international banks to carry out cross-border transactions with Indian firms. After three divisions of the Reserve Bank of India's Foreign Investment Division (FID) were moved to New Delhi, the government can also provide clearer assurances that Mumbai is India's financial nerve centre, rather than Delhi or Gujarat.

Supporting small business growth

Mumbai's SMEs are critical to increasing employment and GDP, but they are largely outside the government's existing purview, which means they face a number of barriers. These include limited access to, or awareness of, affordable bank lending or well-regulated government credits, customs inconsistencies and lack of access to product design.

Since 2016, the Prime Minister's *Startup India* initiative has prompted action at the state government level to improve conditions for start-ups. A new central-government-financed fund of funds to invest in venture capital funds has been created, while simplified patent applications and shortened company setup times have been promised. But if Mumbai is to build an ecosystem to rival others in Asia, let alone in North America, it requires an even wider overhaul of central government policy to empower SMEs, over 90% of which are unregistered. Future measures may include relief from central excise and service taxes; exemption from income tax for early stage businesses; support for early stage investor classes; and a reduction in the rate of bank finance interest (Deodhar, 2014; SME Connect, 2014; Reuters, 2016).

Proactive project involvement for second airport in Navi Mumbai

The central Airports Authority of India (AAI) possesses a 13% stake in Navi Mumbai International Airport, while central ministries possess final say on approval. The AAI partners with state development agency CIDCO on this important project, as a joint venture, but there are major uncertainties about the private finance, which is exacerbating delays. The central authorities will need not only to ensure wise financial decision-making, but also to facilitate the construction of rail connections to the new airport, as well as better port links (Naik, 2014).

Key actors and mechanisms that enable Mumbai to make progress with the nation state

A leadership reform agenda is beginning to take shape in Mumbai. There is a strong consensus among local government, central government agencies, business leaders and regional bodies of the need for a stronger institutional framework. Most institutions recognise that Maharashtra state will continue to play a critical role. Different solutions include a city CEO, a mayor for the metropolitan region, a co-ordination unit and a reform to foster inter-institutional collaboration and integration.

Bombay First is a non-profit initiative of private corporates under the umbrella of Bombay Chamber of Commerce and Industry, India's oldest chamber of commerce. Modelled on London First, it was designed to bring private sector expertise into the debate about how Mumbai could overcome its constraints and become a more competitive city. Bombay First has continued the historic role of Mumbai's industrial houses, banks and chambers of commerce in the city's urban development and governance challenges. It has been influential in making the case to central government (and state government) for making Mumbai more globally competitive through changes in regulation and investment in quality of life. It has undertaken comprehensive diagnosis of Mumbai's develop- ment and future needs, and commissions important studies that engage with the national tier (Chattaraj, 2012b). Its work highlights the role of business leadership in engaging with government institutions to promote increased investment, metropolitan thinking and economic development strategy. Meanwhile, the Citizens' Action Group has been appointed by the state to strategise and monitor initiatives for Mumbai city development.

Conclusion

Mumbai faces many critical strategic questions as it attempts to find a more sustainable and productive path in the 21st century. Its future as a financial centre is unclear because of previous policy delays and failures. There is, as yet, no concrete proposition for how Mumbai will serve India's future growth, and what its roles will be in the rapidly changing Asian system of cities. The city also urgently needs a robust regional planning and policy perspective that prepares new business and employment clusters in the north and east, including media, medicine, logistics, biotechnology, electronics, wholesale and service sectors.

Central government policy in India can create the conditions for Maharashtra and other Indian states to act in the long-term interest of cities rather than short-term political imperatives. But so far it has not fully recognised the role of cities in India's development and does not co-operate with a wide span of Mumbai's institutions other than Maharashtra state itself. Its lack of prescrip- tive support has led to disjointed narratives and a tendency to react to unin- tended consequences. This has led to growing calls for reforms that would empower urban governments and allow for the entire governance system to be reorganised.

Most of Mumbai's imperatives cannot be achieved without an improved contract with higher tiers of government. Engagement of senior officials and spe- cial representatives from the Government of India will be essential to future progress (Sivaramakrishnan, 2015). Any resolution of its fragmented governance system will entail a metropolitan authority being set up with at least some exec- utive power, which would likely require constitutional reform. If Mumbai is ever to realise its economic potential, it will need simple durable reforms from higher tiers of government that can make the region's challenges more coherent and empower urban governments to deliver more projects. A proposal in November 2014 by the Chief Minister of Maharashtra to create a senior co-ordinator 'CEO' of Mumbai was briefly mooted, but for such a leader to co-ordinate effectively would require the whole system of governance to be recalibrated.

Under the current Modi administration, a new agenda has been established around smart cities, development corridors to Bangalore and Delhi and private sector partnerships for urban infrastructure projects. There is a great deal of optimism about the role that national policy can play in supporting Mumbai's financial sector and small business growth. These agendas will only be optimised in Mumbai if attached to a broader reform to the system of planning and implementation. At the same time, constitutional changes to strengthen the leadership, technical capacity and resources of local bodies, and regulatory reforms to support coastal and rail development, would be very welcome for Mumbai to avoid becoming permanently locked into an unsustainable and unequal growth model.

8

New York: Adapting to 'emergency back-up' federalism

Daniele Pieroni (2014), licensed under CC BY 2.0

World Cities and Nation States, First Edition. Greg Clark and Tim Moonen.
© 2017 John Wiley & Sons, Ltd. Published 2017 by John Wiley & Sons, Ltd.

New York City is a global capital of business and finance, and the major gateway to the Western Hemisphere for professional and creative talent. Sometimes described as the definitive city of the 20th century, it has recovered from multiple setbacks (fiscal, environmental, security and financial) in the first years of the 21st, and continues to set a benchmark for what it means to be a successful global city. With a GDP at $1.4 trillion by PPP, the functional New York region is currently the second largest metropolitan economy in the world, and is more productive than any of its international peers, due to it being a first-mover in investing in ICT, absorbing demand for skilled workers and making organisational reforms (Table 8.1). In recent decades the city has strengthened its position in a diverse set of business and innovation clusters, and is sustained by world-class civic institutions, a deep spirit of enterprise and much-improved school education and public space. It benefits from a powerful Mayor–Council citywide government model that is better resourced and more unified than in most American cities. New York's urban development has also extended across the borders of two other states (New Jersey and Connecticut) to form the 23 million person 'tri-state' area, the 'New York region'.

The success of New York in previous generations means there is a global spotlight on how it adjusts to the changing character of both the global economy and American politics. In this chapter we highlight how it is beginning to feel the effects of unmanaged regional growth and a chronic underinvestment in housing and infrastructure. Wages for the median resident have stagnated for some time, and the city is witnessing a decline in the number of medium-skilled jobs that threaten its reputation as a symbol for upward mobility.

New York faces up to new challenges in an American system where there is no direct constitutional link between New York City and the federal tier. Instead, the state governments, which historically are not located in large commercial centres, play a more direct mediating role. The New York State government in Albany provides financial aid for the City while also drawing large fiscal resources from taxable activity within it, and as a result the city/state relationship has a sustained and negotiated character. American political traditions also mean local actors and the private sector play a prominent role in urban and economic development. The responsibilities of higher tiers of government are mainly to maintain a positive currency, tax, trade and immigration environment, and to provide additional finance to ensure good connectivity, infrastructure capacity and occasional investment in housing and education systems (Figure 8.1).

Table 8.1: New York metropolitan region's size and economic performance

% of national population	% of national GDP	GVA per capita vs national average (1)	City global competitiveness rank	Country global competitiveness rank	Annualised employment growth 2000–14	Annualised GDP growth 2000–14	% of national employment
5%	8%	1.28	1	3	0.4%	1.2%	5.4%

Source: Parilla *et al.*, 2015; OECD Stat., 2014; World Economic Forum, 2015; EIU, 2012.

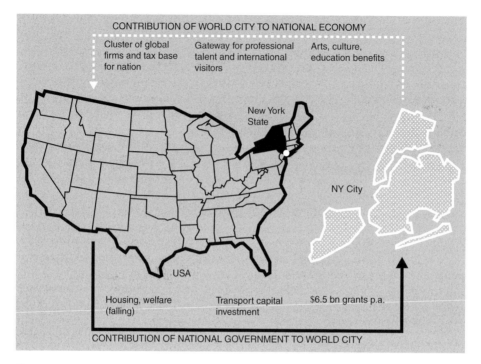

CONTRIBUTION OF WORLD CITY TO NATIONAL ECONOMY

Cluster of global firms and tax base for nation

Gateway for professional talent and international visitors

Arts, culture, education benefits

New York State

NY City

USA

Housing, welfare (falling)

Transport capital investment

$6.5 bn grants p.a.

CONTRIBUTION OF NATIONAL GOVERNMENT TO WORLD CITY

Figure 8.1:   Reciprocity between New York City and the United States federal government.

We also observe in this chapter that the US federal system arrangements mean that federal government does not take a leadership role in the direction of its major cities. There has been no broad framework resembling a 'national urban policy' in the US for over 30 years, with national urban programmes instead focusing upon small-area-based initiatives for community-led housing and economic development. The federal government did previously play a substantial role in investing in affordable housing programmes and many of these were utilised in New York City. The gradual loss of this investment stream into New York over the past 20 years has contributed to New York's affordable housing crisis. The federal tier has also withdrawn from many financing responsibilities and focused primarily on security, immigration and healthcare challenges.

Instead, it is the federal support that New York City tends to receive in response to major crises that emerges as a recurrent theme of this chapter. There have been three such major crises since 2000: the terrorist attacks of 9/11, the 2008 global financial crisis and subsequent recession and Hurricane Sandy in 2012. These three events each provoked a major response from the federal government to respond to the national interest in ways that directly involved investment and support for New York and its business and citizen communities. Such emergency assistance has been very welcome but does not mask the fact that New York and other leading American cities are not treated as esteemed partners in pursuit of national goals.

History of the city and nation state relationship up to 2000

New York had favourable relations with the federal government in the mid-20th century. In the late 1940s, the federal tier began to direct money to cities in a targeted manner, with money flowing directly from Washington to New York City and others. The City was a major proponent of the new public housing system and succeeded in gaining almost a third of national grants between 1949 and 1964. Under the Johnson administration, New York proved to be a guinea pig for federal War on Poverty projects to tackle crime and cohesion by allowing communities to administer funds (for example, Mobilization for Youth and the Community Action Program). Later, funds from the Urban Development Action Grant passed during the Carter presidency were used to leverage private investment to stimulate urban renewal in areas of Lower Manhattan and Brooklyn (Berg, 2007).

A new NYC Federal Affairs Office in Washington in 1970 and the City's congressional delegation were effective in putting New York's case to the federal level for grant funds. The success in influencing federal officials actually meant the City became very financially dependent on the federal tier for money to deliver key services, despite the lack of constitutional obligation for the federal tier to do so. From 1975 to 1978, it provided 78% of the city's public transport capital budget. After initial reluctance to help the City in the fiscal crisis of 1975, the Ford administration eventually signed the New York City Seasonal Financing Act to extend $2.3 billion of federal loans. This contributed positively to the alleviation of the city's financial problems, but the period created a rift in city–federal relations that persists until today (Green and Moore, 1988; Roberts, 2006; Forman, 2014).

Federal activity in a still de-populating New York City declined amid the tax cuts of the 1980s, but some successes were achieved. Fiscal discipline was ultimately good for New York City's creditworthiness, but it saw aid to the City effectively cut by $500 million a year between 1981 and 1985. The Metropolitan Transportation Authority (MTA) and welfare programmes were especially affected. Fiscal discipline was a major challenge, although the federal government did provide guarantees on the City's debts, and the city eventually emerged more creditworthy and bankable, albeit more unequal.

Into the 1990s, most federal attention focused on New York's chronic crime and welfare problems, and their effect on job creation and business attraction. State government housing investment, supported by City and federal funds, provided a boost as the city returned to growth. Tougher crime legislation to allow the city to hire 5000 additional police was considered crucial by Mayor Giuliani in turning around the city's reputation for violent crime and in reviving the city's tourism and population. Federal support for public transport increased and helped revive the New York City subway. At the same time, New York's city government consistently defended immigrants as assets rather than liabilities, as federal legislation sought to deny some access to services (New York City, 1997; Golden, 2014).

Evolution of the city's relationship with the federal tier since 9/11

The Bush administration from 2001–2008 was not defined by strong urban initiatives, and the events of 9/11 led to a much greater focus on security and foreign policy. Mayors Giuliani and Bloomberg argued vigorously with Washington for increased anti-terror funds to deal with the specific threat to the city, and for more funds to integrate immigrants. New York City received major funding to reform education under the *Race to the Top* scheme during the Bloomberg administration, as a result of shared commitments with the state government (Medina, 2010; Katz, 2014). But other challenges such as aging public infrastructure, congestion, pollution and housing shortages did not receive substantial financial or regulatory support. City and state governments have had to innovate, whether on tourism and branding initiatives, or on housing, and successive mayors have filled revenue holes by building new apartments on public land owned by the Housing Authority (NYCHA). Overall, the city's leaders have been very successful in diversifying its economy into high technology and creative sectors and retaining New York's reputation as a global leader in spite of limited federal support.

Perhaps the most distinctive support New York City has received in the 21st century has been the federal injections of money to help rescue the city from a series of major setbacks – in 2001, 2008 and 2012. First, federal funds were critical to rebuilding Lower Manhattan after 9/11. As businesses operating in New York found it difficult to buy commercial property insurance that included the risk of terrorism, Congress passed the Terrorism Risk Insurance Act (TRIA) to increase risk coverage. After the 2008 financial crisis, the government issued an unprecedented $700 billion package to ensure the financial system did not collapse, a decision from which the entire New York City economy has benefited. Furthermore, an above-average $7 billion in Recovery Act funds went to programmes benefiting New York schools and buildings. The stimulus has not only helped New York to avoid the collapse of finance and business services, it has also enabled it to diversify its economy at a critical juncture. And most recently, in response to Hurricane Sandy in 2012, federal agencies such as the Army Corps of Engineers and the Federal Emergency Management Agency provided over $13 billion to fund the City's recovery efforts, much of which was administered by the City itself. So, although the federal government has not had a consistent policy to protect and support its leading urban economies, when New York has needed help it has been available (Vogel *et al.*, 2011; New York City, 2016).

These valuable emergency funds have not, however, disguised an ongoing lack of engagement with the City's evolving needs. Federal public transport spending stayed flat despite growing demand, preventing local agencies from expanding the system, while housing and workforce training investment has fallen away. For example, the City's total allocation under the federal Workforce Investment Act dropped from $97 million in 2002 to $63 million in 2013. New York has relied on Congress to resist the worst of the cuts, and a culture of confrontation rather than strategic thinking prevailed (Center for an Urban Future, 2009; Fischer, 2014a). Bruce Katz at the Brookings Institution is not alone in arguing that the federal government has "left the building". Federal priorities around healthcare and defence send a 'de facto signal' to leaders in New York City and elsewhere: "you now run the country and you need to make the principal transformative investments in what drives the economy and makes us an inclusive society" (cited in Goff, 2013). This means that New York State instead plays the key role in supervising the activities of New York City, as the higher-tier government, levying many important taxes in the city that fund state-wide services, and providing essential investment in infrastructure and other amenities.

Today, the federal level retains a small role in public education, safety, public facilities, water and sanitation, and its Low-Income Housing Tax Credit and Section 8 vouchers are key to New York's capacity to supply affordable housing to over 400,000 people. A recent Workforce Innovation and Opportunity Act supports the city's ambitions to match skills to employer demands much more effectively and may reverse a decline in funding. The federal immigrant investor programme of EB-5 visas, administered by U.S. Citizenship and Immigration Services, has enabled a number of big development and regeneration projects to be brought forward in Brooklyn, Manhattan and Staten Island. The EB-5 system has attracted large numbers of Chinese investors in recent years and may have the potential to be expanded to housing projects in the City (Fischer, 2014b; Schlanger, 2014).

The national system of cities: New York City and American metros

For much of the 20th century, the many US federal government initiatives and programmes belied the lack of a coherent national policy for cities and metropolitan areas. During an earlier era of political bipartisanship, the national Advisory Commission on Intergovernmental Relations (ACIR) tried to address issues of metropolitan development. The ACIR sought to address fragmentation in federal grant funding and supported metropolitan consolidation, but polarisation in US party politics marginalised the ACIR over time until its demise in 1996 (Kincaid, 2011). In general, most policy activity was related to poverty reduction and social exclusion, but not as part of a holistic approach, and much of it was undermined by localism and competition. Federal economic policy did not take a strong spatial or urban turn until much more recently (Harvey, 2008).

Under the Obama administration, the federal government has tried to boost its commitment to cities and stimulate economic growth in productive metropolitan regions. The White House Office of Urban Affairs was established in 2009 to take into account policy impacts on metropolitan areas, but the body lacked clear goals and soon lost traction. Nevertheless, a new positive conversation arose about the future of American cities and how to help them succeed as centres of employment and resilience (Mallach, 2010; Holeywell, 2013). The federal Department for Housing and Urban Development has also made some progress on integrating transport, housing and environmental policy. Analysts argue that there is now a less compartmentalised approach and a stronger grasp of the need for urban resilience and sustainability. However, this is sometimes compromised by overlapping legislation that lacks strategic vision and incentivises sprawl and car dependence, such as the Fixing America's Surface Transportation (FAST) Act.

National budgets have tried to bring forward investment in cities but with little success. The proposed national 2015 budget included $302 billion in additional funding over four years, mostly to be spent in cities. This record sum would have relied on new tolls on existing roads, tolls on congested roads and higher and more rigorous corporate taxes, but political resistance meant only a temporary compromise bill was agreed (Associated Press, 2014). The U.S. Department of Transportation's $98 billion budget for 2017 also intended to accelerate the shift towards more integrated and transit-oriented cities, and to properly finance metropolitan planning organisations, but faced a hostile Republican-controlled Congress.

Ongoing challenges where New York needs help from national government

New York City's economy flourished and diversified under Mayor Bloomberg, but it faces more demanding global competition, rising costs and fiscal restrictions that present challenges in the current cycle. The City is looking for a less prescriptive and more engaged and supportive federal approach to cities that makes tangible progress in several areas. As Dan Garodnick from NYC Council has argued, "New York cannot reach its full potential unless the federal government gives us the support we need" (quoted in New York City Council, 2014). Although issues such as the necessary reform of regional transportation agencies are not within the purview of federal government, the main areas where action in Washington shapes New York City's fortunes include immigration, infrastructure development and the economy.

A sustainable arrangement for immigration and talent

The tension in values between New York City and the rest of the country is keenly felt on the topic of immigration. While the legislative record is one of US government hostility to immigration, New York City and the state government have enacted many policies to support immigrant access to services and healthcare, and to protect them from federal investigations. New York City is known as a 'sanctuary city' and its agencies no longer co-operate with the federal government on many requests to detain undocumented immigrants because of concerns of the risks of discouraging immigrants from registering with government systems and institutions (Jorgensen, 2014; New York City, 2015a).

Immigration is part of New York's DNA, and in recent decades has helped propel the city's success in higher education and entrepreneurship, but national opposition has begun to erode the city's reputation for openness to skilled workers, entrepreneurs and students. Given the city's large (37%) foreign-born population, New York's political system is fairly united in support of immigration and distances itself from the federal immigration machinery that seeks to deport large numbers of new arrivals. The City is supported by New York State, which has actively invited immigrants through the federal system and established an Office for New Americans to assist with integration and entrepreneurship (Aon and the Partnership for New York City, 2013; Semple, 2013).

New York political leaders are leading proponents of fairer and more effective immigration reform. Former Mayor Michael Bloomberg continues to co-chair the Partnership for a New American Economy, which leads an effort to reform national immigration policy. In the years ahead, New York's profile as a city that is open to talent and newcomers will likely depend on the federal government debate becoming less antagonistic and more flexible to the human capital needs of its large cities (Jorgensen, 2014).

Co-financing and endorsement of transport infrastructure and high speed rail development

Public transport use has soared over the last two decades, but few major upgrades have been made and Hurricane Sandy highlighted the vulnerability of the city and region's transport systems. Amtrak lacks finance to replace aging rail tunnels linking New York and New Jersey, and a new solution needs to be agreed that would be ready before 2030. The federal government, however, has not increased revenues for transportation for over 20 years. The 2015–2019 capital investment plan is less than one-quarter funded by federal funds, while state funds account for nearly 30%.

New York City's current Mayor Bill de Blasio and the New York City Congressional delegation continue to lobby Washington to encourage federal funding support for subways, light rail, buses, bridges and ferries. In 2015 they successfully argued to stop an $80 million annual cut to public transport in New York City up until the 2020s, highlighting the already high commuter congestion in the city. The FAST Act supports additional funding for Bus Rapid Transit and the second phase of the Second Avenue Subway (Freemark, 2014; Young, 2014; New York City, 2015b).

The federal government has also acknowledged the need for a regional high-speed rail system connecting New York to Boston and beyond. In principle, this could reduce travel time between these two cities to less than one hour, and to one and a half hours between New York and Washington DC. The possibility of making these cities commutable would have a major impact on the productivity of the entire region and could combine the unique political, financial and scientific capabilities of the three cities. Recent legislation allows Amtrak to increase rail funding in the Northeast Corridor. However, for high-speed rail, at a slated cost of over $100 billion, the cities and federal government will need to broker an unprecedented financial package, for which the political conditions do not look immediately likely (Callegari, 2014; Ahn and Russell-Einhorn, 2015).

At the same time, New York's airport system capacity, punctuality and quality are uncompetitive and urgently require modernisation. Investment in terminals and transport links is urgent. Currently, Newark, LaGuardia and JFK airports all rank in the bottom 20 in the US for federal grant funding per passenger. The City urgently relies on federal investment in modern satellite air traffic controls to support greater flight volume efficiency. Management and scheduling failures within the Federal Aviation Administration have been a major reason for new technology delays which contribute to congestion in the system (Knauth, 2013; Partnership for New York City, 2013; Global Gateway Alliance, 2014; Sitt and Sigmund, 2014).

New York argues that it requires the federal government to contribute to capital investment in accordance with the region's vital importance to long-term national prosperity, and develop robust project delivery structures to make sure long-term programmes are implemented. Federal loan guarantees are also sought in order to mobilise private sector lenders (Cassidy, 2014; Schned *et al.*, 2014). There is a view that the federal government can do a great deal more to catalyse private investment in and around rail stations, whether through credit enhancement authorities or changes in regulation. It is also not inconceivable that the federal tier could endorse a more bespoke application of transport investment to reflect the specific needs and priorities of each city.

Improved regulatory environment to promote economic development

The federal tier does not play a direct role in economic development, but its laws do not provide the City with all the resources and flexibility it needs to make strategic investments in its economy. Complex business tax codes, for example, slow the pace of economic growth, and significant R&D funding from the federal government for sectors such as biotechnology has disappeared (Tyrangiel, 2014; Wylde, 2014). More broadly, concern is growing that the tax and cost framework in New York is no longer as attractive as it once was and risks causing the city to shed jobs to other locations.

Re-investment to manage and reduce polarisation

The federal government has many of the most effective tools for welfare, healthcare, housing aid and food assistance and any comprehensive set of solutions in these areas depends on federal input. The rise in low-skill and low-income jobs in New York is pronounced, and federal programmes contribute much less to the housing and welfare challenge than they used to. The City's Housing Authority (NYCHA) is in serious deficit after federal investment declined by a third in a decade, and now accounts for more than half of all the public housing infrastructure work needed nationally.

For New York's new ten-year housing plan to be implemented, the federal department for Housing and Urban Development will need to help with finance, regulatory relief and cross-agency harmonisation (Dicken, 2007; Forman, 2014; Katz, 2014; Torres and Jones, 2014). Mayor Bill de Blasio has insisted that federal support in these areas is essential, arguing that "if the cavalry would show up once in a while, we could do so much for our people" (quoted in CBS New York, 2013).

New York's inequality challenge has a very regional dimension, but federal housing loan regulations make it hard to meet the growing demand for mixed-use and walkable communities across the region. Currently, 81% of federal loans and loan guarantees nationwide support single-family home ownership. The lending framework disincentivises the medium-rise redevelopment and re-investment of poor low-rise neighbourhoods in suburban areas. New York's ability to build high-quality and inclusive spaces depends on federal adjustments to commercial caps and on engaging a wider mix of developers (Regional Plan Association, 2016).

Climate change assistance and policy leadership on climate change mitigation

In the aftermath of Hurricane Sandy, New York City Mayor Michael Bloomberg proposed a $20 billion long-term plan to protect New York City from the future storms and extreme weather brought on by climate change. City capital funding aims to pay for much of the coastal protection, but additional federal government assistance is required for a large share, while changes to federal policy on flood insurance and retrofitting have been advocated. A step change in federal policy can also help set higher standards, disclose more data connected to climate change and provide confidence for long-term investment strategies (Timm, 2013; NYC Planning, 2014; Robinson, 2014).

Key actors and mechanisms that enable New York to make progress with the nation state

New York City Mayors and federal politicians from within the region play the major role in advocating for federal policy in Washington DC. The political system's reliance on campaign contributions means that the Mayor uses the support of wealthy donors to raise awareness of the City's needs. Current Mayor Bill de Blasio has continued former Mayor Bloomberg's lead in working actively to bring a congressional focus back to necessary investments in education, public transport and housing in New York and other major US cities.

The Mayor of New York City is always a well-known national figure and can communicate with federal officials directly with confidence of gaining at least a certain degree of access. The Mayor will periodically visit Washington to meet members of the federal administration and Congressional leaders. Mayoral requests at the national level are not usually financial but relate to policy changes in areas where New York is especially affected, such as immigration, climate change, terrorism and gun control. Very often, Mayors will use the television or print media to make points to federal government. NYC Mayors also create ad hoc alliances with other big-city mayors to argue for changes in drugs, gun, immigration and environmental legislation, where urban opinion often diverges from the national electorate.

The New York region is a functional 'tri-state' region of 31 counties in New York, New Jersey and Connecticut that is growing rapidly and requires very high upfront capital investments in key infrastructure projects and greater co-ordination. There is no empowered governmental institution to co-ordinate the New York region, and few bodies that operate across state boundaries (apart from the Port Authority that manages key parts of regional transport infrastructure). A careful mix of federal support, new financing tools and inter-state government collaboration usually has to be assembled to deliver on these projects. The Port Authority, MTA and the Regional Plan Association (RPA) all play important roles in the region. The RPA is an independent body which does not form part of New York City Hall. It seeks to influence long-term planning for the region. RPA's funding model is based on gifts and foundations, which allows its research and advocacy to be non-partisan, participatory and evidence-led. It also draws support from a wide range of stakeholders across the tri-state region's business, philanthropic, civic and planning communities.

Business leadership organisations play a decisive role in building political relationships with senior national politicians in New York, not least because of their importance to political campaign fundraising. Three important institutions are the Partnership for New York City, founded in 1979, the Real Estate Board of New York City and the Regional Plan Association. The Partnership for New York City makes a powerful case in Washington for infrastructure investment and the business environment.

New York City's mostly Democrat congressional delegation is influential in periods when there is a Democratic Party majority in the House of Representatives. It is especially effective during periods of crisis in New York City (for example, 9/11 and Hurricane Sandy) in ensuring aid is supplied quickly and fully, and that improved infrastructure is subsequently built. In recent years, New York Senators such as Charles Schumer and Kirsten Gillibrand have been important in galvanising support for Wall Street in Washington, using outside advocacy groups and the news media. Recently, they have also helped secure significant federal grants for terrorism prevention, response and recovery. Meanwhile, the New York City Federal Affairs Office is part of the Mayor's Office and closely tracks federal activity and lobbies executive and legislative officials on issues where the Mayor is not required or available.

New York is also prominent within the US Conference of Mayors (and, to a lesser extent, the National League of Cities), which offers a collective voice for cities to make the case for the federal government to retain its existing financial responsibilities. In 2014, Mayor de Blasio was at the forefront of the organisation's issue of a report on income inequality and the founding of a Cities of Opportunities Task Force to address the issue. New York has recently supported efforts in cities to introduce an enhanced minimum wage, better broadband and improved pre-school services, as the city leadership senses a window of opportunity to achieve policy breakthroughs despite federal government inaction.

Conclusion

New York has grown nearly a million jobs in the past 20 years and is still on nearly every measure a highly successful world city. But there is now a widespread perception that the city's relationship with the federal government is weaker than ever. Indeed, of the 12 cases featured in this book, it may well be New York that now has the most remote and fragmented relationship with its national tier, and which has experienced the most intergovernmental dysfunction and disinvestment. Given the high-profile setbacks the city has faced and its obvious future imperatives, New York would now almost certainly benefit from the federal government once again becoming more involved and taking leadership on airport and air traffic control investment, housing investment, inter-city transport, R&D funding and the platform for international trade. Currently, the city's flexibility to address economic, social and environmental challenges is constrained by federal regulations and programmes that are rigidly prescriptive and siloed.

Any hypothetical 'new deal' between New York City and federal government would go far beyond issues of money, and would have to cement the city's openness framework. Although the federal government supported New York's financial sector in the initial aftermath of the financial crisis, departmental attempts to rein in the industry through legislation such as the Dodds–Frank Act have had wider effects on New York's competitiveness. National immigration policies are also proving a deterrent to the city's reputation as an open city to skilled workers and students. As jobs and business operations are increasingly able to move to lower-cost, more business-friendly cities, New York's long-held and long-cherished global leadership in financial services is no longer a certainty.

New York's future also hinges on creative solutions for the wider metropolitan region, but unlike some of its peers there are few mechanisms for achieving co-ordination or consensus. New York's long-term competitiveness will depend on the emergence of substantive tools and upfront capital investments to shape regional development. Greater federal recognition of the metropolitan perspective will be essential in this respect to incentivise inter-state and intergovernmental collaboration.

It is likely that the ongoing partisanship and sclerosis at federal level will continue for some time to come, feeding both policy gridlock and future unanticipated problems and tensions in the American political system. If this is the case, the ability and appetite of political leaders to make real legislative step changes to support leading US cities, and New York in particular, will be highly circumscribed. Instead, New York may have to rely on softer and subtler means of negotiation and influence to achieve progress. The increased participation of former and current city leaders in federal agencies, and the roll-out of smarter technology and data transparency, are examples of ways in which better policy can emerge and others can be given scope to lead and innovate. Many other instances of improvisation and negotiated collaboration to overcome institutional disadvantages will be necessary. In the next cycles, New York's capacity for re-invention will be tested to its limits.

9

São Paulo: The quest for recognition and reform

World Cities and Nation States, First Edition. Greg Clark and Tim Moonen.
© 2017 John Wiley & Sons, Ltd. Published 2017 by John Wiley & Sons, Ltd.

São Paulo is Brazil's command and control centre for domestic and international companies, and the country's major centre for business capitalisation, real estate, innovation, R&D and decision-making. The City of São Paulo itself is home to 6% of the Brazilian population and generates around double that share of national GDP (Table 9.1). Now a 21 million person metropolitan region, population growth has begun to abate, but city systems have still not come to terms with the earlier 50-year surge of in-migration. The city still has a substantial infrastructure deficit and major investment needs in its housing, rail, water, sanitation and flood defence systems.

As São Paulo has emerged as Latin America's principal business region, policy-makers at all levels have come to agree that the city needs to invest in urban quality to sustain an economic transition into services and higher-value industries. While the service sector now supplies a majority of jobs, industry and commerce still have a very strong presence, especially compared to neighbouring Rio de Janeiro. At the same time, the city's monocentric spatial structure is a source of congestion, low productivity and regional imbalances. There is a huge mismatch between the location of homes and jobs, with the city centre containing nearly a fifth of jobs but only 4% of the population. Over the last decade, São Paulo has tried to initiate the first long-term planning perspective that would take into account the chronic problems of slum housing, social and environmental vulnerability and the need to engage citizens more effectively. This has had patchy success due to institutional constraints that militate against plan longevity.

The city of São Paulo is a 12 million person municipality the size of Greater London. It is also the capital of São Paulo State, the so-called economic 'locomotive' of Brazil whose own government is the middle tier of a three-tier federal structure. The city is one of 39 municipalities in a sprawling 8000 km² metropolitan region, each of which has its own mayor and council. There is no metropolitan government, and only loose co-operation. São Paulo is an example of a world city where the relationship with federal government is by no means automatic and instead requires tactical and dedicated leadership. As with New York and Mumbai, this chapter details how successive federal governments have rarely prioritised investment in the city and still do not identify São Paulo's distinct economic role or growth needs. Although it is Brazil's business capital and major wealth generator, São Paulo is more usually perceived as a tax resource for poorer areas than as a platform for national competitiveness.

In this chapter, we illustrate how federal reforms – such as the creation of a Ministry for Cities – and funding disbursements during the last economic boom began to help São Paulo make inroads into long-term problems of housing, access

Table 9.1:   São Paulo's metropolitan statistics

% of national population	% of national GDP	GVA per capita vs national average (1)	City global competitiveness rank	Country global competitiveness rank	Annualised employment growth 2000–14	Annualised GDP growth 2000–14	% of national employment
10%	18.3%	1.29	62	75	2.2%	1.9%	8.7%

Source: Parilla *et al.*, 2015; IBGE, 2016; World Bank, 2014; World Economic Forum, 2015; EIU, 2012.

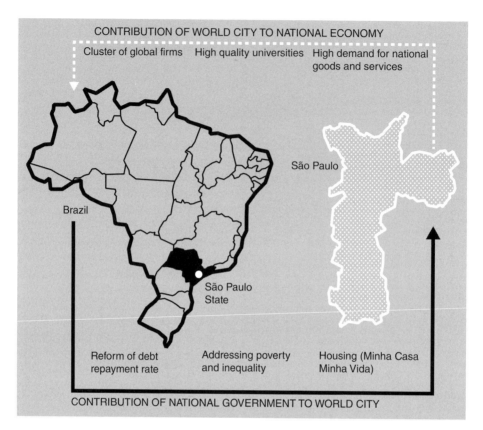

Figure 9.1:　Reciprocity between São Paulo and the Brazilian federal government.

and exclusion. Little by little, a blended, partnership approach appears to be emerging that combines federal, state and city budgets to deliver more housing and create more density (Figure 9.1). The chapter also touches on the persistent challenges of implementation, partly due to the siloed 'single sector' application of federal policies that do not join up across social, economic and environmental departments, and partly also due to the failure to engage the private sector. We highlight the impact of short electoral mandates and political friction between polarised tiers of government, which produce a low co-ordination equilibrium and have left São Paulo with a mounting investment deficit and an inadequate metropolitan governance system to cope with its rapid urbanisation. Under these conditions, São Paulo as a world city has had to innovate and advocate in interesting ways to gain the attention, support and concessions of higher-level ministries.

History of São Paulo's relationship with its nation state up to 2000

Brazil's early federal system left considerable power in the hands of state governments. São Paulo State was one of the major holders of political power until 1930, when power was centralised and the federal bureaucracy expanded.

Subsequently, federal governments had a long and largely unsuccessful record of discouraging urbanisation in the thriving industrial centre of São Paulo. Federal policies to alter the urban system failed to actively develop other areas of the country or to enact measures that would have distributed wealth more evenly (Meade, 2010).

As São Paulo grew rapidly after 1950, attempts to build metropolitan-level frameworks were ineffective. São Paulo was designated a metropolitan region by the federal government in the 1970s as part of its Metropolitan Action Program. The EMPLASA planning agency was established, followed by a metropolitan planning agency, but this body lacked political capital. In the same way, the National Commission for Metropolitan Regions and Urban Policy (CNPU), which was created in 1974, lacked power to co-ordinate other agencies and influence investment policy (Martine, 1989).

Since the 1988 Federal Constitution (FC), the government has changed its approach to São Paulo and Brazil's cities as part of the democratisation process. The FC provided the first constitutional framework for the development of land and urban management, and formally recognised the principle of autonomy for municipal governments and the social function of urban land. In the 1990s, some of the principles of the FC began to shape urban policy in São Paulo. Urban master plans were signed at the local level and citizen involvement in municipal decision-making increased. Political de-centralisation and public–private partnerships were popular solutions advocated for city dilemmas.

In general, the regional and global reach that São Paulo's economy has acquired has not been especially attributable to federal government investment or supportive state structures. Instead, its internationalism is built into the city's commercial and cultural diversity and industrial and export pre-eminence. It is the state rather than the federal government that tends to be the more influential partner of São Paulo, and the two governments work effectively together, especially when there is political alignment. Even when different political parties hold office, there are recent signs that a spirit of agreement and compromise between city and state levels can be forged. Endowed with strong powers by Brazilian constitutional law and with a strong standing within the Brazilian federation, São Paulo State engages with the 39 metropolitan municipalities on a 1-to-1 or small group basis, and is a major investor in infrastructure, transport and, until recently, water systems.

Changes in São Paulo's relationship with higher tiers of government since 2000

Since 2000, São Paulo's urban poor have received more federal support in the form of housing and, to a certain extent, better educational opportunities, access to credit, transport links and recreational spaces. Much of the change is attributed to the 2001 City Statute, whose constitutional principles on urban policy have given Brazilian municipalities legal and fiscal tools to implement master plans and enter into private and voluntary sector partnerships. For example, the National Fund for Social Housing, created in 2005 as part of a series of regulatory and institutional reforms in the urban sector, spearheads the federal financing of housing projects. The Fund encourages local governments in São Paulo metropolitan region to create satisfactory sectoral plans (Federal Government of Brazil, 2005).

The federal social housing programme *Minha Casa Minha Vida* has made some impact in reducing São Paulo's metropolitan housing deficit. As with other national urban programmes, the central city of São Paulo did not initially participate much, partly because of high land costs, and it continued to draw mostly on a variety of other public housing programmes. Other cities in the metropolitan area have been more successful at leveraging the *Minha Casa Minha Vida* funds. The scheme has been more successful in high-growth, medium-sized cities, helping to curb the proliferation of favelas, albeit much of the new housing is in single-use districts and disconnected from transport systems. In São Paulo itself, however, very few units have been delivered although many are planned, and there is wide debate about whether the quality and location of housing are suitable.

In 2013 the Ministry of Cities announced $18 billion (R40 billion) of investment in urban transport in the state of São Paulo from the federal budget and subsidised interest rates for other governments and the private sector to take advantage of, as part of an Urban Mobility Pact for the city. This investment was due to consist mostly of a loan to the state government (which is often crucial to long-term financing of major projects), with a small proportion directly invested by the federal level. Significant funds were earmarked to expand São Paulo's public transport network, specifically the subway and train networks, including to the airport, and to implement effective and popular mitigation measures such as special bus lanes that dramatically reduce commute times on key routes (Xinhua, 2013; Federal Government of Brazil, 2014; Prefecture of São Paulo, 2014a). However, very few of the promised funds were ultimately transferred due to Brazil's 2015–16 recession, stalling the city's much-needed infrastructure modernisation and its attempt to alter long-term spatial dynamics. The transition towards more sustainable transport has also been made more difficult by legislation to limit taxes on car production since 2008. This has seen car ownership in São Paulo rise significantly, adding a significant layer of congestion and road infrastructure costs to the city's already imbalanced use of land (Agência PT de Notícias, 2014).

Political alignment between the new Mayor of São Paulo and the Brazilian federal government is an important catalyst for co-operation and progress. Without it, there is a tendency for projects to be discontinued when there is a handover of power. São Paulo's local plans have to be consistent with federal policies in order to attract financial and political support. São Paulo State is currently governed by the PSDB party, but both the city of São Paulo and the federal government are led by the PT party. After the election of Mayor Fernando Haddad in 2012, both governments spoke of the need for a transition towards establishing a working routine between the city and federal administrations. Haddad stated that, "São Paulo is a global, worldly city, and as such it needs to be more in line with the state and federal governments, for the sake of the well-being of its people" (cited in Rocha, 2012). *São Paulo 2040*, the city's first long-term strategic vision, was not actively pursued by the mayor due to political differences, but it has influenced subsequent urban legislation and plans.

Strategic alignment with the state and federal governments is recognised to be more of a priority than it has been in the past. Frequent elections make it difficult for governments to achieve the alignment necessary for reform. Short-term political mandates also render investment choices and horizons short-termist. In São Paulo, this has resulted in a chronic investment deficit that has continued to grow over time. Governments have had to adapt and improvise to this deficit, often by using urban operations to sell construction rights to build at higher densities in order to generate infrastructure capital.

By the standards of many emerging world cities, governance in São Paulo has been fragmented and weakly co-ordinated. The planning and investment relationships between the federal, state and municipal governments have been untidy, and not always well joined up with the private sector and civil society. 'Whole-city' integrated planning and financing solutions remain some way off because São Paulo's growth has spilt over historic borders, leaving an institutional vacuum. It is common to find a complex and negotiated mixture of federal, state and municipal involvement in many of São Paulo's largest projects.

The national system of cities: São Paulo and Brazil

Brazil's urbanisation began earlier and accelerated faster than in most emerging nations. The promotion of immigration from Europe, followed by modernisation in the coffee sector and then industrialisation in the country's southeast, meant that Brazil rapidly urbanised after 1930. But Brazil's 20th century governments repeatedly and unsuccessfully tried to discourage urbanisation because of perceived social costs. Later, a turbulent economic decade between 1983 and 1993 – which saw five changes in currency – severely slowed the growth of the larger cities, including São Paulo. The rate of rural–urban migration continues to decline.

1988 was a watershed year in the country's approach towards its cities. The culmination of the Urban Reform Movement was the Federal Constitution (FC), which effectively assigned Brazil's local governments the responsibilities (and some of the tools) for urban management, equity and affordability. The FC effectively made urban policy a centrepiece of the country's democratic evolution (Table 9.2). The autonomy it granted to municipalities was praised for its ambition, but metropolitan-level powers were not prescribed and instead were left to state governments to delegate (Fernandes, 2007).

In the 1990s, as the principles of the FC began to shape urban policy, many cities and local governments enacted master plans and environmental legislation for the first time. Both right- and left-wing representatives promoted their own brand of citizen engagement in the way municipal decisions were made. Political de-centralisation, public–private partnerships and citizen participation were popular solutions to Brazilian city dilemmas (Gohn, 1999). The city of Curitiba was one to seize these opportunities to make big changes to its urban fabric. It soon became Brazil's leading example of a well-planned city with a high quality of life and sustainable mobility.

Table 9.2:   Brazil's urban policy and development timeline, 1987–2014

1987	Establishment of the Urban Reform National Forum comprising civil society entities.
1988	New Federal Constitution with two chapters dedicated to urban themes for the first time.
1989	New State Constitution regulates the specific context of the territory.
2001	City Statute guarantees the provisions of the 1988 Federal Constitution, enshrining the concept of the social function of property.
2003	Ministry of Cities and National Conference of Cities (*ConCidades*) created.
2004	Establishment of National Council of Cities as consultative body of MOC. National Programme for Urban Land and Property Regularisation.
2005	New laws regulating urban environmental sanitation and social housing, reversing trend toward privatisation.
2007	*Plano de Aceleração do Crescimento* begins new cycle of urban infrastructure investment.
2009	Establishment of *Minha Casa Minha Vida* housing stimulus programme.
2009	*Plano Municipal de Habitação* (PMH) defines guidelines, programmes, financial and human resources for implementation up to 2024.
2010	*Plano Municipal de Saneamento Básico*, integrated with the PMH, lays down goals and necessary investments to be respected by the Water and Sanitation concession signed later that same year, for a period of 30 years.

In 2001 the constitutional principles of urban policy were enacted in the City Statute. This breakthrough, which gave citizens the 'right to the city', dramatically reduced politically motivated practices in urban management and improved cities' legal and fiscal tools to deliver their master plans. The progress that the City Statute set in motion has set the standard in Latin America and across other developing economies (Wilson Center, 2009).

Brazil has become a much more metropolitan country in the last half century. Metropolitan regions now account for over 60% of the population, up from 20% in the 1950s. These regions generate 60% of national income, collect 70% of all municipal taxes and account for nearly half of all municipal investments. Much of the metropolitan dynamic is taking place in the north and west of Brazil, shifting from the established southeastern centres. The largest 15 cities in Brazil are the most diverse economies, but smaller cities are witnessing a significant population influx, albeit with attendant challenges of infrastructure, poverty and under-employment (Martine and McGranahan, 2013; World Bank, 2015).

Brazil's move towards a more focused national urban policy has accelerated since 2003 when the Ministry for Cities (MoC) was established. The MoC is divided into four secretariats: housing, environmental sanitation, public transport and mobility, and land and urban programmes. Each is supervised by an executive secretariat with a remit to build capacity in the municipalities. It defines the National Urban Development Policy, although the planning and management of São Paulo's urban development are delegated to municipal governments, as is the case with all of Brazil's cities.

National urban policy in Brazil has continued to focus principally on delivering services rather than on economic development. The priority has been to raise standards of living in cities by providing housing and basic services, but this has not been accompanied by mechanisms to address economic performance, productivity, Brazil's urban hierarchy or the economic functions of cities. The role of city competitiveness and trade capability is not a major part of the national urban discourse. This means that there is little public case made at the national level to invest in cities such as São Paulo on the basis that it would improve job creation. The result is slow progress in adjusting the municipal debt ceiling and interest rates to allow larger local governments to invest in their own development.

A 2007 federal growth plan called *Plano de Aceleração do Crescimento* (PAC) slightly increased investment in urban logistics, energy, social services and housing, in an attempt to break with the path of austerity outlined previously by the IMF. This cycle of investment has had some impact in reducing poverty in the larger cities and extending government service provision, although the city and state budgets remain responsible for the lion's share of investment in slums, sanitation infrastructure and housing. PAC has also raised ambitions among Brazil's medium-sized growing cities to avoid the problems experienced by their larger counterparts and become more sustainable and competitive areas.

Unlike some other world cities, São Paulo's commercial success has not drawn resentment from other Brazilian cities, not least because it has shared many of the same challenges with other cities – education, transport, environment, housing and crime. The city's reputation – energetic and ambitious – contrasts with that of Rio de Janeiro, but although the two are not politically well connected, tension between them is, in many respects, not as marked as in other emerging nations (Chao, 2014).

São Paulo municipality received R14.3 billion in federal transfers in 2013, compared to R18.5 billion in local tax revenue. As a share of its overall financial base, São Paulo is less supported by federal government than other Brazilian cities. Its 'revenue generation' index stands at 1.59 – for every dollar received by the federal government, São Paulo generates R1.59 from its own tax base. As such, it receives less support than Rio de Janeiro, whose ratio stands at 1.47, Belo Horizonte at 0.78 and Salvador at 0.88 – the latter two being unable to raise as much in local taxation as they receive in government transfers. Although São Paulo's vibrant economy means it is able to raise much more money locally than other cities – especially through its property tax, services tax (ISS) and value-added tax (ICMS) – this has meant that the federal level does not provide the enhanced support that other world cities receive for playing unique functions in their national economy (Table 9.3).

Table 9.3: Selected revenue sources for São Paulo and its peers, 2013 ($US billion)*

	Total own tax revenue	Total State transfers	Municipal property tax	ITBI (municipal real estate transaction tax)	ISS (municipal levy on services)	ICMS (State tax on the circulation of products and services)	IPVA (vehicle tax)
São Paulo	6.7	5.1	2.0	0.5	3.6	2.5	0.7
Rio de Janeiro	3.0	2.6	0.6	0.3	1.7	0.8	0.2
Belo Horizonte	0.9	1.3	0.3	0.1	0.3	0.3	0.1
Salvador	0.6	0.8	0.1	0.1	0.3	0.2	0.1

* Based on 2013 exchange rate
Source: Meu Municipio, 2016.

São Paulo benefits from slightly more freedom in deciding how to allocate its resources. São Paulo can decide where slightly more than half of its revenue goes, whereas for most other Brazilian cities more than half of spending is decided by higher tiers of government. From a wider perspective that considers the relative fiscal advantages other world cities possess, São Paulo has not been granted particularly generous spending autonomy within the Brazilian system.

Ongoing challenges where São Paulo needs help from national government

After high-profile protests against the poor state of São Paulo's public services – transport, education and healthcare – the federal government is under significant pressure to deliver improved systems in partnership with São Paulo state and municipal governments. Federal loans and funding will play a role in improving services, but federal officials have to balance this against a need to show fiscal restraint.

Reduce the city's fiscal constraints and recognise long-term investment needs

São Paulo is disadvantaged by a series of fiscal and debt arrangements, but national-level dialogue on fiscal issues adopts a zero-sum game approach to the way transfers are distributed and rarely examines opportunities for giving cities greater revenue autonomy. The city's problematic fiscal arrangements have at least four dimensions:

- **High net fiscal outflows.** Each year the city raises R200 billion in total tax revenues, but a much smaller proportion is reinvested in the city. Although this imbalance is common in large and successful cities, many agree with Odilon Guedes, member of São Paulo's Regional Economic Council, that "[t]he permanent transfer of wealth from our city to the federal government is enormous and unfair" (Guedes, 2012).
- **City debt.** Seventy per cent of São Paulo's R66 billion ($26 billion) tax liability is owed to the federal government because of a 1997 bailout. This sum has been repaid at rates of up to 9% p.a. plus inflation, despite a renegotiation in 2000 that attempted to ease the debt strain. This rate was finally reduced by the Senate to 4% p.a. plus inflation (consumer price index) in November 2014. Nevertheless, repayment requirements, due by 2030, eat into the city municipality's annual budget of R36.8 billion ($13.25 billion). The main sources of income are the ISS service tax ($3.6 billion), the transfer of ICMS value-added tax ($2.5 billion) and property taxes ($2 billion). But almost 10% of expenditure ($1.3 billion) is allocated to servicing debt, with nearly $0.8 billion on repayments and $0.5 billion on amortisation (Figure 9.2). Expenditure on repayments alone is twice as a high as the Brazilian municipal average, reaching nearly 6% of expenditure (compared to under 3% in Rio de Janeiro), even

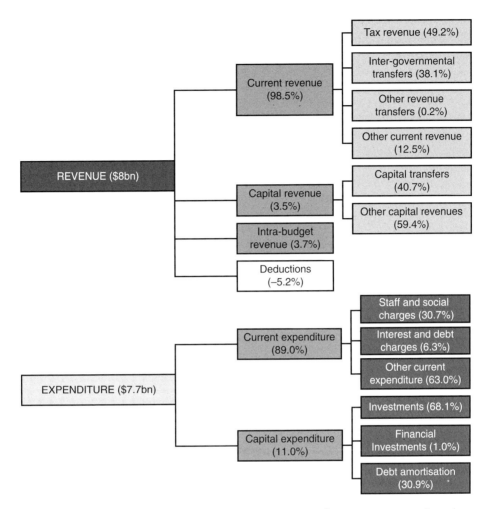

Figure 9.2: Balance of revenue and expenditure in São Paulo city government (based on 2014 figures and exchange rates).

though no major infrastructure items have recently been brought forward through this debt service (Folha de Sao Paulo, 2012; Guedes, 2012; Meu Municipio, 2016).

- **Borrowing restrictions.** Because São Paulo's debt exceeds 120% of net current revenue, national law prevents it from seeking loans from national or international financing organisations for key projects (Guedes, 2012).
- **Institutional fragmentation.** Low financial capacity and weak institutional recognition within Brazilian fiscal federalism prevent a system of metropolitan-wide financing from operating effectively in São Paulo's regional governance framework (Sudjic *et al.*, 2008).

Currently, there is limited recognition of São Paulo's economic role and fiscal needs. Within the federal government, only a small number of departments (for example, the Ministry of Finance and the internal revenue service) possess a strong grasp of São Paulo's role as an economic and tax-raising unit. São Paulo requires reforms that can support its long-term investment needs. The recalibration of the rate of repayment in November 2014 will help free up resources for investment elsewhere to improve delivery standards more in line with citizen expectations. There is, however, scope for a retroactive reset of the repayment rate back to 2000 (Coppola, 2013).

São Paulo is actively looking to become more autonomous financially, in order to create programmes and solutions without relying so much on higher tiers of government. A greater share of the gas tax would constitute one incremental reform. The Mayor also tried to increase property taxes in 2013 to reflect the rapid rise in land prices. Although it was initially suspended by the São Paulo Court of Justice, the Court later decided to maintain the effects of the law, allowing the property taxes to increase in value (Dos Santos Val, 2013; Ministério das Cidades, 2013; Valor, 2013).

Proactive support for infrastructure systems modernisation

A previous generation of urban energy, water and sanitation infrastructure is becoming inefficient and requires modernisation. São Paulo's citizens are also dissatisfied with the quality of transport services and the high fares. São Paulo has critical investment requirements in at least four sectors. Water systems need overhauling due to spiky demand, drought, water catchment issues and supply and maintenance challenges. Sewage collection and treatment is a priority as only just over 80% of sewage is collected and more than a fifth is not treated. Flood defence systems are required to manage the city's many vulnerable and precarious areas. Rail network expansion is also needed, as it is viewed as the major mechanism to integrate management of the metropolitan area given huge vehicle congestion. However, federal investment has not yet been carried out in anticipation of future health, economic development and environmental challenges, and is still largely reactive.

Effective economic management, government efficiency and transparency

São Paulo is beginning to make the transition from industrial powerhouse to business and knowledge hub, with signs that its industrial base is plateauing. The speed of this transition is slowed by a low level of legal certainty and predictability, and a mixed confidence in the public sector to manage investment effectively. The regime of licensing, certification and regulation has encouraged pervasive corruption in an attempt to bypass procedures.

The city's competitiveness in growing sectors depends partly on federal government managing inflation, improving government efficiency and transparency in order to incentivise private sector investment and project leadership in the redevelopment of key centres. The privatisation of Guarulhos Airport for R16 billion ($6 billion) in 2012 has illustrated the ability of deregulation to improve efficiency, raise the investment rate and increase the productivity of existing assets (Jovem Pam, 2014; Winter, 2014).

Approval for metropolitan initiatives and governance reform

São Paulo's metropolitan region has fragmented into sub-regional arrangements, and collaboration between municipalities is only sporadic. The lack of competent metropolitan management of water, flood, drainage, transport and housing systems is a major constraint on the city's productive growth. Building on a 1973 law that defined and recognised Brazilian metropolitan areas, central government finally recognised metropolitan areas in a 2015 Metropolitan Statute after ten years of discussions and intervention by the Brazilian Supreme Court. The law demands that the federal states create metropolitan regions and puts in place instruments for shared governance among the municipalities. But the original text to create a federal fund to finance the metropolitan initiatives was vetoed by the President because of concerns other priority areas may be neglected (Mattos Filho, 2015). Most commentators view the Statute as a promising step forward if it can be followed up with clarity about how federal government will help support metropolitan initiatives.

Holistic approach to informal housing challenge

Despite ongoing progress at delivering more and better social housing, including through the federal programme *Minha Casa Minha Vida*, close to a quarter of the São Paulo metropolitan area housing is classified as unregistered. A partnership between City Hall and the federal government (Ministry of Planning and the Department of Heritage) is arranging the transfer of large plots of land to the City for affordable housing construction. At the same time, the Municipal Housing Plan defines the 'precarious settlement upgrading programme' as its most important priority, but there are concerns the approach does not fully incorporate the housing deficit challenge within an integrated urban development agenda (Prefecture of São Paulo, 2014b).

Mayor Fernando Haddad's administration has struggled to deliver a pledge of 55,000 affordable housing units. The Mayor's 15-year master plan committed to over 45,000 units a year by 2030, one third affordable, and to give the public sector greater control over the character of the city's development given the number of stand-alone, weakly integrated towers that have been built. The plan aims to densify in the city centre and around public transport nodes, and $33\,km^2$ Zones of Special Social Interest have been earmarked in primarily low- or medium-density areas. These Zones are a pioneering model in Latin America but have a poor track record of attracting private capital to build lower-income housing, and rely on planned transport lines coming online. Without more channels for public investment in public housing, and these seem unforthcoming in the aftermath of Brazil's economic contraction, affordability will remain a serious challenge in São Paulo (Holmes, 2016).

Key actors and mechanisms that enable São Paulo to make progress with the nation state

São Paulo is just one of thousands of municipalities that the federal government works with, which makes it hard for it to attract attention. Although Brazil's larger cities can gain privileged access to engage with ministers, there is no customised relationship with São Paulo. The relationship depends on city leaders being proactive in proposing projects and scalable solutions.

Brazil's Ministry of Cities is an important enabler of constructive debate and reform around the country's urban challenges. It organises gatherings of mayors nationwide and international seminars for officials in its leading cities to learn from experts who have experience at building metropolitan governance. It employs several staff who are former members of São Paulo's municipal government, owing to their skills and experience of large-scale urban challenges. Some commentators observe stronger informal networks between the two institutions over the past decade, and more examples of shared working on projects. There are occasional strong links between senior city leaders and federal government, as current Mayor Fernando Haddad served as Minister of Education in the federal government for seven years under successive Presidents Lula and Dilma Rousseff. Unlike in some other large federal countries, city mayors enjoy a substantial profile in Brazil, and federal governments have to work in negotiated partnership with them to achieve national goals.

São Paulo's business leadership is currently working to form a business board that can make the investment case to central government to adjust the fiscal model. It is attempting to mobilise the city's corporate strength in law, banking and real estate to marshal a business agenda like London First, one that can take a leadership role in the alliance against corruption and over-regulation.

The National Conference of Cities (ConCidades) represents all 3400 Brazilian municipalities, with over 2500 delegates elected to debate the National Urban Development Policy. The recognition of this body and its inclusion in the political process signals the government's attempt to build a participatory urban system. The most recent biannual conference, in November 2013, provided an important channel for dialogue between the Ministry, local governments and civil society around the process of urban reform.

São Paulo itself cannot afford to bring forward big programmes, but it can innovate with demonstrator projects to give confidence to private sector investors and state/federal ministries. The city is engaging with universities to build new, innovative models of slum upgrading, social housing, industrial zones and redevelopment that already act as an inspiration to national schemes, as well as cities in countries supported by the Cities Alliance, such as India and South Africa.

Conclusion

São Paulo is set to remain Latin America's leading world city for some time but it continues to suffer from many financial and political handicaps. Although the city is a major tax revenue generator, most funds are re-invested elsewhere by federal tiers. With Brazilian municipal borrowing regulations so constraining, and without substantive new revenue instruments, São Paulo risks becoming locked into a permanent state of under-investment.

As we find in other federal nations, co-ordination with the federal government is quite intermittent in São Paulo, and tends to take place through large, all-purpose national investment projects. Although recent city leaders have managed to occasionally bridge political divides, party political alignment across at least two of the three tiers of government is still usually a prerequisite to achieving more substantial progress. Recent overdue government reforms to recognise metropolitan areas and renegotiate the city's interest rates are welcome, but federal financial mismanagement has now jeopardised future pipelines of investment. More broadly, São Paulo and other big Brazilian cities will only be able to bring about transformative change when constraints around debt ceilings and revenue tools are lifted.

São Paulo's situation partly reflects the lack of popular recognition of the challenges of metropolitan areas in Brazilian public life, which ultimately results in the absence of impetus to improve the metropolitan management of essential city systems. The city's capacity to expedite projects depends on increased legal certainty, predictability, transparency and trust. An overhaul is needed of regulations at different tiers of government to allow reinvestment in the urban core. One potentially important trend is the growing role of business leadership to build a common reform agenda around transparency, safety and business friendliness.

10

Toronto: Building capacity to renew the 'city that works'

Booledozer (2016), licensed under CC BY 2.0

World Cities and Nation States, First Edition. Greg Clark and Tim Moonen.
© 2017 John Wiley & Sons, Ltd. Published 2017 by John Wiley & Sons, Ltd.

For more than 30 years Toronto has been Canada's world city, and North America's second most globalised urban economy after New York. Since the 1960s it has established itself as an open and pluralist international city anchored around a rich mix of business clusters and world-class universities. The city operates in a ten-province federal system, and is the provincial capital of Ontario, hosting a strong provincial government and administrative presence. Greater Toronto accounts for just over a sixth of national population and GDP (Table 10.1). The City of Toronto, the provincial government and federal Government of Canada all share responsibility and resources for different dimensions and aspects of urban development.

In Canada, the federal government is not licenced to intervene directly in individual city affairs, but this chapter shows that it does collaborate more systematically than in other federal examples by sharing programme costs and jurisdictional responsibilities. Its agencies help fund Toronto's outstanding universities and many of their research programmes; they have also helped facilitate integration of immigrants and improve Toronto's business climate (Figure 10.1). More recently, sound national macroeconomic policy has enhanced the reputation of Toronto's banking sector and financial risk management. Toronto's high quality of public services (especially health and education) is a significant draw for mobile talent. In this chapter we explore the way in which relationships between the city and federal levels evolve informally and are shaped, to a large extent, by the changing impulses of federal leadership. The distinctive contribution of Toronto business and civic alliances in the last decade is also emphasised.

Like other world cities in federal systems, Toronto's outward expansion has tended to outpace attempts to create new city boundaries. The City of Toronto is one of 25 municipalities in the Greater Toronto area, a 6 million person metropolitan region with a high level of jurisdictional fragmentation. After a golden age of successful development in the 1970s and 1980s, Greater Toronto's economic and productivity growth is now held back by congestion, housing shortages and weak clustering. Investment and co-ordination issues have left Toronto metropolitan region with low capacity to tackle these challenges. This chapter points to the mixed results of provincial government amalgamation and the indifference and inability of the federal tier to intervene around the scale of Toronto's governance.

Toronto certainly has intergovernmental challenges moving forward, which partly reflect the agrarian and resource-based origins of Canada's economy and society. Canadian federalism does not have a focused and integrated approach to the distinctive needs and opportunities of its five major cities. Urban policy initiatives have tended to appear fleetingly and become diluted over time. In addition,

Table 10.1:   Toronto's metropolitan area: key statistics

% of national population	% of national GDP	GVA per capita vs national average (1)	City global competitiveness rank	Country global competitiveness rank	Annualised employment growth 2000–14	Annualised GDP growth 2000–14	% of national employment
19.5	19	1.02	12	13	1.8%	0.4%	20%

Source: Parilla *et al.*, 2015; OECD Stat., 2014; World Economic Forum, 2015; EIU, 2012.

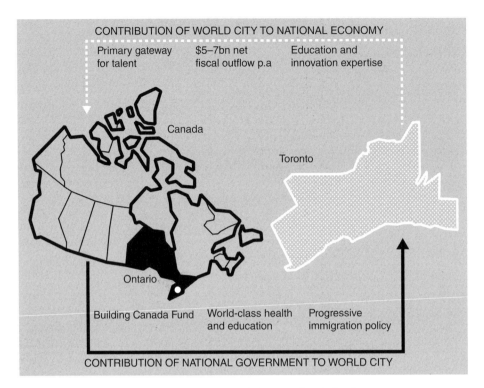

Figure 10.1:   Reciprocity between Toronto and the Canadian federal government.

the city lacks an adequate and predictable fiscal base to manage demand and plan innovation-led urban development. A change in leadership at the city and national levels in 2015 promises a period of more effective alignment and advocacy.

History of Toronto's relationship with the nation state

Toronto is among a minority of top-tier world cities in not having always been a national centre for culture, trade and commerce. It also operates in a de-centralised federal structure that accords significant financial and political power to the Ontario provincial government. As a result, Toronto's relationship with the Canadian State is not always consistent and occasionally fragmented (Dewing and Young, 2006).

Apart from two short spells as the nation's capital (1849–1852; 1856–1858), Toronto was always a secondary city to the larger, more established Montreal and the more powerful Federal Capital, Ottawa. It was only after 1945 that immigration and steady, well-managed growth created the depth of knowledge, skills and experience to become an international centre. After a long campaign for de-centralised and democratic municipal government, a two-tier government system was devised by the province in 1954 to manage citywide services and regional projects for the then Metropolitan Area of Toronto.

A series of changes in the 1960s and 1970s – some led by government – contributed to a golden age for Toronto. The signing of the US–Canada Auto Pact in 1965 transformed the entire car manufacturing sector across southwest Ontario as US companies opened branches and trade multiplied. Later, in 1976, the secessionist movement in Quebec inspired fears that business would be disadvantaged as a consequence, and led to a more consolidated shift in high-order employment from Montreal to Toronto. Throughout the period, federal loans and housing corporations – such as the Central Mortgage Housing Corporation (now Canada Mortgage and Housing Corporation) – were key to financing major redevelopment as Toronto emerged into a modern and functional 'city that works'. The CMHC's low-interest loans to developers and its financing of non-profit housing created much of the affordable housing in Greater Toronto.

Since the 1980s, the dynamic has become less centralised and a more intergovernmental approach has prevailed. Federal government withdrew from mass social housing first under the Conservative government of Brian Mulroney (1984–1993) and then the Liberal government of Jean Chrétien (1993–2003). Its main area of intervention in Toronto became transport and systems infrastructure. One review has noted that Canada's federal system now has a more informal and less paternalistic ethos that encourages city and provincial governments to pursue their own interests. This means that the federal tier is flexible "as to when, how, and under what conditions they will pursue cooperative solutions" (Bakvis *et al.*, 2009).

As Toronto became Canada's undisputed financial capital in the late 1980s, the federal government tried to redistribute prosperity to the rest of Canada, but State incentives proved to be no match for Toronto's industrial agglomeration and large skilled labour force. At the same time, the continuing growth of the Toronto region meant that the boundary of the area defined as 'Metro Toronto' was increasingly the hub of a much larger and inter-dependent 'Greater Toronto' region where 'Metro Toronto' was just half of the population (Filion, 2009).

The 1998 City of Toronto Act was instituted by the Ontario provincial government to amalgamate the city from six municipalities into one, and 'download' responsibility onto it to run public programmes. Although these downloads were initially fairly revenue neutral, the cost of maintaining the social housing stock has gradually required more investment. The challenge inherent in the amalgamation was that it focused on the consolidation of local government in the historically defined 'Metro Toronto' area and failed to organise the rapidly emerging 'Greater Toronto' region, where many of the new challenges surfaced. It was also too small to take a lead on transport and land-use strategy for the whole Toronto area, so the province retained a key role.

Toronto in the 21st century: A mixed record of federal–city relationships

Since the 1998 reform, the federal and provincial governments have continued to play an active and positive role in maintaining Toronto's attractiveness to business, immigrants and to international talent. But the city's reform process is incomplete and both upper tiers have effectively presided over a growing invest-ment deficit in infrastructure, public transport, housing and social services.

Since the 1998 reform, attempts to solve political-administrative fragmenta-tion across the Greater Toronto area have been partial and inadequate. Within the central city, under the term of Mayor David Miller, who sought a 'new deal' with federal government, the City succeeded in reforming the City of Toronto Act. In 2006, the Mayor was given enhanced powers to lobby federal ministries, appoint committee chairs and lead the budget process in order to solve the annual fiscal crisis. In practice, the Act only provided the City with limited leeway to adopt a municipal income and sales tax (Slack and Bird, 2013; Joy and Vogel, 2015). Subsequently, however, the City successfully passed a land trans-fer and vehicle registration tax, generating combined revenue of over \$350 mil-lion annually. But the 1998 amalgamation did not encompass the surrounding suburbs, and there continue to be problems organising horizontally for regional economic and transport priorities. For instance, Metrolinx – formerly the Greater Toronto Transportation Authority – was established in 2006 to deliver quick-win regional projects. Although Metrolinx has managed to purchase many key rail corridor lines, its lack of executive or revenue-raising powers has placed it at the mercy of municipal politics. Elsewhere, the provincial govern-ment has attempted to structure collaboration through inter-municipal plan-ning mechanisms and service boards. These alternatives do not have the scope to devise and implement region-wide strategies, or to advocate for reform with a single voice.

Municipal lobbying for more federal investment in transport and infrastruc-ture has yielded periodic success for Toronto. In 2002, the federal government created the Infrastructure Canada Program and the Canada Strategic Infrastructure Fund, which ultimately triggered over \$1 billion of joint capital investments in public transport (Joy and Vogel, 2015). Then, in 2007, the federal tier began to offer a stable and predictable (albeit limited) source of revenue to city infrastructure in the form of the Building Canada Fund and a share of the Gas Tax. Much of the resulting investment in hard infrastructure was very wel-come, even if it was not part of a strategic process. Since the recession, the fed-eral government has taken many important steps to make the country and Toronto more competitive. It renewed the Building Canada Plan, which provides an unprecedented level of funding (C\$53 billion up to 2023) to municipalities, and is ensuring that key projects such as the Union Station Revitalization and the regional GO Transit Package will be completed. Also, in 2015, Mayor John Tory won a promise of \$2.6 billion from the federal Public Transit Fund to finance one third of the Smart Track surface subway project, although the tim-ing of this envelope of money is, like others, uncertain. In general, federal fund-ing has comprised 20 to 40% of funding for many large projects, and indicates its commitment to nation-building, but its total contribution amounts to a very small (<5%) share of municipal financing.

Toronto's concentration of high-quality universities and research institutes means it has also benefited from successive federal research funding programmes. Launched in 1989, the federal Networks of Centers of Excellence (NCE) pro-gramme has created partnerships at the centre of some of Toronto's high-tech clusters – notably clean energy, ICT and life sciences. The Canadian Institutes of Health Research, the Natural Sciences and Engineering Research Council and the Social Sciences and Humanities Research Council contribute a significant slice of teaching hospital research funds. Since 2006, federal government has invested more than C$11 billion ($10 billion) in science, technology and innovation, and recent funding schemes support Toronto's cutting-edge research in neuroscience, cancer and stem cells. Canada Excellence Research Chairs (CERC) has also helped attract international researchers, while Toronto's universities also benefit from a new Canada First Research Excellence Fund (Crawford, 2012; University of Toronto, 2013; Gertler, 2014; Kazakov, 2014; Zeng, 2014).

Integration of immigrants remains a shared government priority. A multi-level Canada–Ontario Immigration Agreement (COIA) was implemented in 2006 which gave nearly $1 billion to help immigrants to the state settle and integrate. A separate Memorandum of Understanding for the City of Toronto was created, acknowledging its special role in integrating migrants. Such intergovernmental innovation has been supported by high-performing civic partnership networks (for example, the Toronto Region Immigrant Employment Council and DiverseCity) which try to enhance immigrant employability and provide pathways to leadership roles in business and the public sector.

Box 10.1: Waterfront Toronto

Waterfront Toronto is a unique governance experiment in Toronto, in a system where no single level of government holds enough authority or resources to deliver redevelopment by itself. It consists of a joint federal–provincial–municipal development corporation that was established in 2001 to transform Toronto's waterfront in preparation for hosting major events. The three tiers of government established Waterfront Toronto in a decision made permanent by legislation in Ontario province. Rather than grant the new corporation control over land assets, a multi-year funding plan was agreed in 2005 that earmarked C$500 million from each level of government to invest in an 8 km^2 area of brownfield contaminated land that had been neglected for over a century (Environment Canada, 2008).

Waterfront Toronto has effectively combined the financial resources and oversight of the federal government, the province's authority over housing and land-use and the local expertise and interests of municipalities (see Figure 10.2). The corporation has had to maintain very regular contact with ministers and leaders at all levels in order to secure over 80 separate 'contribution agreements' with government partners. This multi-level application and negotiation for funds has given it credibility and largely insulated it from the changing whims of different political leaders, and allowed it to focus on the patient task of building high-quality public space that boosts Toronto's image as a global city (Department of Finance Canada, 2013; Bozikovic, 2014). Indeed, Toronto's selection to host the 2015 Pan-Am Games was widely attributed to the waterfront development, which was home to the athletes' village.

(Continued)

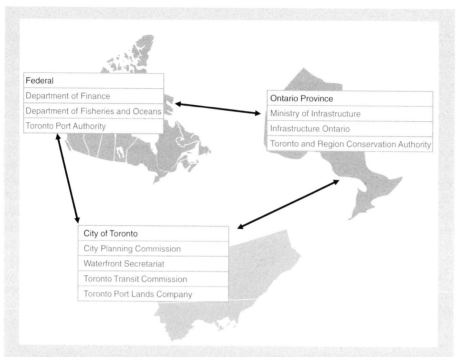

Federal
Department of Finance
Department of Fisheries and Oceans
Toronto Port Authority

Ontario Province
Ministry of Infrastructure
Infrastructure Ontario
Toronto and Region Conservation Authority

City of Toronto
City Planning Commission
Waterfront Secretariat
Toronto Transit Commission
Toronto Port Lands Company

Figure 10.2:   The range of institutions collaborating on Toronto's waterfront (based on Eidelman, 2013).

Waterfront Toronto has had to overcome many hurdles to become the success story it is today. Quarterly meetings of the Intergovernmental Steering Committee were suspended in 2009, and high-level intergovernmental dialogue faded. Requests for new powers for Waterfront Toronto have not been granted because of intergovernmental distrust, and many projects have been slow to be approved. But despite these setbacks, the co-operation and engagement across the three levels of government have raised expectations that future tri-governmental endeavours of this size could be successful. The project continues to receive considerable interest from the responsible federal minister and the federally owned Port Authority. $1.3 billion of shared funding has yielded over $3 billion in economic output, and Waterfront Toronto has since sought another ten years of funding worth over $1.6 billion (Eidelman, 2013).

The federal government has also made important steps to improve Canada's business environment. Its commitment to fiscal discipline, which may soon achieve a balanced budget, boosts business confidence and allows revenues to be directed towards growth and jobs. The tax regime has become a competitive advantage, without substantially compromising Canada's high-quality public services that are a key attraction to immigrants across the skill spectrum, and mark Toronto out as a socially conscious world city. A 2013 federal Canada Job Grant has also helped Toronto workers access up to a year of training for an available job, offering a guaranteed role attached to the State-sponsored scheme.

Despite these important contributions, the lack of vertical co-ordination of policy programmes results in ad hoc interactions and incoherent initiatives. There remains no single mechanism or institution to align the three tiers (federal, provincial, municipal). Federal or provincial governments have tended to offload fiscal and service delivery responsibilities to Toronto's municipalities, and the long-term effect is under-resourcing that has begun to resemble the situation seen in American cities south of the border.

The national system of cities: Toronto and Canada

Canada's urban system is witnessing a growing concentration of population, jobs and knowledge in the largest cities, partly at the expense of the smaller centres. Each of the major cities is becoming highly specialised. Toronto has emerged as the major centre for finance, culture and productive innovation; Vancouver is a uniquely attractive tourism and logistics centre, taking a lead on sustainability; Montreal is a renewed and vibrant city of knowledge; Calgary is a booming commodities region beginning to diversify its economy; and Ottawa is the political capital (Wolfe, 2014).

Political arrangements make it difficult to give Canada's leading quartet of cities due status or stature. Although Canada's urban system is now driven by growth in four cities – Toronto, Calgary, Montreal and Vancouver – there is no political will to designate these cities as the 'Big Four'. The federal government has no constitutional authority to assign large cities specific taxing powers to address their growth and infrastructure needs. Indeed, in 1971 the Pierre Trudeau administration created a Ministry of State for Urban Affairs, but this institution was soon shut down because of resistance from provincial governments which claimed their constitutional responsibility for municipal affairs was being infringed (Spicer, 2011).

New national urban agendas have been proposed but their support for Canada's largest cities has proven limited. In the mid-2000s, under Prime Minister Paul Martin, a greater national focus on urban issues led to the restructuring of the Cabinet to create a more effective Cities Secretariat. This initiative was eventually diluted within a new ministry headed by a Minister for Cities and Communities, which did not prioritise the dynamic role played by Canada's large cities.

Toronto's leadership organisations have periodically tried to mobilise a national urban agenda that spells out actions for urban growth. Although the federal government lacks the influence held by national governments in non-federal countries, Toronto has called upon it to provide a national focus on important city initiatives, and engage actors in a rigorous process. In the 2010s, the federal tier has come under increasing pressure to reassess and strengthen its relationship with Toronto and other large cities, because these cities are now seen as the crucibles of Canada's challenges of competitiveness, polarisation and social diversity. Canada's NDP opposition party confirmed its ambition to increase the federal role to support cities in 2013, and urban issues were prominent in Canada's 2015 election debate. The victorious leader of the Liberal party, Justin Trudeau, committed to a big investment programme to deliver infrastructure investment and swept the board in Toronto in particular (Shaker, 2004; Mulcair, 2013; Spicer, 2015).

Canadian cities do not have an organisational structure through which to put forward their needs to national government. Each has varied, but usually fairly limited, ability as a metropolitan region to legislate, raise revenue and enforce goals. The Federation of Canadian Municipalities gives a collective voice to urban areas, but outcomes from its advocacy are mixed. At the same time, a joined-up approach to the city region is largely missing in Canada. In Toronto's case, despite the amalgamation of the city, at the regional level municipalities often operate in isolation and have few incentives to pursue joint objectives. The lack of effective regional governance is a barrier to investment and planning. Large Canadian cities therefore share overlapping challenges and needs in relation to higher tiers of government (Federation of Canadian Municipalities, 2013).

Ongoing challenges where Toronto needs help from national government

The division of powers in Canadian politics means that federal government tends to intervene in Toronto's development on an ad hoc rather than a strategic basis (Wang, 2014). The weight of political representation in favour of rural areas in some provinces also means that, despite Canada being an urban majority country, urban agendas have not been consistently applied at the federal level. Spikes of federal enthusiasm for social housing or infrastructure projects make long-term planning difficult. The collection of urban data is also compromised after the federal government replaced the mandatory Census with a voluntary survey (Vinodrai and Moos, 2015). If the national government can adopt a more sustained leadership position that recognises Canada's large cities, it has the power to be a counterweight to the paternalistic city–provincial relationship and to allocate finance more effectively.

Aligned investment in infrastructure to address growing transport deficit

There is widespread recognition that the public transport deficit is Toronto's major concern. There has been almost no new investment in public transport for the last two decades and traffic jams cost Toronto up to $10 billion a year in lost economic activity. National building plans have been a step forward but their thin spread across the country means their impact in Toronto is fairly small (Oved, 2014). Many political leaders in Toronto have highlighted that progress on congestion and public transport depends on reliable engagement with provincial and federal partners.

Toronto needs federal government to apportion available funding to the city's transport needs in a way that aligns with provincial plans and disbursements. The city has a new transport agenda, which is geared around the Smart Track surface rail line, two light-rail lines on the waterfront and north–south, and electrification of regional trains. This reflects a desire in

Toronto to pursue multiple projects at once to address the deficit quickly (Kinney, 2016). For any of these to gain momentum, Toronto needs not only support for innovative financing solutions but also firm provincial alignment for accessing GO Transit infrastructure funds (Church, 2013). Federal support for public transport would relieve much of the pressure for the city to augment its own revenue streams.

Promote long-term revenue solutions

Canadian municipalities lack their own finance tools and rely on occasional largesse from either their provincial government or the federal government. For Toronto in particular, the overall fiscal picture is facing serious medium-term pressure. The City's fiscal challenge is visible in at least three ways. First, municipalities are responsible for ownership and maintenance of core infrastructure but collect just 10% of tax money, with the rest collected by the federal and provincial governments. In some cases, the cost of provincial collection is perceived to be as great as the revenue new taxes would create, which has disincentivised the city council from voting for more taxing powers. Second, federal government currently transfers large resources out of Ontario province for redistribution around Canada. The province has a 39% share of the population, but receives only 34% of federal transfers, a deficit of around $12–13 billion annually. Third, the City possesses a fairly inelastic property tax and small land transfer and billboard taxes, but these do not cover its complex service and infrastructure spending demands (Toronto Region Board of Trade, 2012).

The City of Toronto is also vulnerable to reductions in provincial and federal government transfers. Provincial (C$1.9 billion) and federal (C$200 million) transfers account for 23% of the City's C$9.7 billion operating revenues, and this share has grown because of the rise in infrastructure funding and the slow growth in other revenue sources (for example, property taxes). Gradual expiry of federal housing agreements and the elimination of provincial compensation for the city's social service costs will leave large holes in an already strained budget (Slack and Cote, 2014).

The City of Toronto therefore requires a stronger and more predictable fiscal base if it is to manage *new* infrastructure needs and maintain existing systems, as well as lead innovation-driven urban development. This means that, like London, Toronto can benefit from a reform at the provincial level that would allow it to retain and re-invest a larger share of the money it generates. A more effective taxing power would make it less dependent on higher tiers of government. Options include an enhanced property tax, as proposed by Mayor John Tory, vehicle registration taxes or a progressive income tax. In the longer term, some have even proposed that Toronto should have provincial powers over regional issues such as infrastructure, and a much more direct relationship with the federal government (Lu, 2010). Urbanist Richard Florida has argued that, "Toronto needs the resources of a province to become a truly global city" (Florida in Tapscott, 2014).

Positive trade policy in order to increase productivity growth

Toronto's GDP and labour productivity growth has been modest over the past two decades, despite its sector strengths. One reason is the lack of traded clusters. The Canada–EU Comprehensive Economic & Trade Agreement (CETA) is an example where regulatory co-ordination can support trade and innovation. Other potential agreements include the Trans-Pacific Partnership and smoother interprovincial trade deals (Toronto Region Board of Trade, 2014a). The national tier is needed to set the tone for Canadian businesses to become more exposed to markets outside of North America and identify opportunities in Asia and South America.

Increased support for immigrant settlement and labour market efficiency

Toronto's economy depends on the attraction of talent, but there are barriers to the integration of new arrivals into the labour market that result in the unemployment and under-employment of skilled foreign workers. Toronto has taken steps to become a 'sanctuary city' for 200,000 undocumented residents, many of whom are employed, amid federal inaction. At the same time, Toronto faces a labour shortage as the 'baby boomer' generation retires, while younger workers in the region still struggle to gain access to good jobs. From Toronto's perspective, the federal tier may need to play a more effective role in circulating up-to-date labour market information to match skills to jobs. More clarity around the refugee resettlement process has also emerged as an important priority in response to the ongoing Syrian refugee challenges in 2015–16.

Investment to grow science and creative clusters

Federal and provincial government grants and funding streams can invigorate Toronto's scientific research strengths. Federal government decisions – such as to build the replacement for Ottawa's aging Health Canada facilities in the remote city of Winnipeg – are not always conducive to effective clustering for innovation. Federal subsidies are also critical to the survival and vitality of the city's creative and cultural sectors. Their potential removal threatens their longer-term competitiveness. Toronto's car sector, which is still a major contributor to the southern Ontario economy, is now also vulnerable, challenged by competition from Mexico. It will need careful management and research as Toronto makes a transition towards advanced manufacturing.

Contribute fairly to meet affordable housing challenge

Since 2013, the city's *Close the Housing Gap* campaign has aimed to push the federal and provincial governments to contribute their fair share of funding for social housing capital repairs, and to make long-term funding available for social and affordable housing (City of Toronto, 2013).

Vigorous and effective championing of Toronto as a world city

National leaders have not yet made a compelling and sustained case for Toronto as Canada's world city (Mulcair, 2014). This is partly a communication problem, as organisations duplicate or have different priorities. Toronto requires national messages about economic development that highlight the country's other strengths beyond natural resources, in order to complement the work done regionally by Invest Toronto and the Greater Toronto Marketing Alliance.

Key actors and mechanisms that enable Toronto to make progress with higher tiers of government

Toronto representatives routinely meet, engage and lobby federal and provincial ministers. The federal minister of finance has been an important target of advocacy, with former Minister of Finance Jim Flaherty (2006–2014) also appointed Minister Responsible for the Greater Toronto Area. The Mayor of Toronto's role is to champion funding models and solutions to provincial and federal governments. The challenge is to get federal, provincial and Toronto officials to talk productively about the city's needs, especially in relation to transport and infrastructure funding.

The Federation of Canadian Municipalities runs campaigns such as *Fixing Canada's Housing Crunch*, which aim to convince the federal government to establish robust national strategies on themes such as housing, policing, roads and green innovation. It organises the Big Cities Mayors' Caucus, which meets two to three times annually to discuss affordable housing and infrastructure programmes in order to show the federal government that they are willing partners for the future (Federation of Canadian Municipalities, 2016).

Consider Canada City Alliance is a recent partnership of 11 economic development agencies from Canada's large cities that works to promote the country as a destination for international trade and investment. The Alliance has collaborated with national government on trade missions in order to capitalise on Canada's current business climate advantages (Paradis, 2013).

During phases of weak Toronto city leadership, a number of new organisations have stepped up to fill the policy vacuum. Perhaps most significant is the Toronto Region Board of Trade. Canada's largest urban chamber of commerce, with 12,000 members, has become an influential opinion shaper on Toronto's business and public policy issues. It is very active in advocating for economic development, sustainable infrastructure and strengthening city regional governance. It has helped build a shared recognition that the Toronto region is the appropriate competitive unit, and that a regional, unified development agency would yield positive outcomes. The Board has lobbied federal government intensively for financing of the region's transportation plan and for funding for immigrant training (Toronto Region Board of Trade, 2014b).

At the same time, the Greater Toronto Civic Action Alliance (formerly Toronto City Summit Alliance) has emerged as an innovative coalition dedicated to promoting the region and offering an additional source of leadership in encouraging federal and provincial governments to recognise cities' leading role in the national economy. Since 2002 it has become an umbrella organisation for initiatives on immigration, green space, arts and R&D, and lobbies provincial and federal governments to encourage action (Relph, 2013).

Toronto's universities are an important source of ideas and leadership. One influential department on intergovernmental issues is the Institute of Municipal Finance & Governance. The IMFG is an academic think tank within the University of Toronto that provides high-profile research to engage Canadian politicians and electorates on their cities' fiscal and governance challenges. Its papers and presentations are widely circulated among government, academic, corporate and community leaders.

Conclusion

Toronto originally became a world city as a legacy of a long phase of consistent infrastructure investment. But despite its ongoing success and global excellence, the city has been under-invested for some decades now. Despite recent increases to federal grants for capital infrastructure and provincial delegation of some local taxing powers, the city and region face major fiscal barriers in trying to address the infrastructure deficit. Fragmented financing arrangements lead to ad hoc rather than strategic planning for the city's future.

No federal agencies currently analyse, monitor or support Toronto's assets as an aspiring world city. There is a need for a more explicit administrative and policy focal point for the urban engines of the national economy, instead of siloed departmental structures. Toronto can also benefit from federal initiatives to encourage productivity growth through trade in order to support the transition into high-value sectors.

In future, the dispersed governments and sectors in Greater Toronto will need to combine resources to speak with a unified voice to higher tiers of government, and in co-operation with a firmer and more ambitious national network of large Canadian cities. Mayor John Tory's affiliation with influential regional alliance Civic Action, and strong working relationships with provincial and federal governments, has the potential to yield a period of more effective regional alignment and advocacy.

Section IV Mixed blessings: City-states and special status cities

11

Hong Kong: A laboratory for a globalising nation

Exploringlife (2015), licensed under CC BY 2.0

World Cities and Nation States, First Edition. Greg Clark and Tim Moonen.
© 2017 John Wiley & Sons, Ltd. Published 2017 by John Wiley & Sons, Ltd.

For well over a century Hong Kong has been one of the most open city markets in the global economy, and within the Asia-Pacific it is still the leading financial services hub and decision-making centre for global firms. The city has a deep culture as an entrepôt of trade and entrepreneurship, supported by its deepwater port, its British legal and financial frameworks and its bilingual status. Having made the journey from trading port to labour-intensive industry, high-value-added production and finally to internationally traded services and supply chain management, Hong Kong retains a large pool of agile companies in trade, wholesale, retail and personal services that serve Asian and global markets. It is also Asia's leading city for higher education institutions and among the ten most visited cities in the world. Over the last 30 years, Hong Kong has established itself as the business and capital-raising gateway into and out of what is now the world's second largest economy, China (Table 11.1). Its appeal derives from the fact that it combines unique access to Chinese products and markets with a very trusted and stable business climate that operates to globally recognised standards. Hong Kong has also become the managerial centre for the mainland Pearl River Delta (PRD), a phenomenally productive region for export manufacturing that has been described as the 'world's factory'.

For the last 20 years Hong Kong has been a world city with highly distinctive governance arrangements, as one of two 'special autonomous regions' under the sovereignty of the People's Republic of China (the other is Macau). This status was created as part of the 'one country, two systems' model introduced in 1997 and guaranteed until at least 2047. Hong Kong retains very considerable powers under this model, and has no local government 'beneath' the city, only 18 district councils that advise the government. The city has a large and powerful bureaucracy whose numerous agencies and departments deliver services and strategies that have been highly effective compared to many of its peer cities. However, the central government retains a key say in Hong Kong governance; the city's Executive Council is led by the Chief Executive, who is ultimately appointed by the Chinese State Council and reports directly to it.

Despite the rhetoric and controversy that surrounds Hong Kong's relationship with China, this chapter highlights the ways in which the two are interdependent (Figure 11.1). Hong Kong manages an enormous manufacturing economy on the Chinese mainland, and its stock exchange is a key source of international capital. Its financial experience has helped China to manage its financial resources and risks. Government leaders typically recognise the assets of Hong Kong's unique trading experience, legal framework, company

Table 11.1: Hong Kong: key statistics

% of national population	% of national GDP	GVA per capita vs national national average (1)	City global competitiveness rank	Country global competitiveness rank	Annualised employment growth 2000–14	Annualised GDP growth 2000–14	% of national employment
0.5	4	4.4	4	7	1.1%	3.3%	0.4

Source: Parilla *et al.*, 2015; World Bank, 2014; World Economic Forum, 2015; EIU, 2012.

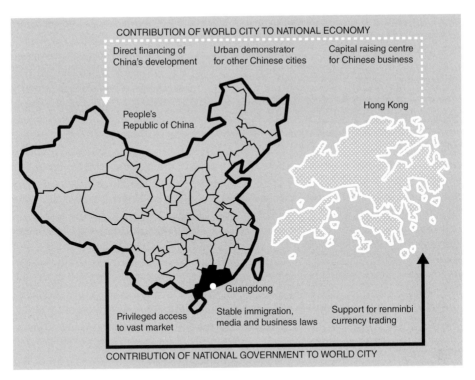

Figure 11.1: Reciprocity between Hong Kong and the Chinese central government.

performance, mature capital markets and global network, especially as China begins a transition towards a long period of potentially slower growth. As a result, Hong Kong has, in fact, received careful and timely support from the Chinese central government through most of the two decades since the handover of power. Helped by national Five Year Plans and personality-driven policies, the city has been able to successfully open up a vast market as an economic hinterland, and has retained its own policies on immigration, currency and media. Central government supported its ambition to be the largest offshore renminbi centre, and continues to invest in high-speed rail connectivity. Until recently, assurances about the process of constitutional reform have helped encourage foreign investment.

Beijing's desire to retain its role as gatekeeper to Hong Kong's leadership makes this one of the most fractious and potentially volatile relationships between a world city and its nation state. Political uncertainty exacerbates other concerns about Hong Kong's future roles in the Asia-Pacific urban system and the city's capacity to manage housing and affordability pressures. The city will require greater confidence about its future and opportunities for more participatory decision-making. But this chapter also points out the decisive role central government will have to play in Hong Kong's consolidation as a global renminbi trading centre, integration with Shanghai's stock exchange and the ongoing market and infrastructure integration with the PRD region. Reassurance and license from the centre will enable the city to continue to differentiate its global offer and grow its distinctive role as a laboratory for urban development in the rest of the nation state.

History of Hong Kong's relationship with Beijing

Hong Kong's relations with the Chinese state extend back over 150 years. As the then British colony gained credibility as a reliable, low-tariff and commercially diverse trading and trans-shipment centre, and a staging post for Chinese emigration, a new Chinese business elite took advantage of opportunities to embed the colony into pre-existing Chinese and Asia-Pacific finance networks. The city became the preferred local head office location for expanding multinational corporations, who valued the commercial intelligence and political influence Hong Kong possessed through its links to London. It also became a base and headquarters for Chinese revolutionaries such as Sun Yat-Sen in the 1890s, indicative of the close engagement Hong Kong had with Chinese politics. Hong Kong continued to be a haven for refugees fleeing China in the 1930s and 1940s.

Although economic ties waned during the Cultural Revolution, a tacit diplomatic agreement between the UK and China allowed Britain to retain its presence and influence as long as Chinese interests were not challenged. The arrival of wealthy entrepreneurs from Shanghai, many of whom possessed great industrial and technical know-how, saw Hong Kong's businesses begin to build their own industries to serve the post-war economy. The refugee population soon filled new jobs in the labour-intensive electronics, plastics and textiles sectors, where Hong Kong became a first-mover in Asia. The international activity of firms in these sectors was largely financed by local British banks that had the financial resources and expertise to optimise the export process. As a British colonial 'protectorate', the Hong Kong government initially adopted a liberal economic policy with few long-term capital-intensive investments or planned sector and technology advances. The city was successfully competing on its strategic location and the entrepreneurial flexibility of so-called 'guerrilla' business strategies that quickly identified and exploited short- and medium-term profit opportunities (Clark and Moonen, 2014). As wage and production costs grew, Hong Kong moved into higher-value sectors such as banking, insurance and shipping.

After 1949, Hong Kong's location made it the natural place for commercial and political representatives to gain information and intelligence about China. More than 100 countries now have consul-generals or vice-consuls stationed in the city, many of them along the northern fringe of Hong Kong Island. Hong Kong also developed a vibrant media sector with a freer flow of information and less governmental interference than in some other leading Asian cities.

Its British jurisdiction, legal and policymaking apparatus, and its adherence to British accounting standards and other professional qualifications, has been a source of stability and predictability for international trading firms who used the city as a regional headquarters and meeting place. These foundations, laid long ago, remain important. The city's legal system is a central pillar of resilience against the rise of alternative global financial centres. Hong Kong's relationships with London and New York continue to be important ingredients of its global embeddedness.

Economic integration began to accelerate in the 1980s with the opening up of the mainland economy. The lifting of the moratorium on foreign banks in 1978 and the opening of the Shenzhen Special Economic Zone in 1980 effectively triggered a new phase in Hong Kong's evolution. The city's industrial base relocated to the neighbouring PRD region for cost reasons. The new access to a large workforce in growing cities such as Shenzhen and Guangzhou meant that Hong Kong was able to manage and finance a huge number of manufacturing joint ventures. Hong Kong capital flooded into the regional subcontracting market that became essential to global supply chains of consumer goods. Hong Kong benefited greatly from growth on the mainland, which resulted in many newly listed mainland companies listing on the HKSE, a huge rise in Chinese tourism, a very large deposit base of RMB and a soaring domestic export market (Fung, 2008, 2011).

It is no exaggeration to say that Hong Kong played a decisive role in the transformation of the Chinese economy. Its manufacturing and import/export firms began to employ tens of millions of workers on the Chinese mainland (mainly Guangdong), and became responsible for intermediating the lion's share of China's external trade and foreign direct investment by 2000. As China's budget and expenditure have grown, Hong Kong has been a key source of international capital, and its financial know-how has helped China to manage its financial resources and risks more prudently.

Changes in the relationship since the 1997 handover

The difficult years after the 1997–8 Asian Financial Crisis posed a big challenge for the Chinese central government to prove the success of the 'one country, two systems' model. For the most part, it has kept its promise to uphold the mandate and treat Hong Kong as a separate country from an immigration and currency standpoint, with more liberal media laws in keeping with its commercial and banking status. Beijing's interpretation of electoral provisions in the Basic Law, and later its commitment to universal suffrage by 2017, provided a degree of certainty about the process of constitutional reform in a way which did not hinder flows of foreign investment into Hong Kong, given the city's democratic advantages (China Daily, 2004).

Many commentators wrongly predicted a decline in Hong Kong's international hub status, due to political uncertainty and the Asian financial crisis. But the city's post-1997 status as a globalised gateway to mainland China has actually fostered an expansion of international influence and urban investment. The city responded by proactively sponsoring a new cycle of redevelopment to strengthen and diversify its services offering. As a result of the 2003 Closer Economic Partnership Arrangement (CEPA), Hong Kong goods and services were able to access mainland markets, boosting patterns of integration. Many strategic initiatives were brought forward to upgrade key infrastructures, urban development and culture. Its status as an autonomous region has been highly attractive to foreign investors seeking access to the Chinese market without the uncertainties of Chinese corporate law (Chiu and Lui, 2009;

Mok and Cheunga, 2011; Horesh, 2013; Government of Hong Kong Trade and Industry Department, 2016).

Hong Kong has remained the primary business and investment gateway into and out of China. Mainland China is by far its largest source of imported goods, growing at a rate of 5–7% per year. The city offers direct access to China's goods and markets but with a business climate and legal system that has world-wide credibility. Hong Kong now hosts the most valuable direct real estate holdings ($800 billion) of any global city, because of mainland Chinese investors. Chinese firms also use Hong Kong as a capitalisation platform – nearly half of the 1600 firms on the HKSE are from the mainland. The city draws more than ever upon the assets and markets of its 57 million person PRD hinterland on the mainland. Hong Kong finance, whether through the stock exchange or private equity firms, is enabling the PRD's transition towards more advanced manufacturing, services and innovation. At the same time, PRD demand for Hong Kong's universities and research capabilities is huge, and is often then deployed just over the border on the mainland. The central government also supports Hong Kong's offshore renminbi ambitions (European Commission, 2014; Savills, 2014).

Demand from China has created new challenges for Hong Kong to manage the costs of being a 'safe' global centre. Hong Kong was, in some respects, unprepared for the effects of regional and national integration after 1997. The phenomenon of wealthy mainland Chinese purchasing real estate for long-term investment in the city has contributed to high housing prices, exacerbated by limited land supply. There are some instances of growing resentment about the scale of immigration and tourism from mainland China (Denyer, 2013).

Central government closely monitors the latest developments in Hong Kong and looks to make timely adjustments on Hong Kong policies accordingly. Several members of the Standing Committee have direct experience with Hong Kong, and are engaged with a high-level working group on the city. Government leaders recognise Hong Kong's unique trading experience, legal framework, mature capital markets, global network and agglomeration of trading activities. They have fully supported a whole range of schemes to encourage shared knowledge, such as internships for Hong Kong students in mainland state companies (Wong, 2002; Tam, 2012; Chun-ying, 2014). Since 2012, the Ministry of Science and Technology has supported Hong Kong's R&D capabilities by establishing national laboratories at six universities in Hong Kong. In 2016, five new Hong Kong branches of the Chinese National Engineering Research Centres (CNERCs) as well as state partner laboratories have begun to conduct research in a range of projects of mutual interest, such as biomedicine, electronic data, robotics, energy and materials (Leung, 2016).

The national system of cities: Hong Kong and China

After 30 years of rapid migration to industrialising cities, two-thirds of China's 40 large cities (greater than 2.5 million population) are in eastern, mainly coastal, China. Economic prosperity is concentrated in these large cities primarily because of their clustered agglomerations and superior access to international export markets. The largest cities have the highest incomes and productivity, and also the highest share of manufacturing. It is significant that cities that are within the orbit of Shanghai, Beijing or Hong Kong are also more prosperous than those that are not.

The World Bank's (Lall and Wang, 2011) simple typology of Chinese cities identifies four kinds of city. At the 'top' of the hierarchy are the big city coastal gateways, the engines of growth that are now pivoting their economies towards quality and innovation (for example, Beijing, Shanghai and Guangzhou). They are supported and complemented by the expanding 'suburban' cities in the regional sphere of influence of these coastal cities (for example, Hangzhou and Tianjin). Then there are the large inland cities outside the main development cluster, but which possess strong advantages of human capital and public amenities (for example, Chongqing and Chengdu). Finally, there are the smaller hinterland cities at the 'bottom' of the urban hierarchy, which have a visible agricultural character. Hong Kong has an oblique relationship with this system as it is, in effect, the primary regional node in the Greater Pearl River Delta, although Guangzhou, in particular, is beginning to compete with Hong Kong for air visitors and in other areas.

Chinese national urban policy has responded to a World Bank warning that China must plan its huge scale of urbanisation more effectively to ensure environmental sustainability and social inclusion. The Bank has highlighted the importance of energy efficiency, clean energy, density and traffic congestion relief. The Chinese government began identifying large regional city clusters as bastions of future sustainable development, given the world city credentials of Shanghai, Beijing and Hong Kong. The PRD, Yangtze River Delta (YRD) and the Baibu Gulf all became the subject of regional plans for the first time in the late 2000s, with the aim of bridging regional divides and creating a single cohesive economic region (Yao and Borsak, 2013; Nan, 2014). Today, China's leading centres of Shanghai, Guangzhou and Beijing are making their own steps towards world city status, which leaves the future character of China's urban system uncertain. Shanghai and its State-owned enterprises have even earmarked an initial 10 billion yuan ($1.6 billion) investment for an upgrade of Lingang New City as a 'mini-Hong Kong' as a test-bed for financial liberalisation. Although it is expected to be many years before its effect on the activities of foreign manufacturers and financial institutions becomes visible, there may be a long-term impact resulting from attempts to replicate Hong Kong's unique attributes and leadership in offshore yuan trading (Ren, 2014).

Today, China is nearly two-thirds of the way through a 60-year urbanisation process. Some have gone as far as to claim the country is about to undergo its second urbanisation revolution – from quantity to quality. Fewer new cities are being built from scratch, with more emphasis instead on reform, renewal and targeted investment. In 2014, the Central Committee of the Communist Party announced a six-year phase of State-led transport and infrastructure construction to consolidate China's urban structure, as part of its *National New-type Urbanisation Plan*. The Plan reaffirms the commitment to 'human-centred and environmentally friendly' urbanisation, and targets a new growth model that is more based on domestic services and consumption. The Plan aims for Hong Kong to be able to reach all large (500,000+) Chinese cities by high-speed rail by 2020.

Recently, the Chinese government has reiterated its ambition for Hong Kong to spearhead national growth and prosperity. The National 12th Five Year Plan (2011–15) dedicated an individual chapter to "Maintaining the Long-term Prosperity and Stability of Hong Kong and Macao" for the first time. The Plan set out the government's intention to consolidate Hong Kong's status as an international hub for financial services, trade and shipping, and especially its offshore renminbi and asset management roles. It also identified six industries where Hong Kong was highly competitive, and a PRD cluster with Hong Kong's financial system at the helm. The Plan has allowed Hong Kong to consolidate its role as a regional headquarters for multinational firms, and to export more services and business management to the mainland (Government of Hong Kong Constitutional and Mainland Affairs Bureau, 2011). Subsequently, in the pre-amble to the 13th Plan, the government has re-affirmed its desire to leverage "the unique strengths of Hong Kong and Macao" and support Hong Kong's ambitions in the same economic sectors (Legislative Council Panel on Commerce and Industry, 2016).

The latest regional infrastructure strategy developed by the Chinese central government is the *One Belt, One Road* initiative, which aims to integrate policy, connectivity, trade and finance across all the nations in the so-called 21st century 'silk road'. This new initiative has important implications for Hong Kong, which already illustrates and embodies how two systems can be integrated in a complementary way. In the 2016 Policy Address, Chief Executive C.Y. Leung spoke of the potential for Hong Kong to use its financial services, trade and logistics expertise to serve the *One Belt, One Road* strategy, as well as for other firms to lead joint ventures with countries along the route (Leung, 2016). With central government permission, Hong Kong also intends to join the new Asian Infrastructure Investment Bank and offer mediation and arbitration services.

Hong Kong's future imperatives and the role of China's central government

Given intense cross-border rail and road integration, Hong Kong is *de facto* moving towards a more unified economic region of collaboration and partnership with the PRD that maximises efficiency and complementarity. The Chief Executive's 2014 Policy Address acknowledged the strategic ambition to "strengthen co-operation with the mainland...in every aspect" (quoted in The Government of Hong Kong, 2014). This even extends to Hong Kong's developers and urbanists creating solutions for cities in the PRD and across China, turning the city into something of a laboratory for Chinese (and Asian) urbanism. Nevertheless, for Hong Kong's future success as a world city, there are several areas where dialogue and problem-solving are necessary.

Clarity over future political arrangements

Hong Kong is witnessing a deepening confrontation over its political future, due to strains between advocates of political liberalisation and Beijing's desire to retain its role as gatekeeper to the city's leadership. Beijing issued its first white paper on the future implementation of the political model in July 2014, stating that, "the high degree of autonomy in Hong Kong is not an inherent power, but one that comes solely from the authorisation by the central leadership." At the same time, Hong Kong government policies to kick start the economy have been delayed by parties in the city's Legislature in protest against China's refusal to compromise in advance of full elections in 2017. This reflects growing polarisation in Hong Kong politics that threatens to impair the city's leadership and strategic capability going forward (Powell, 2014).

The likely political settlement with China is by no means clear, and will need to be managed as long-term investment horizons begin to take into account the expiration of the city's special status in 2047. Hong Kong will need to optimise its political relationship with China to sustain business confidence, and to ensure that the most effective complementary roles with the PRD and with Shanghai are achieved. Even if the Chinese government may not wish to be tied publicly to a long-term vision for the city, Hong Kong requires an open dialogue of ideas and propositions about its future.

Oversee process of deepening integration with Pearl River Delta

Hong Kong's potential to build a free-trade zone with neighbouring Guangdong may be important in its medium-term competitiveness. A zone that would allow Hong Kong-based companies and individuals to freely access Chinese markets would consolidate the city's talent and regulatory advantages over Shanghai and mainland regions (Tong *et al.*, 2013). The city would also benefit from the agglomeration effect of rail links to Macau and Zhuhai. Hong Kong is well positioned to guide the PRD's rapid transition towards innovation-led development if it can steer a careful and mature negotiation of its future with the mainland.

Hong Kong's relationship with Guangdong is shaped by a Joint Conference that is co-chaired by the Chief Executive and the Governor of Guangdong Province. Separate co-operation meetings also take place with Shenzhen, Guangzhou and Zhuhai to build the three pilot free-trade zones in Qianhai, Nansha and Hengqin. Qianhai, in particular, has been much touted since it won the central government's support in 2010 as a pilot for modern services. Located just over the border in Guangdong, it is an example of a Chinese-led policy that needs careful input from Hong Kong in a highly politicised context. With potential investment of up to RMB 400 billion ($65 billion), Qianhai could become a hub for RMB internationalisation and finance reform, and relieve Hong Kong's office space shortages. Central government has been key to introducing incentives to open a channel for the two-way flow of RMB (Colliers International,

2014), but so far little has been achieved other than successful shopping malls which are attracting mainland customers away from Hong Kong.

In addition, despite progress on a third runway at Hong Kong's international airport, capacity constraints remain over the longer term. There is scope to share regional airports, if the political risk is well managed. The central government's new smarter approach to urbanisation may shape the pace and direction of future airport construction and encourage a more shared regional approach to infrastructure development (Hong Kong International Airport, 2011, 2015; Vogel, 2016).

Maintaining Hong Kong's competitiveness as a financial centre during systems integration

The evolution of Shanghai and Hong Kong's complementary finance specialisms will require careful ongoing intervention. The China Securities Regulatory Commission now permits qualified investors from the mainland and Hong Kong to invest freely in stocks listed in each other's stock markets, which can boost Hong Kong's status as a global securities and renminbi trading centre. In order to become recognised as a risk management centre and not just a stock exchange, Hong Kong has introduced currency futures to allow hedging between the renminbi and the euro, the yen, the rupee and the ringgit, with planned gold futures to be settled in renminbi and dollars (Hughes, 2016). Integration, if well managed, also has the potential to boost the portfolio diversity of mainland investors, propel Chinese capital internationally and raise company performance, governance and productivity (Chung and Chow, 2014).

Support for Hong Kong's role as laboratory for Chinese urbanism

Hong Kong is exploring opportunities to extend its influence on the mainland through the stewardship of satellite communities across the border. This may prove part of the solution to the city's housing demand, along with housing development in the New Territories and regeneration on Hong Kong Island. Increased land sales aim to yield 20,000 private apartments for development annually across Hong Kong (Tan, 2014).

Key actors and mechanisms that enable Hong Kong to make progress with the nation state

Hong Kong's Chief Executive plays a critical role in building trust between the city's electorate and the mainland. Part of his remit is to carry messages to Beijing that gauge and communicate public opinion. He also attends meetings with provincial governors and city mayors to discuss future co-operation, particularly in economic development. The Chief Executive meets newly appointed leaders of State ministries and commissions – such as the National Development and Reform Commission (NDRC) and the Minister of Commerce – whenever possible to discuss implementation of Five Year Plans, the CEPA free trade agreement and the internationalisation of mainland firms. In addition to the Chief Executive, Hong Kong's Legislative Council makes requests to visit the mainland to enhance mutual understanding and networks, subject to approval from central government (Chun-ying, 2013).

In 2013 the Financial Services Development Council was established as a senior cross-sector advisory body to engage the sector in ideas for strategic development. Board members include chiefs at JPMorgan, Standard Chartered, HSBC, Citigroup and Hong Kong's Trade Development Council. In exploring new opportunities and challenges to Hong Kong brought about by restructuring in China, its proposals are used in negotiations with central government authorities (Financial Services Development Council, 2014).

Hong Kong's Chambers of Commerce, and many other business and civil society groups, are active in the debate to ensure a prosperous future for Hong Kong. Hong Kong bankers engage with the State Council and China's financial regulators to debate financial sector developments. Senior members of the Hong Kong Monetary Authority and the Hong Kong Association of Banks, as well as firm representatives, are in dialogue with the China Banking Regulatory Commission, the People's Bank of China, the State Council, the Ministry of Finance and the China Securities Regulatory Commission, in order to defend Hong Kong's interests as Beijing undertakes financial reforms. Other professional bodies, such as the Hong Kong Institute of Certified Public Accountants, also have a presence in Beijing and advocate for improved practices. In Beijing, senior CCP officials such as Li Yuanchao, Li Keqiang, Zhang Dejiang, Wang Qishan and Yu Zhengsheng, all have strong links and experience with Hong Kong's business and political communities (Tam, 2012).

In 2013 a Consultative Committee was formed to advise the Hong Kong government on economic and trade co-operation between Hong Kong and mainland China, reorganising the previous Greater Pearl River Delta Business Council. The new Consultative Committee on Economic and Trade Co-operation covers economic and trade issues between Hong Kong and all mainland regions, making relevant policy proposals that will help Hong Kong firms succeed in the Chinese market. The 30–40 member group chaired by former head of the Trade Development Council and Mass Transit Railway Corporation, Mr Jack So, and including many senior business leaders, closely monitors developments in China's liberalising trade zones and will provide guidance for mutual benefit (Swire, 2013; The Government of Hong Kong, 2013).

Hong Kong deputies have been invited in greater numbers to the National People's Congress to discuss the framework for the city's political reform in 2017. In August 2014, 12 Hong Kong representatives attended the NPC's Standing Committee meeting, compared to just two in 2004, as an indication of Beijing's commitment to reform.

Conclusion

Hong Kong's future relationship with its nation state is engulfed in polarising debate on the character of its democracy, in light of Beijing's insistence on having the final say on the city's Chief Executive. Although no outcomes are obvious, future stability will likely involve compromise on electoral reform. Although a long-term plan beyond 2047 would be very difficult to agree and sustain, Hong Kong requires a large and broad-based discussion of options and scenarios for its future. At the same time, it is clear to most informed commentators that the governance system could be strengthened to allow for more participative decision-making and for greater cross-cutting activity.

Integration with the PRD has been a huge boon to Hong Kong over the past 20 years and the intensification of these links, facilitated by central government, promises many benefits for the city. Its companies and entrepreneurs will likely gain greater access to markets in the region, and profit from more productive agglomeration and harmonisation of standards and rules. The central government's plans for urbanisation will shape the pace, direction and collaborative ethos of infrastructure development in the PRD.

Hong Kong has the potential to be the undisputed global renminbi trading hub, plugged in to a dynamic set of Chinese stock exchanges, and with satellite zones for housing, office space and financial services on the mainland to absorb some of its surplus demand. The programme of enormous investment that is set in train by the *One Belt, One Road* strategy gives Hong Kong an opportunity to become a critical supplier of capital and expertise. In principle, these are the ingredients for Hong Kong to sustain its position as the leading centre of finance and knowledge in Asia, and a living laboratory for urbanism in the continent. But the major uncertainty surrounds the decision-making of the Chinese central government, and the extent to which it views control over Hong Kong as essential to long-term national cohesion and security. Widespread fears about the erosion of the city's language, culture and civil liberties reflect the existential anxieties of a semi-autonomous world city at the frontier of a resurgent geopolitical superpower. Despite the successful reciprocity of the last two decades, Hong Kong now faces up to a new cycle of political tension and confrontation which risks compromising the success model that has made it such a dynamic and inclusive world city to date.

12

Moscow: Demand or divergence – the externalities of political centralism

World Cities and Nation States, First Edition. Greg Clark and Tim Moonen.
© 2017 John Wiley & Sons, Ltd. Published 2017 by John Wiley & Sons, Ltd.

Moscow is Russia's economic and political capital and the wealthiest city in the Russian Federation. It is a dense, 12 million person 'federal city' directly recognised by the federal government and with a high level of self-governing powers and fiscal resources. The city's re-emergence as a political centre with global reach hinges on a number of distinctive assets. First, it is the commercial, transport, governmental and management hub city of a large centralised country, and the largest customer and distribution market in Europe. Second, it possesses a large, high-quality, technically proficient labour force. Around 6% of Russia's population live in Moscow, with around a fifth of the city's population working in finance, credit, banking, insurance or science (Table 12.1). Most of Russia's key companies have their headquarters in Moscow, including Sberbank, Russia's largest bank. Despite recent challenges, the city retains an attractive balance of profitability and risk for many investors. Relative to other emerging world cities, Moscow has high standards of health and education, and relatively low crime (Krasheninnokov, 2003; Banki, 2016; Sberbank, 2016).

Like St Petersburg, Moscow is a federal city with the powers of a regional government. The powerful city government administers 12 local districts and maintains a close, complex and largely positive relationship with the federal government. The federal leadership has supported Moscow's ambitions in financial services with a sequence of reforms, while centralisation of government has encouraged firms to cluster in Moscow in order to be close to decision-making, enhancing agglomeration in the capital. Russian state institutions are also major users of Moscow land and infrastructure. The city regularly commits 40% of its tax revenue to the federal budget, below the regional average of over 50%, but cumulatively the second largest amount of any Russian region (Figure 12.1). At the same time, Moscow has high investment needs that cannot be solely addressed by its own resources.

Moscow has been experiencing the strains of rapid car-oriented growth combined with a monocentric transport system and pattern of development. The city is now embarking on a bold programme of transport extension and modernisation, longer-term spatial planning towards an enlarged centre and polycentric development, waterfront renewal and rationalisation of its economic land uses. This chapter highlights the importance to Moscow that national government improves the framework conditions for business and provides incentives for private investment. It appraises the mixed blessing for a world city when its national government is able to make firm and unilateral decisions in its capital's favour, such as the extension of the city boundary to incorporate 'New Moscow',

Table 12.1:   Moscow's metropolitan area: key statistics

% of national population	% of national GDP	GDP per capita vs national average (1)	City global competitiveness rank	Country global competitiveness rank	Annualised employment growth 2000–14	Annualised GDP growth 2000–14	% of national employment
8	29.7	1.84	58	45	2.1%	3.5%	9.7%

Source: Parilla *et al.*, 2015; World Bank, 2014; Russian Federation Federal Statistics Service, 2015; World Economic Forum, 2015; EIU, 2012.

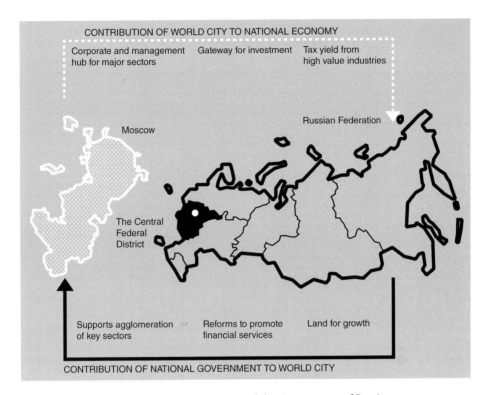

Figure 12.1: Reciprocity between Moscow and the Government of Russia.

the creation of Skolkovo innovation district and the successful bid for the 2018 football World Cup.

Relative to other world cities, a major challenge for Moscow that emerges from this chapter is that very few other Russian cities are able to develop complementary roles. We explain how the limited competences and resources of most other Russian cities reinforce Moscow's role as the key node in the national system, and increase negative side effects associated with a congested/inflationary hub city in a centralised state. The lack of policy attention on how Moscow interacts with other cities and regions in the Russian system, or how national urban policy in Russia will develop, risks locking the country into a path dependency that is less productive and less sustainable than it otherwise could be.

History of the city and federal government relationship in Moscow

Moscow's 20th century political history until 1991 was largely shaped by a centralised and 'bureaucratic' state, whose leadership included the head of the Communist Party Committee in Moscow. Its development from 1924 to 1990 was guided by centrally mandated national plans and economic goals aimed at providing equal services to citizens. Within this system, national elites routinely identified Moscow as the city which should embody the best of the Soviet model, in competition with capitalist cities. Moscow benefited infrastructurally from cycles of renewal, including a glut of tall buildings in the 1950s, designed to put forward Moscow as representative of socialist values. The right to housing was also implemented by Moscow's administration through the mass production of homes and social infrastructure and enormous suburban infrastructure programmes. Living conditions improved drastically from the 1950s onwards with a huge apartment building programme. In 1940, living space per capita in Moscow was just 6.2 square metres but had more than doubled to 13.6 square metres in 1971 (Colton, 1996; Krasheninnokov, 2003). State-funded housing development peaked with the 1970s construction for the 1980 Olympic Games.

Moscow also benefited from Communist government decisions to locate electronics and military technology laboratories in and around the capital. The surrounding Moscow Oblast (region) became increasingly industrialised, and has grown to the extent that today it is an area of 7 million people the size of Denmark. Many of Russia's leading universities, such as Lomonosov Moscow State University (MGU), the Higher School of Economics, People's Friendship University of Russia and MGIMO, Russia's most prestigious specialist humanities and international relations institute, continue to thrive and carry out high-quality research. This legacy has enabled Moscow to pursue leadership in R&D and technology functions in recent years.

Moscow's profile of international engagement was fundamentally shaped by national politics. Although productive trade and diplomatic relationships with Western cities declined after the late 1930s, Moscow became a multi-ethnic and multi-lingual centre for people across the Soviet Union. The State's ambition to industrialise the capital and to create a living showcase for socialist achievements saw strong links also created with China, India and others. As Moscow received favourable allocations of investment, it acquired many physical, commercial, cultural, scientific, educational and institutional assets with which to make a successful transition in the post-Soviet era (Colton, 1996; Kolossov and O'Loughlin, 2004).

Russia's painful process of transition after 1991 triggered new approaches to leadership and management in Moscow. In 1991 the capital was allowed to introduce a popularly elected mayor, and laws brought in up to 1995 gave local governments greater autonomy and powers, many of which were consolidated within the city administration. As Moscow began to experience a construction, office and retail boom, the city government became more powerful and gained a high degree of autonomy in some of its political and economic activities.

Under former Mayor Yuri Luzhkov, Moscow leveraged its political alliance with the federal presidency to retain management of Soviet-era real estate assets during the post-communist transition, and to develop strong private sector connections for city projects. He adopted a distinctive approach to privatisation that favoured mixed forms of ownership to retain city influence as a business partner. The Mayor's team was powerful and unified, and acted as the main channel of communication with the national tier, especially as the local government consisted of a fairly weak city council and network of local leaders. Luzhkov was successful in gaining personal and political support from the federal level to ensure funding streams and to retain partial self-government. Funding for housing, resettlement and development increasingly came from 'off budget' sources, such as housing sales, ground lease rights sales and shares in businesses, rather than from federal or city budgets (Krasheninnokov, 2003; Brie, 2004).

New approaches in the 21st century

Russia's centralised management system has created very high concentrations of companies, capital and talent in Moscow. Russia's historic tradition of centralisation is a form of path dependency, but is accentuated by the benefits that accrue to businesses operating near to Russia's executive and legislative bodies. The desire for proximity to decision-makers has benefited Moscow in terms of tax revenues, foreign trade and highly paid jobs.

Under current Mayor Sergei Sobyanin, Moscow's relationship with national government is strong, and is being used to address challenges of development, healthcare, education and transport. In 2013, Mayor Sobyanin was re-elected on a platform of transforming transport, congestion and rail services. In an autumn 2015 meeting between President Putin and Sobyanin, the Mayor admitted that transport was still the biggest problem facing Moscow. The Mayor explained that authorities had built 400 kilometres of new roads but that the transport system had worsened over the last two decades. However, the Mayor is optimistic about the improved speed of traffic and has highlighted how city authorities have worked with the Transport Ministry, Russian railways and Moscow regional authorities to bring into operation a new railway line to Zelenograd. A new strategic master plan in 2016 lays out major proposals for Moscow's future, overseen by the Deputy Mayor for urban policy and construction, Marat Khusnullin. The plan focuses on transport and on the development of New Moscow and the creation of new polycentric growth nodes (The Kremlin, 2015).

The city's revenue base has been fairly robust. The 2016 budget of 1.6 trillion roubles ($20.7 billion) is expected to rise slightly up until 2018 despite the economic uncertainty across Russia, with social spending strongly protected. The city's debt of approximately $2 billion is set to fall. Moscow's relatively stable finances allow it to make major medium-term investments, for example in housing, where the city is financing one-third of the $60 billion housing programme up to 2018, compared to just $4 billion from the national tier. The pace of housing development has increased and between 2011 and 2016, the city is said to have constructed more than 15 million square metres of housing, peaking in 2015, much of it in former industrial areas and in New Moscow (Department of Urban Planning Policy of Moscow, 2015; TASS, 2015).

Today, the city and national government co-operate quite effectively in many areas. The national government provides Moscow with political support and some funding for its growing role as a world city, while Moscow contributes significantly to the national budget. The share of Moscow's taxes that add to the federal budget is stable at between 39 and 42% each year, compared to over 80% in the wealthy oil and gas extracting regions, and a Russian regional average of 53%.

Moscow's acquisition of global roles since 2000 has been made possible with backing from a national government with a more global perspective. Moscow is the hub of Russia's large and growing corporate sector. As prosperity has grown in Moscow and unemployment has fallen, the city's competitiveness as a financial centre has become seen as pivotal to Russia's long-term development. Disadvantages of legislation, infrastructure, financial regulation and tax regulation have become much more closely scrutinised by national bodies with a view to providing a much more reliable offer by the 2020s (Lane, 2013).

The national leadership has already taken several new steps to support Moscow's aspirations in financial services. In 2010 it gained approval for its plans to abolish capital gains tax, and for the creation of Russia's first patent court. In 2011, the national apparatus approved the merger of Moscow's two exchanges, the RTS and the Micex, to simplify the market structure. Plans also exist to standardise tax rates for foreign-born non-residents and to abolish VAT on margin payments, REPO and derivatives operations. In 2012, Russia finally joined the WTO, a gesture signalling that Russia (and therefore Moscow) is an open economy with a sound institutional framework. Individual investment accounts were introduced from 2015 to boost transparency of financial procedures (Goriaev, 2008; Moscow City Government, 2014a).

While Moscow is an emerging global city with an advanced corporate sector, its status as a key centre for business is periodically undermined by federal foreign policy which heightens geopolitical tensions in the region. Russia's actions in Ukraine and intervention to support Syrian president Bashar al-Assad resulted in financial sanctions against the country. At the time of writing, the Minsk 2 agreement had not been fully implemented by either Russia or Ukraine and EU sanctions remained in place. The current geopolitical tensions provide a serious test to Moscow's ability to project itself as a global centre of commerce. It is likely that if Russia's overall financial situation worsens, living standards in Moscow and other regions will suffer.

In addition to ongoing sanctions, the precipitous fall in the price of oil, from a high of $115 dollars per barrel in June 2014 to around $30–35 dollars in spring 2016 has had a very damaging effect on Russia's federal budget, given that half of it comes from oil and gas. The Russian government has had to revise spending downwards and has had to trim around 10% off most budget headings with the main exception of military spending. There is friction between the big spending departments such as the Defence Ministry and the Ministry of Finance which argues for fiscal restraint. Russia's international reserves have dwindled (see Figure 12.1) and concern is growing that the oil revenue dependent sovereign funds, the Reserve Fund (dedicated to federal budget expenses) and the National Wealth Fund (dedicated to supporting the pension system) will be under severe pressure and risk being expended by 2017–18. The pressure to generate additional funds may prompt a large-scale programme of privatisation whereby the Russian State reduces its stakes in key Russian companies. If this approach is pursued, the State will need to act judiciously to avoid mistakes that famously took place in the 1995 loan-for-shares scandal (Buckley, 2016; Ministry of Finance of the Russian Federation, 2016a, 2016b).

The national system of cities: Moscow and Russia

Russia reached a high threshold of urbanisation at the end of the Soviet era, at 73%, and this figure has stayed roughly the same for the following 25 years. Although new urban settlements have been established, a low birth rate has also prevented the share of urban residents from rising much further. The most visible development in the system of cities in the post-Communist era is the way Moscow has come to play an even more dominant role in the Russian system, at a cost of considerable financial distortions and disparities in less-developed regions.

After 1991, the Kremlin gave regional leaders (for example, mayors in federal cities and governors of regions) powers to run their own regions as part of bilateral power-sharing agreements. The central government has gradually become stronger compared to the regions since 2000, unifying political structures and recommending governors for appointment. Although the financial stabilisation of local self-government has been formally observed, the practical financial autonomy of city municipalities has been constrained, with local taxes in most cities limited to personal asset tax and land tax, with a heavy dependence on transfer payments from regions (Turgel, 2008; KPMG, 2015).

By the early 2000s, Moscow's primacy in Russia's urban system had become clear. Serving as the headquarters for nearly all major companies, Moscow has received the lion's share of direct investment in the 21st century. Procurement spending by the State in Moscow dwarfs that of all other cities (Table 12.2). Per capita income is much more than double the Russian average, and six times larger than the poorest region. The average home loan value in Moscow and the Moscow Region is 3.2 million roubles ($40–50,000), twice the national average. These disparities have created a wide sense of detachment from Moscow among many Russian residents, a trend that is also visible in other world cities (Chebankova, 2010; Becker *et al.*, 2012; Lane, 2013; AHML Research Centre, 2014).

Table 12.2:   State procurement spending in 2013 in the three highest spending regions

	Moscow	**St Petersburg**	**Moscow Oblast**
Sum of contracts	2063 billion RUB ($60 billion)	366 billion RUB ($10.5 billion)	263 billion RUB ($7.5 billion)
Federal procurement spending	1111 billion RUB ($32 billion)	97 billion RUB ($2.8 billion)	62 billion RUB ($1.8 billion)
City procurement spending	552 billion RUB ($16 billion)	154 billion RUB ($4.4 billion)	84 billion RUB ($2.4 billion)
Local government procurement spending	6 billion RUB ($170 m)	7 billion RUB ($200 m)	84 billion RUB ($2.4 billion)

* Based on exchange rate of 35 roubles: 1 dollar.
Source: clearspending.ru

Russia's spatial hierarchy has evolved into an uneven but now quite stable system sometimes described as the 'Four Russias'. This four-level hierarchy breaks down as follows (Zubarevich, 2013):

1. Large cities with post-industrial economies, a highly educated workforce and a growing share of migrants would benefit most from political de-centralisation (21% of population above 1 million, rising to 31% above 500,000 in population).
2. Medium-sized cities and smaller towns, former industrial areas that now supply labour migrants to larger centres and which value stable employment (about 30% of population). This includes the nation's so-called monograds or monotowns, such as Tolyatti, which rely on a single industry and hence are very vulnerable. In Tolyatti, for example, one seventh of the population work for the car company AvtoVAZ. Such dependence is dangerous considering that Russia's car market saw a 36% decline in 2015 (Crowley, 2015; Khrennikov and Lemeshko, 2016).
3. Rural and semi-urban villages with low education and mobility, dependent on agriculture and the public sector, rapidly de-populating (36% of population).
4. Under-developed republics in the northern Caucasus and Siberia, with a different demographic profile characterised by high ethnic/religious volatility.

Despite efforts at integration, there is a clear trend towards growing disparity and specialisation among Russian cities. Moscow, St Petersburg and the oil and gas extracting regions (Kaluga, Sakhalin and Tyumen) have captured nearly all flows of investment and talent, while far eastern and Siberian regions have experienced significant population outflows. This is despite the current Russian government's drive to further develop the far eastern region. Smaller cities, in particular, have declined. As a result, the few high-performing regions have become 'donor' regions in terms of their net fiscal contribution. The reliance on the growth nodes such as Moscow to generate the revenues for national investment is widely accepted, including in Moscow. The way in which powers and responsibilities have become distributed across the federal, regional and local levels has become increasingly distorted and incoherent. The federal level concentrates the lion's share of money but has few direct service delivery responsibilities, while at the regional and local levels, large investment and capacity deficits have appeared as governments try to manage development challenges and provide essential services (Kompalla and Nestmann, 2009; Obrazkova, 2014).

Russia's cities face big challenges in terms of housing, internal and external transport and social service delivery. These have not been fully addressed by federal or regional policy. The federal priority is mainly to ensure uniform standards and to build federal infrastructure, while the regions are responsible for infrastructure such as roads. Municipalities lack financial capacity because of a centralised tax system, and also lack knowledge to develop and implement comprehensive sectoral policies. Their capacity is also held back by the political marginalisation of elected city mayors. Mayors have been in conflict with appointed regional governors, and their leadership has been divided and shared with appointed city managers. As a result, mayors in many Russian cities do not serve out their terms, undermining city government effectiveness (Diappi *et al.*, 2013; Moses, 2013).

The economic downturn of 2008–9 squeezed regional budgets and increased their dependence on transfers from the federal centre. Yet the federal share of total revenues in regional budgets has declined in most cases since 2009 and is below 50% in more than three-quarters of regions. This drop in federal transfers further stretches regional budgets that are suffering from a major profit tax drop and requirements to raise public sector wages. The total debt of regional and municipal governments now stands at 2 trillion roubles ($50 billion). Regions require improved debt reduction tools and a more reliable issuance of federal credits (Kompalla and Nestmann, 2009; Stratfor, 2014).

Russia's regional development policy has stalled and there is no active frame-work for addressing the needs of cities and urban areas. On the one hand, a 2014 federal reform now allows regions to choose from four systems of local govern-ment and aims to help regional and local authorities survive without turning to the federal tier. But on the other hand, the ten-year-old Federal Ministry for Regional Development has been abolished and its powers distributed across other ministries. Although Russia's competitive regions play a key role in accel-erating national development, there is an absence of national urban policy or strategy on how to support and leverage them in order to boost the prosperity of less-competitive urban areas (Zubarevich, 2009; Obrazkova, 2014).

One consequence of this increasing centralisation, fiscal dependence upon larger cities and State-backed industries, increasing path dependency in the development patterns of Russia and a low level of regional development policy is that Moscow and other Russian cities have a priority to build their own agendas for co-operation and knowledge sharing.

Ongoing opportunities and challenges where Moscow can benefit from national government support

The next phase of Moscow's development agenda involves a sequence of ambitious redevelopment and expansion projects that will test the city's delivery capability to the full. Federal government support is important to each of them, in the form of political backing, project collaboration and activation and financial assistance.

Sustained political support through the whole cycle of transport system improvements

Public transport is the most pressing issue facing Moscow. The metro expansion is the essential project in both relieving immediate road congestion and in ena-bling future development patterns that are less monocentric. The city govern-ment has embarked on a once-in-a-century commitment to overcome the strains of monocentric growth by relieving congestion and improving the image and economic vitality of the suburbs.

The 2012–2020 programme of rail and road investments will see the Moscow metro add over 100 kilometres of new subway lines. In 2016, the southern extension of Moscow metro Line 1 was completed. This has led to the opening of the Moscow metro system's 200th station as well as a number of park and ride schemes (Railway Gazette, 2016). A second Metro Circle line will reduce the need for radial journeys and increase orbital travel, encouraging new density and development outside the centre. The total cost of the whole programme – at 4.4 trillion roubles ($60 billion) – will be two-thirds funded from the city budget. The federal budget will allocate around 5–10%, with the rest contributed by private investors such as Mosinzhproekt. Although the federal financial contribution is small, its political support is important in order to deliver projects that are on time, bankable and sustainable (Ernst and Young, 2014).

Release land and increase agency co-operation for Moscow River redevelopment

The renewal of the city's 200 kilometres of river embankments is a major plank of Moscow's effort to improve the city's environment, liveability and urban space. The waterfronts were originally transformed in the 1930s, but today residents lack access to the river for recreational purposes because of its historic role in industrial development and as a transport corridor. Currently, 29% of the riverfront is vacant and underdeveloped, while 17% of the Moscow River frontage area is used for industrial purposes (Samarina, 2015).

The Moscow River development project's completion date is slated for 2035. In total, 40 so-called 'portals' will be created – jetties with social and pedestrian infrastructure. Much of the land scoped for redevelopment is owned or used by federal government – such as military training centres, scientific research institutes and the water area itself. The scale of redevelopment will require a big system-wide effort to improve federal legislation, ministry regulations and the character of city co-operation with federal agencies. The facilitation of land acquisition and the granting of redevelopment powers will be essential to this long-term project (Moscow River, 2014; Samarina, 2015).

Manage macro and regulatory policy to support Skolkovo innovation district

Russia's new 'Silicon Valley' project has been sanctioned and designated by the federal government (Figure 12.2). It aims to build Russia's reputation in advanced industries, research and innovation. Most financing is private and from foundations. Recent developments include the Skolkovo subsidiary unit, the Skolkovo Orbital Launch Centre (SOLC) which is set to send a satellite into space. It will be a research satellite and will be made in conjunction with the Moscow Aviation Institute (MAI). This fits in with more broad federal policy which is keen to boost and reorganise Russia's space programme. Additionally, Skolkovo has also seen the printing of a functioning human organ using a bio 3D printer developed by the centre's researchers (Collinson, 2016; Shustikov, 2016).

Figure 12.2:   Skolkovo Innovation Hub.

The role of federal government at Skolkovo is to provide investors, R&D firms and other project stakeholders with assurances about the tax regime, infrastructure and research facilities and the legal framework. Skolkovo will benefit from clarity from the federal centre on the role of State companies, the need for State planning permits, the relocation of higher education institutions and the role of the tech sector in the future economy (Luhn, 2013; Serdyukova, 2014).

Investment and integrated strategic approach for New Moscow

This is potentially the biggest long-term development project in Moscow's modern history. It has involved a merger with territories southwest of the capital which doubles the size of the city. New Moscow is a minimum 20-year project with the capacity to house 1.5 million people and create one million jobs. The scale of planned growth is enormous, with a total of 700 kilometres of new roads, 45 kilometres of metro lines and 87 parking zones. In 2016 alone, four schools are planned for the New Moscow project as well as 11 kindergartens. A key emerging feature of New Moscow is the construction of low- and medium-rise buildings as opposed to more traditional tower blocks. Moscow's city government has selected a Chinese firm to build the subway that forms the centrepiece to the plan. Prime Minister Dmitry Medvedev is actively engaged with the plans for the project, while President Vladimir Putin has given the project national priority status (Moscow City Government, 2014b; The Kremlin, 2015; Arendator, 2016).

The size and complexity of the project means that progress is incremental. It demands a combination of federal investment and attractive terms for private sector investment, with the Mayor planning to attract over $100 billion of private investment up to 2035 (Moscow City Government, 2014c). The National Wealth Fund has already committed to funding half the $8 billion cost of the four-lane central ring road. Importantly, the federal government needs to help shape a convincing strategic prospectus for the new territories, one that provides confidence for the future to encourage firms and investors to take the risks to relocate. This includes a clear cultural and economic character, and balance between office, commercial and residential development. Mechanisms of interaction are needed between the authorities and developers in New Moscow and the different tiers of government. It had been reported that two-thirds of the building work for the New Moscow project was to be carried out by Turkish construction firms such as Ant Yapi which traditionally have played a major role in Russia's building sector, but geopolitical tensions between Russia and Turkey have made future partnership more uncertain and could delay projects (Nacar, 2015; Ant Yapi, 2016).

Federal government policies can also assist investment flows by strengthening internal institutions and regulations to be conducive to potential investors. Examples include the creation of zones with preferential tax breaks, the freezing of tariffs, a reduction in registration and licensing costs and the formalisation of migrant labour rules.

Effective preparation for the World Cup and international events

Moscow will be the principal host city for the 2018 FIFA World Cup and in the interim will also host the 2016 Ice Hockey World Cup and the 2017 Confederations Cup, which acts as a warm-up tournament for the World Cup. The federal budget will finance around half of the expected cost of the Luzhniki Stadium and Otkrytie Arena redevelopments and road preparations in Moscow. The Luzhniki Stadium reconstruction costs amount to $537 million and have been progressing ahead of schedule. The city government will require the ongoing assistance of the federal tier to ensure that FIFA standards are met, and that the global branding opportunities are not affected by security, hotel, infrastructure or congestion concerns. In a move to try and regulate the costs of hotels in Moscow during the games, Prime Minister Dmitry Medvedev has passed a decree placing a cap on the maximum price of hotels, and similar initiatives will be necessary to ensure the event is successful from a visitor and global audience perspective (The Moscow Times, 2014; Sharkov, 2016).

Address limitations and perceived weaknesses in business and investment friendliness

While Russia overall has improved its position within the World Bank Group Doing Business ranking (51st out of 189 nations surveyed in 2016), corruption remains a major concern in Russia and is a challenge to Moscow's ambition to become a global business hub (Transparency International, 2016; World Bank, 2016). Although Moscow is still rated among the top 15 cities for foreign direct investment potential, relative to its size it underperforms (fDi Markets, 2016).

Key actors and mechanisms that enable Moscow to make progress with the nation state

The city government and federal government have a strong and mutually support-ive relationship that is fostered through high-level leadership networks. There are also a number of areas where Moscow's relationships with other cities and regions are being strengthened. For example, Moscow has become an active leader in the Central Federal District, helping to restore regional co-operation and investment flows between the capital and other regions. Meanwhile, co-ordinating councils for the development of Moscow and St Petersburg as twinned transport hubs are a recent instance of the Ministry of Transport's more effective co-operation with the region (Chebankova, 2010; Ernst and Young, 2014).

Moscow's city government and institutions recognise the capital's position as the leading city in Russia and are committed to sharing knowledge and innova-tions on urban development issues with all other Russian cities. One important platform for collaboration is the annual Moscow Urban Forum (MUF). As part of the MUF's activities, its organising team has arranged international urban dialogues in five Russian regions, inviting many cities to participate. The focus is on exchanging lessons and good practice in urban development and manage-ment. Russian cities also participate actively in the MUF, and the MUF sponsors research about the needs and solutions of Russian cities.

Conclusion

Moscow is an emerging world city that hosts dynamic business activity, entrepre-neurship and cultural institutions. But it is also a dysfunctional city that is highly congested and lacks social capital. Moscow is strongly promoted by federal govern-ment and, in recent years, the city has had the national support and momentum to de-centralise its spatial development through major rail projects, the redevelop-ment of the Moscow riverside and the opportunity to grow in New Moscow. A history of rigid planning is gradually being superseded by more flexible and co-operative management models, but until now a comprehensive strategic approach and long-term stewardship of development sites are still substantively missing. As a result, it is probable that Moscow will repeat some of the mistakes made by other, more established world cities at earlier stages of their development.

Russia is now entering a more challenging phase in its modern history. Complex geopolitical issues and falling energy prices have resulted in a sustained recession in 2015–16 and a much weakened currency and banking sector. It is likely that this will see a reduction in public investment in Moscow's transformation, and increased reliance on private sector involvement. Central government will play an important role in adjusting the enabling framework so that private investment is attracted to play a responsible and judicious role in Moscow's key projects.

Russia's fiscal system has concentrated the declaration of profits in Moscow and requires much of Moscow's tax revenues to be redistributed to other regions through a system of centralised control. Increasing centralisation, fiscal reliance upon larger cities and major revenue-producing industries, growing path dependency in national development patterns and a vacuum in regional development policy all oblige Moscow and other Russian cities need to partner and co-operate more effectively. This will include initiatives for mutual learning and opportunities for other Russian cities. New solutions are especially urgent for Russia's larger regional cities which have serious infrastructure and investment deficits. If they are not addressed, the perception and reality of Moscow as the 'dark star' of the Russian economy may become even more pronounced.

13

Shanghai: Pragmatism in pursuit of global leadership

Daniel Case (2013), licensed under CC BY 2.0

World Cities and Nation States, First Edition. Greg Clark and Tim Moonen.
© 2017 John Wiley & Sons, Ltd. Published 2017 by John Wiley & Sons, Ltd.

Shanghai is mainland China's financial and cultural capital, and arguably the newest member of the global urban elite. The port city has witnessed an extraordinary 30-year period of growth combining industry and services, not only becoming a huge retail and commercial hub but also acquiring expertise in engineering, R&D and design (Chen, 2015). Now a city of 24 million people, Shanghai has made the most dramatic shift from manufacturing to services of any city in China, and its economy increasingly resembles more established global cities (Table 13.1). In a return to its earlier heyday in the early 20th century, the city once again hosts a deep concentration of international banks and is the new home of the BRICS New Development Bank. At the same time, Shanghai functions as a gateway to the enormous Yangtze River Delta manufacturing region.

Shanghai's city government spans one of the largest areas of any world city (6200 km²) and has very extensive powers compared to many more established cities. It is one of the four city municipalities in China to be administratively equal to a province, which places it under direct central government administration. The Chinese Communist Party (CCP) Municipal Committee Secretary still outranks the city Mayor, although both are very powerful positions in a centralised political system, and a gradual and limited shift of leadership responsibilities towards the Mayor is visible. The Shanghai case shows how the nation state has played a decisive role in steering its leading commercial centre's emergence into a world city since 1990. Although the city was rarely used as a pioneer for reform, the State empowered the city government to harness foreign capital in order to upgrade the metropolitan economy very rapidly, granted it more fiscal autonomy to run an expansionary budget policy and gave it stronger planning powers to encourage local government innovation. National decision-makers take regular measures to manage the property market and make national infrastructure decisions (for example, high-speed rail) that shape the pattern of Shanghai's growth. State banks even invest in the city's technology system and issue development loans when necessary. Shanghai's example shows how a world city's success can be an important element of a national government's legitimacy (Figure 13.1).

This chapter reviews Shanghai's distinctive history of pragmatic and opportunist leadership that has been prepared to take risks and negotiate with central government over issues of economic development, talent and trade. In most political cycles since the reform process began, there have been strong personal connections between city and central government, and many city officials graduate to the national tier. Mayors Jiang Zemin (1985–1988) and Zhu Rongji

Table 13.1:   Shanghai's metropolitan area: key statistics

% of national population	% of national GDP	GDP per capita vs national average (1)	City global competitiveness rank	Country global competitiveness rank	Annualised employment growth 2000–14	Annualised GDP growth 2000–14	% of national employment
2	4	1.86	43	28	2.3%	7.1%	1.1%

Source: Parilla *et al.*, 2015; World Bank, 2014; World Economic Forum, 2015; National Bureau of Statistics of China, 2015; EIU, 2012.

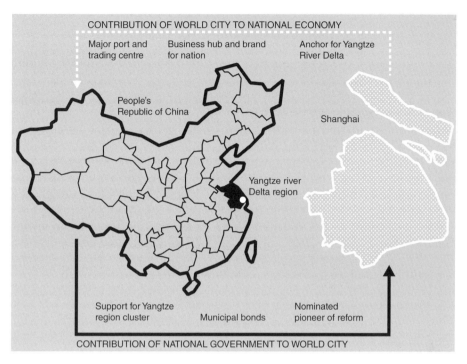

CONTRIBUTION OF WORLD CITY TO NATIONAL ECONOMY

Major port and trading centre

Business hub and brand for nation

Anchor for Yangtze River Delta

People's Republic of China

Shanghai

Yangtze river Delta region

Support for Yangtze region cluster

Municipal bonds

Nominated pioneer of reform

CONTRIBUTION OF NATIONAL GOVERNMENT TO WORLD CITY

Figure 13.1: Reciprocity between Shanghai and the Chinese central government.

(1988–1991) both went on to occupy top national posts, and current President Xi Jinping served as the Shanghai party chief in 2007.

Although central government support for Shanghai has been remarkably successful, it is apparent that new tactics will be required to achieve a more sustainable model of urbanisation. Today, Shanghai is seeking to manage the negative externalities of its exposure to globalisation: the unanticipated speed of migration, the challenges of wage growth in its manufacturing and trade-oriented model and more acute concerns about housing affordability, income inequality and social inclusion. The city is currently in a process of adjustment towards a diversified higher-skilled economy that requires not just hard infrastructure but also 'soft' factors such as talent, IP protection and liveability. It also intends to preserve a large advanced manufacturing base to protect it from over-reliance on financial and other services and to support central government's *Made in China 2025* campaign. How the partnership unfolds between city and central governments has become a litmus test of Shanghai's capacity to transition through successive cycles and become a top-tier world city in the future.

History of Shanghai's relationship with central government

Shanghai was, for a century up to the 1940s, one of the largest financial centres in Asia. The city was one of the first treaty ports to open after the Opium Wars, and developed a distinctive tradition of asserting local autonomy against the

State. From the 1850s on, Shanghai was a trade entrepôt for foreign firms accessing central China and by the end of the century was eastern Asia's main business centre and commodity port. Shanghai was viewed as a glamorous, wild and unruly city and was fundamentally shaped by influences beyond China. The Manchu government was compelled to afford privileges to foreign residents and traders, and the city's civic culture strongly favoured a degree of independence from national bureaucracy (Yeung, 1996; Nijman, 2007).

During the 1920s and 1930s the central State began to tighten its economic grip on international settlements by using State capital. It sought to make its mark on its largest city during a period of political upheaval, and thus took the bold step of creating a dedicated modern municipal government for Shanghai, even commissioning its first master plan. Large-scale infrastructure projects were initiated with a view to unclogging access to the port and bringing the Chinese-controlled part of the city up to the infrastructure standards in the foreign concessions. But the city's port and industrial importance meant the State became reluctant to risk experimentation. Political instability, Japanese occupation and the withdrawal of foreign concessions throughout the troubled 1930s and 1940s halted most of the grandiose plans and stalled the city's development (MacPherson, 1990, 2002; Logan, 2002).

After the Chinese Revolution of 1949, a lack of foreign investment, an insular economy and central government's urbanisation priorities saw Shanghai lose many of its advantages within China's national system. The city was tightly controlled by the central government because it was the largest contributor to China's revenues, providing nearly 25% of national funds. Between 1949 and 1985, Shanghai only received 1% of the revenue it generated for central government for its own municipal infrastructure (Chen, 2009). Much of the central city was gradually converted into an area for government and administrative use. Beijing gave the city support for its State-owned enterprises (SOEs), and industry soaked up most investment capital, leaving little for the maintenance of urban infrastructure such as housing, transport and utilities (Wei and Leung, 2005).

China's market reform and an open-door policy which began in the late 1970s under Deng Xiaoping took time to make its impact in Shanghai. Tight central government control over foreign capital inflows and revenue remittance meant the municipality lacked resources to renew infrastructure. Shenzhen's development was accelerated as the first priority in the early 1980s, although Shanghai's own potential was eventually recognised as it was nominated as one of the 14 open coastal cities in 1984. A pragmatic city government under Mayor Zhu Rongji was primed to seize its opportunity to transform its stagnant State sectors and protect new pillar industries (in particular the car-producing sector). City leaders began to be more assertive in fighting for Shanghai's interests with central government (Yeung, 1996; Thun, 2006). Although Shenzhen and Guangzhou had been initially treated more favourably than Shanghai, the State Council approved the city's Comprehensive Plan of 1986 with the comment that:

"After several decades of hard work, Shanghai should be built into [a] socialist modern metropolis with prosperous economy, advanced science and technology, colourful culture, convenient transport, sensitive information and handsome environment. It should also take the role of 'the important base' and 'the pioneer' in the construction of the modernization of our socialist country" (cited in Zhang, 2014).

Turning Shanghai into a world city rapidly became a Chinese 'State project' from 1990. The establishment of the Pudong New Area and the Shanghai Stock Exchange in 1990 was key, as they allowed foreign banks to trade in renminbi. Soon after, in 1992, the 14th Chinese Communist Party Central Committee called for Shanghai to become the 'dragon head' of the Yangtze River Delta economic region. Pudong was given the biggest support and the highest project size approval limit of any mainland development zone. Other Economic and Technology Development Zones were earmarked in the heart of the city to steer large-scale redevelopment (Chen, G., 2014). These projects gave confidence and momentum to the Shanghai municipal government, which commissioned an influential research report called *Shanghai towards the 21st Century*, that recommended Shanghai become "an international economic central city" by 2010. These ambitions were supported by large increases in central government finances, technology investments and development loans from State banks. There is little doubt that Shanghai's entry into globalisation would not have been so rapid without the State's changed attitude to foreign investment and preferential tax and fiscal autonomy policies from 1990 onwards (Wei and Leung, 2005).

By the mid-1990s, the central government and city government had begun to combine effectively to make Shanghai the productive engine of the Yangtze River Delta region. Many city government officials had graduated to the national tier and were committed to the project of globalising Shanghai, incorporating new ideas into Urban Master Plans and Shanghai's Five-Year Plans. Central government budget strains meant it unloaded some of the financial burden on Shanghai municipality and also transferred more powers for it to generate its own revenue. District-level and municipal governments in Shanghai acquired a range of administrative powers, such as planning, financial management, infrastructure system maintenance and the promotion of foreign trade. Counties were upgraded to districts in order to accelerate urban development. De-centralisation measures created big incentives for Shanghai's local governments to focus on economic development and investment. Under this arrangement, infrastructure investment actually increased more than eightfold in the 1990s (Wu, 2003; Timberlake *et al.*, 2014). Personal links between central government and Shanghai were important to this intense phase of development. President Jiang Zemin and Premier Zhu Rongji were both former leaders in Shanghai, while the Mayor of Shanghai, Xu Kuangdi, had key contacts with central government leadership.

Reforms and cyclical approaches in the Shanghai–Beijing relationship since 2000

In 2001 the State Council approved Shanghai's Master Plan to become an international economic, financial, trade and shipping centre by 2020. This growth model became known as *A Dragon Head; Four Centres* as Shanghai pursued a strategy to leverage its industrial and logistics capabilities and move into high-technology manufacturing. But just as this new approach got underway, the era of warm city–nation state relations began to cool in 2003, when former Shanghai Mayor Jiang Zemin's term as Prime Minister ended. The city lost a strong supporter in central government and the policy relationship became less positive as the State reined in the city government from its reliance on megaprojects and the property market, with limits to bank lending and land use. National leaders investigating corruption and mismanagement also targeted a group of officials with links to the Shanghai government.

This cooling of relations did not lead to significant or lasting divergence about the vision for Shanghai's economic future. The city made a rapid transition into higher-value production and the number of foreign R&D facilities grew much faster in the 2000s compared to the number of branches of overseas investment and finance firms. At the same time, Shanghai focused on the preparation and delivery of global events, such as the 2010 World Expo, which drew tens of millions of visitors, and the Formula 1 Grand Prix. The city's economic ambitions were re-affirmed by the State in 2009 and again in 2013. The central State's *Thousand Talents* programme has allowed Shanghai to capture the benefits of the return and influx of high-quality graduates for sectors such as biotechnology (Shanghai Municipal Government, 2001; Chubarova and Brooker, 2013; Wu and Zhang, 2013). International expansion for Shanghai returned to the central government's agenda after 2009. Shanghai submitted a plan entitled *Accelerating the Development of Modern Services and Advanced Manufacturing in Shanghai and Making Shanghai an International Financial Centre and International Shipping Centre*. The State Council confirmed that Shanghai's internationalisation was "an important measure for our country's modernisation and further reform and opening-up." It endorsed the process in the 2011 Five Year Plan, stating that "[b]y 2020, Shanghai should strive to basically have completed its construction as an international financial centre that is compatible with China's national economic power and the international status of renminbi" (Shanghai Municipal Government, 2011).

The geographical distance between Shanghai and the political capital Beijing has been one important brake on the scale of financial and business agglomeration. The widespread State ownership of key assets, especially in the financial and industrial sectors, works against Shanghai's aspiration for financial services. Most Chinese financial institutions, including the four largest Chinese banks, and large Chinese firms are owned by the central government and headquartered in Beijing. No Chinese bank has relocated to Shanghai since the Bank of Telecommunications moved from Beijing in 1990. Although the largest international banks invariably set up branches and presence in Shanghai, the effect of mainland competition such as that from the Binhai New Area in Tianjin and the Liangjiang New Area in Chongqing may be uncertain in the long term.

In the 2010s, Shanghai's leadership has been committed to supporting the central government's latest reform agenda through initiatives such as a 29 square kilometre free trade zone (FTZ). The zone, which tries to liberalise regulation on commodities trading, futures exchanges, two-way investments and re-insurance, has received strong support so far from central government authorities such as the Ministry of Industry and Information Technology (MIIT), which had previously been opposed to opening up to foreign participation in key sectors. The zone has the potential to boost service industries and productivity in Shanghai and more widely, and is effectively an experiment for a broader programme of internationalisation (Kingwood and Mallesons, 2013; Hogan Lovells, 2014).

The national system of cities: Shanghai and China

In comparison with Japan and Korea, China is not a typical developmental state because of its tradition of administrative de-centralisation. In the first phases of its post-1970s reform, the State also had weaker capacity and was less inclined ideologically to co-operate with the private sector. The State allows cities to pursue their own goals within broadly defined targets and within acceptable bandwidths of macroeconomic policy. Occasionally the State adopts a spatially targeted set of policies that favours certain cities for a period of time, whether Shenzhen, Shanghai or inland centres.

Since the late 1980s China's central government has been heavily engaged in the formation of global cities (Table 13.2). It gave permission for land leasing, which was the critical revenue tool that allowed Chinese cities to finance and manage their development. In Shanghai, land leases and urban land-use taxes soared in the decade from 1999. This tool has also prompted many other city governments to compete in becoming international cities by building ambitious and glamorous projects (Du and Huang, 2014). Many cities have been extremely successful in attracting international investment, but the fiscal and tax structure of Chinese municipalities has begun to create distortions in urban development patterns. Chinese cities generate much of their income by selling

Table 13.2:   China's urban policy and development timeline, 1989–2014

1989	National Urban Planning Law to control big city growth, support "entering the factories but not cities."
1994	Fiscal reform to decentralise system, encouraged city governments to pursue long-term leasing of State-owned land for revenue.
1996	State Council requires master plans for all cities larger than 500,000.
2001	Urbanisation becomes pillar of Five Year Strategy: Town-based industrialisation policy leads to speculative development of industrial parks.
2003	First central government strategy to regenerate deindustrialising areas.
2006	Five Year Plan highlights role of regional city clusters, growth in medium-sized cities.
2007	Eco-Cities advocated by national government.
2009	Shanghai Expo – Better City Better Life.
2011	Green Smart City co-operation established with EU's DG Connect.
2013	Chinese Academy of Social Science (CASS) launches the Ecological City Green Book.
2014	National New-type Urbanisation Plan up to 2020.

Source: Kamal-Chaoui, Leman and Rufei (2009).

development rights to developers and investors at the start of the development process. This encourages the short-term pursuit of cash by selling land a long way from the centre. The land tax structure also incentivises investors to hold onto developments until demand picks up, resulting in an inefficient and over-segregated use of space. At the same time, the system of political promotions, which relies on crude measures of growth to gauge a local politician's success, also inhibits good decision-making about the kind of urban development leaders seek. These frameworks tend to produce cities that have a lot of relatively low-density industry in prime areas and high-density residential in under-served areas. The reform of these 'rules of the game' by national government will be an important agenda in the next decade to enable the specialisation of the largest cities like Shanghai, and the emergence of productive second- and third-tier cities (Tompson, 2015).

Compared to most other national systems, the Chinese urban system is much less concentrated in favour of its leading cities. The share of population and economy in cities such as Shanghai, Beijing, Guangzhou, Tianjin, Shenzhen, Wuhan and others is comparatively low, although gradually converging over time. Given the productivity advantages that accrue to larger cities, it may be prudent for China to encourage the growth of its large cities even further, but it has been reluctant to do so and long-term population caps have recently been recommended. Instead, central government has also gradually recognised the importance of developing productive regional urban linkages around the large cities of Beijing, Shanghai and Hong Kong. The de-centralisation of powers in the 1990s fostered co-operation between Shanghai and other cities in the Yangtze River Delta region (Nanjing, Hangzhou, Wuxi, etc.) to build shared transport infrastructures and energy systems. The industry and commerce bureaus in these cities reached a broad consensus on market access, private sector support, tourism promotion and HR policy, which has helped the region avoid the worst effects of competition and duplication (Du and Huang, 2014). However, this regional networked governance will require deeper levels of co-operation in future as domestic and foreign manufacturers move production elsewhere to escape high land and labour costs. With the risk of capital flight, Shanghai's integration with its regional hinterland cities and provinces will need to become more developed.

The national 2014–2020 urbanisation initiative places big financial pressures on cities to spend on large infrastructure and housing projects. To help with this challenge, central government approved a RMB109 billion ($18 billion) pilot bond issuance programme to ten cities in 2014, including Shanghai. Shanghai's permission to issue municipal bonds may create a new revenue source for its local government and reduce over-reliance on proceeds from the real estate sector. These bonds are a more transparent and responsible long-term option for the city than other local government debt facilities. For many other cities across China as well, they offer a route to avoid capital flight and keep money parked onshore.

One of the biggest challenges for China's future urban system is the resolution of the *hukou* system, which regards migrant workers and families as temporary residents with few or no rights to many basic urban services. *Hukou* has fostered segregation and discrimination, skewed demography and led to under-education of many children in urban and rural areas. It also acts as a deterrent against migration between cities, which has negative effects on city economies. Shanghai has made important steps to reform the *hukou* system and is viewed as an example for others in China, as detailed in the new urbanisation plan. By 2004, Shanghai had already taken a lead in attracting talented migrants and excluding lower-skilled migrants through the introduction of a complex points system. Since 2009, those with renewable residence permits have been able to apply for *hukou* if they can also show they have paid taxes and social security fees for seven years, among other stipulations. Shanghai's annual quota controls population size and helps recruit talent for economic development. Shanghai's recent arrangement, although an incomplete solution that prioritises economic over social objectives, offers more transparency than previous systems. Central government aims to see all large cities gradually regularise access to social security and services, and Shanghai is likely to lead the *hukou* system's evolution over time (Zhang, 2012; Zhao, 2014).

In summary, China's economic and urbanisation model between 1990 and 2015 depended fundamentally on cheap labour, cheap urban land, huge export demand and the under-pricing of environmental externalities (Tompson, 2015). This model proved phenomenally successful at fuelling the growth of cities and the wealth of its residents, but the conditions for this model have now expired. China is now in a phase of uncomfortable readjustment towards a new approach that helps its cities compete for talent, upgrade their environmental performance, incentivise more compact growth and fully integrate migrant populations. Its ability to adapt policies and incentives accordingly will have a big impact on growth patterns in both the Shanghai region and across the country.

Ongoing challenges where Shanghai needs help from national government

Shanghai's trade and investment figures were healthy in 2014, despite a national slowdown, and the city is actively pursuing its goal to consolidate its global status by 2020, as well as contain its population below 25 million. Service industries now account for more than two-thirds of GDP, up significantly from 2010, although the city retains important specialisations in semiconductor materials, robotics, aerospace and maritime construction. As the city undergoes transition, its leadership must continue to follow central government's orders closely. The city's local party chief Han Zheng (the Mayor until 2012) has good personal ties with President Xi Jinping, who firmly believes that Shanghai should spearhead the reform process in China, which hinges on expanding domestic demand and making structural readjustments (FTZ Shanghai, 2014; Shanghai Municipal Government, 2014). Despite being one of China's most competitive cities, Shanghai is not used to being a pioneer of reform, so this process will require careful stewardship. Looking ahead in the short term, there are three areas where Shanghai requires clear, ongoing support and action from central government.

Join up approach to ensure free trade zone becomes a successful experiment

Shanghai still lags some way behind Hong Kong in terms of market development, and much depends on the success of Shanghai's new free trade zone. The zone is supposed to liberalise regulation on commodities trading, futures exchanges, two-way investments and re-insurance, after previous opposition to opening up to foreign participation. It is effectively an experiment for a broader programme of internationalisation in Shanghai.

President Xi Jinping and Premier Li Keqiang have personally endorsed the zone, and central government ministries want Shanghai officials to move forward boldly yet safely with the institutional innovation, but more partnership and risk-sharing is needed to ensure the experiment is carried off effectively. The first two years of the zone were marred by tension between the city and national levels, and in 2015 the Vice Mayor of Shanghai in charge of the zone was investigated for corruption by the Communist Party (Ruwitch and Blanchard, 2015).

The lessons from the free trade zone may be widely applied in the blueprint for others on the mainland. The central government faces the challenge of managing city and investor expectations as demand to create more low-tariff zones increases around the country. A balancing act is required to ensure short-term investor demand is matched by strategic decision-making about which locations to develop and how. In the meantime, Shanghai's leadership is collaborating with Shenzhen to share learning about trade zones, urban management and international standards (Shanghai Daily, date unknown; Yeung and Mak, 2013).

Solutions are also needed for the future roles of State-owned enterprises in a more liberalised system, with capital expected to be redirected towards new, advanced manufacturing and service sectors, as well as quality of life investments (Tian and Ying, 2013; Chen, G., 2014; Lelyveld, 2014). On this issue, city government has the challenge of presenting a compelling case for change to ministry-level regulators and politicians.

Support for convertibility of the renminbi

Central government has been concerned about balancing the gradual relaxation of exchange control, which is critical to China's financial internationalisation and its ability to manage the risks of its export-oriented manufacturing economy. It introduced current account convertibility in 1996, but retains capital account non-convertibility.

Hong Kong was the chosen launch pad for the gradual internationalisation of the renminbi. The State has actively supported the development of Hong Kong as its preferred offshore centre for renminbi-denominated assets, and as a result, Shanghai has been unable to benefit from the one-off opportunity to internationalise the renminbi.

Provide leadership on budget transparency and new city-level revenue tools

Because municipalities such as Shanghai bear a disproportionate burden of infrastructure and welfare spending relative to the revenue they generate, there are regular attempts to bypass restrictions on borrowing. However, Shanghai has not fared very well in terms of gaining concessions from the centre: the share of the revenue that it can claim from stamp duty receipts has been gradually reduced from 50% to 3%. Its newly acquired capacity to issue municipal bonds is, therefore, welcome. The central government can alleviate investor concerns about the new municipal bond market by improving budget transparency, offering more rigorous information on municipalities' fiscal position and setting clearer debt-to-GDP caps to instill discipline (Hu, 2014; The Wall Street Journal, 2014).

Key actors and mechanisms that enable Shanghai to make progress with the nation state

Although the Mayor of the Shanghai municipality is the highest-ranking executive official in the city, the dual system of government means the Mayor has less power than the Shanghai Party Chief, although this imbalance is evolving. Both are nevertheless very powerful, and decision-making power is highly centralised. Both advocate for the city to central ministries and President Xi Jinping.

Mainland economic policies that shape Shanghai's room for manoeuvre are the domain of the State Council and some central government ministries. Shanghai cannot enact policies that attract foreign capital and talent, for example by cutting personal income tax (30% + for many workers), without support from these bodies.

Conclusion

Shanghai has benefited from a highly pragmatic approach to its relationship with central government, whereby it adapts and leverages new national policies in order to consolidate its ambitions to become one of Asia's leading financial and trading cities. It is an example of a world city that is not a capital city but which has, nevertheless, benefited from close political links to central government decision-makers. The national strategy since 1990 has been highly supportive of Shanghai's global credentials, although some of the externalities of its approach are now becoming more visible. Reforms to land, fiscal and migration systems will all have to come forward in the next cycle of China's development if Shanghai is to optimise its role and become a highly specialised and productive global city.

The free trade zone has become a barometer of central government's appetite and capacity to undertake a more substantive reform process that can enable Shanghai to become one of the world's leading financial centres. The relaxation of exchange controls to manage the risks of China's export-oriented economy and the move towards a model of State-owned assets rather than companies, are also preconditions to a more diversified and innovative economy. Successful trialling of different financial instruments will give Shanghai a more responsible long-term alternative to local government debt facilities, and will depend on central government to improve standards of budget transparency and debt-to-GDP caps.

Like other world cities, Shanghai's development is now regional in character, and inextricably tied to the surrounding cities such as Suzhou, Hangzhou and Wuxi. These cities have increasingly shared infrastructure and energy systems and, in principle, play complementary economic roles. In future there are opportunities for deeper regional collaboration and also risks of unmanaged or incoherent growth. Whether and how central government supports the sustainable 'regionalisation' of Shanghai, through such reforms as land taxes and sales regulations, will be key to its ability to withstand the more damaging effects of economic transition that other world cities have had to endure.

14

Singapore: The opportunities and obstacles of city-statehood

William Cho (2011), licensed under CC BY 2.0

World Cities and Nation States, First Edition. Greg Clark and Tim Moonen.
© 2017 John Wiley & Sons, Ltd. Published 2017 by John Wiley & Sons, Ltd.

Singapore is unique among global cities for its status as a city-state. With a population of more than 5.5 million living in an area two-thirds the size of Hong Kong, the city is now among the leading five centres for finance and business services globally, having been a largely impoverished former colonial society half a century ago (Table 14.1). From an unpromising starting point after independence in 1965, Singapore now clearly exemplifies many characteristics of a world city: wealth, stability, cultural diversity, deep networks, leading-edge innovation and inspiration for others. It enjoys widespread acclaim for its quality of life, its sustainability and its emergence as a centre of knowledge and entertainment. The unique speed at which it has established itself as a preeminent world city has given rise to much speculation about how other cities can emulate it and indeed which governance model is best suited to the age of cities (Long, 2015; Mahbubani, 2015; Shen, 2015).

Singapore has only one consolidated government whose 15 ministries perform both urban and State functions. This is a product of its geographical location, political evolution and institutional framework. From this point of view, Singapore offers an important point of comparison with other world cities. Singapore does not have to negotiate relationships between a world city government and a national government in the same way as the other cities.

Despite the conventional narrative that alleges only advantages to Singapore's status as a city-state, in fact it has had to overcome several handicaps of not having a nation state above and around the city. With no higher tier of government, it has not had access to a larger fiscal base for investment capital or transfer payments. Equally, it has not enjoyed the larger diplomatic structures, diverse institutional presence and global reach of a major nation state. Instead, Singapore has contrived to produce these features within a smaller city-state by committing to successive cycles of internationalisation. Since independence, the disadvantages of lack of space, economic isolation, multi-ethnic tension, unemployment, housing shortages, water supply and infrastructure have all been addressed through an outward-facing approach that is open to global corporate investment and expertise.

Singapore's lack of support from a large, powerful national government with a large domestic market has, though, been offset by a highly efficient and unified city-state government. This chapter explains how, without a higher tier of government to answer to, Singapore has been able to mobilise key institutions and a national workforce in pursuit of its goals. Its ability to closely manage trade unions and wage regulations has allowed it the unusual luxury of managing its own labour market to keep wages more competitive than in other industrialising

Table 14.1: Singapore: key statistics

Population	% of national population	% of national GDP	City global competitiveness rank	Country global competitiveness rank	Annualised employment growth 2000–14	Annualised GDP growth 2000–14	% of national employment
5.5 million	100	100	3	2	3.7%	3%	100

Source: Parilla *et al.*, 2015; World Economic Forum, 2015; EIU, 2012.

Asian cities, and of being able to exclude extractive business elites. Control over State-owned firms and banks has allowed it to impose a high savings rate, keep inflation low, focus on re-investment rather than consumption and sustain macroeconomic stability. Over time, these areas have all allowed Singapore to progress more quickly than other aspiring world cities.

Singapore's government and governance history

Singapore is unique among global cities for its status as a city-state. It has only one consolidated government whose 15 ministries perform both urban and State functions – a product of its geographical location, political evolution and institutional framework. From this point of view, Singapore offers an important point of comparison with other world cities in this study. Singapore does not have to negotiate relationships between a world city government and a national government in the same way as the other cities. So, how does that change the environment in which Singapore can develop and pursue its own world city strategy?

The starting point was not promising. In the late 1950s, when the British began to expand self-rule, Singapore possessed a small territory and limited natural resources – especially fresh water. It inherited high poverty, unemployment and population growth rates, a severe housing shortage and a waning entrepôt economy. To cope with this unfavourable starting position, the newly elected People's Action Party (PAP) started to overhaul urban governance, abolishing the Town Council and forming a unitary government with integrated vision across agencies to optimise land and resource use. PAP created the semi-autonomous Housing Development Board (HDB) in 1960 and the Economic Development Board (EDB) in 1961. Their crucial remits were to integrate processes and group all the key actors under one plan, to avoid duplication of policies and optimise the allocation of resources in the face of competing priorities (Centre for Liveable Cities and Civil Service College Singapore, 2014).

Disagreements about water supplies, economic vision and multi-ethnic integration saw Singapore's brief federation with Malaysia disintegrate. Singapore's independence in 1965 was a major risk given its limited endowment of assets, and put it in the unusual situation of entering international markets as a city without a domestic hinterland. But this was the course that Singapore embarked upon (Wee, 2001; Mauzy and Milne, 2002).

Strong and consolidated government was required. Upon full independence in 1965, the government knew it had to re-invent itself to tackle its lack of space, unemployment, housing, water and infrastructure challenges. To address economic isolation, the PAP chose to re-orient Singapore as an outward-facing economy. It opened up to global manufacturing firms in order to provide jobs and benefit from the skills and technology brought in by foreign enterprises. It also maximised its port location in a dense shipping corridor bridging East and West, entering into circuits of global trade as a manufacturer and logistical hub (Huff, 1995; Centre for Liveable Cities and Civil Service College Singapore, 2014).

Internationalisation was an essential ingredient. Singapore's cyclical programme of open economic development has unfolded under highly efficient and unified urban government, with the ability to mobilise key institutions and a national workforce in pursuit of its goals. The rationalisation of government and ability to harness social and economic assets has helped the city-state tackle its infrastructure and sustainability issues at each stage of development (Huff, 1995).

Unlike, many city governments, in Singapore PAP's leadership knew that its political survival hinged on achieving fast and consistent results. This imperative translated into the creation of a highly integrated and coherent form of government, whereby different agencies and departments pursued the same strategic objectives and were carefully organised to complement each other and not pursue different agendas or duplicate their efforts. Co-ordination failures across government were minimised with powerful planning and a 'whole of government' approach to addressing major issues. This required professionalism and self-discipline at the institutional and professional level and the avoidance of a 'silo culture' between ministries in the Singapore government.

Simple power structures have allowed strategic Cabinet decisions to be implemented by departments, agencies and statutory boards. Areas of responsibility and co-operation were strictly defined with a single chain of command and accountability. Sector-specific departments have been re-organised several times since independence to prevent duplication and fragmentation and maximise their effectiveness as the city evolved. For example, the EDB initially provided economic infrastructure and oversaw land planning, but was re-organised specifically to attract global capital, shifting infrastructure and planning to different agencies (Centre for Liveable Cities and Civil Service College Singapore, 2014).

A pragmatic response to resource and land scarcity, and agile and adaptive learning, saw the 'whole of government' approach become formalised in the first Concept Plan in 1971. Concept Plans were translated into Master Plans, which spelt out operational requirements to deliver the strategy and were updated every five years. These updates helped identify issues that needed attention in the short and medium term, in order to achieve long-term strategic aims. Originally, Concept Plans were strictly government designed. However, since the late 1980s, planning has involved first academia and the private sector and, more recently, civil society (Low, 2001; OECD, 2011; Centre for Liveable Cities and Civil Service College Singapore, 2014).

The mobilisation of key institutions

The Singapore government has leveraged the support and control of key institutions to develop a world-class business climate. In 1967, the government brought the trade unions under control of the National Trade Unions Congress (NTUC), and in 1972, it placed wage regulations under the sway of a National Wages Council. This allowed the city the unusual luxury of managing its own labour market to keep wages more competitive in low-value manufacturing than other industrialising Asian nations such as South Korea and Taiwan. It has also been able to favour global firms and SOEs, and so exclude local business elites from power to maintain focus on economic objectives. Control over State-owned firms and banks allowed Singapore to impose a high savings rate, keep inflation low, focus on re-investment rather than consumption and sustain macroeconomic stability. All of these factors have built Singapore's reputation as a stable destination for investment (Huff, 1995; Low, 2001; Mauzy and Milne, 2002; Centre for Liveable Cities and Civil Service College Singapore, 2014).

Singapore's ability to intervene in social policies – usually a role left to national governments – has created a highly educated urban workforce well prepared for new cycles of growth. To ensure an attractive labour force for global firms, Singapore invested heavily in education at all levels, both tertiary and skills-based curriculums. It has also channelled grassroots concerns and associations about access and skills into administrative bodies and has run large numbers of campaigns to influence social behaviour. A supportive media has also allowed Singapore to shape opinion in favour of its open city model, while closely monitoring skills and crime levels to optimise its business environment as the city moved first into high-value services and manufacturing and later towards creativity and innovation (Huff, 1995; Mauzy and Milne, 2002; OECD, 2011; Centre for Liveable Cities and Civil Service College Singapore, 2014).

The impacts of Singapore's unitary government on global city adaptation and success

A unitary government, with all resources dedicated to one city, has allowed Singapore to achieve remarkable results in a comparatively short period of time (see Figure 14.1). Where other cities have struggled to create jobs, affordable housing and sustainably manage resources across successive cycles, Singapore has adjusted exceptionally well in pursuit of rising up the value chain and diversifying its economy.

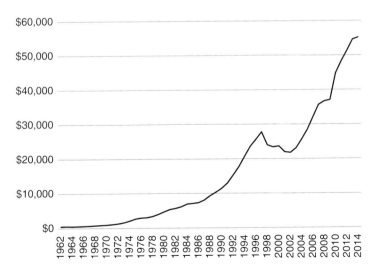

Figure 14.1:   Singapore GDP per capita, 1962–2014.

At the same time, Singapore has not had to navigate the advantages and disadvantages of a nation state sitting above the city. In terms of world city advantages, Singapore has not had a higher tier of government providing a larger fiscal base for investment capital or transfer payments. Equally, it has not enjoyed the diplomatic structures and global reach of a large nation state. However, through dedicated and focused governance, Singapore has contrived to produce these features within a smaller city-state. At the same time, it has suffered from none of the tensions between nation state and world city that exist in the other cities in this study, but has rather internalised such tensions into citywide debates about the nature of the development path and the best means to meet the needs of the Singaporean people.

Economic performance

Singapore's employment patterns have radically improved under independence. Prior to 1965, unemployment hovered around 14% and the economy grew at an average of 5–6% a year. The EDB's stewardship of economic policy allowed it to lead a fully integrated response. It provided infrastructure and subsidised investment and co-ordinated cross-agency input into a single economic framework. From 1968, it acted exclusively as a 'one stop shop' to attract firms, while providing economic intelligence. Economic growth nearly doubled and unemployment fell to around 4% by the mid-1970s. From 1964 to 1979 the share of manufacturing in employment quadrupled (Huff, 1995; Centre for Liveable Cities and Civil Service College Singapore, 2014).

Co-ordinated monitoring and appraisal of the emerging knowledge economy has helped the EDB. Economic Review Committees have directed citywide transitions towards a more knowledge-intensive economy, in partnership with educational establishments. Spatial contiguity and unitary government make cross-departmental reviews and economic development policy implementation considerably easier than the equivalent exercises in large, multi-layered states (Centre for Liveable Cities and Civil Service College Singapore, 2014).

Housing and other infrastructure

Singapore's record of infrastructure management highlights how the city-state has adopted a mixed approach whereby it engages private actors in funding infrastructure development while retaining control over infrastructure development. On the one hand, it has privatised electricity and water provision, but it has also adopted limited privatisation of the port and an airport owned and operated by government-linked companies (GLCs), while the road and water supply systems have been managed by statutory authorities. The city-state's self-governing capacity has allowed it to be flexible in granting GLCs the right to raise funds on the market while also receiving grants and equity investment from government. More than half of infrastructure providers are wholly or majority owned GLCs and statutory authorities. Singapore has always retained overarching control over infrastructure development to ensure that quality remains high and decisions reflect longer-term policy. All key transport authorities have been mobilised to upgrade harbour, airport, telecoms and transport facilities consistently. The integration of different regulatory and infrastructure agencies under the Land Transport Authority has ensured sound oversight of the city's physical network. This systematic approach has meant that international assessments characterise Singapore as having one of the best infrastructure platforms globally (Centre for Liveable Cities and Civil Service College Singapore, 2014; Jones, 2015).

While other global cities often deal with perverse incentives built in at the national level that encourage wasteful land use and sprawl, Singapore's record of land management has been more positive. Extensive house-building programmes and co-ordination with the Urban Renewal Authority and other system agencies (telecoms, utilities, economy and environment) have helped prevent urban fragmentation and supply commercial and public service facilities to self-contained communities, maximising scarce land. Integrated systems have enabled Singapore to deliver larger-scale affordable housing than would have normally been possible: 80% of Singaporeans continue to live in HDB housing, with the city-state boasting one of the highest home-ownership rates in the world, defying the pattern found in dense cities (Centre for Liveable Cities and Civil Service College Singapore, 2014).

Singapore has overcome most of its water supply barriers through its whole-of-government approach. Water management policies were co-ordinated across all levels of government and implemented both at the infrastructure level and by intervening in social habits. In 1972, the NEWater scheme was developed to re-inject recycled water into industry. At a social level, the government ran campaigns to reassure the public that what was once 'sewage' was a renewable resource. In the early 2000s, the agencies overseeing water supply, distribution and recycling were fused. This ensured that the whole water cycle came under one agency. The co-ordination of public utilities, environment, land and transport agencies allowed the development of citywide water catchments to capture rainwater, providing 50% of Singapore's daily supplies. Cross-government efforts have seen Singapore's per capita usage fall by nearly 10% to 157 cubic litres a day between 1994 and 2007 – in contrast to 440 in Los Angeles – with the realistic aim of being completely water independent from Malaysia by 2061 (Chen, Maksimovic and Voulvoulis, 2011).

Singapore's response to climate change also benefits from its own Climate Change Secretariat (NCCS), established under the Prime Minister's Office, to pull all the different stakeholders under one agency. Recently, the city-state created a Resilience Working Group to assess Singapore's vulnerabilities to climate change at a cross-governmental level, and come up with a whole-of-government response by 2016. This level of co-ordination is unique at a city level, and even rare at national tiers of government (OpenGov, 2014a, 2014b).

The role of key institutions

A number of institutions have been critical to Singapore's effective adjustment from a regional hub to a global services provider. These include the PAP, the civil service, the Ministry of National Development (MND), the HDB and the

Urban Redevelopment Authority (URA) which it oversees, the EDB, the Centre for Liveable Cities (CLC) and the Ministry of Environment and Water Resources (MEWR).

The PAP's continuity in power since 1959 means it has been able to plan consistently for the long term, according to economic as well as political cycles. This continuity has allowed it to take difficult but pragmatic and strategic decisions to sustain its vision, often taking an experimental approach to policy that would not be possible in a multi-tier system. Ministers often hold several cabinet posts and have acquired knowledge of cross-government issues. PAP has built effective, low-corruption institutions in order to deliver on its political promises and stay legitimate (Mauzy and Milne, 2002; Quah, 2013; Centre for Liveable Cities and Civil Service College Singapore, 2014; OpenGov, 2014a, 2014b).

At the same time, the Singaporean Civil Service has been a meritocratic and highly effective institution. Because it was bound to the PAP's strategic vision early on, it has consistently delivered on its objectives without the bureaucratic reluctance and resistance often found in other national administrations. Its performance and integrity derive from very rigorous anti-corruption procedures, the recruitment of foreign talent and the proactive employment and retention of high-calibre personnel through a scholarship programme and competitive pay package (Mauzy and Milne, 2002; Quah, 2013; Centre for Liveable Cities and Civil Service College Singapore, 2014). Partly as a result, Singapore's administration ranks amongst the world's least corrupt and most efficient. Transparency International's Corruption Perceptions Index (CPI) placed Singapore 8th in 2015, while Singapore consistently ranks in first place for government effectiveness according to the World Bank (World Bank, 2014; Transparency International, 2016).

The MND has ultimate responsibility for planning in Singapore, and has ensured a very judicious use of land by overseeing the joint efforts of the HDB and URA. The work of these two statutory boards, implementing the Ministry's strategic directives, and their co-operation with other government agencies, has been key in delivering a more integrated approach to planning which has curbed urban fragmentation and sprawl and prevented the duplication of public services across different agencies. The integration of all land planning under a unitary agency has prevented the overlap and competition between different institutions operating at the national, regional and local level which typically constrain cities in larger nation states.

As a statutory board of the Ministry of Trade and Industry, the Economic Development Board has ensured that economic actors across the city work towards the same economic policy. While other global cities often have similar agencies, they do not benefit from the broad powers of the EDB. It can influence macroeconomic trends at the city level, while advising and co-ordinating the delivery of citywide social policies designed to respond to economic trends, such as reforming education for a knowledge-based economy.

Agencies that provide external and comparative evaluation have also become important in Singapore. Set up in 2008 by the MND and MEWR, the Centre for Liveable Cities (CLC) seeks to create and share knowledge on liveable cities by providing research and outreach. It tracks Singapore's performance in terms of liveability, sustainability and competitiveness to inform and feed back into policy making. Although not a unique organisation in this respect amongst global cities, it is a source of tacit and formal knowledge on the mechanics of unitary government, allowing the city-state to continue adapting its unique position by learning from other cities and agencies and drawing from Singapore's past (Centre for Liveable Cities, 2016).

Singapore's future challenges

Singapore's governance model has succeeded in tackling many issues such as sustainability, infrastructure and economic growth with which other cities struggle, but it still has its share of challenges. In many respects, the city-state is at another crossroads as it undergoes a new cycle of economic restructuring and absorbs the effects of weak global demand and faltering emerging economies. Although, unlike other world cities, Singapore does not have development spillover within its national territory, it does face the task of building a constructive and complementary relationship with Indonesia and Malaysia. However, its future challenges can potentially be addressed through its capable city-state government in a more coherent way than they can be addressed in most other world cities.

Solutions to manage future population growth

As a result of increased immigration since the 2000s, Singapore's population has grown rapidly. Forecast to reach almost 7 million people by 2030, the city's transport system is increasingly congested, while house prices have gone up as the HDB has struggled with supply. This has put increasing pressure on land supply, including protected areas. Singapore's government will need new solutions to maintain a high quality of life in the face of these infrastructure and land pressures (Bin, 2013; Cheah, 2013; Centre for Liveable Cities and Civil Service College Singapore, 2014; Centre for Liveable Cities and Shell, 2014; National Research Foundation, 2016).

Financial and liveability equations for an aging society

Singapore's population is also aging. This is not only increasing the dependency ratio but putting pressure on social services as citizen expectations improve, and further increasing the need for immigration, therefore contributing to population growth. Reforms to the way in which services and pensions are delivered are underway, but it is still unclear how the city will find the balance between density and liveability (Cheah, 2013; People's Action Party, 2014).

Effective management of immigration and labour market

Pressure on infrastructure and wages has increased resentment towards low-skilled foreign workers, with riots manifesting this discontent in recent years. The city government faces the challenge of integrating new arrivals and optimising the flow of foreign workers. A recent tightening of Singapore's foreign worker and immigration policy leaves Singapore vulnerable to shortages of qualified manpower in lower-end and high-end industries. How judiciously and flexibly the government selects and integrates immigrants will shape Singapore' status as a forward-looking and inclusive city (Bin, 2013; Chan, 2014).

Singapore continues to take steps to adapt its education system to the knowledge economy, but it is unclear what role the government can play to ensure a strong supply of middle-income jobs for those with mid-tier skills. A two-tier model of highly paid and low-skilled jobs that resembles other world cities has begun to raise questions about the future spectrum of employment. The capacity of local businesses to grow by reducing overhead and land costs will be one factor that shapes Singapore's ability to grow middle-income jobs in the future (Centre for Liveable Cities and Civil Service College Singapore, 2014).

Shift to more innovation-based economic model and engagement of business leadership

Singapore's economic model has relied mainly on international firms and State-owned enterprises to win market share. Local firms have played an auxiliary role as subcontractors and suppliers (Singapore Business Federation, 2016). Many analysts observe that Singapore will have to move on to a more mature economic model that is less dependent on foreign investment and which allows Singapore to build its own thought leadership and innovation platform, mindful of the city's limited and aging workforce. The internationalisation of Singapore-owned and Singapore-based firms will therefore be a key priority in the next 20 years. The government can play an important role by engaging more local firms in procurement and putting local companies at the heart of future economic strategy.

The complexity of economic strategy as an advanced city-state will probably require Singapore's government to build more sustained collaboration with businesses and business leadership organisations. Sector-specific and cluster-specific strategies in particular can benefit from greater consultation with, and feedback from, firms. Singapore's global outreach and branding can also partner more effectively with the private sector in the way that other established world cities do.

Reforms to enhance stock market competitiveness

Singapore's stock market risks falling behind in global terms due to a lack of market capitalisation. As a small stock exchange, around one-fifth of the size of Hong Kong, it has been vulnerable to the downturn in oil and commodity prices, and will have challenges remaining attractive in a dynamic Asian context. The liberation of pension funds from investment restrictions to allow them to enter the stock market is one potential reform that has been proposed.

Conclusion

Fifty years of evidence suggests that Singapore's constitution as both a city and a state has enabled it to be profoundly alert to the imperative to adapt if it is to compete economically and survive politically. This imperative has translated into a highly integrated government where different agencies and departments pursue congruent strategic objectives and are carefully organised to complement each other. Co-ordination failures across government are minimised through a 'whole of government' approach when addressing major development issues. Professionalism and self-discipline at the institutional and professional level and the avoidance of a 'silo culture' have been hallmarks of Singapore government ministries.

The balance sheet of Singapore's achievements indicates the advantages of aligned government. Singapore has arguably made more productive use of its limited land than any other world city, while co-ordination with the Urban Renewal Authority and other system agencies (telecoms, utilities, economy and environment) has helped prevent urban fragmentation and supply commercial and public service facilities to self-contained communities. Integrated systems have enabled Singapore to deliver large-scale affordable housing and majority home ownership, defying the pattern found in high-performing cities.

Singapore has suffered from none of the tensions between nation state and world city that exist in other cities. Rather, it internalises such tensions into citywide debates about the nature of the development path and the best means to meet the needs of the Singaporean people. It is clear that Singapore has been able to defuse tension through its greater scope (compared to other world cities) to intervene in social policies and behaviour – savings, housing, education, skills, health, water usage and crime. The opportunity to experiment with and monitor policies without interference from national levels has helped maintain an appealing business environment and achieve responsive public services.

Singapore's governance model has clearly accomplished a great deal and attracts many admirers, but its advantages are not permanent. With the population approaching 7 million people by 2030, the scale and kind of challenges – increased congestion, an aging population, high expectations of public services and a dwindling supply of middle-income jobs that risks eroding confidence and public trust – require new tools and new approaches. A sustainable set of solutions is sought on immigration, social inclusion, density and liveability. Based on the retrospective view, Singapore's governance system is more capable of adjusting to these challenges than more complex, distributed and dysfunctional governance systems we find in other world cities. But in future, as the Asian system of cities evolves and matures, Singapore may have to learn the skills that have been acquired in other places. In particular, collaborative leadership with non-governmental partners will become a key area that the city will need to expand, following the lead taken in other established world cities.

Section V Conclusion: A New Deal for the 21st century?

15

Adjusting to an age of world cities

Globalisation and urbanisation are mutually reinforcing. As cities take on cross-border functions and become open to international populations, they grow (Table 15.1). The choice is not between growing or not growing, but whether to have growth which is managed or unmanaged. Successive cycles of growth and internationalisation come with side effects or *negative externalities* for which support from national and federal governments, and other higher-tier authorities, becomes essential.

As we have seen in the case of these 12 world cities, the externalities include price inflation, transport congestion, stretched housing and labour markets, infrastructure deficits, environmental vulnerabilities and social divisions. Many world cities have found that there are also too many rigidities in their economic development systems to be agile and responsive to the pace of change since the global financial crisis. Whether that means connecting new residents to jobs, absorbing new wealth-generating sectors near the city centre or responding to the demand of younger adults and older generations for urban living, the pace of change in such cities reveals rigidities quickly. Other cities experience the ongoing rise of the informal economy and high rates of unemployment and under-employment, especially among recent arrivals. The disparities that accumulate from such unplanned and unanticipated growth have become serious. They erode quality of life and the sense of cohesion within the city, and they give rise to opposition and hostility to the entire world city model – among local residents and those farther afield.

World Cities and Nation States, First Edition. Greg Clark and Tim Moonen.
© 2017 John Wiley & Sons, Ltd. Published 2017 by John Wiley & Sons, Ltd.

Table 15.1:   Population and visitor growth in world cities

	Population growth since 2000	**Visitor numbers change since 2010**
Shanghai	+8.1 m	−0.8 m
Mumbai Metro	+3.9 m	+0.75 m
Moscow	+2.3 m	+1 m
São Paulo (city)	+1.6 m	+0.4 m
London	+1.5 m	+4.1 m
Singapore	+1.5 m	+3 m
Toronto (GTA)	+1.4 m	+0.9 m
Tokyo (prefecture)	+1.5 m	+3.61 m
Paris (Île de France)	+1.1 m	+2.79 m
Hong Kong	+0.6 m	+0.5 m
New York City	+0.5 m	+2.8 m
Seoul (metropolitan city)	−0.06 m	+4.3 m

Sources: National Bureau of Statistics of China, 2015; Russian Federation Federal Statistics Service, 2016; IBGE, 2015; GLA Datastore, 2015; Department of Statistics Singapore, 2015; Ontario Ministry of Finance, 2014; Tokyo Metropolitan Government, 2016; INSEE, 2016; Istrate and Nadeau, 2012; Parilla *et al.*, 2015; Census and Statistics Department, The Government of the Hong Kong Special Administrative Region, 2015; Department of Planning New York City, 2015; Seoul Metropolitan Government, 2015; Hedrick-Wong and Choong, 2014, 2015; Bremner, 2010, 2015.

Negative externalities that arise from high demand for cities are not all of the city's own making. Often they are exacerbated by national sectoral policies and co-ordination failures. It is typical for national, federal or state departments to operate as silos, and there are institutional barriers or disincentives to working across them. As the case studies of cities have shown, it is common for there to be no clear spatial dimension to the way national and state departments operate. This results in failures to join up thinking across sectors that should be linked, such as land use and transport, housing and education or immigration and economic development. For world cities, such sectoral rigidities contribute to the suboptimal use of land and unequal social conditions. National fiscal and regulatory policies also have important and often unrecognised spatial consequences. This means that even when planners in world cities try to construct compact and integrated urban environments, the fiscal regimes set in place by higher tiers of government end up encouraging and subsidising sprawl and other kinds of inefficient development (Blais, 2010).

But in the current cycle of the global economy, nearly ten years on from the financial crisis, national governments have begun to recognise that changes to the status quo are needed to allow world cities to effectively serve their citizens and stay competitive. This recognition has not tended to grow organically, but as a result of external catalysts – economic crises, political scandals, environmental disasters, security threats or imminent sporting events. Nation states sense the opportunities and threats associated with the changing centre of economic gravity or with the (dis-) integration of large regions (for example, EU, MERCOSUR, NAFTA), and have had to identify new strategies for their biggest and most globally oriented cities to succeed.

In this chapter we summarise the ways in which national governments have tried to adapt in recent years and reinforce the success of their global cities. We focus on eight areas that seem especially visible from recent international examples:

- Agreement and funding for infrastructure and connectivity projects;
- Step changes to address housing challenges;
- Governance reforms;
- Fiscal and financial tools;
- Reforms to make the city more attractive to business and ready for investment;
- Investment in the city's research and innovation capabilities;
- Advocacy and finance for hosting international events;
- Opening up labour markets.

High-quality infrastructure and connectivity projects

World cities have to pay attention to both internal and external connectivity. External transport links are critical in order to play the international roles required and expected of world cities. Ports, airports, high-speed trains, logistics platforms, motorway networks and all aspects of digital connectivity are critical competitive assets to cities that specialise in sectors that are traded globally. Infrastructure is often among the top three concerns of businesses in world cities and the demand to prevent key systems reaching capacity is high. At the same time, rapid population growth, the imperatives for managed density and the re-ordering of land use that goes with internationalisation depend upon excellent internal connections, especially public transport. The finance and agreement of public transport is a pressing issue in many high-demand world cities. Metro, bus rapid transit and light rail projects provide relief from congestion, and in many cities are viewed as the major mechanism to stimulate development patterns that are less dependent on city centres.

National government financial contributions are often the critical bridge to enabling transport projects to go ahead, but political support is also necessary to deliver projects that are on time and bankable. In Paris, the French central government appointed a Minister for Le Grand Paris in 2008 to oversee a new €27 billion metro and drive through an agreement with the regional government. Although the ministerial position was disbanded, Prime Minister Manuel Valls has retained a strong personal leadership role in the project. The project is mostly funded by taxes on local businesses, housing and property, some of which the State redirects to the delivery agency Société du Grand Paris (SGP). The State is also prepared to finance the SGP if it requires a further injection of capital. The 200-kilometre, 72-station metro system now forms the backbone to Paris's long-term development, including the creation of new neighbourhood 'hubs' along the route, as well as the city's bid for the 2024 Olympic Games.

Many other national governments are making special provision to help their world city improve its transport system and how it is governed. In London, the east–west Elizabeth Line (Crossrail 1) was part-funded by the national department of transport (a £4.7 billion grant from a total package of £15 billion) and in 2016 the Chancellor has given the north–south Crossrail 2 project priority status, with a view to being up and running by the early 2030s. Moscow's own enormous subway expansion which aims to create a more polycentric city receives only a small federal contribution but federal political support is vital for the many projects to be bankable and delivered on time. Meanwhile in Mumbai, central government has made small but important loans for new metro corridors in support of the state government that is providing the lion's share of investment. These examples highlight the role of higher tiers of government as important partners in major infrastructure projects, although not every world city benefits from this level of engagement. New York City has seen delays on subway, streetcar, light rail and BRT projects because of a lack of funding and cost over-runs. Meanwhile the state government insists that the metropolitan transport authority (MTA) exhausts all other available financial options before New York State funding for its capital plan becomes available. The lack of predictable support for necessary projects risks becoming a major disadvantage for world cities seeking to cope with soaring demand.

Step changes to address housing and real estate challenges

The employment opportunities, cultural offer and political stability of many world cities have created unprecedented demand for real estate from domestic and international markets. Rising demand for real estate, from private buyers and investors alike, presents new and unexpected challenges around housing supply and affordability, especially for younger people. The issue of how to increase the rate of supply also brings with it related dilemmas about how to manage land use and maintain education, health services and other social infrastructure.

Housing challenges are acute in land-scarce cities such as Hong Kong, Mumbai and Singapore, but are also very serious in established cities such as London, Paris and New York. To date, it is housing that has arguably proved the externality that world cities in multi-level government systems have most struggled to address. Only a few somewhat smaller cities – including Hamburg and Vienna – have managed to anticipate and push through housing supply at scale through integrated approaches. Cities with fragmented governance and land ownership have made much slower progress, and many national initiatives have had little impact. In São Paulo, for example, the central City has only recently begun to benefit from the federal mass social housing programme *Minha Casa Minha Vida*, after several years of low participation.

Models that rely principally on the market via private sector developers to sustain an elevated rate of supply have only been very partially successful. The institutional and land ownership complexity that prevents sites from being brought forward, infrastructure deficits, the volatility of economic cycles that results in uneven supply and a divergence in interests between asset owners, developers and future residents are all familiar issues in world cities. In fact, it is the city-state of Singapore which has arguably tackled the housing demand associated with being a successful world city better than almost any other. Only 9% of Singaporeans lived in publicly built housing in 1960, but this figure has risen to a remarkable 82% today. Its advantage compared to other cities is that its Housing and Development Board (HDB) has been given extensive powers to acquire and develop land, and has its goals tightly integrated with wider government objectives on density, public transport and quality of life. The HDB has been able to take ownership of land at pre-development value, in order to ensure that the public sector can capture the development gains that come from infrastructure upgrades, something that most other world cities are only just beginning to experiment with. Unlike other cities, the HDB has been able to leverage scale and to control procurement, licensing and permitting processes. Singapore's independence also gives it the freedom to set up its own savings account that allows residents to contribute to and withdraw from a Central Provident Fund to buy homes on long leases. While home ownership has declined in many established world cities, Singapore's has grown from 59% to 91% since 1980, and has become a key source of the government's legitimacy and popularity (Woetzel *et al.*, 2014).

Very few cities can emulate Singapore's model. What most cities in more liberal frameworks require instead is a new set of powers from higher tiers of government that can ultimately enable an increase in the rate of supply. Many cities argue that they need their plans to have the same enforcement status as national or state planning regimes, to allow city leaders to oblige local municipalities to meet targets. Paris has seen a lot of activity in this area. The French Prime Minister has expressed determination to meet an ambitious target of 70,000 units a year. Operations of National Interest have been created to give the government better planning powers in key sites, publicly run property developers have been streamlined into one regional body and the State has set up so-called 'State–Region Contracts' which establish a joint budgetary and planning vision between regions and central government. These are promising instances of innovation, but those responsible for housing in world cities also often need to borrow larger sums for house-building. In certain cities, such as London, devolution of lucrative taxes such as stamp duty is viewed as essential. Whether higher tiers of government will be tempted to approve such kinds of reform in the near future will be very significant. The bending of national frameworks towards a city's specific needs will likely have to be a prerequisite in the next cycle, and many of the practical projects now being considered fall into this bracket.

Meanwhile, in other more planning-oriented cities such as Shanghai, the priorities are usually rather different. They often relate more to reforming the incentive structure built into the land market and the tax-sharing system so as to more effectively prevent sprawl and make better use of prime urban land, including for housing (Pinoncely, 2015). A more advanced case is found in Tokyo, where there is an imperative to encourage more flexible re-use of real estate to stem the surge of vacant housing and contain the infrastructure costs of an aging society (Soble, 2015).

Improvement and expansion of governance in world cities

Nearly always in the evolution of globally oriented cities, existing governance arrangements come to be insufficient to sustain and develop their lead roles within a fast-moving global economy. Often, local government institutions are well run and have acquired professional know-how, but their sound policies may be hampered by the lack of alignment across the whole economic space. Governance fragmentation and duplication are most acute in cities such as Mumbai, but are also very visible in Paris, São Paulo and Toronto (Table 15.2).

Table 15.2: Character of city/metropolitan government in world cities

City	Leadership structure	No. of local governments at city scale	Responsibilities and fiscal powers	No. of local governments at metropolitan scale	Territorial fragmentation (per 100,000 inhabitants)
Hong Kong	Chief Executive; Executive Council assist policymaking.	1	Responsible for all affairs except security/defence. Full legislative powers and control of annual operating expenditure of HK$354 billion ($46 billion).	1	n/a
London	Two-tier, directly elected Mayor/ Greater London Authority	1 City Assembly, 33 boroughs	Transport, police, planning, promotion and economic development; Only 7% of tax paid retained by Mayor and boroughs.	47	0.38 – Low
Moscow	Executive Mayor and 35-member city council. Federal city status with powers of a regional government.	12 districts (okrug) and 146 smaller territories.	Full service delivery roles. Donates 40% of tax revenue to federal budget.	51	Low
Mumbai	Fragmented between Maharashtra Chief Executive, Municipal Council of Greater Mumbai, MMRDA and 15+ other councils and corporations.	1 Municipal Council (Municipal Council of Greater Mumbai)	Institutions lack defined functions; severe problems bringing forward infrastructure investment – e.g. 40% of MMRDA budget unspent due to project implementation delays.	9 municipal corporations and 8 smaller municipal councils + MMRDA + state	Medium
New York	Directly elected citywide Mayor; public corporations (MTA, Port Authority)	1 city, 5 boroughs	Most core services, including education; $82 billion budget, 70% self-funded, $30 billion of non-property taxes.	356	2.13 – Medium
Paris	City of Paris Mayor, Métropole du Grand Paris, Paris Regional Council and President.	20 arrondissement mayors in central City; 130 Communes in the Metropole, 7 other departments in the Region.	$10 billion City budget (transport, affordable housing) and $6 billion regional budget (transport, schools). Fairly high local tax raising and retention. New regional 'green bonds'.	1375	11.42 – High

City	Government structure	Divisions	Service delivery / fiscal	Number	Rating
São Paulo	Municipal Mayor; metropolitan governance fragmented into sub-regional arrangements.	31 sub-prefectures in central city, 1 central city.	Central municipality has full public service delivery roles and is a leader in fiscal innovation. Lack of metropolitan management of key systems; major fiscal outflows and debt repayment challenges.	39 municipalities/ mayors in metropolitan region + state	Medium
Shanghai	Dual structure - CCP municipal secretary and city Mayor. Small number of well co-ordinated bodies and development corporations with close links to the CCP.	1 province divided into 16 districts and 1 county.	Many core service delivery roles. Land sales have enabled very high spending on fixed assets, new tools currently under development.	16 districts and 1 county	Low
Singapore	Cabinet of Singapore led by elected Prime Minister, answers to 87 Parliamentary MPs.	No local government; advisory bodies based on 23 electoral divisions.	Complete fiscal and decision-making autonomy.	n/a	n/a
Seoul	Metropolitan government and directly elected Mayor.	25 autonomous districts (gu).	Education, crime, welfare and infrastructure; some special fiscal rights but highly centralised revenue collection.	965	3.87 – Medium
Tokyo	Tokyo Metropolitan Government governs 13 million person prefecture; powerful elected Governor.	23 self-governing wards and 26 suburban 'cities'.	Many core service delivery functions. Direct taxation in 23 wards; corporation, residents and property taxes.	235	0.65 – Low
Toronto	Directly elected Mayor and 44-member City Council.	Single-tier municipality; 4 regional municipalities.	Bus services, social services, police; $10 billion operating budget, 40% funded from property tax.	50	0.72 – Low

Sources: de Blasio, 2016; City of Toronto, 2016; IBGE, 2015; Île-de-France Regional Council, 2011; Île de France Regional Council, 2014; Mairie de Paris, 2015; OECD Stat, 2014; Phadke, 2014; PwC, 2015; Russian Federation Federal Statistics Service, 2015.

Even in cities where powerful citywide governments are well established, such as New York, London and Tokyo, it is not an easy task to organise investment, institutions and policies to solve problems at the right scale. The alignment of investment, policy and institutions is complex but imperative.

Leadership and institutional frameworks

Over the past 25 years there has been more attention paid by many nation states to strengthening world cities' governance systems. In the cycles of reform since 1990, Russia and Korea were among the first to enact municipal self-government legislation for their lead cities. Moscow gained an elected mayor in 1991 and Seoul's mayor became directly elected as part of an official policy of Seoul's *segyehwa*, or internationalisation. Not too much later, after a hiatus of over a decade without a citywide government, in 1997 Britain's New Labour government agreed to create a Greater London Authority and a directly elected mayoral system (Table 15.3).

In federal systems, state or provincial governments have often been the ones to take the lead in enhancing governance arrangements. In Toronto, the provincial government amalgamated the city's six municipalities nearly 20 years ago and gave it responsibility to run public programmes. In German cities such as Stuttgart and Hanover, completely new and accountable metropolitan institutions were created with full competences agreed with the states of Baden-Wuerttemberg and Lower Saxony, respectively. And in India, Maharashtra's Chief Minister has voiced interest in creating a senior co-ordinator position to integrate Mumbai's many city agencies.

World cities have shown they can survive fundamental changes to their institutional framework if the governance deal is well designed and builds in flexibility for the future. In the most radical case, Hong Kong has received many benefits from the Chinese central government commitment to a 'one country, two systems' model agreed in advance of independence in 1997. For the most part, the government has kept its promise to uphold the mandate and treat Hong Kong as a special case – a separate country from an immigration and currency standpoint, with more liberal media laws. Beijing's interpretation of electoral provisions in the Basic Law, and later its commitment to universal suffrage by 2017, provided some certainty about the process of constitutional reform in a

Table 15.3: Recent 'elected mayoral systems' created or expanded by higher tiers of government

City	Year created	First Mayor
Paris	1977	Jacques Chirac
Moscow	1991	Yuri Luzhkov
Seoul	1995	Cho Soon
Toronto (amalgamation)	1998	Mel Lastman
London	2000	Ken Livingstone

way which did not hinder flows of foreign investment into the city. Contrary to many predictions, Hong Kong was able to expand its international influence after 1997 because of the success of the model and the opportunities for integration with the Pearl River Delta. Its status for the last two decades has been highly attractive to foreign investors seeking access to the Chinese market without the uncertainties of Chinese corporate law. It is only in the last two years that tensions have arisen as Beijing has been determined to retain its role as gatekeeper to the city's leadership.

One of the most high-profile governance reforms to have taken place recently is in Paris. Although the entire urbanised area is inside the boundaries of the Île-de-France region, until 2016 it had no urban-wide authority that addressed the metropolitan scale. The new métropole incorporates the city of Paris and the three surrounding départements within an area half the size of Greater London, and gradually it is likely to gain powers of taxation, planning, land use, social housing and economic development. The concern is that 'Grand Paris' – whose leadership is composed of more than 200 councillors – becomes a complex fifth layer of government in an overcrowded system and is unable to galvanise support for increasing the pace and scale of change. With an initial budget of €4 billion, most of which is redistributed to municipalities, the institution has very limited independent investment capacity. France's national leadership will likely need to engage closely with the progress of the new institution to ensure it fulfils its remit (Bessis, 2016).

Across all the world cities surveyed in this book there is an interesting correlation between the centralisation of national political systems and the empowerment of city governments (see Figure 15.1). In centralised nation states

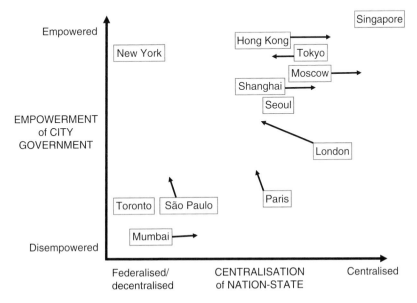

Figure 15.1: Indicative relationship between empowerment of world cities' governments and the centralisation of nation states (Arrows indicate direction of travel).

such as Russia, Japan, Korea and China, their world cities often have fairly empowered city or metropolitan government structures, with a wide span of control, access to a range of fiscal tools and favourable net fiscal flows. Often, these advantages were granted after periods of political or social upheaval. But centralisation is no guarantee of an empowered world city government. London has limited ability to finance projects or to enforce its strategic ambitions, and Paris has a limited metropolitan framework, although in both cases the situation is changing.

In many de-centralised nation states, world cities have not acquired a powerful institutional self-governing structure. Paternalistic relationships with state or provincial governments, and a lack of political or popular will to recognise metropolitan-scale problems, mean that cities such as Toronto, São Paulo and Mumbai have sprawled, are fragmented and are still unable to address the next phase of their evolution as world cities comprehensively. Sprawl and complex governance are also visible in the New York region, but in its case city leaders have managed to gain control over a large and diversified set of taxes and have set high standards of bold and innovative city management.

Inherited political systems are not binding for world cities. World cities can become more empowered even within centralising systems, as Moscow appears to be doing. London is gradually becoming a more empowered metropolitan government just as the British political framework becomes slightly less centralised. At the opposite end of the spectrum, cities such as Mumbai and São Paulo show signs that they are beginning to gain greater self-governing capacity even within highly de-centralised political systems. For all world cities, their capacity to break out of traditions that become less favourable over time, and to steer more positive development paths, is linked to their dialogue and advocacy with other tiers of government.

Governance systems at the wider regional level

World cities are growing well beyond their historic borders. As functional economic regions they are experiencing steady population growth which threatens the functionality of existing systems. There are new costs of regional sprawl, growing risks of regional exclusion and a concern to reduce energy consumption. In most cases, cities' ability to address these challenges is hampered by leadership and co-ordination failures between the city and the region that have been overlooked by national departments (Table 15.4). There have only been a small number of examples – such as Auckland – where the national government has led the creation of an empowered regional authority.

Some national governments have begun to take an active interest in their world cities' regional and spatial growth needs (Arretche, 2013). At the boldest end of the spectrum, we find governments that have unilaterally increased the geographical boundary of their world city. This has taken place in Moscow, where the national government made the unprecedented step of merging the city with sparsely populated territories southwest of the capital. This move to create 'New Moscow' effectively doubles the size of the city and provides

Table 15.4:   Status of regional governance in 12 world cities

City	Region	Regional tier of government?	Status of regional governance
Hong Kong	Greater Pearl River Delta	No	Some regional collaboration, mostly on infrastructure. Development Plans drawn up by central government.
London	Greater South East	No	No regional framework – Greater London has periodic meetings with 100+ authorities in wider South East.
Moscow	Moscow + Moscow Region	Yes (separate)	Region entirely separate to Moscow city government, weak co-ordination, contingent on central government impetus.
Mumbai	Mumbai Metropolitan Region	No	Fragmented – led by Maharashtra State. Limited powers of MMRDA.
New York	New York Region	No	Spans 3 states, very little co-ordination, RPA's non-binding plan promoted through networks
Paris	Île de France	Yes (integrated)	Region in charge of transport, planning and spatial development land use, complex negotiated implementation with City, metropole, inter-municipal bodies etc.
São Paulo	São Paulo Metropolitan Region	No	No regional entity, just basic planning functions.
Seoul	National Capital Region	No	No structured co-operation between SMG and wider region but many cross-border initiatives.
Shanghai	Yangzte River Delta	No	Very large city-regional government, some economic and transport co-ordination with surrounding municipalities.
Singapore	Singapore – Johor Bahru (Malaysia)	No	Weak regional co-operation with Malaysia – limited agreements on transport and water.
Tokyo	Tokyo Capital Region	No	No formal regional entity but some ad hoc co-operative efforts.
Toronto	Greater Toronto Area	No	Region is widely recognised but no governance framework. Cross-regional transport and spatial growth strategies. Business and civic bodies fill gaps.

potentially much-needed room to relieve congestion, with an intention to house 1.5 million people eventually if enough private investment can be attracted. The initiative is long term in nature and builds upon international experience such as Navi Mumbai, which began in the early 1970s, and the development of the New Territories in Hong Kong. Russia's sovereign wealth fund has already committed to financing half the cost of a four-lane central ring road, while a metro connection is underway. Although Russian government ministries will no longer be relocated to the new territory, as first mooted, the increased land provides valuable opportunities to create a more polycentric city and raise standards of living. The move does not, however, address Moscow's relationship with the surrounding Moscow Region, whose authority does not extend to the city itself. This situation contrasts with cities such as Paris, where the Île-de-France region includes the central city, which makes it possible to undertake a more integrated form of regional planning.

Other world cities have a longer history of regional planning but have yet to receive backing from higher tiers of government to build government structures accordingly. Mumbai's Metropolitan Region Development Authority (MMRDA) is more than 40 years old, having been created by the Maharashtra state government to plan for expansion beyond the city's historic peninsula. It has become a highly competent long-term planning body that relies on the sale of land holdings to help finance specific projects. But MMRDA's powers only extend to planning and transport, and not to other city systems. There are strong calls to finally widen its span of authority and strengthen its mandate to co-ordinate a shared regional vision.

The risk of unmanaged regional growth also looms large in New York. Access to economic opportunity is declining across its 'tri-state' region, and investment from New York State and federal governments in housing, density, amenities and rail infrastructure lags behind what is necessary to adapt to New York's future economy. The region has a highly credible and experienced Regional Plan Association that produces strategies for the region, but the RPA has no implementational authority. Although territorial expansion and metropolitan consolidation are not plausible options for New York, the region needs higher tiers to increase the capacity of its large institutions, especially the Metropolitan Transportation Authority and the Port Authority.

By contrast, cross-regional collaboration and engagement in London has begun to improve since 2013. Greater South East workshops and summits aim to establish more productive ways of co-ordinating strategy and infrastructure investment. More than half of the 156 local authorities in the region have attended the summits so far. In agreeing to focus on how to address the regional barriers to housing delivery, and on better sharing of data, the region has made small steps towards a more collaborative ethos (GLA, 2015).

The regional dimension of governance for large and fast-growing cities is an important and neglected imperative for higher-tier governments to address. Where reforms have been undertaken in the past 30 years they are generally perceived as positive but inadequate. To remain successful, such reforms need to be adaptable and continuous so that the governance can continue to adjust to the changing shape and character of the urban area.

More broadly, governance reforms and upgrades at citywide, metropolitan and regional levels are an important ongoing task for nearly all world cities. They can have a significant impact on world cities' capacity to build a unified vision, to raise their international profile and to unlock new development pathways. Larger and still fast-growing world cities urgently need integrated governance and to re-align institutions with new geographies, while others with more settled spatial patterns often need more extensive sources of finance and fiscal autonomy. The experiences of London, Paris and even Hong Kong show that national governments are sometimes willing to agree new governance for individual cities. In general, however, preferential treatment for one city is politically difficult to achieve, and also may have long-term ramifications in terms of broader inter-city co-operation. Leaders in many world cities are realising that it is better to ask for governance reform as part of wider sub-national reforms (see Chapter 16).

Fiscal and investment systems

Independent and self-sustaining revenue sources are almost unheard of among world cities – only Singapore and Hong Kong possess them. Even a comparatively empowered city government such as New York, which raises over 70% of its budget through its own funds, is reliant on $12 billion of state government grants for areas such as school and pre-school education, and on $8 billion of federal government grants (de Blasio, 2014). This, of course, does not include the other state and federal spending that is allocated entirely separately. Other world cities, even those that have gained some improved taxing powers, are much more restricted and struggle to raise the finance both to modernise their city systems and to cope with operating costs.

There are a number of dimensions in which world cities are still fiscally disempowered:

- **Net fiscal outflows**. World cities invariably raise a greater sum of total tax revenue for the State than is re-invested by central government allocations, despite local government obligations to own and maintain infrastructure. Although this is to be expected and is widely viewed as a fair trade-off, there are many examples where the net outflows are seen as excessive, to the extent that they inhibit the world city's capacity to grow and ultimately increase revenue for the rest of the country. Prominent examples include São Paulo, Seoul and London. In São Paulo, the central city is less supported by federal government compared to other Brazilian cities. Although it generates income through its property, services and value-added taxes, there is a sense that the federal level does not provide the enhanced support commensurate with the city's functions and responsibilities in Brazil's economy.
- **Investment and borrowing restrictions**. Some world cities are trapped in highly unsatisfactory debt repayment situations that squeeze their room to invest in future infrastructure items. São Paulo, for example, has been repaying debts to federal government at rates of up to 9% per annum plus inflation. Interest rates were finally reduced by the Senate in November 2014, but its scale of debt disqualifies it from seeking many other sources of debt finance (Escola de Governo, 2014). In this and other cases, the world city is not treated especially differently in recognition of the unique demands placed upon it.
- **Inelastic taxes**. Many established world cities depend on fairly inelastic property taxes that do not rise in accordance with increased spending demands. The costs of social housing and housing supply more broadly have grown, but national governments have often withdrawn from this area, notably in the US, Canada and the UK.
- **Competing for 'trophy' projects**. In systems where central government collects or controls a majority of tax revenues, world cities often have to 'bid' against other cities for financial support for glamorous projects that will attract government interest and attention. Tokyo, Paris, New York and Toronto have all recently bid for the Olympics, while Moscow has bid for the football World Cup and São Paulo for the EXPO, among many others. In London, the process of bidding for trophy projects began with the regeneration of its Docklands in the 1980s, and continues until more recently with projects

such as Crossrail, the 2012 Olympics and Crossrail 2. The advantages of one-off disbursements for prestigious developments tend to be offset by uncertain time-frames and the constraints on preparing for future growth. In order to overcome this deficit, London took the step of creating a Finance Commission which made a persuasive case for expanding the capital's share of self-retained taxes from 7% to around 12%.

Other issues include cities' limited experience of delivering big and complex projects in productive partnership with the private sector. For some cities there is a deficit not so much of infrastructure funding *per se* but of bankable projects that are attractive to investors. This can be due to unpredictable revenues or political risk concerns, but also the inflexibility of traditional financing models with regards to multi-sector projects. In terms of public capital investment, there is also weak alignment and clarity between different envelopes of funding at the national, state and city levels.

As a result of this array of challenges, world cities have become a lot more active in debates about fiscal and investment systems with their national and state governments. They are exploring both the creation of new taxes and different ways to share existing taxes (London, Paris). They are pursuing new or increased forms of debt financing and a new generation of PPPs (São Paulo). Some are experimenting with municipal bonds to diversify revenue sources and prevent over-reliance on a fragile revenue stream (Shanghai). And there are new mechanisms of value capture finance being looked at and tested, such as tax increment financing and air rights (Toronto, São Paulo, Moscow).

Many, if not most, world cities require a higher investment rate and greater investment capacity. Not all of the fiscal or tax challenges can be solved by a simple national government reform, but many solutions require a national-level dialogue that rejects a hostile, 'zero-sum game' approach to cities' fiscal contributions, and examines opportunities for greater revenue autonomy. World cities' ability to make progress on achieving a fairer or more advantageous fiscal arrangement depends on a better grasp among leaders and the public about the best level of fiscal autonomy.

Business friendliness and investor readiness

There is now sharper awareness of the competitive dynamics between world cities in different nations, along with increased observation of the failure of regional redistribution policies, coupled with recognition of the unequal effects of globalisation. These have triggered more proactive policy responses from developed nation state governments (for example, France, Japan and Korea) to make their world cities more competitive and inclusive. The overhaul of regulation in key strategic sites in world cities is one response to make cities more open to business, entrepreneurs and tourists, alongside a more holistic approach to the education and skills system to prepare younger residents for the competitive labour market.

For emerging world cities, national governments focus on getting the business basics right in order to become attractive places for investment and business location. Their future ability to compete in higher-value knowledge sectors depends on how well their national governments manage inflation and improve public sector efficiency, legal certainty and transparency, so as to incentivise the private sector to invest and take the lead on key projects. A national inquiry into Mumbai's future finance competitiveness more than ten years ago identified exactly these shortfalls, but little progress was then made. Others have made bigger strides, including by altering the ownership and management structure of key national infrastructure if there is a strong case to do so. In São Paulo, the privatisation of Guarulhos Airport for R16 billion ($6 billion) in 2012 provided a signal in Brazil about the potential of deregulation to raise the investment rate and increase the productivity of existing assets.

One of the most striking recent examples of national experimentation to open up a world city has been in Shanghai. A Free Trade Zone was established on the city's outskirts in 2013 with central government approval to test the liberalisation of the national financial system. The Zone was designed to increase the role of the yuan currency in global transactions and to allow two-way investments in a range of sectors. Despite presidential endorsement and active central government impetus, at the time of writing the Zone has been mired in bureaucratic caution and strains in the partnership between municipal government and central government departments represented on the State Council. As emerging economies experience a slowdown in growth, central governments such as Beijing are proving hesitant to pursue liberalisation of investment in order to deter capital outflows, and this has implications for how emerging world cities such as Shanghai can establish themselves as international financial centres (South China Morning Post, 2014; Wan *et al.*, 2014).

Investment in research and innovation

With technology and science-led industries now in a rapid phase of global integration, many more world cities are seeking to become science and technology hubs. National and state governments play a key role in deciding where the facilities that underpin such hubs are located. National research grants and decisions about where to locate scientific institutions can substantially affect the technology and innovation ecosystems in world cities. The influence of education and higher education reforms is also felt over the medium and longer terms.

The use of government designations of major new innovation sites is increasingly visible, as a way of altering the spatial economy of the city. One example is Paris's own 'Silicon Valley', Paris-Saclay, which has been accelerated by the French government naming it an 'Operation of National Interest.' Central government is heavily represented in the public co-ordination agency that brings together universities and local politicians, and the Prime Minister's Office oversees much of the investment. In such cases, where the State plays a steering role, there is sometimes concern that a top-down technocratic approach risks alienating local actors and paralysing the process of synergistic innovation.

But the State's involvement also provides confidence for institutions to relocate and for investors to commit capital, and these have to be carefully balanced.

Toronto is one world city that has really benefited from successive federal research funding programmes. Launched in 1989, the federal Networks of Centers of Excellence (NCE) programme has been a partner in several of Toronto's high-tech clusters – including clean energy, ICT and life sciences. At the same time, the Canada Excellence Research Chairs (CERC) has helped attract international researchers. The Canadian Institutes of Health Research, the Natural Sciences and Engineering Research Council and the Social Sciences and Humanities Research Council provide a large slice of Toronto's teaching hospital research funds. Since 2006, federal government has invested more than C$11 billion ($10 billion) in science, technology and innovation, and recent funding schemes support Toronto's cutting-edge research in neuroscience, cancer and stem cells. Federal funding streams have ultimately helped turn Toronto's high-quality universities and research institutes into world-class strengths (Crawford, 2012; University of Toronto, 2013; Kazakov, 2014; Zeng, 2014).

For world cities where the State has played the decisive role in higher education, reforms to open up the sector to the market have to be pursued carefully and judiciously by national governments. Deregulation in order to meet certain targets has had the inadvertent effect of lowering standards and creating an over-supply of an uncompetitive product, as has happened with some of Japan's higher education reforms (Kan, 2016). A lack of investment to support universities and research institutes can also result in an over-supply of highly qualified candidates and a detachment from private industry. National governments have tended to be more successful in this area when they avoid high-profile 'signature' initiatives and build a long-term strategic perspective that takes into account resources and capabilities in their cities' key research institutions.

Support for hosting global events

Global events are once-in-a-generation opportunities for world cities to raise their profile, alter their brand and bring forward infrastructure development. The highest profile events – such as the Olympic Games and the football World Cup – focus global attention on world cities' physical modernisation and cultural vitality. Many other international events – such as political assemblies, sporting championships and regional multi-sport games – offer opportunities for cities to interact with new 'customers' and enter new markets. For events to be branding successes rather than failures, they require close co-operation with national governments to ensure infrastructure projects are completed on time, technical standards are met and visitor experiences are positive.

Although the cost–benefit analysis of major events is widely contested, they have certainly been catalysts of infrastructural transformation in many world cities. The 1988 Olympics and 2002 World Cup in Seoul, the 1998 World Cup and 2016 European Championships in Paris, the 2009 Shanghai EXPO and the 2012 London Olympics all provided rare opportunities to regenerate ex-industrial areas in partnership with national agencies. Such events often create essential new capacity for the growth of new sectors and urban restructuring. At the same time, they are identity-building exercises that signal new edges of a city's offer. Perhaps most importantly, they are an important means through which investment in the world city can become a national priority for a fixed period of time. The fixed deadlines are often important in unlocking and accelerating key infrastructure and other investments.

Sometimes national or federal initiatives to support a regeneration process can result in increased capacity to host international events in future. In the case of Waterfront Toronto, Canada's three tiers of government took the unusual step of creating a joint development corporation to develop the site. Intergovernmental dialogue broke down at one point and mutual distrust curtailed the powers for the development agency, slowing down progress. Nevertheless, a federal minister and the federally owned Port Authority continue to engage productively, and the combined weight of the government 'contribution agreements' has ultimately produced high-quality public space that successfully hosted the 2015 Pan-Am Games athletes' village.

Open labour markets

When international firms operate in globalised clusters that serve markets in many countries from a single location within a world city, they require labour markets that are open to international talent. Most world cities therefore strongly prefer to be within a country that has some degree of openness to international workers and also to have universities and other specialist institutions that are able to recruit students internationally.

Many world cities have difficulty staying open to talent over multiple cycles. As a self-governing city-state, Singapore is one of the few exceptions. Its unique government arrangement has enabled it to leverage the support and control of key institutions to develop and sustain a world-class business climate. The city-state's effective management of trade unions and wages has allowed it the unusual luxury of managing its own labour market to keep wages more competitive at each successive stage of internationalisation. It has also been able to favour global firms and State-owned enterprises and maintain focus on economic objectives. Its ability to intervene in social policies – usually a role left to national governments – has created a highly educated urban workforce well prepared for new cycles of growth. To ensure an attractive labour force for global firms, Singapore has invested heavily in education at all levels, both tertiary and skills-based curriculums. It has closely monitored skills and crime levels to optimise its business environment as the city moved first into high-value services and manufacturing, and later towards creativity and innovation (Huff, 1995; Low, 2001; Mauzy and Milne, 2002; Centre for Liveable Cities and Civil Service College Singapore, 2014).

There are many other areas where cities are beginning to work in more fruitful collaboration with national governments. One of the most important is climate change. The now widespread culture of cities transparently sharing best practices has made national governments begin to see cities as credible partners on the issue, although many national administrations still deny or play down the potential implications of a changing climate. Where nation states have been supportive, they have adapted their regulatory and taxation frameworks to incentivise cities to expand renewable energy and energy-efficient buildings (Andrews, 2016).

Another challenge that has become more apparent is the way in which the rapid growth in immigration (and in visitor numbers) creates challenges of social cohesion and labour market integration. Open world cities such as Toronto and New York have an under-employed (and sometimes undocumented, but often skilled) base of foreign labour that is ignored or excluded by national policies, and so requires innovation and investment by the city itself. The issue of immigration also often reveals the tension in values between world cities and the rest of their country. This arose very clearly in London during the 2016 national referendum debate about a 'Brexit' from the European Union, with Londoners voting by a clear margin to remain while most of the rest of England and Wales voted to leave. In the case of New York, the City openly refuses to comply with federal directives on migration because they are viewed as counter-productive. New York leaders have been active in trying to shape opinion and change minds about national immigration policy, and their future success at doing so will partly determine how much it will continue to be perceived as a city that is still open to talent and newcomers. This issue is one of the most difficult areas for world cities to achieve sustained national support, and leadership and innovation over how the national conversation on immigration evolves will be critical.

Making practical progress with national governments

From the case studies, it is obvious that mayors of world cities usually play a vital leadership role if and when multiple levels of government sit down and talk productively about the needs of their city. Successful mayors raise awareness, champion funding models, find allies in the private and civic sectors, gain the trust and confidence of national ministers and convince them that their city deserves consideration (Table 15.5). The role of individual city leaders in London, Tokyo, São Paulo, Moscow, New York and Shanghai has been cited as influential in setting agendas with national governments and at securing one-off deals and larger reforms. Indeed, many prospective mayoral candidates in these cities run on the basis that they have the access to and credibility with national decision-makers to get things done.

There are a number of other elements that appear important if cities are to make headway in their relationship with national government.

- **New institutions.** Several world cities have created new expert committees and multi-sector institutions to improve the evidence base for future decisions. In 2013, Hong Kong established a Financial Services Development Council as a senior cross-sector advisory body that explores new opportunities associated with Chinese financial reform, and its proposals are used in negotiations with central government authorities (Financial Services Development Council, 2014). This extends existing efforts from banking and accountancy

Table 15.5: Channels of communication and advocacy between world cities and national governments

	Relationship and dialogue with national government	Role of business and civic leaders
Hong Kong	Chief Executive builds trust between electorate and mainland government. Senior CCP officials have experience in city; HK Legislative Council builds inter-city networks, subject to approval; new Financial Services Development Council advocates with central government.	Accountants and bankers dialogue with China Banking Regulatory Commission, People's Bank of China, the State Council and Ministry of Finance to defend financial sector interests.
London	Charismatic Mayor has platform and profile to speak for the entire city; usually benefits from political alignment; long-term infrastructure plan to highlight finance needs; new alliance with secondary cities.	London First has channels of communication with central government and advocates on Crossrail 2, airport expansion, China visas, housing supply; national arts and cultural institutions make economic case for funding support.
Moscow	Strong, mutually supportive relationship, fostered through high-level leadership networks.	Business elites have sponsored key projects such as Skolkovo Management School and Innovation District.
Mumbai	Limited relationship; Maharashtra Chief Executive is key point of contact.	Bombay First makes the case for de-regulation and investment to make Mumbai more liveable and competitive.
New York	High-profile Mayor has direct access to lobby for better policy on immigration, gun control, terrorism etc.; ad hoc alliances with other big-city mayors.	Important roles played by Partnership for New York City, Real Estate Board and Regional Plan Association.
Paris	Leaders and agencies in central City government; complex negotiation with Île de France regional council; consultation with expert planning agencies.	Chambers of Commerce work separately to advise on strategic processes; emerging public–private model at regional council level.
São Paulo	Modest but improving; shared working on demonstration projects; stronger informal networks as many Ministry of Cities staff are ex-members of municipal government.	Emerging business leadership makes investment case to adjust fiscal model and marshals a business-friendliness agenda.
Shanghai	Strong personal connections between city Mayor, CCP municipal party chief, the State Council and central ministries; many city officials graduate upwards.	Involvement of overseas Chambers of Commerce on investment issues but little strategic input on urban priorities.
Singapore	Fully integrated city/national government that adopts 'whole of government' approach.	Limited but growing partnership in smart cities and 'living lab' agendas.
Seoul	Mayor advocates for greater fiscal and political autonomy. Negotiations with Ministry of Security and Public Administration on devolution of powers.	Limited.
Tokyo	Governor Masuzoe is a powerful advocate and has a co-operative relationship with Prime Minister Abe. Research Institutes provide evidence on competition and pro-globalisation approach.	Small role, mainly via Chamber of Commerce, major firms and State-owned companies; growing in the lead up to 2020 Olympics.
Toronto	Mayor champions funding models for infrastructure to upper-tier governments; Federal Minister of finance also responsible for the Greater Toronto Area; Consider Canada City Alliance collaborates with federal government on trade missions.	Toronto Region Board of Trade, Canada's largest urban Chamber of Commerce, lobbies federal government intensively for money for transport and immigrant training; Greater Toronto Civic Action Alliance lobbies on immigration, green space, R&D, strong links with new Mayor.

associations to engage with the State Council and China's financial regulators to defend Hong Kong's interests and advocate for improved practices.

- **Business leadership.** Business leadership groups have become important actors in cities where governance is dysfunctional or where interaction between different tiers of government is strained. The most established and mature business leadership groups lobby state or national governments intensively for political reform and financial support, and help build a shared recognition that world cities need to be co-ordinated beyond the city's political boundaries. Toronto's regional Board of Trade has become an influential opinion shaper on business and public policy issues, and is an active advocate for economic development, transportation infrastructure and the regional dimension of governance. In London over the last 20 years, London First has built good channels of communication with central government and urges the national tier to be bold and decisive on infrastructure hardware and openness to emerging markets.
- **Civic coalitions** offer an additional source of leadership in world cities and lobby higher tiers to recognise the environmental and cultural needs of vibrant world cities. Toronto's CivicAction and New York's Regional Plan Association are examples of highly credible civic institutions that use their research and strong networks to advocate for short-term reform (on issues such as public space, immigration and arts funding) and long-term development strategy.

    Universities and academic-affiliated think tanks are becoming a more important source of ideas and leadership in the renegotiation of city terms with higher tiers of government. One example is the Institute of Municipal Finance & Governance in Canada. Based at the University of Toronto, its research successfully engages Canadian politicians and electorates with information about their cities' financial and governing capacity relative to need and to international peers.

- **National departments and units.** Many national governments in centralised states take a direct ministerial interest in their world cities, monitoring developments closely and making regular policy adjustments. These periods of engagement are very often led by individual personalities who are personally committed to a cities agenda. The paradigm shift that has occurred in London and the UK in the last five years is partly the result of Chancellor George Osborne becoming convinced of the case for a new approach to London and the northern cities. This resulted in the subsequent commitment of the UK Treasury to move the agenda of devolution and infrastructure forward much more quickly than usual. Elsewhere, some countries have had national ministers with special responsibility for their world city, as in Canada, where two federal ministers of finance previously had responsibility for the Greater Toronto Area. France has had several ministers for Grand Paris and Hong Kong benefits from the fact that several members of China's seven-member Central Standing Committee have direct experience with the city and are engaged with a high-level working group that oversees city affairs. The experience of senior political officials with their world city's business and political communities is often viewed as an important informal factor in the way national governments are responsive to the city's needs.

Conclusion

For all world cities, investment in growth management and tackling the externalities of consistent growth has become a pre-condition to their ongoing success and prosperity. Their ability to perform world city functions (governmental, financial, corporate, retail, cultural and tourist functions) requires that investment keeps track of population growth and the overall growth in demand. This is not a simple, one-off task. The ability of world cities to provide benefit to nations is multi-cyclic in its character, in that it has to be shaped over several political and economic cycles.

The evidence from many recent examples suggests that world cities are only in a position to invest and manage their growth if there is a stable agreement in place with higher tiers of government. In such agreements, state and national governments explicitly recognise their largest and most globally oriented cities and focus on long-term growth challenges rather than short-term imperatives. In so doing they identify the mechanisms through which their world cities can finance the big projects that shape growth and unlock capacity. They also adjust their sectoral policies to make it possible for world cities to align planning, land use, investment and infrastructure in order to manage growth. A long-term focus also identifies the importance of sustaining a positive business climate and remaining committed to a high quality of life. In order to deliver this long-term agenda, world cities depend on national governments having trust and confidence in their city leaders, sometimes supported by advocacy and evidence from civic and business groups. Incremental and ongoing adjustments to governance appear to be highly significant if world cities are to manage their growth equitably at a wider metropolitan scale. Critically, the partnership between a world city and its national government also rests on consensus that the world city continues to provide a net benefit to the nation as a whole. This sensitive issue has become more frequently debated and is the subject of Chapter 16.

16

Unintended consequences: Making world cities work for nations

National and sub-national governments are clearly critical partners in the ongoing development and adaptation of world cities. But many tensions are beginning to appear in these vertical relationships as the leading cities become semi-detached from their national economies and develop their own distinct demographic and cultural character. Some of these tensions were visible in the UK referendum decision to vote 'Brexit' and leave the European Union, but they can also be found in many other countries as their world cities are increasingly perceived to symbolise the negative and disruptive effects of globalisation. Other cities and rural areas observe a built-in bias in the economic and political system and seek to correct what they perceive as the distortions in the national development model. At the same time, the under-performance of other regions creates its own knock-on effects on the world city itself, including many of the negative externalities associated with excess demand that were highlighted in Chapter 15.

In this chapter we examine the range of advantages and disadvantages that world cities are deemed to bring to national economies and societies. Although the pros and cons vary in each context, we argue that leaders in world cities and national governments have little option but to address the disadvantages head on and create alliances for a collaborative set of solutions. We then review the latest national policies that have been designed for their wider system of cities, and the efforts among world cities and other groupings of cities to work together to solve entrenched challenges and argue effectively for substantive reform from the national tier.

The advantages and disadvantages of having a world city

Over the last four decades nation states have come to realise, some faster than others, than world cities have a number of impacts on the rest of their country. Some of these impacts are perceived as advantageous and others are viewed as disadvantageous (Table 16.1).

On the positive side, there are a number of factors which are repeatedly cited in favour of world cities. In emerging nations, they have played a decisive role in the transformation of national economies, operating as intermediaries in a large share of nations' external trade and foreign investment, and managing the financial risks involved. In more established countries they act as suppliers of capital and as drivers of productivity and specialisation. In all cases, world cities appear to function as an interface between the domestic and international economy in ways that, over time, raise corporate performance and governance. At least ten positive spin-offs of world cities are cited:

- The density of firms and workers in world cities encourages the **sharing of infrastructure, services and information** with businesses around the country. Evidence on agglomeration indicates that productivity tends to grow with city size. Large, diverse cities have the capacity to achieve scale spillovers that have increased productivity effects on the whole national economy.

Table 16.1:   Advantages and disadvantages of world cities to their nation states

Advantages	Disadvantages
Agglomeration spillovers for workers and firms in world city and beyond	Brain drain from rest of nation to world city
Re-distribution of tax revenue from world city to other regions	Over-concentration in key world city sectors (eg finance, services, real estate)
Nationally dispersed supply chain development from world city functions	Excessive influence of world city on macro-economic and industrial policy
Up-skilling of domestic firms through expertise in world city	Global turbulence in world city promotes volatility in national economy
Demand for goods and services produced domestically from world city	Preferential treatment of world city within national infrastructure investment
World city acts as gateway for trade, investment, students and visitors	Failure of mobile capital to invest in less dynamic regions, preferring world city
World city acts as 'escalator' for talent to develop that can serve other regions	Perceived lack of fiscal re-distribution to meet welfare needs of lagging regions
Increases overall levels of entrepreneurship in world city and nation	Two-tier housing market at national level
World city provides a strong business brand for nation	Lack of access to finance sand expertise in rest of nation

- **Taxation revenue** on world cities' high-value industries, in particular financial and business services but also creative and high-technology industries. The redistribution of this revenue to the rest of the country is vital to investment in public services and in raising overall standards of living, especially in regions that lag well behind the national average.
- World cities possess **financial expertise and trade and export management** capabilities that facilitate the employment of workers in productive industries, many of which are located in the wider hinterland of the world city. Experienced companies based in world cities are able to broker complex financial and trade deals that reduce risk and improve corporate performance. This phenomenon is very well established in Hong Kong but is also visible in Moscow, Mumbai, São Paulo and Shanghai, among others.
- They foster **supply chain development** regionally and nationally. The rise of new technologies adds momentum to the search for efficiency gains and the relocation of parts of value chains within national borders. In general, world cities drive specialisation and trade benefits within national supply chains, although many nation states have not yet thought through their growth strategies through the lens of supply chains. The ability of other cities and non-urban locations to tap into these supply chains depends on the quality of their physical and human infrastructure (Coyle and Rosewell, 2014).
- The global firms that world cities host **help domestic firms learn** about new techniques, products and processes. There is good evidence that global companies that are integrated into the local economy play an important role in vertical knowledge transfer to smaller local partners and suppliers of intermediate inputs, both in established and emerging countries. Local industry competition to serve multinational companies is a major driver of technological improvements. The evidence of horizontal spillovers between multinational and local firms within the same industry is understandably more mixed, but there are many important examples of tacit knowledge transfer taking place hosted by globally oriented cities (Rand, 2015).
- Spending by the large affluent and high-net-worth populations in world cities increases **demand for certain kinds of national goods and services**. Demand for medical care, retail, children's education and construction have all increased considerably and the resources and talent in these sectors are often drawn from around the region and the country.
- They are **visitor and tourist gateways** to the rest of the country for customers who otherwise would not visit. Most world cities are an entry point for visitors interested in cultural tourism elsewhere in the nation, and encourage visitors to stay longer and visit other cities. They are especially important for long-distance air travellers who can connect directly to some cities but not others. In the same vein, world cities also function as connectivity hubs that provide access to national transport networks (Ram, 2016).
- They are '**escalator regions**' for upskilling ambitious workers who arrive from across the country, and who then take their acquired knowledge and proficiency to secondary and tertiary cities later in their career (Fielding, 1992). In the case of London, the city has functioned as an escalator since at least the 1970s and this role has intensified recently. In Japan, the next largest cities such as Osaka, Nagoya, Fukuoka and Hiroshima function as 'siphon cities'

that recruit bright students from nearby regions and later channel them to Tokyo after graduation. The benefits that accrue to women in particular have become more visible and the capital increasingly illustrates an 'escalator' effect as older migrants 'step off' and return to the provinces later in life (Fielding, 2014a). Meanwhile, in Shanghai and Seoul, this escalator role is also recognised as increasingly influential (Fielding, 2014b; Kim, Doh and Kim, 2015). In Toronto, the escalator effect is less pronounced but still visible (Newbold, 2015). The evidence so far suggests that second-tier cities are not subject to nearly as much speculative migration of talented young people, and more frequently rely on suitable jobs already waiting in situ (Champion, 2013; Champion, Coombes and Gordon, 2013).

- World cities have **high levels of entrepreneurship** and can diffuse new firms and sectors into the national economy. A large international dataset finds consistently higher prevalence of entrepreneurship in world cities compared to their countries, with only a small number of exceptions where there are large business constraints, such as Milan and Tokyo. Their cultural diversity also applies to the management of small companies, and this has been shown to be an important source of product innovation compared to cities where leadership and management are more homogeneous. In cities such as London, New York and others, diversity also enables cities to develop links with international markets which is an important catalyst for innovation and iteration. Other analysts have also argued that the high degree of tolerance and individualism often found in world cities, especially Anglo-Saxon cities, is also a spur for entrepreneurial activity (Acs, Bosma and Sterberg, 2008; Sobel, Dutta and Roy, 2010; Nathan and Lee, 2013; Florida, 2015).
- World cities provide important '**business brands**' for nations by being identified as leading business cities. The business brand of cities such as Hong Kong, Tokyo, Istanbul and Zurich is superior to their countries and provides a positive point of perception for external investors (IPSOS-MORI, 2013; Saffron, 2015).
- Although world cities are often criticised for the brain drain effects they cause, in many emerging countries they can help to **reverse brain drain** by attracting 'returnees' who had previously left to work in high-end industries in North America and Europe (Chacko, 2007). The phenomenon of returning entrepreneurs is especially visible in Mumbai, Hong Kong, Shanghai and Seoul, as well as smaller world cities such as Tel Aviv and Taipei (Kenneya, Breznitzc and Murphree, 2012).

The (perceived and actual) negative externalities of having a world city

World cities also create externalities within their nations. As we have detailed, national governments have tended to become more 'open' to international economic flows since the 1980s, and many of the benefits accrue to their world cities. But after one or two cycles of exposure to globalisation, national government, political representatives, national media and national electorates frequently observe costs or externalities that appear in the wider nation. The 'pull factors' in world city areas are perceived to result in over-concentration, disparity and dysfunction. The most commonly cited negative externalities of world cities include:

- **Brain drain**. The way world cities 'suck in' younger talent and professional labour from the rest of the nation accelerates social and economic gaps, both between urban and rural areas and between the world city and other cities. Korea is an example where severe brain drain towards the Seoul capital region has acted as a major deterrent to companies considering relocating their R&D and their managerial functions to second cities. For many emerging nations, the internal 'brain drain' to their world cities is now viewed as a more serious challenge than the external brain drain to other countries. In more established cities, there is concern that upwardly mobile talent in world cities increasingly does not 'get off' at the top of the 'escalator' and return to lower-income regions, intensifying the skills gaps. This has implications for other cities' specialised sector competitiveness, and the social cohesion in cities that have lost much of their young adult population (Duke *et al.*, 2006; Massey, 2007).
- **Over-concentration of financial and business service sectors**. As agglomeration intensifies, many commentators argue that higher-value sectors have become too concentrated in the world city at the expense of other regions. This process has also begun to occur in other sectors that historically have been more dispersed (for example, digital and creative industries). Attempts to de-concentrate certain industries away from the world city mirror efforts in the 1950s through to the 1980s to do the same with manufacturing, with mixed results. There are also similar debates in the real estate industry, as investment companies come to view world cities as saturated with capital and look for better value elsewhere.
London is a prime example of the world city being viewed as over-concentrating higher-value sectors. A divide between the capital and the rest of the country has been noticed since the late 19th century – London's GDP per capita was twice that of the West Midlands in 1911. The gap grew again in the 1920s and 1930s, and then later from the 1980s. After the global financial crisis, the national political conversation was dominated by talk of 'rebalancing the economy', based on the belief that the British economy was too asymmetric and threatened long-term stability and prosperity. This also incorporated the idea that London was too dependent on financial services and had promoted a model of short-term consumption (75% of GDP) over long-term investment. The agenda of rebalancing has informed the policy response of central government since 2010 and has been at the crux of the 'Northern Powerhouse' concept which aims to make northern cities more self-sufficient and less dependent on the UK exchequer (Gardiner *et al.*, 2013).
- **Government monetary policy bias**. The concentration of wealth and capital in world cities is viewed to have distorting spatial, economic and environmental effects. Monetary policy is sometimes viewed to be too oriented around the world city because of the concern to head off house price booms, to the detriment of the rest of the country. The fact that in many world cities the value of the property stock in inner city districts rivals large swathes of the rest of the country makes governments wary. But long-range studies in many countries have shown that central bank policy to keep interest rates low has potentially destabilising by-products that contribute to financial crises. The unequal structure of the housing market in general is also viewed in some countries to be a deterrent against labour migration between different regions (Jordà, Schularick and Taylor, 2015).

- **Volatility**. The exposure of world cities to the global economy leads to volatility that has an amplified impact on much of the country when sharp downturns occur. The temporary collapse of globally plugged-in industries, or capital flight from heavily invested cities, presents very serious risks to the whole country.
- **Disproportionate per capita expenditure on infrastructure**. World cities' capacity to compile investable projects can mean that national government part-financing of projects happens more regularly than in other less bankable cities. In London, for example, planned public infrastructure investment allocated there is currently more than three times the average in other UK regions. For world cities that are more productive than the rest of the country, even when rail links to other cities are proposed or developed, there is concern that this merely serves to increase the magnetism of the world city at the expense of others.
- **Easier access to finance**. The clusters of banks and venture capital firms that world cities tend to host is seen to give nearby small and growing firms much greater advantages to get their business off the ground, while companies elsewhere are relatively starved of capital. Many of the incubator and accelerator communities for the new innovation economy are oriented around capital cities with global functions rather than smaller centres.
- **Insufficient fiscal redistribution**. World cities generate a high proportion of national income tax and in nearly all years are net donors to national government revenue. But there is a perception that net fiscal outflows are still not enough to tackle the ever-growing welfare needs in other regions. Concerns of this kind are regularly expressed in Moscow/Russia, São Paulo/Brazil and other countries where the disparities between world cities and nation states are very large.

Many of the aforementioned negative externalities are linked to a related factor: undue political influence of world cities on national governments. World cities are perceived to be more successful at lobbying politicians to spend money on large infrastructure projects that serve their needs over the rest of the country. They are also seen to receive a lot of help after serious economic or security setbacks (for example, financial bail-outs, climate or terrorist disasters). Many analysts argue that world cities are beneficiaries of investment favouritism because they have more political leverage over national government policies, and because decision-makers come into greater day-to-day contact with their contemporary problems. This is viewed as a particular problem in politically centralised countries such as the UK, Korea and France. In the UK, for example, economic development experts argue that "spatial economic imbalance...has to do with the progressive concentration of economic, political and financial power in London and its environs" and that little will change "without 'decentering' the key institutional structures that make up the UK's national political economy" (Martin *et al.*, 2014: 1).

The extent to which all the above negative externalities are real or perceived is widely debated. But what is clear is that many of the disparities between world cities and their nation states are set to grow before they shrink. In the UK, the larger British cities outside London have been physically regenerated after industrial decline, at least in their city centres, but have struggled to achieve significant social and economic uplift. London's economy is forecast to grow by 27% in real terms between 2015 and 2025, compared to 14% in the north of England, with nearly as large a gap in job creation. New York City and the next largest American cities have been growing jobs and wages more quickly than the US economy as a whole for the past decade and appear likely to continue doing so (Martin, Gardiner and Tyler, 2014; Shearer *et al.*, 2016).

This is not just an Anglo-Saxon phenomenon. The economic divide between rural China and the largest coastal cities such as Shanghai, Beijing and Guangzhou is growing, and made more complicated by the exclusionary *hukou* system of citizenship. The large wealth and lifestyle gap with smaller cities is set to result in higher fiscal demands placed on China's most globally oriented cities. Meanwhile, the gaps between French cities are not as large, and many secondary French cities have been more successful, but they have not grown access to economic opportunity in their suburbs and national attempts to prepare them for global competition were held back by a lack of funding. One of the only exceptions to the performance disparity is Seoul, which has not outperformed the rest of Korea in recent years, although much of its growth takes place in the wider capital region instead, where many R&D functions are located. Moreover, Korea's six other metropolitan cities besides Seoul struggle with population decline, a narrow economic base and unappealing city centres (China Economic Review, 2013; Ji-Yoon, 2015).

These phenomena are borne out in the available GDP data on secondary cities (Table 16.2). China and the United States are among the only countries where the majority of secondary cities after their main world city perform above the national average (Germany is another). The more even balance of prosperity tends to be in federal countries, while in centralised countries such as Japan and the UK only a small minority of second cities has been able to sustain a productive economy. But even in federal countries there are clear signs that many medium-sized cities are not functioning as complementary engines of growth and productivity.

The concerns of ever-increasing disparity pose a major challenge to the viability of the world city model. Disparity in many cases breeds resentment and discontent, especially in the centralised political systems (less so in federal cases such as Toronto and São Paulo). It can result in the rise of political parties opposed to the world city model and subsequent decisions that are unfavourable to their success (protectionism, excessive regulation, immigration caps, withdrawal from intergovernmental treaties). The under-performance of second-tier and smaller cities also has direct negative implications for world cities as it further intensifies demand to access the world city, creates unanticipated congestion and reduces the potential for effective complementarities across the national system.

Leaders in world cities have little option but to make the case that some of the externalities and perceived biases can be amended with the right policies and intervention, without the nation state needing to reject the world city model entirely. They may also have to admit that some systemic advantages are hard to change but are more than offset by the benefits of a world city to economic vitality. This admission may form part of an acceptance among nation states that world cities will inevitably increase inter-regional disparities, and even alter the spatial character of a nation for good. The task of world cities, then, is to build alliances that can manage and leverage these changes for the long-term national good. In the next section, we review:

Table 16.2: Performance of second cities in national economies*

	National GDP per capita (PPP)	Leading global city GDP per capita (PPP)	Number of cities above national GDP average**	Cities (above, below)
USA	$54,600	New York: $70,000	8/10	**Los Angeles, Chicago, Dallas, Houston, Washington, Boston, Philadelphia, San Francisco,** Miami, Atlanta.
China	$12,900	Shanghai: $24,000 (Hong Kong $57,200)	7/10	**Beijing, Tianjin, Chengdu, Guangzhou, Shenzhen, Zhengzhou, Wuhan**, Chongqing, Shijiazhuang, Haerbin
Brazil	$16,000	São Paulo: $20,600	4/10	**Brasilia, Curitiba, Campinas**, **Grande Vitoria** Rio de Janeiro, Belo Horizonte, Porto Alegre, Recife, Fortaleza, Salvador
India	$5,900	Mumbai: $7,000	2/5	**Delhi, Chennai,** Kolkata, Hyderabad, Bangalore
Canada	$44,800	Toronto: $45,700	2/7	**Calgary, Edmonton**, Montreal, Vancouver, Ottawa, Quebec City, Winnipeg
Korea	$35,300	Seoul: $34,300	1/4	**Busan-Ulsan**, Daegu, Daejon, Gwangju
Japan	$37,400	Tokyo: $43,600	2/10	**Nagoya, Shizuoka,** Osaka-Kobe, Kitakyushu-Fukuoka, Sapporo, Kumamoto, Sendai, Hiroshima, Okayama, Niigata
France	$40,400	Paris: $57,200	1/8	**Lyon**, Lille, Marseille, Nice, Toulouse, Bordeaux, Strasbourg, Nantes
United Kingdom	$39,500	London: $57,200	1/10	**Bristol,** Birmingham, Manchester, Leeds, Liverpool, Nottingham, Glasgow, Sheffield, Newcastle, Cardiff-Newport

* Insufficient data for Russian cities. Number of cities selected based on data availability and relevant size categories.
Source: IMF, 2016 and Parilla *et al.*, 2015.

- The latest national policies that have been designed to create a more harmonious and sustainable system of cities, often with the support of their most globally connected cities.
- The collaborative efforts between world cities and other national cities to create their own solutions and engage higher tiers of government.

National frameworks to support the wider system of cities

The ideal scenario for world cities and nation states is a system of cities that can adjust so that each can benefit from changes brought about by globalisation. World cities and other cities rely on national frameworks and policies that are designed to help all cities to succeed, and which optimise the specific combination of cities within national territory. For such frameworks to emerge, it is usually a prerequisite for national government policies to recognise the mega-trends of urbanisation and globalisation, and then create the conditions for institutions to act in the long-term interest of cities rather than short-term political imperatives. Many national policies and regulatory and institutional frameworks are unintentionally anti-urban; they encourage sprawl, or they incentivise unhelpful internal competition, or they place legal and other rigidities in the way of co-operation at the local level. Most state and national governments operate with powerful sectoral ministries that may be highly competent but have the unintended consequences of militating against cross-sectoral and integrated solutions at city and metropolitan level.

A common theme for world cities is that national governments do not fully recognise the role of cities in their country's development, especially their economic role as the primary engines of prosperity in the 21st century. Until recently, most have treated their country's urban challenges as welfare and safety problems rather than as priorities for strategic economic attention. There is also a tendency not to trust local authorities to act appropriately or decisively. Periodic changes to the macroeconomic framework may have helped globalising sectors in world cities, but without the systems (land use, energy, governance) in place to support and manage the growth that followed. When national governments fail to provide direction or confidence, this often leads to disjointed narratives and a tendency to be reactive rather than proactive. What cities beyond the world city are now asking for are:

- Legislation that recognises cities as engines of growth and endorses the metropolitan dimension of their challenges;
- Increased powers for city and regional leaders to take a lead on growth management;
- New programmes and pipelines of infrastructure investment;
- Deregulation to attract investment to a broader range of cities;
- Relocation of functions to support rebalancing.

National policies and laws to recognise cities

There is no doubt that national governments are becoming more alert to the needs of their cities, and no longer favour an entirely equalised, 'spatially blind', approach. France's Maptam law effectively acknowledges the metropolitan character of its 12 leading cities. This gives Lyon and Marseille, in particular, stronger economic development and planning powers to address fragmentation, and takes steps to prevent Paris from being treated with undue favouritism when it comes to national approaches to urban challenges (Gittus, 2015). Meanwhile in Korea, city-regions are now recognised as single economic units through which economies of scale can be most productively achieved. And in Brazil, after the 2001 City Statute gave its cities valuable tools to implement master plans and enter into new partnerships, a new law agreed by national congress has established the first mechanisms for developing metropolitan regions in an integrated way.

These programmes and policies are very welcome for having raised the profile or investment rate in cities. Most commentators, however, argue that they do not necessarily ensure effective implementational capacity in major national cities, or simplify the complex relationships and processes between national and city governments. This highlights the fact that government initiatives are not a substitute for a clear spatial strategy, or for genuinely improved institutional mechanisms for government co-operation and delivery.

One country whose cities have largely benefited from consistent and regularly updated national urban policy is China. Its latest *National New-type Urbanisation Plan* makes clear that the next phase of urban growth has to have a greater focus on quality of life and environment. The Plan provides confidence about inter-city links, and aims for Hong Kong to be within reach of all large Chinese cities by high-speed rail by 2020. The leading cities are given clear strategic direction with target clusters, and productive regional linkages among the cities near Shanghai, Beijing and Hong Kong have been achieved (Legislative Council Panel on Commerce and Industry, 2016). However, certain externalities have emerged amid this top-down approach. The *hukou* system has fostered segregation, skewed demography and fostered under-education for many children in urban and rural areas. It also acts as a deterrent against migration between cities, which has negative effects on city economies. The model of relying on cheap labour, cheap urban land, huge export demand and the under-pricing of environmental externalities has begun to reach its limits (Tompson, 2015). China's ability to adapt its national policies and incentives will be critical if both its most globalised cities and the regional centres are to become more productive and integrated.

Increasing city and city-regional powers beyond the world city

In centralised systems it is common for second cities to seek to emulate some of a world city's autonomy and governing powers. Over the last decade, London's directly elected metropolitan mayoral system has become an attractive model for several other large British cities, because of the potential it brings for a stronger negotiating voice with central government and the mandate it offers to implement strategic decisions. London's incremental acquisition of greater powers helped inspire the creation of a Combined Authority in Greater Manchester and is now pursued by several other city regions. Over the past four years the UK Cabinet Office has partnered closely with cities on a one-to-one basis to identify bespoke solutions, resulting first in 'City Deal' packages of spending reform and more recently the devolution deals with the larger second cities.

In a similar vein, Japan's second cities have begun to make the case for their own devolution deals, and although Osaka's initial efforts were defeated in a referendum, there remains strong political appetite for greater autonomy. In Korea, mayors of the larger second-tier cities have called for the establishment of a tiered system that would give them more autonomy, through an increase of local consumption tax that they view as necessary if they are to shoulder the growing welfare burden (Im, 2015).

Infrastructure programmes

In countries where leadership, co-ordination and finance in metropolitan areas have proven challenging, national governments have tended to prioritise infrastructure programmes and projects in order to rebalance growth.

Probably the most high-profile national infrastructure strategy in recent times is China's *One Belt, One Road* initiative. It aims to radically transform China's overland links through western China to central Asia and Europe. This has massive implications for the growth of large inland cities such as Chongqing and Xi'an, which are major rail gateways in this initiative. The strategy is already giving impetus for more integrated development in the inland region – especially between Chengdu, Chongqing, Xi'an and Kunming which are now actively collaborating. *One Belt, One Road* also has the potential to allow Hong Kong to use its financial services, trade and logistics expertise to serve China's next cycle of development (Leung, 2016).

In India, national infrastructure agendas have helped drive an increase in capital investment in cities nationwide over the past decade. The JNNURM investment programme was the first demand-driven approach to cities, releasing large sums for urban projects, and has been followed up by the Smart City Mission, AMRUT and others which reflect an increased awareness of specific urban infrastructure needs and a desire to see growth in a wider group of cities. Under the current Modi administration, the mobilisation of private finance and alignment of funding with state governments has been a priority, and public capital spending has risen substantially to encourage states to complement national infrastructure efforts with their own plans. A new $4 billion National Investment and Infrastructure Fund operates as a fund of funds and will soon be an equity investor. The signs are more promising for India's cities than they have been for some time, but some observers note that mechanisms to ensure timely implementation by the states will be paramount (Nair, 2015; Bonislawski, 2016; Knowledge at Wharton, 2016).

Infrastructure items for second cities are sometimes also brought forward in tandem with greater decision-making autonomy. In the UK, the national government has identified the so-called 'Northern Powerhouse' as an opportunity to raise productivity in the country's northern city regions, arguably as well as growing political support for the Conservative Party in a part of the country where it has not been successful. The Northern Powerhouse has become the defining moniker for the project of economic rebalancing, accompanied by the city region devolution deals. There are fierce debates about whether the priority catalytic infrastructure is the high-speed line to London (HS2) or the road and rail links between the northern cities (including HS3). Given the cynicism and skepticism that surrounds British government attempts to address the North–South and London–UK divide, it is likely that the project's success will rely on visible 'quick wins' that create momentum and optimism.

As urban issues become more prominent in national political debate, national parties increasingly make promises that are linked to urban infrastructure improvements. In Canada, the victorious leader of the Liberal Party in the 2015 election, Justin Trudeau, committed to a big investment programme to deliver infrastructure investment and swept the board in Toronto in particular (Spicer,

2015). This programme follows from previous phases of investment for cities yielded from a national Gas Tax Fund and a Building Canada Fund, which were seen as welcome but inadequate relative to rising need. Infrastructure has also been at the heart of the Brazilian federal approach to urban development under the PT Party. Brazil's Growth Acceleration Programme (PAC) is now ten years old and has focused on urban logistics, energy, social services and housing in an attempt to reduce poverty. Although PAC has its critics, it has been effective in some of Brazil's medium-size, fast-growing cities as they seek to avoid the problems experienced by São Paulo in previous cycles. This has been followed by a so-called Urban Mobility Pact to finance major transport projects in response to protests at poor-quality public services. But not all national governments are able to pass major infrastructure spending plans because of political conflict. In the United States, major spending bills have been watered down and national initiatives have mostly been geared to investing in the research infrastructure for smart cities and driverless cars (The White House, 2015).

In all of these cases, one of the imperatives for national governments is to develop not just new sources of infrastructure investment for cities, but long-term strategies around which the investment is channelled. Often, infrastructure funds are distributed on a per capita basis and do not take a view about strategic needs of some cities over others. This means that, over a 10–15 year cycle, infrastructure that is not planned strategically may beget as many challenges as it solves.

Deregulation to attract investment to other cities

It is now common for national governments to recognise that second cities need to become more friendly to business and open to investment. The Korean government has relaxed development restrictions in the green belt of many of its largest cities. New legislation that allows some mayors to abolish green belts altogether is designed to encourage foreigners to invest as well as foreign workers to join and stay long term in Korean firms (Kim, 2015). Meanwhile, Japan's National Strategic Special Zones initiative features Osaka, Niigata and Fukuoka strongly as well as Tokyo, and aims to make it much easier for foreign companies to settle and for entrepreneurs to start up. These are likely just the beginning of a broader stage of reform to allow these second cities to compete internationally.

Relocation of capital city functions

Some countries have contemplated relocating their capital city not just for political reasons but also to achieve more balanced national development. Brazil and Nigeria both relocated their capitals in order to reduce congestion, make more effective use of inland regions and encourage national unity. More recently, Seoul is nearly a decade into a national project to relocate government ministries and semi-public bodies away from the capital to Sejong City in the centre of Korea. This decision is the latest in a long line of de-concentration policies, and is not without controversy as many analysts identify inefficiencies as different departments become physically separated, and many political officials continue to live in Seoul. So far, the relocation has not added political momentum for a broader programme of de-centralisation, but it does represent a bold attempt to move the centre of political gravity closer to Korea's other population centres.

Collaboration between world cities and other cities in their nations

Leaders in most world cities recognise that collaboration with other large cities in their nation states can help make a more powerful case for national reform. For these reasons, we observe several new or enhanced alliances and networks of cities at the national level. National legislators in several countries (for example, Brazil, the UK and India) are discussing or have approved (for example, France and Canada) reforms that involve all of their major metropolitan areas. Most nation states do not have an organisational vehicle through which large cities can put forward their needs to higher tiers of government, despite the fact they share very similar challenges and needs. Major cities and regions ally on housing and infrastructure, de-centralisation reform and economic development, but deliberations in many of these gatherings are rarely binding and have a more consultative character (Paradis, 2014).

Some cities have noticeably begun to make progress at building collaboration with other cities in their nation state. London is one of the clearer examples. Perceptions of London's unfair advantages in the UK system are fuelled in part by the distinctive under-performance of England's secondary cities. Only one of the eight English 'core cities' (Bristol) has a per capita output above the national average, a rare situation among developed nations. Despite the potential for deep division, London has learnt to build alliances with these second cities. In 2014, the Mayor of London and the London boroughs united with the ten UK core cities (including Cardiff and Glasgow) for the first time to call for changes to the current government finance formula (London Councils, 2014). Advocacy from the core cities often now takes place in London with the capital's direct support. Leaders of these cities reject a knee-jerk 'anti-London' position on the basis that additional freedoms for *all* cities is the best route to unlocking their economic potential. In their 2015 report *Unlocking the Power of Place*, the core cities re-iterated that "the solution should not be to undermine London, but to completely reset the UK's ambition for infrastructure investment", through new financial instruments and devolved funds (Core Cities, 2015: 27). Given that the deficit between tax raised and public spending in the UK's second cities is still more than £50 billion per year, an important case has been made for the national government to close the productivity gap in order to protect the national balance sheet. This joint agenda has informed UK Chancellor George Osborne's plans to devolve powers in customised arrangements to regions such as Greater Manchester, the West Midlands, Sheffield and the North East.

The performance gap between the world city and other national regions is perhaps most visible in Moscow. Few other Russian cities, apart from St Petersburg, have been able to build complementary roles in the urban system, and most lack the capacity or resources to shape their own longer-term investment and development needs. This imbalance risks causing unsustainable congestion effects in the capital. In the absence of a clear national regional development strategy, Russian cities have had to start building their own agenda for co-operation and knowledge-sharing. Moscow has become an active leader in the Central Federal District, helping to restore regional co-operation and investment flows between itself and other regions. The annual Moscow Urban Forum provides a rare platform for other Russian cities to access international urban expertise, exchange lessons and build solutions to their profound problems collaboratively.

But it is still fair to say that most national groups of cities do not yet have a fully functioning organisational structure through which to put forward their needs to national government. Advocacy groups such as the Federation of Canadian Municipalities, Brazil's ConCidades and Japan's Forum for Consultations offer a collective voice to urban areas, but their effectiveness is viewed as fairly modest. This is why new bodies representing the larger cities have come to the fore. One example is the Consider Canada City Alliance. It brings together the 11 largest cities to market themselves with a clearer message for investment and trade opportunities (in lieu of coherent national championing for the big cities), so these cities can ultimately grow their jobs base. These new platforms for the larger urban areas are proving more effective in some countries, especially when they partner with and receive the blessing of national-level agencies, as in the case of Canada and the UK. It has also been suggested that national governments should encourage non-institutional stakeholders (especially business leadership bodies, civic groups and resident representatives) to become more active in the governance structure to make the leadership and networks of second cities more resilient and responsive.

World cities into the future

The activity of governing world cities is, and will continue to be, a shared endeavour involving two, three, four or even five levels of government. Substantial and active co-operation between city governments and ministries of the national government is usually a prerequisite not only to the world city's successful adjustment to change, but also to the ability of other cities to find their own paths to sustainable and competitive futures.

The evidence from across the countries surveyed in this book, and others, indicates that public trust and confidence in the evolving urban dynamics set in train by globalisation can be improved with the help of a robust national urban policy. National frameworks that outline an inclusive vision of urbanisation and create predictability around long-term public infrastructure priorities and funding streams appear to offer benefits for both world cities and other cities. This kind of multi-cycle approach allows cities to understand how they should compete in global supply chains and complement the most globally oriented cities. Even in federal systems, the national tier still has responsibility to co-ordinate with state and local partners to create lasting policy and identify viable funding mechanisms.

Taking a longer view, the kind of tensions and disparities that are emerging between world cities and the other cities and rural areas in the nation state are only just beginning. New forms of dialogue between groups of cities and with higher tiers of government will need to be sustained over multiple political and economic cycles, as disparities may get more acute before they get better. The speed and purpose with which national governments adjust to the effects of world cities on the rest of the country, and make a firm stand to defend those cities with global functions, will likely become a major dimension of 21st century political leadership. It may even, in some cases, become critical to the future integrity of the nation itself.

Conclusion

In this book we have emphasised that there is no one-size-fits-all solution to the 21st century challenges facing world cities and how they might engage and partner with their nation state. Every world city is on its own growth trajectory and inherits its own distinctive history and political discourses with national government. In addition, each world city is in a dynamic regional 'system of cities' that will see regions such as Asia-Pacific and Latin America change greatly in their character and balance of powers over the next 50 years. Given that the frameworks and the opportunities for change are so different, this book does not advocate that cities can learn directly from each other's experience. It observes only that world cities and nation states appear to address development problems more effectively when there is a culture of partnership rather than partition between them. But the mechanisms and catalysts for building partnerships and making progress will always be unique to each city, which is one of the reasons why cities are such interesting places to study and analyse.

The political system in which world cities sit constitutes perhaps the biggest point of difference for how they can approach intergovernmental issues in future. What is noticeable about world cities in a unitary system is that they all have a direct and constant relationship with their central government. The extent to which top-down management and interference occurs around big projects and local decision-making, of course, varies, but this group of cities – including London, Paris, Tokyo and Seoul – are using the profile of their city leaders and their champions in the civic and business sectors to establish a permanent dialogue on the city's investment, governance and business climate needs. In these unitary systems, we have seen that it is not uncommon for political officials to take roles in both the world city and the national government during their careers, while national politicians tend to more routinely confront the issues and dilemmas of the world city. As a result, what we now see in many of these cases is a national government that recognises its responsibilities and obligations around housing, infrastructure planning, public land, business costs and regulation. This may not guarantee that incumbent governments always make choices that are conducive to successful agglomeration, or that they actively pursue reforms that result in real fiscal autonomy for their world cities. But it does offer avenues for world cities to negotiate and build coalitions horizontally and vertically in pursuit of incremental gains.

The situation for world cities in federal systems is almost entirely different and cannot be directly compared. In this book we have seen how the relationship in federal arrangements is often remote, sporadic and supportive only in moments of crisis or electoral imperative. It is not uncommon for federal intervention to be, at best, inefficient and insufficient or, at its worst, unhelpful and counter-productive. Examples may include federal immigration laws in New York and federal policies for security and cultural infrastructure in Brussels. Rarely does it make sense for world cities to go 'cap in hand' to the federal tier for money to finance major projects, or to request reforms to governance, boundaries or departmental powers. On these issues, diplomacy takes place with state or regional governments. So the relationship with the nation state will always be more limited and mediated. But these world cities cannot 'go it alone.' This book has highlighted that many of them risk becoming locked into negative path dependencies of under-investment and unmanaged metropolitan growth that will threaten their competitiveness and liveability in the coming decades. The nature of any 'new deal' between world cities and federal government will require a durable national strategy for the future of cities, full recognition of the priority of the metropolitan scale and positive signalling about future federal investment in smart technology, high-speed transport and integrated systems.

The future journey of world cities in 'special relationships' with higher-tier governments will also have a path of its own. For cities that have a privileged status within the national system, as do Moscow and Shanghai, the vertical governmental issues are rather different than in conventional unitary or federal arrangements. Investment and infrastructure needs are mostly addressed quite effectively, and there are few demands for greater fiscal autonomy. Instead, the future relationship will hinge on how well the world city and national government partner on programmes of national reform – to open their economies, incentivise the right kind of growth and ensure that redevelopment is handled effectively. These cities' success will also depend on strategies to avoid excessive demand and inflation in the world city and curb rising disparities with other national cities. Meanwhile, for other cities in special circumstances, most notably Hong Kong, political co-existence will be the challenge around which city and national governments may have to find common ground in the decades to come. All told, the advantages for 'special' cities are obvious in certain cycles of globalisation and economic growth, but in other cycles can also create externalities and these will have to be met by a renewed focus and application among city and national leaders.

By most measures, the history of world cities and nation states is a short one. There are no definitive maxims for how they ought to co-exist, and little can be taken for granted as to how their relationships will evolve in future, especially given the likely disruptors of climate change, digital technology and geopolitical conflict. What is clear is that although the century of the nation state is over, it casts a long shadow on this century of cities. The extent to which the long wave of global urbanisation will, in hindsight, come to be viewed as a success for human development will, in no small part, be down to how well nation states and their world cities team up and work together.

References

Chapter 1   Introduction: Clash of the centuries?

Allain-Dupre, D. (2015). *Capacity Building in Public Sector Investment Across Levels of Government*. Conference of the Committee of the Regions, April 15 2015, An Investment Plan for Europe: Joining Forces Panel D. Innovation and quality in local public investment. Available at http://cor.europa.eu/en/events/Documents/20150415_dorotheeallaindupre.pdf. Accessed 2016 Jan 15.

Arretche, M. (2013). Governance and Finance in Two Brazilian Metropolitan Areas. In Slack, E. and Chattopadhyay, R. (eds) *Finance and Governance of Metropolitan Areas in Federal Countries*. Oxford: Oxford University Press, pp. 49–76.

Bunnell, T. (2002). Cities for Nations: Examining the City-Nation State Relation in Information Age Malaysia. *International Journal of Urban and Regional Research*, **26**(2): 284–298.

Clark, G. and Moonen, T. (2013). *The ten traits of globally fluent Metro areas*. The Brookings Institution. Available at http://www.brookings.edu/~/media/Research/Files/Reports/2013/06/26-global-metro-traits/TenTraitsIntnl.pdf?la=en. Accessed 2016 Mar 16.

Census and Statistics Department, The Government of the Hong Kong Special Administrative Region (2015). *Hong Kong Population Projections 2015–2064*. Available at http://www.censtatd.gov.hk/hkstat/sub/sp190.jsp?productCode=B1120015. Accessed 2016 Jan 20.

Department of Statistics Singapore (2015). *Population Trends 2015*. Available at https://www.singstat.gov.sg/docs/default-source/default-document-library/publications/publications_and_papers/population_and_population_structure/population2015.pdf. Accessed 2016 Jan 20.

Dowling, J. (2014). Concern for security, nationalism and trust in government are all on the rise in a national survey. *Sydney Morning Herald*. Available at www.smh.com.au/federal-politics/political-news/concern-for-security-nationalism-and-trust-in-government-are-all-on-the-rise-in-a-national-survey-20141028-11d3bk.html#ixzz3Hw10P5Ap. Accessed 2016 Mar 16.

EMPLASA (2016). *Indicadores: Região Metropolitana de São Paulo*. Available at http://www.emplasa.sp.gov.br/Emplasa/Indicadores/gsp.asp. Accessed 2016 Jan 19.

Geographical Information Authority of Japan (2014). *2014 prefectural city by area adjustment*. Available at http://www.gsi.go.jp/KOKUJYOHO/MENCHO/201410/opening.htm. Accessed 2016 Jan 20.

Greater London Authority (2015). *2014 Round Population Projections*. Available at http://data.london.gov.uk/dataset/2014-round-population-projections. Accessed 2016 Jan 20.

Hashi, Y. (2014). Tensions in Asia Stoke Rising Nationalism in Japan. *Wall Street Journal*. Available at http://online.wsj.com/articles/SB10001424052702304610404579403492918900378. Accessed 2016 Jan 16.

Herrschel, T.J. (2014). *Cities, State and Globalisation*. London: Routledge.

Hill, R.C. and Fujita, K. (2011). The Nested City. In Jacobs, A. J. J (ed.). *The World's Cities: Contrasting Regional, National, and Global Perspectives*. Routledge: London, pp.119–128.

IBGE (2015). *Estimativas da populacao residente no Brasil e unidades da federacao com data de referencia em 1 de Julho de 2015*. Available at ftp://ftp.ibge.gov.br/Estimativas_de_Populacao/Estimativas_2015/estimativa_dou_2015_20150915.pdf. Accessed 2016 Jan 19.

INSEE (2016a). *Estimation de la population au 1er Janvier par région, département, sexe et âge de 1975 à 2015*. Available at http://www.insee.fr/fr/themes/detail.asp?reg_id=99&ref_id=estim-pop. Accessed 2016 Jan 20.

INSEE (2016b). *Panorama Ile de France*. Available at http://www.insee.fr/fr/themes/document. asp?reg_id=20&ref_id=23769. Accessed 2016 Jan 20.

Municipal Corporation of Greater Mumbai (2015). *Year Book 2015*. Available at http://mcgm. gov.in/irj/go/km/docs/documents/home/Year%20Book%202015/English%20Year%20 Book%202015%20(PART%20I).pdf. Accessed 2016 Jan 19.

National Bureau of Statistics of China (2015). *China Statistical Yearbook of 2014*. Available at http://www.stats.gov.cn/tjsj/ndsj/2014/indexeh.htm. Accessed 2016 Jan 19.

OECD Stat. (2016). *Metropolitan areas*. Available at https://stats.oecd.org/Index.aspx? DataSetCode=CITIES. Accessed 2016 Jan 19.

Office for National Statistics (2013). *Population estimates for UK, England and Wales, Scotland and Northern Ireland mid-2012*. London: ONS. Available at http://www.ons.gov.uk/ons/ regional-statistics/region.html?region=East+of+England#tab-data-tables. Accessed 2016 Jan 20.

Office for National Statistics (2014). *2012-based Subnational Population Projections for Regions in England. Sub-national population projections*. London: ONS. Available at http:// ons.gov.uk/ons/taxonomy/index.html?nscl=Sub-national+Population+Projections#tab-data-tables. Accessed 2016 Jan 20.

Ontario Ministry of Finance (2014). *Ontario Population Projections Fall 2014. Based on the 2011 census*. Available at http://www.fin.gov.on.ca/en/economy/demographics/projections/ projections2013-2041.pdf. Accessed 2016 Jan 19.

Parilla, J., Trujillo, J.L., Berube, A. and Ran, T. (2015). *Global Metromonitor 2014: An uncertain recovery*. Washington D.C.: The Brookings Institution. Available at http://www.brookings. edu/~/media/Research/Files/Reports/2015/01/22-global-metro-monitor/bmpp_GMM_final. pdf?la=en. Accessed 2016 Feb 15.

Parnreiter, C. (2013). The global city tradition. In Acuto, M. and Steele, W. (eds) *Global City Challenges: Debating a Concept, Improving the Practice*. New York: Palgrave Macmillan, p. 24.

Russian Federation Federal Statistics Services (2014). *Regions of Russia: Socio-economic indicators*. Available at http://www.gks.ru/wps/wcm/connect/rosstat_main/rosstat/ru/ statistics/publications/catalog/doc_1138623506156. Accessed 2016 Jan 20.

Russian Federation Federal Statistics Services (2015). *Evaluation of the resident population of Moscow January 1, 2015*. Available at http://moscow.gks.ru/wps/wcm/connect/rosstat_ts/ moscow/ru/statistics/population/. Accessed 2016 Jan 20.

Seib, G.F. (2014). Growing Nationalism Could Prove Disruptive. *Wall Street Journal*. Available at http://online.wsj.com/articles/SB10001424052702304811904579585743845367658; http://www.ft.com/cms/s/0/df0add1e-3fef-11e4-936b-00144feabdc0.html. Accessed 2016 Jan 15.

Seoul Metropolitan Government (2015). *Seoul Statistical Tables: The population projections*. Available at http://english.seoul.go.kr/get-to-know-us/statistics-of-seoul/seoul-statistics-by-category/. Accessed 2016 Jan 20.

Statistics Bureau of Guangdong Province (2015). *Guangdong Statistical Yearbook*. Available at: http://www.gdstats.gov.cn/tjnj/2015/directory/content.html?20-01-0. Accessed 2016 Jan 20.

Statistics Korea (2016). *Metropolitan and provincial status indicators*. Available at http:// www.index.go.kr/potal/main/EachDtlPageDetail.do?idx_cd=2729. Accessed 2016 Jan 20.

Tilly, C. (1990). *Coercion, Capital, and European States, AD 990–1990*. Oxford: Blackwell.

Tokyo Metropolitan Government (2014). *Tokyo's population (estimated)*. Available at http:// www.toukei.metro.tokyo.jp/jsuikei/js-index.htm. Accessed 2016 Jan 19.

United Nations, Department of Economic and Social Affairs, Population Division (2014). *World Urbanization Prospects: The 2014 Revision*. Available at http://esa.un.org/unpd/wup/ highlights/wup2014-highlights.pdf. Accessed 2016 Jan 20.

United States Census Bureau (2014). *Annual Estimates of the Resident Population: April 1, 2010 to July 1, 2014 – United States – Metropolitan and Micropolitan Statistical Area; and for Puerto Rico*. Available at http://factfinder.census.gov/faces/tableservices/jsf/pages/ productview.xhtml?src=bkmk. Accessed 2016 Jan 20.

Waltz, K. (1999). Globalization and Governance. *PS: Political Science & Politics*, **32**(4): 693–700.

World Bank (2009). *Systems of Cities, harnessing urbanization for growth and poverty alleviation – The World Bank Urban and Local Government Strategy*. New York: World Bank.

Chapter 2   Cities and nation states: The story so far

Acuto, M. (2013). *Global Cities, Governance and Diplomacy*. London: Routledge, pp. 2, 25–26.

Amen, M., Toly, N., McCarney, P. and Segbers, K. (eds) (2011). *Cities and Global Governance*. Surrey: Ashgate.

Ardalan, K. (2004). Liberalism and neoliberal capitalist globalization: Contradictions of the liberal democratic state. *GeoJournal*, **86**(1): 33–44.

Barber, B. (2013). *If Mayors Ruled the World: Dysfunctional Nations, Rising Cities*. New Haven: Yale University Press, p. 6.

Beaverstock, J.V. (2011). German Cities in the World City Network. Some Observations. *Raumforschung und Raumordnug*, **69**(1): 13–18.

Braudel, P. (1991). *The Mediterranean and the Mediterranean World in the Age of Philip II, Volume 1*. Berkeley: University of California Press.

Bunnell, T. (2015). Antecedent Cities and Inter-referencing Effects: Learning from and Extending Beyond Critiques of Neoliberalisation. *Urban Studies*, **52**(11): 1983–2000.

Chase, S. (2013). Federal budget gives a boost to auto sector. *The Globe and Mail*. Available at www.theglobeandmail.com/report-on-business/federal-budget-gives-a-boost-to-auto-sector/article16807848/. Accessed 2016 Feb 16.

Coatsworth, J., Cole, J., Hanagan, M., Perdue, P., Tilly, C. and Tilly, L. (2015). *Global Connections: Politics, Exchange and Social Life in World History*. Cambridge: Cambridge University Press.

Comstock, M. (2012). For Cities to Walk the Walk, National Governments Need to Pave the Way. *World Bank Sustainable Cities*. Available at http://blogs.worldbank.org/sustainablecities/trade/for-cities-to-walk-the-walk-national-governments-need-to-pave-the-way. Accessed 2016 Feb 15.

Curtis, S. (2014). Cities in a Global Order. *The World Financial Review*. Available at http://www.worldfinancialreview.com/?p=2861. Accessed 2016 Feb 15.

Curtis, S. (2016). *Global Cities and Global Order*. Oxford: Oxford University Press.

Dyson, K., Featherstone, K. and Michalopoulos, G. (1998). Strapped to the mast: EU central bankers between global financial markets and regional integration. In Coleman, W.D. and Underhill, G.R.D. (eds). *Regionalism and Global Economic Integration: Europe, Asia and the Americas*. London and New York: Routledge.

Frankopan, P. (2015). *The Silk Roads: A new history of the world*. London: Bloomsbury.

Friedmann, J. (1986). The world city hypothesis. *Development and Change*, **17**(1): 69–83.

Fukuyama, F. (1989). The End of History? In The National Interest (1992). *The End of History and the Last Man*. New York: The Free Press.

Germain, R.D. (1997). *The International Organization of Credit: States and Global Finance in the World-Economy*. Cambridge: Cambridge University Press.

Giersig, N. (2008). *Multilevel urban governance and the European City: discussing metropolitan reforms in Stockholm and Helsinki*. Wiesbaden: VS Verlag.

Gordon, I. (1999). Internationalisation and Urban Competition. *Urban Studies*, **36**: 5–6, 1001–1016.

Herrschel, T.J. (2014). *Cities, State and Globalisation*. London: Routledge.

Hill, R.C. (2004). Cities and nested hierarchies. *International Social Science Journal*, **56**(181): 373–384.

Hill, R.C. and Fujita, F. (2003). In Jacobs, A.J. (ed.) (2013). *The World's Cities: Contrasting Regional, National, and Global Perspectives*. New York: Routledge, p. 119.

Hill, R. C. and Kim, J.W. (2000). Global cities and developmental states: New York, Tokyo and Seoul. *Urban Studies*, **37**: 2167–2195.

Horsman, M. and Marshall, A. (1994). *After the Nation-State: Citizens, tribalism, and the new world disorder*. London: Harper Collins.

Istrate, E. and Nadeau, C.A. (2012). *Global Metro Monitor 2012: Slowdown, recovery and inter-dependence*. Washington D.C.: The Brookings Institution. Available at http://www.brookings.edu/~/media/research/files/reports/2012/11/30-global-metro-monitor/30-global-monitor.pdf. Accessed 2016 Feb 15.

Jessop, B. (1997). The entrepreneurial city: Re-imaging localities, redesigning economic govern-ance, or restructuring capital? In Jewson, N. and MacGregor, S. (eds). *Realising Cities: New Spatial Divisions and Social Transformation*. London: Routledge, pp. 28–41.

Katz, B. and Bradley, J. (2013). *The Metropolitan Revolution: How Cities and Metros Are Fixing Our Broken Politics and Fragile Economy*. Washington, D.C.: Brookings Institution Press.

Knox, P. and Taylor, P. (1995). *World Cities in a World-System*. Cambridge: Cambridge University Press.

Kübler, D. and Rochat, P. (2013). Governance and Finance of Large Metropolitan Areas in Federal Systems: Switzerland. In Slack, E. and Chattopadhyay, R. (eds). *Governance and Finance of Metropolitan Areas in Federal Systems*. Oxford University Press: Toronto, pp. 254–289.

Kynge, J. and Wheatley, J. (2015). Emerging Markets: Fixing a broken model. *The Financial Times*. Available at http://www.ft.com/cms/s/0/945c837e-4fc7-11e5-b029-b9d50a74fd14.html?siteedition=uk#axzz3kR1qiOem. Accessed 2016 Feb 15.

Lachmann, R. (2002). *Capitalists in Spite of Themselves: Elite Conflict and Economic Transitions in Early Modern Europe*. Oxford: Oxford University Press.

Lachmann, R. (2010). *States and Power*. Cambridge: Policy Press.

Langley, P. (2002). *World Financial Orders: An Historical International Political Economy*. London: Routledge, p. 140.

Massey, R. (2007). *World City*. Cambridge: Polity, p. 35.

McNeely, C. (1995). *Constructing the Nation-state: International Organization and Prescriptive Action*. London: Greenwood Press.

Mount, H. (2015). Modern London is the true heir of ancient Greece. *Financial Times*. Available at www.ft.com/cms/s/0/f948e1ec-7182-11e5-9b9e-690fdae72044.html. Accessed 2016 May 24.

NYC Mayor's Office of Operations (2010). *The Impact of the American Recovery and Reinvestment Act on New York City: Highlights from One Year of Implementation*. Available at www.nyc.gov/html/ops/nycstim/downloads/pdf/human_services_council_presentation_mayors_office_of_operations.pdf. Accessed 2016 Feb 15.

OECD (2005). *OECD Territorial Reviews: Seoul, Korea 2005*. Paris: OECD.

OECD (2006). *OECD Territorial Reviews: Competitive Cities in the Global Economy*. Paris: OECD.

OECD (2010). *Cities and Climate Change*. Paris: OECD.

OECD (2013). *SYNOPSIS: Third Ministerial Meeting of the OECD Territorial Development Policy Committee*. Paris: OECD.

OECD (2016). *Trends Shaping Education*. Paris: OECD.

Ohmae, K. (1995). *The End of the Nation State: The Rise of Regional Economies*. New York: Simon and Schuster Inc.

Parnreiter, C. (2013). The global city tradition. In Acuto. M. and Steele, W. (eds). *Global City Challenge: Debating a Concept, Improving the Practice*. New York: Palgrave Macmillan, p. 24.

Pirenne, H. (1925). *Medieval Cities: Their Origins and the Revival of Trade*. Princeton: Princeton University Press.

Poggi, G. (2004). Theories of state formation. In Amenta, E., Nash, K. and Scott, A. (eds). *The Wiley-Blackwell Companion to Political Sociology*. Oxford: Blackwell.

Polese, M. (2005). Cities and National Economic Growth: A Reappraisal. *Urban Studies*, **8**: 1429–1451.

Robinson, J. (2002). Global and World Cities: A View from Off the Map. *International Journal of Urban and Regional Research*, **26**(3): 531–554.

Rohlen, T. (2002). Cosmopolitan Cities and Nation States: Open Economics, Urban Dynamics, and Government in East Asia. *Discussion Papers*. Asia Pacific Research Centre, Stanford University.

Sassen, S. (1999). Embedding the global in the national: Implications for the role of the state. In Smith, D.A., Solinger, D.J. and Topik, S. (eds). *States and Sovereignty in the Global Economy*. London: Routledge.

Sassen, S. (2000). *Cities in a World Economy*, 2nd edition. New York: Sage Publications.

Sassen, S. (2001). *The Global City: New York, London, Tokyo*, 2nd edition. Princeton: Princeton University Press.

Sassen, S. (2005). The global city: introducing a concept. *Brown Journal of World Affairs*, **11**(2), 29. Available at <http://www.saskiasassen.com/pdfs/publications/the-global-city-brown.pdf>. Accessed 2015 Nov 4.

Singapore Ministry of Finance (2009). *Budget Highlights Financial Year 2009: Keeping Jobs Building for the Future*. Available at www.mof.gov.sg/budget_2009/speech_toc/downloads/ FY2009_Budget_Highlights.pdf. Accessed 2016 Feb 16.

Slack, E. and Côté, A. (2014). *Comparative Urban Governance. Future of Cities*. Working Paper. London: Government Office for Science.

Smith, A. (1776). *The Wealth of Nations*. London: Penguin.

Smith, D.A., Solinger, D.J. and Topik, S. (eds) (1999). *States and Sovereignty in the Global Economy*. London: Routledge, pp. 7–8.

Smith, N. (2002). New globalism, new urbanism: Gentrification as global urban strategy. *Antipode*, **34**(3): 434.

Taylor, P. (1995). World Cities and territorial states: The rise of and fall of their mutuality. In Knox, P. and Taylor, P. (eds). *World Cities in a World-System*. Cambridge: Cambridge University Press.

Therborn, G. (2011). End of a paradigm: The current crisis and the idea of stateless cities. *Environment and Planning A* 2011, **43**: 272–285.

Tilly, C. (1990). *Coercion, Capital, and European States, AD 990–1990*. Oxford: Blackwell.

Tompson, W. (2015). *OECD Urban Policy Reviews: China 2015*. Presentation at Sciences Po, Campus de Reims, March 2015. Available at http://www.slideshare.net/CentreforCities/ city-horizons-what-does-the-future-hold-for-chinas-cities. Accessed 2016 Feb 15.

Turok, I. and Parnell, S. (2009). Reshaping Cities, Rebuilding Nations: The Role of National Urban Policy. *Urban Forum*, **20**: 157–174.

Watson, V. (2013). The Postcolonial Dimension. In Acuto, M. and Steele, W. (eds). *Global City Challenge: Debating a Concept, Improving the Practice*. New York: Palgrave Macmillan.

Weber, A. (1899). *The Growth of Cities in the Nineteenth Century*. New York: MacMillan.

World Bank (2009). *Systems of Cities, harnessing urbanization for growth and poverty alleviation – The World Bank Urban and Local Government Strategy*. Washington D. C.: The World Bank.

World Bank Institute (2014). *Why Local Governments Need to Care About Municipal Finances*. Available at https://olc.worldbank.org. Accessed 2016 May 24.

Xu, J. and Yeh, A.G. (eds) (2011). *Governance and Planning of Mega-City Regions*. London: Routledge.

Young, G. (2008). *The Fiscal Relationships between Capital Cities and their National Governments*. Washington D.C.: Brookings Institution.

Zhang, L.Y. (2014). Dynamics and Constraints of State-led Global City Formation in Emerging Economies: The Case of Shanghai. *Urban Studies*, **51**(6): 1162–1178.

Chapter 3   London: From centralism to negotiated growth management

AECOM (2015). *London 2065*. Available at http://www.aecom.com/wp-content/uploads/2015/10/ AECOM_Cities_London_2065_Manifesto.pdf. Accessed 2016 Feb 10.

Agnew, H. and Jenkins, P. (2016). Three scenarios for the City after Brexit. *Financial Times*. Available at www.ft.com/cms/s/0/5efe1f9a-484f-11e6-b387-64ab0a67014c.html. Accessed 2016 Jul 29.

Airports Commission (2015). *Airports Commission: Final Report*. Available at https://www. gov.uk/government/uploads/system/uploads/attachment_data/file/440316/airports-commission-final-report.pdf. Accessed 2016 Feb 11.

BBC (2015). George Osborne: Councils to keep £26bn in business rates. *BBC News*. Available at: http://www.bbc.co.uk/news/business-34445311. Accessed 2016 Feb 11.

BBC (2016). David Cameron: We'll directly commission 13,000 new homes. *BBC News*. Available at http://www.bbc.co.uk/news/uk-politics-35217418. Accessed 2016 Feb 11.

Blinder, S. (2015). UK public opinion toward immigration: Overall attitudes and level of concern. *The Migration Observatory at the University of Oxford.* Available at http://www. migrationobservatory.ox.ac.uk/briefings/uk-public-opinion-toward-immigration-overall-attitudes-and-level-concern. Accessed 2016 Feb 10.

Brown, R. (2016). *Strange Days – London after the EU Referendum.* London: Centre for London.

CAA (2014). *Airport Data from 1990 Onwards.* Available at https://www.caa.co.uk/Data-and-analysis/UK-aviation-market/Airports/Datasets/UK-Airport-data/Airport-data-1990-onwards/. Accessed 2016 Feb 11.

Chakrabortty, A. (2013). London's economic boom leaves rest of Britain behind. *The Guardian.* Available at http://www.theguardian.com/business/2013/oct/23/london-south-east-economic-boom. Accessed 2016 Feb 11.

Champion, T. (2008). The 'escalator region' hypothesis and the regional cities of England: A research agenda. *Presentation for LSE SERC Urban and Regional Economics Seminar.* Available at http://cep.lse.ac.uk/seminarpapers/31-10-08-CHA.pdf. Accessed 2016 Feb 11.

Clark, G. (2015). *London 1991–2021: The Making of a World City.* Chichester: Wiley.

Communities and Local Government Committee (2014). *First Report Devolution in England: The case for local government.* UK Parliament. Available at http://www.publications.parliament. uk/pa/cm201415/cmselect/cmcomloc/503/50301.htm. Accessed 2016 Feb 10.

Communities and Local Government Committee (2016). *Devolution: The next five years and beyond.* London: House of Commons.

Crossrail (2016). *Funding.* Available at http://www.crossrail.co.uk/about-us/funding. Accessed 2016 Feb 11.

EIU (2012). *Hot Spots: Benchmarking Global City Competitiveness.* London: The Economist. Available at http://www.economistinsights.com/sites/default/files/downloads/Hot%20 Spots.pdf. Accessed 2016 Jan 19.

Freedland, J. (2014). London is Ukip's worst nightmare. *The Guardian.* Available at http:// www.theguardian.com/commentisfree/2014/may/23/london-ukip-nightmare-labout-tories-local-elections-farage. Accessed 2016 Feb 11.

Gainsbury, S. and Neville, S. (2015). Austerity's £18bn impact on local services. *Financial Times.* Available at http://www.ft.com/cms/s/2/5fcbd0c4-2948-11e5-8db8-c033edba8a6e. html#axzz3xdje0RF7. Accessed 2016 Feb 11.

GLA (2015). *Land and Development: London Land Commission.* Available at https://www. london.gov.uk/what-we-do/housing-and-land/land-and-development/london-land-commission. Accessed 2016 Feb 11.

Gordon, I.R. and Travers, T. (2010). London: Planning the ungovernable city. *City, Culture and Society,* **1**(2): 49–55.

HM Government (2014). *London Growth Deal.* Available at https://www.gov.uk/government/ uploads/system/uploads/attachment_data/file/398867/23_London_Enterprise_Panel_and_ Greater_London_Growth_Deal.pdf. Accessed 2016 Feb 11.

HM Government (2015). *£58m Expansion of Growth Deal Boosts Local Plan for London Economy.* Available at https://www.gov.uk/government/uploads/system/uploads/attachment_ data/file/399384/London_Factsheet.pdf. Accessed 2016 Feb 11.

HM Treasury (2014). Chancellor: 'We need a Northern powerhouse', *HM Treasury press release.* 23 June 2014.

Holman, N., Fernandez-Arrigoitia, M., Scanlon, K. and Whitehead, C. (2015). *Housing in London: Addressing The Supply Crisis.* London: LSE London.

Hopkirk, E. (2016). Kerslake: Even housebuilders doubt government's housing commitment. *BD Online.* Available at http://www.bdonline.co.uk/kerslake-even-housebuilders-doubt-government's-housing-commitment/5079884.article. Accessed 2016 Feb 11.

Lehrer, N. (2015). Why Paris became the Jihadi Jackpot. *The Nation,* November 17. Available at http:// www.thenation.com/article/why-paris-became-the-jihadi-jackpot/. Accessed 2016 Feb 11.

LEP (2016). *A Growth Deal for London.* Available at https://lep.london/publication/growth-deal-london. Accessed 2016 Feb 11.

London Assembly (2016). *Economy Committee – 6 July 2016 Transcript of Item 3 – Brexit and the London Economy.* Available at www.london.gov.uk/moderngov/documents/b14586/ Minutes%20-%20Appendix%201%20-%20Transcript%20Wednesday%2006-Jul-2016%20 14.30%20Economy%20Committee.pdf. Accessed 2016 Jul 29.

London Finance Commission (2013). *Raising the capital: The report of the London Finance Commission.* Available at https://www.london.gov.uk/sites/default/files/gla_migrate_files_destination/Raising%20the%20capital_0.pdf. Accessed 2016 Feb 11.

Massey, D. (1979). In what sense a regional problem?. *Regional Studies,* **13**(2): 233–243.

McGough, L. (2016). Three questions the new London Finance Commission needs to answer. *Centre for Cities.* Available at www.centreforcities.org/blog/three-questions-new-london-finance-commission-needs-answer. Accessed 2016 Jul 29.

Metro Dynamics (2016). *AdiEU: The Impact of Brexit on UK Cities.* Available at http://static1.squarespace.com/static/55e973a3e4b05721f2f7988c/t/577a9b87be65944fd9c7907e/1467653000392/AdiEU+-+4+July.pdf. Accessed 2016 Jul 29.

OECD Stat. (2014). *Metropolitan areas.* Available at https://stats.oecd.org/Index.aspx?DataSetCode=CITIES. Accessed 2016 Jan 19.

ONS (2013). *Non-UK Born Population of England and Wales Quadrupled Between 1951 and 2011.* Available at http://www.ons.gov.uk/ons/rel/census/2011-census-analysis/immigration-patterns-and-characteristics-of-non-uk-born-population-groups-in-england-and-wales/summary.html. Accessed 2016 Feb 11.

Parilla, J., Trujillo, J.L., Berube, A. and Ran, T. (2015). *Global Metromonitor 2014: An uncertain recovery.* Washington D.C.: The Brookings Institution. Available at http://www.brookings.edu/~/media/Research/Files/Reports/2015/01/22-global-metro-monitor/bmpp_GMM_final.pdf?la=en. Accessed 2016 Feb 15.

Pickford, J. (2013). Politics: Running the 'ungovernable' city. *The Financial Times.* Available at http://www.ft.com/cms/s/2/75ae6d62-7d14-11e2-adb6-00144feabdc0.html#axzz3zqoXX8FW. Accessed 2016 Feb 11.

PwC (2016). *The potential economic impact of Brexit for London, the UK and Europe.* Available at http://pwc.blogs.com/press_room/2016/07/the-potential-economic-impact-of-brexit-for-london-the-uk-and-europe.html. Accessed 2016 Jul 29.

Rogers, S. and Blight, G. (2012). London 2012: What's the real price of the Olympic games? Visualised. *The Guardian.* Available at http://www.theguardian.com/sport/datablog/interactive/2012/jul/26/london-2012-price-olympic-games-visualised?guni=Graphic:in%20body%20link. Accessed 2016 Feb 11.

Sheffield Political Economy Research Institute (2015). Public Infrastructure Investment & Business Activity in the English Regions. Brief No.15. Available at http://speri.dept.shef.ac.uk/wp-content/uploads/2015/08/SPERI-Brief-No.15-Public-infrastructure-investment-business-activity-in-the-English-regions.pdf. Accessed 2016 Feb 25.

Sullivan, C. (2016). London's surplus public sector land 'can take 130,000 homes'. *Financial Times.* Available at http://www.ft.com/cms/s/0/c2635fc4-c1fd-11e5-993a-d18bf6826744.html#axzz3zqoXX8FW. Accessed 2016 Feb 11.

Taylor, P., Evans, D., Hoyler, M., Derudder, B. and Pain, K. (2009). The UK Space Economy as Practised by Advanced Producer Service Firms: Identifying Two Distinctive Polycentric City-Regional Processes in Contemporary Britain. *International Journal of Urban and Regional Research,* **33**(3):700–718.

The Economist (2016). Gotham on Thames. February 27. Available at http://www.economist.com/news/finance-and-economics/21693610-many-britons-think-london-too-big-it-really-too-small-gotham-thames. Accessed 2016 Feb 27.

Topham, G. (2016). Government backs TfL plan to run London's commuter rail services. *The Guardian.* Available at http://www.theguardian.com/uk-news/2016/jan/21/tfl-londons-commuter-rail-services-department-for-transport. Accessed 2016 Feb 11.

Transport for London (2016). *How we are funded.* Available at https://tfl.gov.uk/corporate/about-tfl/how-we-work/how-we-are-funded. Accessed 2016 Feb 11.

Travers, T. (2004). *The Politics of London: Governing and Ungovernable City.* Basingstoke: Palgrave Macmillan.

Travers, T. (2015). *London Boroughs at 50.* London: Biteback Publishing.

World Economic Forum (2015). *The Global Competitiveness Report 2015–16.* Geneva: World Economic Forum. Available at http://www3.weforum.org/docs/gcr/2015-2016/Global_Competitiveness_Report_2015-2016.pdf. Accessed 2016 Jan 19.

YouGov (2016). *YouGov / Evening Standard Survey Results: Fieldwork: 1st – 5th July 2016.* Available at https://d25d2506sfb94s.cloudfront.net/cumulus_uploads/document/4s7vvulwm6/EveningStandardResults_London_SadiqMayor_EURef_Housing_Independence_Website.pdf. Accessed 2016 Jul 29.

Chapter 4 Paris: Manufacturing a metropolis amid institutional complexity

ANRU (2016). *Nouveau programme national de renouvellement urbain: L'état d'avancement du programme au 14 janvier 2016*. Available at http://www.anru.fr/index.php/fre/Programmes/Programme-National-pour-la-Renovation-Urbaine/L-etat-d-avancement-du-programme-au-14-janvier-2016. Accessed 2016 Jan 29.

Béhar, D. (2013). Les paradoxes du rôle de l'État dans la gouvernance du Grand Paris. *Métropolitiques*. Available at http://www.metropolitiques.eu/Les-paradoxes-du-role-de-l-Etat.html. Accessed 2016 Jan 29.

Bowie, D. (2013a). *Governing Metropolitan Regions Within a Localist Agenda*. Report of second seminar, Institut d'Urbanisme de Paris, Université Paris – Est Creteuil 22nd February 2013. Available at www.regionalstudies.org/uploads/Governing_Metropolitan_Regions_within_a_Localist_agenda.Creteuil_summary.REVISED.28.3.doc. Accessed 2016 Jan 29.

Bowie, D. (2013b). *Report of the third seminar of the RSA research network on governing metropolitan regions within a localist agenda*. Available at http://webcache.googleusercontent.com/search?q=cache:dABWNT5L1dYJ:www.regionalstudies.org/uploads/RSA_Berlin_event._Summary_report.doc.REV.16.1.14.docx+&cd=2&hl=en&ct=clnk&gl=uk. Accessed 2016 Jan 29.

Cole, A. (2014). Not saying, not doing: Convergences, contingencies and causal mechanisms of state reform and decentralisation in Hollande's France. *French Politics*, **12**: 104–135.

Crouch, C. and Le Galès, P. (2012). Cities as national champions?. *Journal of European Public Policy*, **19**(3): 405–419.

Delourme, V. (2015). Vendredi, c'est Grand Paris. *Libération*. Available at http://www.liberation.fr/france/2015/12/31/vendredi-c-est-grand-paris_1423771. Accessed 2016 Jan 29.

Deraëvea, S. (2014). Pôles métropolitains: The French approach towards inter-city networking. *Regional Studies, Regional Science*, **1**(1): 43–50.

EIU (2012). *Hot Spots: Benchmarking Global City Competitiveness*. London: The Economist. Available at http://www.economistinsights.com/sites/default/files/downloads/Hot%20Spots.pdf. Accessed 2016 Jan 19.

EPAPS (2016). *Paris–Saclay–Enjeux: Projet Urbain*. Available at http://www.epaps.fr/enjeux/un-projet-urbain/. Accessed 2016 Jan 29.

Floc'h, B. (2015). Le Cambridge français sur les rails, malgré les réticences. *Le Monde.* Available at http://www.lemonde.fr/education/article/2015/12/24/le-cambridge-francais-remise-sur-les-rails_4837908_1473685.html#04IRlafPgKogFKeH.99. Accessed 2016 Jan 29.

Gittus, S. (2015). Que change la loi NOTRe pour les collectivités territoriales?. *Le Monde.* Available at http://www.lemonde.fr/les-decodeurs/visuel/2015/05/28/que-change-la-loi-notre-pour-les-collectivites-territoriales_4642897_4355770.html#lS7XFAhgJLtWgf2U.99. Accessed 2015 Jan 29.

Gonguet, J.P. (2014). Valls remet le Grand Paris sur ses rails. *La Tribune*. Available at http://www.latribune.fr/actualites/economie/france/20141014trib21ff7038a/valls-remet-le-grand-paris-sur-ses-rails.html. Accessed 2016 Jan 29.

House, J. (2014). *Controlling Paris: Armed Forces and Counter-Revolution, 1789–1848*. New York: New York University Press.

Husson, L.E. (2015). Région, département, commune: qui s'occupe de quoi désormais?. *Challenges*. Available at http://www.challenges.fr/politique/elections-regionales/20150729.CHA8246/region-departement-commune-qui-s-occupe-de-quoi-desormais.html#Compétences regions. Accessed 2016 Jan 28.

IAU île-de-France (2015). *Les contrats de développement territorial (CDT)*. Available at http://www.iau-idf.fr/savoir-faire/nos-travaux/amenagement-et-territoires/amenagement/les-contrats-de-developpement-territorial-cdt.html. Accessed 2016 Jan 29.

île-de-France (2015). *État-Région: d'ici 2020, 7,3 milliards d'euros d'investissements publics*. Available at http://www.iledefrance.fr/fil-actus-region/etat-region-2020-73-milliards-euros-investissements-publics. Accessed 2016 Jan 29.

île-de-France (2016). *Création du conseil stratégique pour l'attractivité et l'emploi*. Available at http://www.iledefrance.fr/decisions-du-cr/creation-du-conseil-strategique-attractivite-emploi. Accessed 2016 Jan 28.

Jerome, B. (2014). Grand Paris: Valls veut augmenter certaines taxes pour financer les transports. *Le Monde*. Available at http://www.lemonde.fr/politique/article/2014/10/13/grand-paris-valls-veut-augmenter-certaines-taxes-pour-financer-les-transports_4505018_823448. html#K6yT410KsmxttUcJ.99. Accessed 2016 Jan 28.

Jerome, B. (2015). Métropole du Grand Paris: des compétences limitées et des pouvoirs contestés. *Le Monde*. Available at: http://www.lemonde.fr/politique/article/2015/12/29/metropole-du-grand-paris-des-competences-limitees-et-des-pouvoirs-contestes_4839045_823448. html#bfGxUF3ug6AcUyml.99. Accessed 2016 Jan 28.

Le Figaro (2014). Réforme régions: ultimatum des élus régionaux. *Le Figaro*. Available at http://www.lefigaro.fr/flash-actu/2014/05/12/97001-20140512FILWWW00357-reforme-regions-ultimatum-des-elus-regionaux.php. Accessed 2016 Jan 28.

Lefevre, C. (2012) In Kantor, P., Lefèvre, C., Saito, A., Savitch, H.V. and Thornley, A. (eds). *Struggling Giants: City-region Governance in London, New York, Paris, and Tokyo*. Minneapolis: University of Minnesota Press.

Lehrer, N. (2015). Why Paris became the Jihadi Jackpot. *The Nation*, Nov. 17. Available at http://www.thenation.com/article/why-paris-became-the-jihadi-jackpot/. Accessed 2016 Feb 11.

Les Echos (2016). Nouveau Grand Paris : l'avancement du projet. *Les Echos*. Available at http://www.lesechos.fr/industrie-services/dossiers/0203204107550-nouveau-grand-paris-l-avancement-du-projet-671896.php. Accessed 2016 Jan 28.

Mérot, G. (2015). J.F. Carenco: Paris–Saclay travaille pour l'avenir de la France. *Le Journal du Grand Paris*. Available at https://www.lejournaldugrandparis.fr/pour-j-f-carenco-paris-saclay-travaille-pour-lavenir-de-la-france/. Accessed 2016 Jan 29.

Métropole du Grand Paris – Mission de Préfiguration (2015). Les Acteurs en presence. Available at http://www.prefig-metropolegrandparis.fr/Y-voir-clair-dans-le-Grand-Paris/Les-acteurs-en-presence. Accessed 2016 Jan 29.

Mission Interministérielle pour le projet Métropolitan Aix-Marseille-Provence (2015). *Aix-Marseille-Provence Métropole mode d'emploi: Présentation du cadre institutionnel à destination des acteurs locaux*. Available at http://www.mouvement-metropole.fr/Public/Files/home_resource_doc/doc_institutionnel_ca43c5aa12.pdf. Accessed 2016 Jan 28.

MobiliCities (2015). Grand Paris: Manuel Valls précise le calendrier CDG Express. *MobiliCities*. Available at http://www.mobilicites.com/011-4251-Grand-Paris-Manuel-Valls-precise-le-calendrier-de-CDG-Express.html. Accessed 2016 Jan 28.

Mouvement Métropole (2015). *Loi NOTRE: Mission Interministérielle pour le projet Métropolitan Aix-Marseille-Provence*. Available at http://www.mouvement-metropole.fr/newsletter/voir/id/4-juillet-2015/categorie/19-energies/article/28-loi-notre.sls. Accessed 2016 Jan 29.

OECD (2013). *Towards more inclusive growth in the metropolitan area of Aix-Marseille: International insights*. Paris: OECD. Available at http://www.oecd.org/regional/regional-policy/Summary-Aix-Marseille.pdf. Accessed 2016 Jan 29.

OECD Stat. (2014). *Metropolitan areas*. Available at https://stats.oecd.org/Index. aspx?DataSetCode=CITIES. Accessed 2016 Jan 19.

Parilla, J., Trujillo, J.L., Berube, A. and Ran, T. (2015). *Global Metromonitor 2014: An uncertain recovery*. Washington D.C.: The Brookings Institution. Available at www.brookings.edu/~/media/Research/Files/Reports/2015/01/22-global-metro-monitor/bmpp_GMM_final. pdf?la=en. Accessed 2016 Feb 15.

Pumain, D. (1997). City size dynamics in urban systems. In van der Leeuw, S.E. and Mcglade, J. (eds). *Time Process and Structured Transformation in Archaeology*. London: Routledge, pp. 97–117.

République Française (2014). *Grand Paris: "passer des promesses à la concrétisation"*. Available at http://www.gouvernement.fr/grand-paris-passer-des-promesses-a-la-concretisation. Accessed 2016 Jan 29.

République Française (2015). *Grand Paris, capitale du 21e siècle*. Comité interministériel – 15 Octobre 2015 présidé par Manuel Valls, Premier Ministre: Dossier de Presse. Available at http://www.societedugrandparis.fr/wp-content/uploads/2015/10/15-octobre-2015-cim-grand-paris-dossier-de-presse.pdf. Accessed 2016 Jan 29.

République Française (2016). *Le Commissariat Général à l'Investissement*. Available at http://www.gouvernement.fr/le-commissariat-general-a-l-investissement. Accessed 2016 Jan 29.

Société du Grand Paris (2014). *Philippe Yvin nommé president du Directoire*. Available at http://www.societedugrandparis.fr/actualite/philippe-yvin-nomme-president-du-directoire. Accessed 2016 Jan 28.

Société du Grand Paris (2015). *Ministères de tutelle*. Available at http://www.societedugrandparis.fr/entreprise/acteurs/ministeres-de-tutelle. Accessed 2016 Jan 28.

Subra, P. and Newman, P. (2008). Governing Paris – Planning and political conflict in Île-de-France. *European Planning Studies*, **16**(4): 521–535.

Vie Publique (2015). *Paris: Collectivité Territoriale Spécifique*. Available at http://www.vie-publique.fr/decouverte-institutions/institutions/approfondissements/paris-collectivite-territoriale-specifique.html. Accessed 2016 Jan 28.

Wiel, M. (2015). Remettre la démarche du Grand Paris sur de bons rails. *Métropolitiques*. Available at http://www.metropolitiques.eu/Remettre-la-demarche-du-Grand.html. Accessed 2016 Jan 29.

World Economic Forum (2015). *The Global Competitiveness Report 2015–16*. Geneva: World Economic Forum. Available at http://www3.weforum.org/docs/gcr/2015-2016/Global_Competitiveness_Report_2015-2016.pdf. Accessed 2016 Jan 19.

Chapter 5   Seoul: Lessons from de-centralisation and de-concentration

An, J. (2016). War of nerves as Bak Won-sun, Bak Geun-hye [argue] over budget responsibility. *Jugan Hyeondae News*. Available at http://www.hyundaenews.com/sub_read.html?uid=19869&section=sc5&section2=%BB%E7%C8%B8%C0%CF%B9%DD. Accessed 2016 Feb 25.

Bak, Y. (2015). Special administrative session of government to discuss 'Lotte situation' tomorrow – Jaebeol corporate governance reforms will be pushed on. *MBC News*. Available at http://imnews.imbc.com/replay/2015/nw1800/article/3745447_17808.html Accessed 2016 Feb 25.

Chosun Ilbo (2016). Seoul's Population Aging Rapidly. *Chosun Ilbo*. Available at http://english.chosun.com/site/data/html_dir/2016/01/07/2016010701772.html. Accessed 2016 Feb 25.

Davis, D. (2015). A Conversation with KDI's Joon-Kyung Kim on Korea's Growth Potential. *Asia Foundation*. Available at asiafoundation.org/in-asia/2015/02/25/a-conversation-with-kdis-joon-kyung-kim-on-koreas-growth-potential/. Accessed 2016 Feb 25.

Douglass, M. (2000). Mega-urban Regions and World City Formation. *Urban Studies*, **37**(12): 2315–2335.

EIU (2012). *Hot Spots: Benchmarking Global City Competitiveness*. London: The Economist. Available at http://www.economistinsights.com/sites/default/files/downloads/Hot%20Spots.pdf. Accessed 2016 Jan 19.

Hill, R.C. and Kim, J.W. (2000). Global cities and developmental states: New York, Tokyo and Seoul. *Urban Studies*, **37**: 2167–2195.

Im, S. (2015). Mayors of large cities say 'we should establish three different levels of city, along with other measures, to expand our autonomy'. *Yeonhap News*. Available at http://www.yonhapnews.co.kr/bulletin/2015/04/16/0200000000AKR20150416166400053.HTML. Accessed 2016 Feb 25.

KBS News (2016). Seoul municipal budget policy set in accordance with civic groups. *KBS News*. Available at http://news.kbs.co.kr/news/view.do?ncd=3215976. Accessed 2016 Feb 25.

Kim, C. (2006). *Urban and Metropolitan Management of Seoul: Past and Present*. Presentation at World Bank Institute Workshop on Metropolitan Management Challenges in China. Available at http://info.worldbank.org/etools/docs/library/238544/3_1Kim_Seoul_onlyEN.pdf. Accessed 2016 Feb 25.

Kim, H.J. (2015). Investment, greenbelt rules to ease up. *Korean Joongang Daily*. Available at http://koreajoongangdaily.joins.com/news/article/article.aspx?aid=3003893&cloc=joongangdaily%7Chome%7Cnewslist1. Accessed 2016 Mar 16.

Kim, S. and Winkler, M. (2013). Seoul mayor says cooperating with north to produce leverage. *Bloomberg*. Available at http://www.bloomberg.com/news/articles/2013-08-27/seoul-mayor-sees-south-cooperation-with-north-creating-leverage. Accessed 2016 Feb 25.

Korea Research Institute for Human Settlements (2013). *Growth Management of the Capital Region: A Primer on Korean Planning and Policy*. Korea Research Institute for Human Settlements. Available at http://eng.krihs.re.kr/publication/gBbsView.do;jsessionid=977F92 2EBC8768FE786802B20FE6AEDC?cate=pkpp&seq=28. Accessed 2016 Feb 25.

Kwaak, J. (2014). Seoul Mayor: Politicians Should Eliminate Themselves. *Wall Street Journal*. Available at http://blogs.wsj.com/korearealtime/2014/02/24/seoul-mayor-politicians-should-eliminate-themselves/. Accessed 2016 Feb 25.

Kyunghyang Shinmun (2012). Seoul's 'New Town' policy's concept and direction are correct. *Kyunghyang Shinmun*. Available at http://libweb.anglia.ac.uk/referencing/harvard.htm. Accessed 2016 Feb 25.

Lee, S. (2014). *Regional Development Strategy in Korea*. Presentation, Study Visit Program for NAOG and Senior Officials from Mongolia LOGOD.

Mun, Y. (2008). The Joseon Governor-General's Imitation of Western Corporatism and Colonial Transformation: Financial Corporatism Legislation. *Journal of Korean Social Studies*, **32**: 309–332.

OECD (2005). *OECD Territorial Reviews: Seoul, Korea*. Paris: OECD.

OECD (2012). *OECD Urban Policy Reviews: Korea 2012*. Paris: OECD.

OECD Stat. (2014). *Metropolitan areas*. Available at https://stats.oecd.org/Index.aspx? DataSetCode=CITIES. Accessed 2016 Jan 19.

Oh, Y. (2014). Toward mature local economy. *Joongang Daily*. Available at http://koreajoongangdaily.joins.com/news/article/article.aspx?aid=2990209. Accessed 2016 Feb 25.

Parilla, J., Trujillo, J.L., Berube, A. and Ran, T. (2015). *Global Metromonitor 2014: An uncertain recovery*. Washington D.C.: The Brookings Institution. Available at http://www.brookings.edu/~/media/Research/Files/Reports/2015/01/22-global-metro-monitor/bmpp_GMM_final.pdf?la=en. Accessed 2016 Feb 15.

Park, H. (2013). Market principles should drive urbanization: expert. *Korea Herald*. Available at http://www.koreaherald.com/view.php?ud=20131213000832&mod=skb. Accessed 2016 Feb 25.

Ryder, A. (2015). Governmental Devolution as a Motor of Local Development. In Buček, J. and Ryder, A. (eds). *Governance in Transition*. London: Springer, pp. 65–91.

Seoul Metropolitan Authority (2015). *Budget spending survey*. Available at http://libweb.anglia.ac.uk/referencing/harvard.htm. Accessed 2016 Feb 25.

Seoul Metropolitan Authority (2016a). *Citizen budget participation proposals*. Available at http://www.seoulmetro.co.kr/page.action?mCode=A100000000&cidx=732. Accessed 2016 Feb 25.

Seoul Metropolitan Authority (2016b). *Budget allocation breakdown*. Available at http://finance.seoul.go.kr/archives/33432. Accessed 2016 Feb 25.

Shin, C. (2008). Relations Between the State and Labour under Bak Jeong-hee and Jeong Gwan-ha. *Journal of Labour Research*, **16**: 81–120.

Snyder, N., Hernandez, E., Maxwell, L., Hester, S. and Kapucu, N. (2012). Metropolitan Governance Reforms: The Case of Seoul Metropolitan Government. *European Journal of Economic and Political Studies*, **5**(2): 107–129.

Song, M. (2015). Stockholder equality vs. the essential character of domestically-produced products. *Newscham*. Available at http://www.newscham.net/news/view.php?board=news&nid=99370. Accessed 2016 Feb 25.

Symons, T. (2015). What can England's new mayors learn from the transformation of Seoul city government?. *Nesta*. Available at http://www.nesta.org.uk/blog/what-can-englands-new-mayors-learn-transformation-seoul-city-government. Accessed 2016 Feb 25.

Tait, J. (2005). *Segyehwa: The Globalization of Seoul*. University of Calgary, Canada.

World Economic Forum (2015). *The Global Competitiveness Report 2015–16*. Geneva: World Economic Forum. Available at http://www3.weforum.org/docs/gcr/2015-2016/Global_Competitiveness_Report_2015-2016.pdf. Accessed 2016 Jan 19.

Yeonhap News (2014). Finance minister urges local governments to prioritize economy. *Yeonhap News*. Available at http://english.yonhapnews.co.kr/business/2014/09/01/91/0502000000AEN20140901000751320F.html?faca3500. Accessed 2016 Feb 25.

Yoon, J. (2014). Factories to be allowed in former 'green belt' areas. *Korea Times*. Available at http://www.koreatimes.co.kr/www/news/biz/2014/03/488_153243.html. Accessed 2016 Feb 25.

Chapter 6   Tokyo: Shared global aspirations and blunted reforms

Bertumen, M. (2014). Tokyo Governor Masuzoe Seeks to Open the City to Foreign Workers. *Tokyo Weekender*. Available at http://www.tokyoweekender.com/2014/05/tokyo-governor-masuzoe-seeks-to-open-the-city-to-foreign-workers/. Accessed 2016 Feb 4.

Chan, K.W. and Boland, A. (2012). Cities of East Asia. In Brunn, S., Hays-Mitchell, M. and Zeigler, D.G. (eds). *Cities of the World: World Regional Urban Development*. Lanham: Rowman and Littlefield Education.

Child Hill, R. and Fujita, K. (1993). In Child Hill, R. and Fujita, K. (eds). *Japanese Cities in the World Economy*. Philadelphia: Temple University Press.

EIU (2012). *Hot Spots: Benchmarking Global City Competitiveness*. London: The Economist. Available at http://www.economistinsights.com/sites/default/files/downloads/Hot%20Spots. pdf. Accessed 2016 Jan 19.

Foster, M. (2015). Is Japan losing focus on special economic zones?. *Japan Today*. Available at www.japantoday.com/category/business/view/is-japan-losing-focus-on-special-economic-zones. Accessed 2015 Feb 8.

Fujita, K. (2011). Financial Crises, Japan's state regime shift, and Tokyo's urban policy. *Environment and Planning A*, **43**: 307–327.

Fujita, K. (2015). The landscape of Tokyo power. *International Journal of Urban Sciences*, **19**(1): 82–92.

Fujita, K. and Child Hill, R. (2005). *The World Bank Policy Research Paper No. 3507: Innovative Tokyo*. Washington D.C.: The World Bank. Available at https://www.msu.edu/user/hillrr/ InnovativeTokyo%20Text.pdf. Accessed 2016 Feb 4.

Hill, R.C. and Fujita, K. (2009). Osaka's Tokyo Problem. *International Journal of Urban and Regional Research*, **19**(2): 181–193.

Hill, R.C. and Kim, J.W. (2000). Global Cities and Developmental States: New York, Tokyo and Seoul. *Urban Studies*, **37**: 2167.

Inagaki, K. (2015). Olympic Task to Reinvent Tokyo's Heart. *Financial Times*. Available at http://www.ft.com/cms/s/2/0e30b356-b378-11e4-9449-00144feab7de.html. Accessed 2016 Feb 4.

Kakiuchi, E. (2013). Japan: Tokyo. In Shirley, I. and Neill, C. (eds). *Asian and Pacific Cities: Development patterns*. London: Routledge.

Kashiwa-No-Ha Smart City (2015). *A New Vision for the Cities of Tomorrow*. Available at http://www.kashiwanoha-smartcity.com/en/concept/whatssmartcity.html. Accessed 2016 Feb 4.

Masuda, H. (2014). The Death of Regional Cities: A Horrendous Simulation Regional Cities Will Disappear by 2040 A Polarized Society will Emerge. *Discuss Japan*. Available at http:// www.japanpolicyforum.jp/archives/politics/pt20140120152454.html. Accessed 2016 Feb 4.

Masuzoe, Y. (2014). Policy speech by the Governor of Tokyo, Yoichi Masuzoe, at the third regular session of the Tokyo Metropolitan Assembly, 2014. Available at: http://www.metro.tokyo.jp/ ENGLISH/GOVERNOR/SPEECH/2014/1202/index.htm. Accessed 2016 Feb 4.

McDearman, B., Clark, G. and Parilla, J. (2013). The 10 Traits of Globally Fluent Metro Areas. The Brookings Institution. Available at http://www.brookings.edu/research/reports/2013/06/26-global-metro-traits-mcdearman-clark-parilla. Accessed 2016 Feb 4.

Moore, J. (2014). Japan's urban–rural divide. *The Diplomat*. Available at http://thediplomat. com/2014/02/japans-rural-urban-divide/. Accessed 2016 Feb 4.

Nikkei (2014). Think tanks envision Tokyo as low-tax financial center. *Nikkei Asian Review*. Available at http://asia.nikkei.com/Politics-Economy/Policy-Politics/Think-tanks-envision-Tokyo-as-low-tax-financial-center. Accessed 2016 Feb 4.

Obe, M. (2014). Companies Urged to Get Out of Tokyo. *The Wall Street Journal*. Available at http://blogs.wsj.com/japanrealtime/2014/05/14/companies-urged-to-get-out-of-tokyo/. Accessed 2016 Feb 4.

OECD (2011). *OECD Regions at a glance: Regions as drivers of competitiveness*. Available at http:// www.oecd-ilibrary.org/sites/reg_glance-2011-en/03/06/index.html;jsessionid=1s2dvipa67ub0. delta?contentType=&itemId=/content/chapter/reg_glance-2011-11-en&containerItemId=/ content/serial/19990057&accessItemIds=/content/book/reg_glance-2011-en&mimeType=text/ html. Accessed 2016 Feb 4.

OECD Stat. (2014). *Metropolitan areas*. Available at https://stats.oecd.org/Index.aspx? DataSetCode=CITIES. Accessed 2016 Jan 19.

Oshugi, S. (2011). The Large City System of Japan. *Papers on the Local Governance System and its Implementation in Selected Fields in Japan No.20*. Available at http://www3.grips. ac.jp/~coslog/activity/01/04/file/Bunyabetsu-20_en.pdf. Accessed 2016 Feb 4.

Parilla, J., Trujillo, J.L., Berube, A. and Ran, T. (2015). *Global Metromonitor 2014: An uncertain recovery*. Washington D.C.: The Brookings Institution. Available at http://www.brookings. edu/~/media/Research/Files/Reports/2015/01/22-global-metro-monitor/bmpp_GMM_final. pdf?la=en. Accessed 2016 Feb 15.

Pham, C., (2015). *Tokyo Smart City Development in Perspective of 2020 Olympics: Opportunities for EU–Japan Cooperation and Business Development*. Tokyo: EU–Japan Centre for Industrial Co-operation. Available at: http://www.eu-japan.eu/sites/eu-japan.eu/ files/Smart2020Tokyo_Final.pdf. Accessed 2016 Feb 4.

Saito, A. (2003). Global City Formation in a Capitalist Developmental State: Tokyo and the Waterfront Sub-centre Project. *Urban Studies*, **40**: 283.

Saito, A. (2012). State-Space Relations in Transition: Urban and Regional Policy in Japan. In Park, B.G., Hill, R.G. and Saito, A. (eds). *Locating Neoliberalism in East Asia: Neoliberalizing Spaces in Developmental States*. London: Blackwell.

Saito, A. (date unknown). *Rethinking Urban Politics in Japan: Critical (non)reaction to New Urban Politics*. Available at: http://paperroom.ipsa.org/papers/paper_15453.pdf.Accessed 2016 Feb 4.

Sato, S. and Urabe, E. (2014). Osaka City Plans Subway Operator Initial Offering to Chase Tokyo. *Bloomberg*. Available at http://www.bloomberg.com/news/articles/2014-04-13/ osaka-city-plans-subway-operator-initial-offering-to-chase-tokyo. Accessed 2016 Feb 4.

Soble, J. (2015). A sprawl of ghost homes in aging Tokyo suburbs. *The New York Times*. Available at http://www.nytimes.com/2015/08/24/world/a-sprawl-of-abandoned-homes-in-tokyo-suburbs.html?_r=0. Accessed 2016 Feb 4.

Sorensen, A. (2002). *The Making of Urban Japan: Cities and Planning from Edo to the Twenty First Century*. London: Routledge.

Sorensen, A. (2003). Building world city Tokyo: Globalization and conflict over urban space. *The Annals of Regional Science*, **37**: 519–531.

Stevens, A. (2013). Growth in second tier cities: Urban policy lessons from Japan. *Briefing for Core Cities Group, November 2013*. Japan Local Government Centre. Available at http:// www.corecities.com/sites/default/files/images/publications/Growth%20in%20second %20tier%20cities%20-%20urban%20policy%20lessons%20from%20Japan_0.pdf. Accessed 2016 Feb 4.

Tabuchi, H. (2013). The Olympics of the Future. *The New York Times*. Available at http:// www.nytimes.com/2013/11/09/business/international/olympic-games-give-japan-a-chance-to-show-its-mettle.html?pagewanted=all&_r=3&. Accessed 2016 Feb 4.

Tasker, P. (2014). Tokyo's new governor wins super-job – and super-headaches. *Nikkei Asian Review*. Available at http://asia.nikkei.com/Viewpoints/Geopolitico/Peter-Tasker-Tokyo-s-new-governor-wins-super-job-and-super-headaches. Accessed 2016 Feb 4.

Tateno, M. (2014). Tokyo Gov. Masuzoe to face crunch time later this year. *Nikkei Asian Review*. Available at http://asia.nikkei.com/Politics-Economy/Policy-Politics/Tokyo-Gov.-Masuzoe-to-face-crunch-time-later-this-year. Accessed 2016 Feb 4.

The Association of Mayors and Designated Cities (2016). *News*. Available at http://www.siteitosi. jp/index.html. Accessed 2016 Feb 4.

The Economist (2014). Flaming Out: The decline of Toru Hashimoto. *The Economist*. Available at http://www.economist.com/news/asia/21599401-decline-toru-hashimoto-flaming-out. Accessed 2016 Feb 4.

The Japan Times (2016). Tokyo governor lashes out at Abe administration for Olympic stadium turmoil. *The Japan Times*. Available at: http://www.japantimes.co.jp/news/2015/07/20/ national/politics-diplomacy/tokyo-governor-lashes-abe-administration-olympic-stadium-turmoil/. Accessed 2016 Feb 4.

The Mainichi (2015). Hashimoto's make-or-break tactics prove a success in Osaka double election. *The Mainichi*. Available at http://mainichi.jp/english/articles/20151123/p2a/00m/ 0na/014000c. Accessed 2016 Feb 4.

The Mainichi (2016). Tokyo's Setagaya Ward predicts 1 million population in 2040. *The Mainichi*. Available at http://mainichi.jp/english/articles/20160304/p2a/00m/0na/013000c. Accessed 2016 Feb 4.

The Prime Minister of Japan and His Cabinet (2014). The Forum for Consultations between the National and Regional Governments. *The Prime Minister in Action*. Available at http://japan.kantai.go.jp/96_abe/actions/201406/11kunitochiho.html. Accessed 2016 Feb 4.

Tokyo Metropolitan Government (2015a). Policy speech by the Governor of Tokyo, Yoichi Masuzoe, at the first regular session of the Tokyo Metropolitan Assembly, 2015. Available at http://www.metro.tokyo.jp/ENGLISH/GOVERNOR/SPEECH/2015/0218/index.htm. Accessed 2016 Feb 4.

Tokyo Metropolitan Government (2015b). *Tokyo Metropolitan Government: Bureau of Finance*. Available at http://www.zaimu.metro.tokyo.jp/bond/en/ir_library/ir/ir_document/ir_document2015.pdf. Accessed 2016 Feb 4.

Tokyo Metropolitan Government (2015c). Policy speech by the Governor of Tokyo, Yoichi Masuzoe, at the third regular session of the Tokyo Metropolitan Assembly, 2015. Available at http://www.metro.tokyo.jp/ENGLISH/GOVERNOR/SPEECH/2015/0918/contents04.htm. Accessed 2016 Feb 4.

Tsukamoto, T. (2013). Urban Regeneration and neo-liberal state reform: Changing roles of cities in the Japanese Developmental State. In Leary, M. and McCarthy, J. (eds). *The Routledge Companion to Urban Regeneration*. London: Routledge.

Waley, P. (2007). Tokyo-as-World-City: Reassessing the Role of Capital and the State in Urban Restructuring. *Urban Studies*, **44**: 1465.

World Economic Forum (2015). *The Global Competitiveness Report 2015–16*. Geneva: World Economic Forum. Available at http://www3.weforum.org/docs/gcr/2015-2016/Global_Competitiveness_Report_2015-2016.pdf. Accessed 2016 Jan 19.

Chapter 7 Mumbai: The opportunity costs of leadership and co-ordination failure

Babar, K. (2015a). Higher charge on extra FSI may hit redevelopment in Mumbai suburbs. *The Economic Times*. Available at http://economictimes.indiatimes.com/wealth/news/higher-charge-on-extra-fsi-may-hit-redevelopment-in-mumbai-suburbs/articleshow/46128210.cms. Accessed 2016 Feb 9.

Babar, K. (2015b). Maharashtra's decision to scrap Mumbai's 'Development Plan 2034' to delay many projects. *The Economic Times*. Available at http://economictimes.indiatimes.com/articleshow/47021173.cms?utm_source=contentofinterest&utm_medium=text&utm_campaign=cppst. Accessed 2016 Feb 9.

Birkinshaw, M. (2014). India's urban direction: Learning from the Renewal Mission (JNNURM). *South Asia @ LSE*. Available at http://blogs.lse.ac.uk/southasia/2014/06/04/indias-future-urban-pathways/. Accessed 2016 Feb 8.

Bonislawski, A. (2016). Reimagining India's Big Cities with Smart Development. *Blueprint*. Available at https://blueprint.cbre.com/reimagining-indias-big-cities-with-smart-development/. Accessed 2016 Feb 9.

Business Insider India (2015). Modi Govt sets up Investment and Infrastructure fund for Rs 40k Crores. Available at http://www.businessinsider.in/Modi-Govtsets-up-Investment-and-Infrastructure-fund-for-Rs-40k-Crores?articleshow/50368865.cms. Accessed 2016 Feb 9.

Business Standard (2016). After Delhi, Mumbai might try odd–even plan to reduce pollution. *Business Standard*. Available at http://www.business-standard.com/article/current-affairs/bjp-sena-divided-over-launch-of-odd-and-even-car-number-formula-in-mumbai-116010700842_1.html. Accessed 2016 Feb 9.

Chattaraj, S. (2012a). Bombay First and the Mumbai Transformation Project: A state–business partnership to transform Mumbai. *Sixth Urban Research and Knowledge Symposium 2012*. Available at http://siteresources.worldbank.org/INTURBANDEVELOPMENT/Resources/336387-1369969101352/Chattaraj.pdf. Accessed 2016 Feb 9.

Chattaraj, S. (2012b). *Shanghai Dreams: Urban Restructuring in Globalizing Mumbai.* Unpublished dissertation, Princeton University.

Clark, G. and Moonen, T. (2014). *Mumbai: India's Global City – A case study for the Global Cities Initiative: A joint project of Brookings and JPMorgan Chase.* Global Cities Initiative. Available at https://www.jpmorgan.com/cm/BlobServer/global_cities_mumbai_dec2014.pdf?blobkey=id&blobwhere=1320660418097&blobheader=application/pdf&blobheadername1=Cache-Control&blobheadervalue1=private&blobcol=urldata&blobtable=MungoBlobs. Accessed 2016 Feb 9.

Deodhar, P. (2014). 3 Ways to Boost SMEs so that India becomes the factory to the world. *Money Life.* Available at http://www.moneylife.in/article/india-as-factory-for-the-world/38648.html. Accessed 2016 Feb 9.

Desai, G. (2016). BMC to miss DP 2034 deadline again. *DNA India.* Available at http://www.dnaindia.com/mumbai/report-bmc-to-miss-dp-2034-deadline-again-2168698. Accessed 2016 Feb 9.

Dhoot, V. (2015). Modi government revives 42 stalled projects worth Rs 1.15 lakh crore. *The Economic Times.* Available at http://economictimes.indiatimes.com/news/economy/infrastructure/modi-government-revives-42-stalled-projects-worth-rs-1-15-lakh-crore/articleshow/47579787.cms. Accessed 2016 Feb 9.

EIU (2012). *Hot Spots: Benchmarking Global City Competitiveness.* London: The Economist. Available at http://www.economistinsights.com/sites/default/files/downloads/Hot%20Spots.pdf. Accessed 2016 Jan 19.

Fraser, R. (date unknown). How India has achieved polycentricity, and what secondary cities can do to optimize it. *Asia Development Dialogue.* Available at http://asiadialogue.org/how-india-has-achieved-polycentricity-and-what-secondary-cities-can-do-to-optimize-it/. Accessed 2016 Feb 8.

Gómez-Ibáñez, J. and Masood, S. (2007). *Vision Mumbai.* Cambridge: Kennedy School of Government Graduate School of Design. Available at http://isites.harvard.edu/fs/docs/icb.topic146244.files/Vision_Mumbai_April_07_version.pdf. Accessed 2016 Feb 9.

Guha, R. (2003). The Battle for Bombay. *The Hindu.* Available at http://www.thehindu.com/thehindu/mag/2003/04/13/stories/2003041300240300.htm. Accessed 2016 Feb 9.

Gumber, A. (2014). In Urbanising Maharashtra, Massive Task Ahead For BJP. *IndiaSpend.* Available at http://www.indiaspend.com/uncategorized/in-urbanising-maharashtra-massive-task-ahead-for-bjp-36898. Accessed 2016 Feb 9.

Lewis, C. (2016). Tenants of large, old flats face 200 times rent hike. *The Times of India.* Available at http://timesofindia.indiatimes.com/city/mumbai/Tenants-of-large-old-flats-face-200-times-rent-hike/articleshow/50590484.cms. Accessed 2016 Feb 9.

Mohanty, P. (2014). *Cities and Public Policy: An Urban Agenda for India.* London: Sage.

Nagpal, N. (2015). Scrapping DP 2034: What Mumbai really needs. MagicBricks. Available at http://content.magicbricks.com/industry-news/mumbai-real-estate-news-industry-news/scrapping-dp-2034-what-mumbai-really-needs/81231.html. Accessed 2016 Feb 9.

Naik, Y. (2014). Case crunch 'severely affecting' Navi Mumbai Airport Project; ministry. *Mumbai Mirror.* Available at http://www.mumbaimirror.com/mumbai/others/Cash-crunch-severely-affecting-Navi-Mumbai-airport-project-Ministry/articleshow/34747249.cms. Accessed 2016 Feb 9.

Nair, S. (2015). India's concerns at Habitat III. *The Indian Express.* Available at http://indianexpress.com/article/india/india-news-india/indias-concerns-at-habitat-iii/. Accessed 2016 Feb 9.

Parilla, J., Trujillo, J.L., Berube, A. and Ran, T. (2015). *Global Metromonitor 2014: An uncertain recovery.* Washington D.C.: The Brookings Institution. Available at http://www.brookings.edu/~/media/Research/Files/Reports/2015/01/22-global-metro-monitor/bmpp_GMM_final.pdf?la=en. Accessed 2016 Feb 15.

Pethe, A., Tandel, V. and Gandhi, S. (2012). Understanding issues related to polycentric governance in the Mumbai Metropolitan Region. *Public Finance and Management,* **12**(3): 182–203.

Phadke, M. (2015a). 2 new Metro lines may get Maharashtra cabinet nod today. *The Indian Express.* Available at http://indianexpress.com/article/cities/mumbai/2-new-metro-lines-may-get-maharashtra-cabinet-nod-today/#sthash.Asj75OTu.dpuf. Accessed 2016 Feb 9.

Phadke, M. (2015b). Asian bank may partially fund two new Metro corridors. *The Indian Express.* Available at http://indianexpress.com/article/cities/mumbai/asian-bank-may-partially-fund-two-new-metro-corridors/#sthash.zuUSDBrD.dpuf. Accessed 2016 Feb 9.

Planning Commission: Steering Committee on Urban Development and Management (2011). *Report of the Working Group on Financing Urban Infrastructure.* Available at http://planningcommission.gov.in/aboutus/committee/wrkgrp12/hud/wg_Financing_rep.pdf. Accessed 2016 Feb 9.

Rao, N. (2015). *Reshaping City Governance.* London: Routledge.

Ren, X. and Weinstein, L. (2013). Urban Mega-Projects and Scalar Transformations in China and India. In Samara, T., Shenjing, H. and Chen, G. (eds) *Locating Right to the City in the Global South.* London: Routledge, pp. 107–126.

Reuters (2016). India's Modi Launches $1.5 Billion Fund for Startups. *Fortune.* Available at http://fortune.com/2016/01/16/modi-india-startup-fund/. Accessed 2016 Feb 9.

Saldanha, A. (2016). Disaster Risks Grow As India's Cities Flounder. IndiaSpend. Available at http://www.indiaspend.com/cover-story/disaster-risks-grow-as-indias-cities-flounder-79985. Accessed 2016 Feb 9.

Sankhe, S., Vittal, I., Dobbs, R., Mohan, A., Gulati, A., Ablett, J., Gupta, S., Kim, A., Paul, S., Sanghvi, A. and Sethy, G. (2010). *India's Urban Awakening: Building Inclusive Cities, Sustaining Economic Growth.* McKinsey Global Institute. Available at http://www.mckinsey.com/global-themes/urbanization/urban-awakening-in-india. Accessed 2016 Feb 9.

Sharma, N. (2016). Worried over progress of PM Modi's pet projects Swachh Bharat, Smart City, babus asked to travel to states. *The Economic Times.* Available at http://articles.economictimes.indiatimes.com/2016-01-06/news/69564379_1_swachh-bharat-mission-pet-projects-implementation. Accessed 2016 Feb 9.

Sharma, P. (2014). Serving the Cities: An Indian Scenario. *IOSR Journal of Humanities and Social Science*, 19(1): 15–22.

Shukla, P.R., Pathak, M., Mittal, S. and Dhar, S. (2015). *Promoting Low Carbon Transport in India – Scenarios and Roadmap for Intercity Transport in India: The Role of High Speed Rail.* UNEP. Available at http://www.unep.org/transport/lowcarbon/PDFs/Role_of_High_Speed_Rail_Final.pdf. Accessed 2016 Feb 9.

Sikarwar, D. (2015). Government sets up Rs 40,000 crore National Investment and Infrastructure fund, CEO likely by January-end. *The Economic Times.* Available at http://articles.economictimes.indiatimes.com/2015-12-30/news/69402712_1_infrastructure-fund-sovereign-wealth-funds-finance-minister-arun-jaitley. Accessed 2016 Feb 9.

Singh, R.K. (2015). Modi's infrastructure splurge revives investment in India. Reuters. Available at http://in.reuters.com/article/india-economy-investment-modi-industrial-idINKCN0S71MO20151013. Accessed 2016 Feb 9.

Sivaramakrishnan, K.C. (2015). *Governance of Megacities: Fractured Thinking, Fragmented Setup.* Oxford: Oxford University Press.

Slack, E. (2014). *Innovative Governance Approaches in Metropolitan Areas in Developing Countries.* Presentation to UN Habitat Global Expert Group Meeting on Urban Development Financing: The Challenge of Local Governments in Developing Countries. Available at http://munkschool.utoronto.ca/imfg/uploads/285/slack_presentation_on_innovative_governance_approaches_june_2014.pdf. Accessed 2016 Feb 9.

SME Connect (2014). *SME Connect Volume 4 Issue 16.* Available at http://www.smeconnect.in/issues/VOL4_ISSUE16.pdf. Accessed 2016 Feb 9.

The Financial Express (2015). Cabinet approves NIIF structure. Available at http://www.financialexpress.com/article/economy/cabinet-approves-niif-structure/110417/. Accessed 2016 Feb 9.

The Indian Express (2014). Urban issues higher on agenda compared to rural in state assembly. Available at http://indianexpress.com/article/cities/mumbai/urban-issues-higher-on-agenda-compared-to-rural-in-state-assembly/. Accessed 2016 Feb 9.

The Indian Express (2016). Govt seeks to amend Rent Control Act to keep out larger houses. *The Indian Express.* Available at http://indianexpress.com/article/cities/mumbai/govt-seeks-to-amend-rent-control-act-to-keep-out-larger-houses/#sthash.okQXJPrV.dpuf. Accessed 2016 Feb 9.

The Times of India (2014). Govt plans to attract private players to help develop Smart Cities. *The Times of India*. Available at http://timesofindia.indiatimes.com/business/india-business/Govt-plans-to-attract-private-players-to-help-develop-Smart-Cities/articleshow/44735719.cms. Accessed 2016 Feb 9.

World Bank (2014). *Data by country*. Available at http://data.worldbank.org/. Accessed 2016 Feb 9.

World Economic Forum (2015). *The Global Competitiveness Report 2015–16*. Geneva: World Economic Forum. Available at http://www3.weforum.org/docs/gcr/2015-2016/Global_Competitiveness_Report_2015-2016.pdf. Accessed 2016 Jan 19.

Yglesias, M. (2015). The most important urban policy story in the world is happening in India. *Vox Business & Finance*. Available at http://www.vox.com/2015/2/20/8072575/mumbai-fsi-reform. Accessed 2016 Feb 9.

Zérah, M.H. (2014). Transforming Mumbai, or the challenges of forging a Collective Actor. In Lorrain, D. (ed.). *Governing Megacities in Emerging Countries*. Farnham: Ashgate.

Chapter 8   New York: Adapting to 'emergency back-up' federalism

Ahn, M. and Russell-Einhorn, M.L. (2015). A vision of high-speed rail in America: Time for a national conversation?. The Brookings Institution. Available at http://www.brookings.edu/blogs/techtank/posts/2015/06/29-high-speed-rail-innovation. Accessed 2016 Feb 11.

Aon and the Partnership for New York City (2013). *New York City as a Destination of Choice for Talent*. Available at http://www.pfnyc.org/reports/2013-Aon-PFNYC-%20Report.pdf. Accessed 2016 Feb 11.

Associated Press (2014). Obama signs $10.8 billion temporary highway funding bill. *PBS Newshour*. Available at http://www.pbs.org/newshour/rundown/obama-signs-10-8-billion-temporary-highway-funding-bill/. Accessed 2016 Feb 11.

Berg, B. (2007). *New York City Politics: Governing Gotham*. New Jersey: Rutgers University Press.

Callegari, J. (2014). LIA makes cross-sound connection a priority. *Long Island Business News*. Available at http://www.longislandassociation.org/assets/downloads/Long%20Island%20Business%20News%20LIA%20makes%20cross%20sound%20connection%20a%20priority_1.pdf. Accessed 2016 Feb 11.

Cassidy, M. (2014). Murphy eyes federally backed loans to speed projects. *CT Post*. Available at http://www.ctpost.com/local/article/Murphy-eyes-federally-backed-loans-to-speed-5675703.php. Accessed 2016 Feb 11.

CBS New York (2013). De Blasio Out To Change Federal Government's Relationship With NYC. *CBS New York*. Available at http://newyork.cbslocal.com/2013/12/12/mayor-elect-bill-de-blasio-to-make-another-announcement/. Accessed 2016 Feb 11.

Center for an Urban Future (2009). *50+1: A Federal Agenda for New York City*. Available at https://nycfuture.org/pdf/51_Things_the_Obama_Administration_Should_do_for_New_York_City.pdf. Accessed 2016 Feb 11.

Dicken, P. (2007). *Global Shift: Mapping the changing contours of the world economy*. London: Sage.

EIU (2012). *Hot Spots: Benchmarking Global City Competitiveness*. London: The Economist. Available at http://www.economistinsights.com/sites/default/files/downloads/Hot%20Spots.pdf. Accessed 2016 Jan 19.

Fischer, J. (2014a). *8 Ideas for improving and expanding NYC's workforce development system*. Center for an Urban Future. Available at https://nycfuture.org/research/publications/8-ideas-for-improving-and-expanding-nycs-workforce-development-system. Accessed 2016 Feb 11.

Fischer, J. (2014b). *The Federal Workforce Overhaul: Good News for New York City!* Center for an Urban Future. Available at https://nycfuture.org/research/publications/the-federal-workforce-overhaul-good-news-for-new-york-city. Accessed 2016 Feb 11.

Forman, A. (2014). *Caution Ahead: Overdue Investments for New York's Aging Infrastructure*. Center for an Urban Future. Available at https://nycfuture.org/pdf/Caution-Ahead.pdf. Accessed 2016 Feb 11.

Freemark, Y. (2014). With no new rail tunnel on the horizon under the Hudson, New York faces a looming transport crisis. *The Transport Politic*. Available at http://www.thetransportpolitic.

com/2014/10/06/with-no-new-rail-tunnel-on-the-horizon-under-the-hudson-new-york-faces-a-looming-transport-crisis/. Accessed 2016 Feb 11.

Global Gateway Alliance (2014). *New Study: JFK, Newark and La Guardia lose out in Federal Grant Program.* Press release. Available at http://media.wix.com/ugd/f2e928_96295b6108ef 423583472f9232062aff.pdf. Accessed 2016 Feb 11.

Goff, C. (2013). Q & A with Bruce Katz: Building a new economy from the bottom up. *NewStart.* Available at http://newstartmag.co.uk/features/q-a-with-bruce-katz-building-a-new-economy-from-the-bottom-up/. Accessed 2016 Feb 11.

Golden, A. (2014). *Governance of regional transit systems: Observations on Washington, New York and Toronto.* Wilson Center. Available at https://www.wilsoncenter.org/sites/default/files/CI_140625_governance_v4_0.pdf. Accessed 2016 Feb 11.

Green, C. and Moore, D. (1988). Public Finance. In Benjamin, G. and Brecher, C. (eds). *The Two New Yorks: State–City Relations in the Changing Federal System.* New York City: Russel Sage Foundation.

Harvey, V. (2008). Presentation: *National Urban Policy in the United States.* Available at http://www.planning.org.au/documents/item/2078. Accessed 2016 Feb 11.

Heuvel, K.V. (2014). 'It's Simply Mission Critical': Mayor Bill de Blasio on the Revival of an Urban Agenda. *The Nation.* Available at http://www.thenation.com/article/its-simply-mission-critical-mayor-bill-de-blasio-revival-urban-agenda/. Accessed 2016 Feb 11.

Holeywell, R. (2013). Whatever Happened to the Office of Urban Affairs?. *Governing.* Available at http://www.governing.com/blogs/fedwatch/gov-federal-office-of-urban-affairs-still-exist.html. Accessed 2016 Feb 11.

Jorgensen, J. (2014). Council Passes Bills to Stop Cooperation With Federal Immigration Detainers. *Observer.* Available at http://observer.com/2014/10/council-passes-bills-to-stop-cooperation-with-federal-immigration-detainers/. Accessed 2016 Feb 11.

Katz, B. (2014). Julian Castro's Big Job. *Politico Magazine.* Available at http://www.politico.com/magazine/story/2014/05/julian-castro-hud-107059_Page2.html#ixzz3CaC7B1R2. Accessed 2016 Feb 11.

Kincaid, J. (2011). The U.S. Advisory Commission on Intergovernmental Relations: Unique Artifact of a Bygone Era. *Public Administration Review*, **71**(2): 181–189.

Knauth, D. (2013). Delays Threaten FAA's $40B Air Traffic Control Overhaul. *Law 360.* Available at http://www.law360.com/articles/497460/delays-threaten-faa-s-40b-air-traffic-control-overhaul. Accessed 2016 Feb 11.

Mallach, A. (2010). *Facing the Urban Challenge: The Federal Government and America's Older Distressed Cities.* Washington D.C.: The Brookings Institution. Available at http://www.brookings.edu/~/media/research/files/papers/2010/5/18%20shrinking%20cities%20mallach/0518_shrinking_cities_mallach.pdf. Accessed 2016 Feb 11.

Medina, J. (2010). New York Wins Nearly $700 Million for Education. *The New York Times.* Available at http://www.nytimes.com/2010/08/25/nyregion/25nyrace.html?ref=nyregion&_r=0. Accessed 2016 Feb 11.

New York City (1997). *Archives of Rudolph W. Giuliani Twentieth Annual National Legal Conference on Immigration and Refugee Policy.* Available at http://www.nyc.gov/html/records/rwg/html/97a/legal.html. Accessed 2016 Feb 11.

New York City (2015a). Mayor de Blasio Announces Plan to Improve Immigrant Access to Health Care Services. *Office of the Mayor: News.* Available at http://www1.nyc.gov/office-of-the-mayor/news/701-15/mayor-de-blasio-plan-improve-immigrant-access-health-care-services. Accessed 2016 Feb 11.

New York City (2015b). Statement from Mayor Bill de Blasio on Federal Transportation Bill. *Office of the Mayor: News.* Available at http://www1.nyc.gov/office-of-the-mayor/news/906-15/statement-mayor-bill-de-blasio-federal-transportation-bill. Accessed 2016 Feb 11.

New York City (2016). *NYC Recovery: Sandy Funding Tracker.* Available at http://www1.nyc.gov/sandytracker/#overview. Accessed 2016 Feb 11.

New York City Council (2014). Press Release: July 21, 2014. Available at http://council.nyc.gov/html/pr/072114fed.shtml. Accessed 2016 Feb 11.

NYC Planning (2014). Department of City Planning Releases Comprehensive Guide to Retrofitting Buildings against Future Floods. Press Release. Available at http://www.nyc.gov/html/dcp/html/about/pr100814.shtml. Accessed 2016 Feb 11.

OECD Stat. (2014). *Metropolitan areas*. Available at https://stats.oecd.org/Index.aspx?DataSetCode=CITIES. Accessed 2016 Jan 19.

Parilla, J., Trujillo, J.L., Berube, A. and Ran, T. (2015). *Global Metromonitor 2014: An uncertain recovery*. Washington D.C.: The Brookings Institution. Available at http://www.brookings.edu/~/media/Research/Files/Reports/2015/01/22-global-metro-monitor/bmpp_GMM_final.pdf?la=en. Accessed 2016 Feb 15.

Partnership for New York City (2013). *NYC Jobs Blueprint*. New York: Partnership for New York City. Available at http://www.pfnyc.org/reports/2013-blueprint-web.pdf. Accessed 2016 Feb 11.

Regional Plan Association (2016). *More People Want Walkable Communities, but Outmoded Regulations Get in the Way*. Available at www.rpa.org. Accessed 2016 May 26.

Roberts, S. (2006). When the City's Bankruptcy Was Just a Few Words Away. *The New York Times*. Available at http://www.nytimes.com/2006/12/31/nyregion/31default.html?_r=0. Accessed 2016 Feb 11.

Robinson, D. (2014). Upstate forgotten as New York City grabs attention in climate change warnings. *Albany Business Review*. Available at http://www.bizjournals.com/albany/news/2014/06/24/upstate-forgotten-as-new-york-city-grabs-attention.html?page=all. Accessed 2016 Feb 11.

Schlanger, D. (2014). New York City and the Future of EB-5 Funding. *Commercial Observer*. Available at https://commercialobserver.com/2014/10/new-york-city-and-the-future-of-eb-5-funding/. Accessed 2016 Feb 11.

Schned, D., Kennedy, A. and Barone, R. (2014). *Getting Back on Track: Unlocking the Full Potential of the New Haven Line*. New York: Regional Plan Association. Available at http://library.rpa.org/pdf/RPA-Getting-Back-on-Track.pdf. Accessed 2016 Feb 10.

Semple, K. (2013). New York City Increases Its Resistance to Federal Entreaties on Foreign-Born Detainees. *The New York Times*. Available at http://www.nytimes.com/2013/12/06/nyregion/city-increases-its-resistance-to-federal-entreaties-on-foreign-born-detainees.html?_r=0. Accessed 2016 Feb 11.

Sitt, J. and Sigmund, S. (2014). Bring LaGuardia out of the Third World. *CNN*. Available at http://edition.cnn.com/2014/02/10/opinion/sigmund-laguardia-biden-third-world/. Accessed 2016 Feb 11.

Timm, J. (2013). Bloomberg's $20B plan to protect NYC from climate change. *MSNBC*. Available at http://www.msnbc.com/morning-joe/bloombergs-20b-plan-protect-nyc-cli. Accessed 2016 Feb 11.

Torres, R. and Jones, D. (2014). With federal funding at 'starvation levels', the New York City Housing Authority needs the city and state to step in to stem the agency's recent decline. *Daily News*. Available at http://www.nydailynews.com/new-york/city-state-act-rescue-nycha-article-1.1914034. Accessed 2016 Feb 11.

Tyrangiel, G. (2014). US Cities Leading the Way: Milken 2014 Global Conference. *The Planning Report*. Available at http://www.planningreport.com/2014/05/07/us-cities-leading-way-milken-2014-global-conference. Accessed 2016 Feb 11.

Vogel, C., Michaels, C. and Wileden, L. (2011). *The end of an arra*. Center for Urban Future. Available at https://nycfuture.org/pdf/End_of_an_ARRA.pdf. Accessed 2016 Feb 10.

World Economic Forum (2015). *The Global Competitiveness Report 2015–16*. Geneva: World Economic Forum. Available at http://www3.weforum.org/docs/gcr/2015-2016/Global_Competitiveness_Report_2015-2016.pdf. Accessed 2016 Jan 19.

Wylde, K. (2014). What the new state budget means for business. *Crain's*. Available at http://www.crainsnewyork.com/article/20140413/OPINION/140419955/what-the-new-state-budget-means-for-business. Accessed 2016 Feb 11.

Young, E. (2014). Hudson Rail Tunnels Have Up to 20 Years Left, Amtrak Says. *Bloomberg*. Available at http://www.bloomberg.com/news/articles/2014-05-05/hudson-rail-tunnels-have-up-to-20-years-left-amtrak-says. Accessed 2016 Feb 11.

Chapter 9   São Paulo: The quest for recognition and reform

Agência PT de Notícias (2014). Faixas exclusivas reduzem em média 38 minutos por dia o tempo de viagem de quem usa transporte público. Agência PT de Notícias. Available at http://www.capital.sp.gov.br/portal/noticia/3463. Accessed 2016 Feb 12.

Chao, L. (2014). Intense Versus Laid-Back: São Paulo vs. Rio. *The Wall Street Journal.* Available at http://www.wsj.com/articles/intense-versus-laid-back-sao-paulo-vs-rio-1402526368. Accessed 2016 Feb 12.

Coppola, G. (2013). Brazil Stocks Rebound From Protests With Sao Paulo Fix-It Mayor. *Bloomberg.* Available at http://www.bloomberg.com/news/articles/2013-09-26/brazil-stocks-rebound-from-protests-with-sao-paulo-fix-it-mayor. Accessed 2016 Feb 12.

Dos Santos Val, S. (2013). *A metrópole brasileira: origens e perspectivas.* Available at www.cp2.g12.br/UAs/se/departamentos/sociologia/pespectiva_sociologica/Numero4/Artigos/sylvio.pdf. Accessed 2016 Feb 12.

EIU (2012). *Hot Spots: Benchmarking Global City Competitiveness.* London: The Economist. Available at http://www.economistinsights.com/sites/default/files/downloads/Hot%20Spots.pdf. Accessed 2016 Jan 19.

Federal Government of Brazil (2005). Law No. 11.124, of 16 June 2005. Available at http://www.planalto.gov.br/ccivil_03/_ato2004-2006/2005/lei/l11124.htm. Accessed 2016 Feb 12.

Federal Government of Brazil (2014). *São Paulo recebe investimentos para nova linha do metro.* Available at http://www.brasil.gov.br/infraestrutura/2014/01/empreendimento-foi-selecionado-pelo-programa-de-aceleracao-do-crescimento-pac-grandes-cidades. Accessed 2016 Feb 11.

Fernandes, E. (2007). Implementing the urban reform agenda in Brazil. *Environment and Urbanization*, **19**: 177.

Folha de Sao Paulo (2012). In 12 years, SP paid R$ 17.7 billion in interest for Union. Folha de Sao Paulo. Available at http://folhaspdados.blogfolha.uol.com.br/2012/10/29/em-12-anos-sp-paga-r-177-bilhoes-em-juros-para-uniao/. Accessed 2016 Feb 12.

Gohn, M.G. (1999). *O future das Cidades.* Available at www.lite.fae.unicamp.br/revista/gohn.html. Accessed 2016 Feb 12.

Guedes, O. (2012). É urgente renegociar a dívida de São Paulo. Escola de Governo: Artigos. Available at http://www.escoladegoverno.org.br/artigos/1984-qe-urgente-renegociar-a-divida-de-sao-pauloq. Accessed 2016 Feb 12.

Holmes, C. (2016). São Paulo Is Betting Better Urban Planning Can Solve a Housing Crisis. *Next City.* Available at https://nextcity.org/features/view/sao-paulo-housing-crisis-master-plan-zeis-haddad-habitat-iii. Accessed 2016 Feb 12.

IBGE (2016). *Population projection for Brazil and federal units.* Available at http://www.ibge.gov.br/apps/populacao/projecao/index.html. Accessed 2016 Jan 20.

Jovem Pam (2014). Dilma elogia resultado de privatização do aeroporto de Guarulhos, SP. *Jovem Pam.* Available at http://jovempan.uol.com.br/noticias/brasil/sao-paulo/dilma-elogia-resultado-de-privatizacao-do-aeroporto-de-guarulhos-sp.html. Accessed 2016 Feb 12.

Klink, J. (2008). Building urban assets in South America. In *South American Cities: Securing an Urban Future.* London: LSE Urban Age. Available at https://lsecities.net/publications/conference-newspapers/south-american-cities-securing-an-urban-future/. Accessed 2016 Feb 12.

Martine, G. (1989). The nature and impacts of population redistribution policies in Brazil. In *Population policy in Sub-Saharan Africa: drawing on international experience. Papers presented at the seminar organized by the IUSSP Committee on Policy and Population, in Kinshasa, Zaire, 27 February – 2 March 1989.* Liege: International Union for the Scientific Study of Population [IUSSP].

Martine, G. and McGranahan, G. (2013). The legacy of inequality and negligence in Brazil's unfinished urban transition: Lessons for other developing regions. *International Journal of Urban Sustainable Development*, **5**(1): 7–24.

Mattos Filho (2015). New legislation on urban conglomerates and metropolitan regions. Memorandum to clients. Available at http://www.mattosfilho.com.br/EscritorioMidia/memoinfra280115en.pdf. Accessed 2016 Feb 12.

Meade, T. (2010). *A Brief History of Brazil.* New York: Infobase Publishing.

Meu Município (2016). *Per do município.* Available at http://www.meumunicipio.org.br/meumunicipio/municipio/330455#comparacao. Accessed 2016 Feb 16.

Ministério das Cidades (2013). *Doze propostas para criação do Fundo Nacional de Desenvolvimento Urbano são discutidas na 5ª Conferência.* Ministério do Cidades. Available at www.cidades.gov.br/index.php/o-ministerio/noticias/3954-doze-propostas-para-criacao-do-fundo-nacional-de-desenvolvimento-urbano-sao-discutidas-na-5o-conferencia.html. Accessed 2016 Feb 12.

Parilla, J., Trujillo, J.L., Berube, A. and Ran, T. (2015). *Global Metromonitor 2014: An uncertain recovery*. Washington D.C.: The Brookings Institution. Available at http://www.brookings.edu/~/media/Research/Files/Reports/2015/01/22-global-metro-monitor/bmpp_GMM_final.pdf?la=en. Accessed 2016 Feb 15.

Prefecture of São Paulo (2014a). Faixas exclusivas reduzem em média 38 minutos por dia o tempo de viagem de quem usa transporte público. Agência PT de Notícias. Available at http://www.capital.sp.gov.br/portal/noticia/3463. Accessed 2016 Feb 12.

Prefecture of São Paulo (2014b). Parceria entre Prefeitura e Governo Federal disponibiliza áreas da União para construção de moradia popular. Notícias. Available at http://www.prefeitura.sp.gov.br/cidade/secretarias/habitacao/noticias/?p=172617. Accessed 2016 Feb 12.

Rocha, A. (2012). A new Arab in the City Hall. *Brazil-Arab news agency*. Available at http://www2.anba.com.br/noticia_servicos.kmf?cod=19184228&indice=50. Accessed 2016 Feb 12.

Sudjic, D. *et al.* (2008). *South American Cities: Securing an Urban Future*. London: LSE Cities. Available at https://lsecities.net/publications/conference-newspapers/south-american-cities-securing-an-urban-future. Accessed 2016 Feb 12.

Valor (2013). Haddad diz que só vai aumentar IPTU acima da inflacao em 2015. *Valor.* Available at http://www.valor.com.br/politica/3378442/haddad-diz-que-so-vai-aumentar-iptu-acima-da-inflacao-em-2015. Accessed 2016 Feb 12.

Wilson Center (2009). *Democracy and the City: Assessing Urban Policy in Brazil*. Available at www.wilsoncenter.org/sites/default/files/CUSP_Brazil_web.pdf. Accessed 2016 Feb 12.

Winter, B. (2014). Main battleground in Brazil election – Its biggest city. Reuters. Available at http://uk.reuters.com/article/uk-brazil-election-saopaulo-idUKKBN0FK1KX20140715. Accessed 2016 Feb 12.

World Bank (2014). *Data by country*. Available at http://data.worldbank.org/. Accessed 2016 Feb 9.

World Bank (2015). *Metropolitan Governance in Brazil*. Washington D.C.: World Bank.

World Economic Forum (2015). *The Global Competitiveness Report 2015–16. Geneva: World Economic Forum*. Available at http://www3.weforum.org/docs/gcr/2015-2016/Global_Competitiveness_Report_2015-2016.pdf. Accessed 2016 Jan 19.

Xinhua (2013). Brazil to invest in mass transit in Sao Paulo. *Xinhua News*. Available at http://news.xinhuanet.com/english/business/2013-10/26/c_132831890.htm. Accessed 2016 Feb 12.

Chapter 10   Toronto: Building capacity to renew the 'city that works'

Bakvis, H., Baier, G. and Brown, D. (2009). *Contested Federalism: Certainty and Ambiguity in the Canadian Federation*. Oxford: Oxford University Press.

Bozikovic, A. (2014). Shored up: How Toronto's waterfront redevelopment is going right. *The Globe and Mail*. Available at www.theglobeandmail.com/news/toronto/shored-up-how-toronto-waterfront-redevelopment-is-going-right/article19784844/?page=all. Accessed 2016 Feb 12.

Church, E. (2013). De facto Toronto mayor Norm Kelly seeks talks with Ottawa. *The Globe and Mail.* Available at http://www.theglobeandmail.com/news/toronto/de-facto-toronto-mayor-norm-kelly-seeks-talks-with-ottawa/article16070831/. Accessed 2016 Feb 12.

City of Toronto (2013). *Close the Gap Housing Campaign*. Available at http://www1.toronto.ca/wps/portal/contentonly?vgnextoid=a9e1bfd927a71410VgnVCM10000071d60f89RCRD. Accessed 2016 Feb 12.

Crawford, M. (2012). Innovation in Canada: Bright Ideas, Bright Future. *Area Development*. Available at http://www.areadevelopment.com/Canada-Investment-Guide/Location-Canada-2012/how-Canadian-government-supports-innovation-rd-36342822.shtml. Accessed 2016 Feb 12.

Department of Finance Canada (2013). *Evaluation of the Toronto Waterfront Revitalization Initiative*. Available at www.fin.gc.ca/treas/evaluations/twri-irsrt-eng.asp. Accessed 2016 Feb 12.

Dewing, M. and Young, W. (2006). *Background paper: Municipalities, the Constitution and the Canadian Federal System*. Library of Parliament. Available at http://www.parl.gc.ca/Content/LOP/researchpublications/bp276-e.htm. Accessed 2016 Feb 12.

Eidelman, G. (2013). *Three's Company*. MOWAT School of Public Policy and Governance, University of Toronto. Available at https://mowatcentre.ca/wp-content/uploads/publications/79_threes_company.pdf.

EIU (2012). *Hot Spots: Benchmarking Global City Competitiveness.* London: The Economist. Available at http://www.economistinsights.com/sites/default/files/downloads/Hot%20Spots.pdf. Accessed 2016 Jan 19.

Environment Canada (2008). *Evaluation of the Federal Government's Participation in the Toronto Waterfront Revitalization Initiative.* Available at http://ec.gc.ca/doc/ae-ve/2008-09/638/p2_eng.htm. Accessed 2016 Feb 12.

Federation of Canadian Municipalities (2013). *The State of Canada's Cities and Communities 2013.* Ottawa: Federation of Canadian Municipalities. Available at http://www.fcm.ca/Documents/reports/The_State_of_Canadas_Cities_and_Communities_2013_EN_web.pdf. Accessed 2016 Feb 12.

Federation of Canadian Municipalities (2016). *About us.* Available at http://www.fcm.ca/home/about-us.htm. Accessed 2016 Feb 12.

Filion, P. (2009). Growth and decline in the Canadian urban system: The impact of emerging economic, policy and demographic trends. *GeoJournal,* **75**: 517–538.

Gertler, M. (2014). A Big Step Forward. *U of T Magazine.* Available at http://magazine.utoronto.ca/presidents-message/a-big-step-forward-ontario-university-differentiation-canada-first-research-excellence-fund-meric-gertler/. Accessed 2016 Feb 12.

Joy, M. and Vogel, R.K. (2015). Toronto's governance crisis: A global city under pressure. *Cities,* **49**: 35–52.

Kazakov, V. (2014). New Government of Canada funding supports brain health research at U of T Medicine. *U of T News.* Available at http://www.news.utoronto.ca/new-government-canada-funding-supports-brain-health-research-u-t-medicine. Accessed 2016 Feb 12.

Kinney, J. (2016). Toronto Unveils Ambitious New Transport Plans. *Next City.* Feb 16. Available at https://nextcity.org/daily/entry/toronto-new-transit-plans. Accessed 2016 Mar 3.

Lu, V. (2010). Should Toronto go it alone?. *The Star.* Available at http://www.thestar.com/yourtoronto/yourcitymycity/2010/03/16/should_toronto_go_it_alone.html. Accessed 2016 Feb 12.

Mulcair, T. (2013). *It's time: An urban agenda for our cities and communities.* Speech by Tom Mulcair to the Federation of Canadian Municipalities AGM (Vancouver). Available at http://www.ndp.ca/news/its-time-urban-agenda-our-cities-and-communities. Accessed 2016 Feb 12.

Mulcair, T. (2014). *Building Prosperity in Toronto for the 21st Century.* NDP. Available at https://www.bot.com/Portals/0/unsecure/Newsroom/Speeches/20140620ThomasMulcair.pdf. Accessed 2016 Feb 12.

OECD Stat. (2014). *Metropolitan areas.* Available at https://stats.oecd.org/Index.aspx?DataSetCode=CITIES. Accessed 2016 Jan 19.

Oved, M.C. (2014). The challenges facing John Tory's SmartTrack proposals. *The Star.* Available at http://www.thestar.com/news/city_hall/toronto2014election/2014/10/27/the_challenges_facing_john_torys_smarttrack_proposals.html. Accessed 2016 Feb 12.

Paradis, C. (2013). Opening Remarks to the Consider Canada City Alliance Event. Speeches. Government of Canada. Available at http://news.gc.ca/web/article-en.do?nid=731909. Accessed 2016 Feb 12.

Parilla, J., Trujillo, J.L., Berube, A. and Ran, T. (2015). *Global Metromonitor 2014: An uncertain recovery.* Washington D.C.: The Brookings Institution. Available at http://www.brookings.edu/~/media/Research/Files/Reports/2015/01/22-global-metro-monitor/bmpp_GMM_final.pdf?la=en. Accessed 2016 Feb 15.

Relph, E. (2013). *Toronto: Transformations in a City and Its Region.* Philadelphia: University of Pennsylvania Press.

Shaker, P. (2004). *More Than Money: The New Deal for Cities and a Federal Urban Lens.* Canadian Centre for Policy Alternatives. Available at http://www.policyalternatives.ca/sites/default/files/uploads/publications/National_Office_Pubs/more_than_money.pdf. Accessed 2016 Feb 12.

Slack, E. and Bird, R. (2013). Merging municipalities: Is bigger better?. *Institute on Municipal Finance and Governance Papers on Municipal Finance and Governance. No. 14.* University of Toronto.

Slack, E. and Cote, A. (2014). Is Toronto Fiscally Healthy? A check-up on the city's finances. *IMFG Perspective No.7.* Available at http://munkschool.utoronto.ca/imfg/uploads/288/0.pdf. Accessed 2016 Feb 12.

Spicer, Z.D. (2011). The Rise and Fall of the Ministry of State for Urban Affairs: Exploring the Nature of Federal–Urban Engagement in Canada. *Canadian Political Science Review*, **5**(2): 117–126.

Spicer, Z. (2015). What will Trudeau's urban agenda look like?. *Policy Options.* Available at http://policyoptions.irpp.org/2015/10/30/will-trudeaus-urban-agenda-look-like/. Accessed 2016 Feb 12.

Tapscott, D. (2014). What can a Toronto mayor actually do to create jobs?. *The Star.* Available at http://www.thestar.com/opinion/commentary/2014/05/25/what_can_a_toronto_mayor_actually_do_to_create_jobs.html. Accessed 2016 Feb 12.

Toronto Region Board of Trade (2012). *Meeting the Challenge: Growth in an Age of Deleveraging 2012 Provincial Pre-Budget Submission – February 2012.* Toronto: Toronto Region Board of Trade. Available at https://www.bot.com/portals/0/unsecure/advocacy/BudgetSubmissions/Provincial/TBoT%202012%20Provincial%20Pre-Budget%20Submission%20Feb%2029.pdf. Accessed 2016 Feb 12.

Toronto Region Board of Trade (2014a). *2015 Federal Pre-Budget Submission August 5, 2014.* Toronto: Toronto Region Board of Trade. Available at https://www.bot.com/portals/0/unsecure/advocacy/BudgetSubmissions/Federal/TRBOT-2015-Pre-Budget-Submission-Paper.pdf. Accessed 2016 Feb 12.

Toronto Region Board of Trade (2014b). *Discussion Paper: Think Twice, Vote Once – Decision 2014.* Toronto: Toronto Region Board of Trade. Available at https://www.bot.com/portals/0/unsecure/advocacy/ThinkTwiceVoteOnceDiscussionPaperSummary.pdf. Accessed 2016 Feb 12.

University of Toronto (2013). *Economic Impact Report.* Toronto: University of Toronto. Available at http://universityrelations.utoronto.ca/gicr/files/2013/07/economic-impact-2013.pdf. Accessed 2016 Feb 12.

Vinodrai, T. and Moos, M. (2015). The Higher ED Blog: Counting Matters. Available at http://economicdevelopment.org/2015/10/the-higher-ed-blog-counting-matters/. Accessed 2016 Feb 1.

Wang, J.E. (2014). *The Missing Link of Metrolinx: Examining the Regional Governance of Transit Planning in the Greater Toronto and Hamilton Area.* Major Research Paper: The Graduate School of Public and International Affairs – University of Ottawa. Available at https://www.ruor.uottawa.ca/bitstream/10393/31058/1/WANG%2c%20Jason%20Edwin%2020141.pdf. Accessed 2016 Feb 12.

Wolfe, D. (2014). *Innovating in Urban Economies: Economic Transformation in Canadian City-Regions.* Toronto: University of Toronto Press.

World Economic Forum (2015). *The Global Competitiveness Report 2015–16.* Geneva: World Economic Forum. Available at http://www3.weforum.org/docs/gcr/2015-2016/Global_Competitiveness_Report_2015-2016.pdf. Accessed 2016 Jan 19.

Young, G. (2008). The Fiscal Relationships between Capital Cities and their National Governments. The Brookings Institution. Available at http://www.brookings.edu/~/media/Research/Files/Reports/2008/12/18-dc-revitalization-garrison-rivlin/chapter_3.PDF. Accessed 2016 Feb 12.

Zeng, X. (2014). Federal funding cuts to science felt in university research labs. *The Toronto Observer.* Available at http://torontoobserver.ca/2014/03/19/federal-funding-cuts-to-science-felt-in-university-research-labs/. Accessed 2016 Feb 12.

Chapter 11   Hong Kong: A laboratory for a globalising nation

Cheung, T., Cheung, P. and So, P. (2014). Hong Kong sending unprecedented 12 deputies to NPC committee meeting. *South China Morning Post.* Available at http://www.scmp.com/news/hong-kong/article/1577872/hong-kong-sending-unprecedented-12-deputies-npc-committee-meeting?cd=16&hl=en&ct=clnk&gl=uk. Accessed 2016 Feb 19.

China Daily (HK edition) (2004). Hong Kong Community Hails Clarification. *China Daily (HK edition).* Available at http://china.org.cn/english/China/92411.htm. Accessed 2016 Feb 19.

Chiu, S. and Lui, T.L. (2009). *Hong Kong: Becoming a Chinese Global City*. London: Routledge.

Chun-ying, L. (2013). *Putting heads together for better economic development*. Office of the Chief Executive of the Hong Kong Special Administrative Region. Available at http://www.ceo.gov.hk/eng/blog/blog20130315.html. Accessed 2016 Feb 19.

Chun-ying, L. (2014). *Mainland internships offer Hong Kong students opportunity to pursue their dreams*. Office of the Chief Executive of the Hong Kong Special Administrative Region. Available at http://www.ceo.gov.hk/eng/blog/blog20140610.html. Accessed 2016 Feb 19.

Chung, C. and Chow, B. (2014). Stock Connect brings HK to the fore. *China Daily Europe*. Available at http://Europe.chinadaily.com.cn/epaper/2014-11/21/content_18954102.htm. Accessed 2016 May 26.

Clark, G. and Moonen, T. (2014). *Hong Kong: A globally fluent metropolitan economy*. The Brookings Institution and JP Morgan Chase. Available at https://www.jpmorganchase.com/corporate/Corporate-Responsibility/document/Hong_Kong-A_globally_fluent_metropolitan_city-final.pdf. Accessed 2016 Mar 16.

Colliers International (2014). *The Rise of Qianhai: An Opportunity or a Challenge?* Available at http://www.colliers.com/en-gb/hongkong/-/media/Files/MarketResearch/APAC/HongKong/White-Paper/Qianhai-Aug-2014.pdf. Accessed 2016 Feb 19.

Denyer, S. (2013). Hong Kong squirms in the shadow of China, its overpowering big brother. *The Washington Post*. Available at https://www.washingtonpost.com/world/hong-kong-squirms-in-the-shadow-of-china-its-overpowering-big-brother/2013/12/09/cc9e48c0-5dd0-11e3-8d24-31c016b976b2_story.html. Accessed 2016 Feb 19.

EIU (2012). *Hot Spots: Benchmarking Global City Competitiveness*. London: The Economist. Available at http://www.economistinsights.com/sites/default/files/downloads/Hot%20Spots.pdf. Accessed 2016 Jan 19.

European Commission (2014). *Joint report to the European Parliament and the Council: Hong Kong Special Administrative Region: Annual Report 2013*. Available at http://eeas.europa.eu/delegations/hong_kong/documents/press_corner/20140513_1_en.pdf. Accessed 2016 Feb 19.

Financial Services Development Council (2014). *Annual report 2013/14*. Available at http://www.fsdc.org.hk/sites/default/files/Annual%20Report-TC%20%26%20E.pdf. Accessed 2016 Feb 19.

Fung, V. (2008). *Hong Kong's Economic Integration with the Mainland: The Opportunities, Challenges and Solutions*. Presentation to Business and Professionals Federation of Hong Kong on 16 April 2008. Available at http://www.funggroup.com/eng/knowledge/presentations/06.pdf. Accessed 2016 Feb 19.

Fung, V. (2011). *The Economic Outlook of Hong Kong in the Context of China's 12th Five-Year Plan*. Speech by Dr Victor Fung to the Students and Professionals at Savantas Liberal Arts Academy on 21 May 2011. Available at http://www.funggroup.com/eng/knowledge/presentations/07.pdf. Accessed 2016 Feb 19.

Government of Hong Kong Constitutional and Mainland Affairs Bureau (2011). *The HKSAR's Work in Complementing the National 12th Five-Year Plan*. The Government of the Hong Kong Special Administrative Region. Available at http://www.cmab.gov.hk/en/issues/12th_5yrsplan.htm. Accessed 2016 Feb 19.

Government of Hong Kong Trade and Industry Department (2016). *Mainland and Hong Kong Closer Economic Partnership Arrangement (CEPA)*. The Government of the Hong Kong Special Administrative Region. Available at http://www.tid.gov.hk/english/cepa/cepa_overview.html. Accessed 2016 Feb 19.

Hong Kong International Airport (2011). Five Airports in the Greater Pearl River Delta Sign MOU: Airports to Expand to Meet Demand for Future Growth. Press Release. Available at https://www.hongkongairport.com/eng/media/press-releases/pr_1025.html?jskey=16431. Accessed 2016 Feb 19.

Hong Kong International Airport (2015). *Our Shared Future: Annual Report*. Available at https://www.hongkongairport.com/eng/pdf/media/publication/report/14_15/1415_Annual_Report_EN.pdf. Accessed 2016 Feb 19.

Horesh, N. (2013). Development trajectories: Hong Kong vs. Shanghai. *Asian-Pacific Economic Literature*, **27**(1): 27–39.

Hughes, J. (2016). Hong Kong Exchange adds new renminbi futures. *The Financial Times.* Available at http://www.ft.com/cms/s/0/3f26f7aa-da0e-11e5-98fd-06d75973fe09.html. Accessed 2016 Feb 25.

Lall, S. and Wang, H.G. (2011). China Urbanization Review: Balancing Urban Transformation and Spatial Inclusion. *Eyes on East Asia and Pacific* **6**. Washington D.C. World Bank. Available at http://siteresources.worldbank.org/INTEASTASIAPACIFIC/Resources/226262-1291126731435/EOEA_Somik_Lall_Hyoung_Gun_Wang_March2011.pdf. Accessed 2016 Feb 19.

Legislative Council Panel on Commerce and Industry (2016). Enhancing the Co-operation Relations between Hong Kong and the Mainland – Retention of a Directorate Post in the Constitutional and Mainland Affairs Bureau. Available at http://www.legco.gov.hk/yr15-16/english/panels/ci/papers/ci20151215cb1-279-3-e.pdf. Accessed 2016 Feb 19.

Leung, C.Y. (2016). *The 2016 Policy Address.* Available at http://www.policyaddress.gov.hk/2016/eng/pdf/PA2016.pdf. Accessed 2016 Feb 21.

Mok, K.H. and Cheunga, A. (2011). Global aspirations and strategising for world-class status: New form of politics in higher education governance in Hong Kong. *Journal of Higher Education Policy and Management,* **33**(3): 231–251.

Nan, S. (2014). *Changing Role of Central Government in City Planning.* Presentation. Available at www.chinaplanning.org/Conferences/4thIACP/keynote/Shi_nan.pdf. Accessed 2016 Feb 19.

Ning, Z. (2014). Building a bridge to financial future. *China Daily.* Available at http://europe.chinadaily.com.cn/epaper/2014-05/23/content_17535336.htm. Accessed 2016 Feb 21.

Parilla, J., Trujillo, J.L., Berube, A. and Ran, T. (2015). *Global Metromonitor 2014: An uncertain recovery.* Washington D.C.: The Brookings Institution. Available at http://www.brookings.edu/~/media/Research/Files/Reports/2015/01/22-global-metro-monitor/bmpp_GMM_final.pdf?la=en. Accessed 2016 Feb 15.

Powell, B. (2014). Hong Kong Protests: Will there be another Tiananmen Square massacre? *Newsweek.* Available at http://europe.newsweek.com/hong-kong-protests-will-there-be-another-tiananmen-square-massacre-273979?rm=eu. Accessed 2016 Feb 19.

Ren, D. (2014). Shanghai earmarks 10bn yuan for facelift that includes 'mini Hong Kong'. *South China Morning Post.* Available at http://www.scmp.com/business/economy/article/1509926/shanghai-marks-10b-yuan-citys-facelift. Accessed 2016 Feb 19.

Savills (2014). Best addressed: Alpha Cities. *Candy GPS Report.* Available at http://www.savills.co.uk/promotions/candy-gps-spring-report-2014/alpha-cities.aspx. Accessed 2016 Feb 19.

Swire, M. (2013). Hong Kong Forms Mainland Trade Cooperation Committee. *Tax-News.* Available at: http://www.tax-news.com/news/Hong_Kong_Forms_Mainland_Trade_Cooperation_Committee____62296.html#sthash.Ouwu8DYD.dpuf. Accessed 2016 Feb 19.

Tam, T. (2012). Fixing Hong Kong's ailing relationship with Beijing under the new guard. *South China Morning Post.* Available at http://www.scmp.com/news/hong-kong/article/1090760/fixing-hong-kongs-ailing-relationship-beijing-under-new-guard. Accessed 2016 Feb 19.

Tan, H.A. (2014). Hong Kong to Raise Land Sales to Meet Home Targets, Tsang Says. *Bloomberg.* Available at www.bloomberg.com/news/2014-02-26/hong-kong-to-raise-land-sales-to-meet-home-targets-tsang-says.html. Accessed 2016 Feb 19.

The Government of Hong Kong (2013). Appointments to Consultative Committee on Economic and Trade Co-operation between Hong Kong and the Mainland announced. Press releases. Available at http://www.info.gov.hk/gia/general/201310/07/P201310070248.htm. Accessed 2016 Feb 19.

The Government of Hong Kong (2014). *The 2014 Policy Address: Support the needy, let youth flourish, unleash Hong Kong's potential.* Available at www.policyaddress.gov.hk/2014/eng/pdf/PA2014.pdf. Accessed 2016 Feb 19.

Tong, S., Lee, S. and Chan, V. (2013). Hong Kong Needs Closer China Ties, Blackstone's Leung Says. *Bloomberg.* Available at http://www.bloomberg.com/news/articles/2013-11-12/hong-kong-needs-regional-tie-for-shanghai-fight-blackstone-says. Accessed 2016 Feb 19.

Vogel, B. (2016). Hong Kong and Shenzhen pledge closer co-operation. *IHS Airport 360.* Available at http://www.ihsairport360.com/article/7355/hong-kong-and-shenzhen-pledge-closer-co-operation. Accessed 2016 Feb 19.

Wong, Y.C.R. (2002). The Role of Hong Kong in China's Economic Development. *Asia Growth Research Institute Working Paper Series* Vol. 2002-26. Available at http://www.agi.or.jp/user03/927_186.pdf. Accessed 2016 Feb 19.

World Bank (2014). *Data by country*. Available at http://data.worldbank.org/. Accessed 2016 Feb 9.

World Economic Forum (2015). *The Global Competitiveness Report 2015–16*. Geneva: World Economic Forum. Available at http://www3.weforum.org/docs/gcr/2015-2016/Global_Competitiveness_Report_2015-2016.pdf. Accessed 2016 Jan 19.

Yao, K. and Borsak, R. (2013). World Bank chief urges China to better manage urbanization. Reuters. Available at www.reuters.com/article/2013/09/18/us-china-worldbank-idUSBRE98H0C420130918. Accessed 2016 Feb 19.

Chapter 12   Moscow: Demand or divergence – the externalities of political centralism

AHML Research Centre (2014). *The Housing and Mortgage Market in 2013*. AHML Russia. Available at http://www.ahml.ru/common/img/uploaded/files/agency/reporting/quarterly/report4q2013_en.pdf. Accessed 2016 Feb 24.

Ant Yapi (2016). *Projects Abroad: Ongoing projects*. Available at http://www.antyapi.com.tr/default-en.aspx#!/projects/projects-abroad/ongoing-projects. Accessed 2016 Feb 24.

Arendator (2016). New Moscow will receive more than 1 million square feet in shopping centers and warehouses. Arendator. Available at http://www.arendator.ru/news/146058-novaya_moskva_poluchit_ecshe_bolee_1_mln_kv_m_tc_i_skladov/. Accessed 2016 Feb 24.

Bank of Russia (2016). *International Reserves of the Russian Federation*. Available at http://www.cbr.ru/eng/hd_base/Default.aspx?Prtid=mrrf_m. Accessed 2016 Feb 24.

Banki (2016). *Banks*. Available at http://www.banki.ru/banks/. Accessed 2016 Feb 24.

Becker, C., Mendelsohn, S.J. and Benderskaya, K. (2012). *Russian urbanization and changing spatial structure in the Soviet and post-Soviet eras*. Urbanisation and emerging population issues Working Paper 9, IIED. Available at http://pubs.iied.org/pdfs/10613IIED.pdf. Accessed 2016 Feb 24.

Brie, M. (2004). The Moscow Political Regime. In Evans, A. Jr. and Gelman, V. (eds) *The Politics of Local Government in Russia*. Oxford: Rowman & Littlefield.

Buckley, N. (2016). Putin's proposals to privatise Russian groups appear badly flawed. *The Financial Times*. Available at http://www.ft.com/cms/s/0/666589a8-d586-11e5-8887-98e7feb46f27.html#axzz414hPbxSO. Accessed 2016 Feb 24.

Chebankova, E. (2010). *Russia's Federal Relations*. London: Routledge.

Coatsworth, J., Cole, J., Hanagan, M., Perdue, P., Tilly, C. and Tilly, L. (2015). *Global Connections: Politics, Exchange and Social Life in World History*. Cambridge: Cambridge University Press.

Collinson, S. (2016). Skolkovo Foundation to launch its first research satellites in October. Skolkovo. Available at http://sk.ru/news/b/articles/archive/2016/02/10/skolkovo-foundation-to-launch-its-first-research-satellites-in-october.aspx. Accessed 2016 Feb 24.

Colton, T. (1996). *Moscow: Governing the Socialist Metropolis*. Cambridge: Harvard University Press.

Crowley, S. (2015). Monotowns and the political economy of industrial restructuring in Russia. *Post-Soviet Affairs* DOI:10.1080/1060586X.2015.1054103. Available at http://www.tandfonline.com/doi/abs/10.1080/1060586X.2015.1054103?journalCode=rpsa20. Accessed 2016 Feb 24.

Department of Urban Planning Policy of Moscow (2015). *Moscow State Housing Programme for 2012–18*. Available at http://dgp.mos.ru/state-programs/se-dwelling/. Accessed 2016 Feb 24.

Diappi, L., Bolchi, P. and Slepukhina, I. (2013). *The emerging structure of the Russian urban system: A classification based on self-organizing maps*. ERSA conference papers. Available at http://www-sre.wu.ac.at/ersa/ersaconfs/ersa13/ERSA2013_paper_01135.pdf. Accessed 2016 Feb 24.

EIU (2012). *Hot Spots: Benchmarking Global City Competitiveness*. London: The Economist. Available at http://www.economistinsights.com/sites/default/files/downloads/Hot%20Spots.pdf. Accessed 2016 Jan 19.

Ernst and Young (2014). *The road to 2030: A survey of infrastructure development in Russia*. Available at http://www.ey.com/Publication/vwLUAssets/EY-russia-infrastructure-survey-2014-eng/$File/EY-russia-infrastructure-survey-2014-eng.pdf. Accessed 2016 Feb 24.

fDi Markets (2016). *European Cities and Regions of the Future 2016/17*. Available at http://www.fdiintelligence.com/Rankings/European-Cities-and-Regions-of-the-Future-2016-17. Accessed 2016 Feb 21.

Goriaev, A. (2008). *Creating an international financial center in Russia*. Moscow: Ministry of Economic Development of Russian Federation.

Khrennikov, I. and Lemeshko, A. (2016). Russia Car-Market Drop Forecast to Continue After 36% Plunge. Bloomberg. Available at http://www.bloomberg.com/news/articles/2016-01-14/russia-car-market-drop-forecast-to-continue-after-36-plunge. Accessed 2016 Feb 24.

Kolossov, V. and O'Loughlin, J. (2004). How Moscow is becoming a capitalist mega-city. *International Social Science Journal*, **56**(181): 413–427.

Kompalla, P. and Nestmann, T. (2009). The Russian Regions: Moscow is not everything. Deutsche Bank Research. Available at http://www.dbresearch.com/PROD/DBR_INTERNET_EN-PROD/PROD0000000000248042.pdf. Accessed 2016 Feb 24.

KPMG (2015). *Doing Business in Russia: Your roadmap to successful investments*. KPMG in Russia and the CIS. Available at http://www.kpmg.com/RU/en/IssuesAndInsights/ArticlesPublications/Documents/Tax_2e.pdf. Accessed 2016 Feb 24.

Krasheninnokov, A. (2003). *Urban Slums Report: The Case of Moscow*. Moscow Architectural Institute, Russia. Available at http://www.ucl.ac.uk/dpu-projects/Global_Report/pdfs/Moscow.pdf. Accessed 2016 Feb 24.

Lane, D. (2013). Dynamics of Regional Inequality in the Russian Federation: Circular and Cumulative Causality. *Russian Analytical Digest* No. 139. Available at http://www.css.ethz.ch/content/dam/ethz/special-interest/gess/cis/center-for-securities-studies/pdfs/RAD-139-2-8.pdf. Accessed 2016 Feb 24.

Luhn, A. (2013). Not Just Oil and Oligarchs. *Slate*. Available at http://www.slate.com/articles/technology/the_next_silicon_valley/2013/12/russia_s_innovation_city_skolkovo_plagued_by_doubts_but_it_continues_to.2.html. Accessed 2016 Feb 24.

Ministry of Finance of the Russian Federation (2016a). *Reserve Fund: Mission*. Available at http://old.minfin.ru/en/reservefund/mission/. Accessed 2016 Feb 24.

Ministry of Finance of the Russian Federation (2016b). *National Wealth Fund: Mission*. Available at http://old.minfin.ru/en/nationalwealthfund/mission/. Accessed 2016 Feb 24.

Moscow City Government (2014a). *Individual investment accounts to help attract investors*. Available at http://v1.investinmoscow.cnews.ru/ru/news/byid/individualnye_investitsionnye_scheta_pomogut_privlech_investorov. Accessed 2016 Feb 26.

Moscow City Government (2014b). Groundbreaking ceremony for the Central Ring Road: Construction of the Central Ring Road launched in Moscow. Press release. Available at http://www.mos.ru/en/press-center. Accessed 2016 Feb 24.

Moscow City Government (2014c). Sobyanin plans to attract 7 trillion roubles for New Moscow in 20 years. Press release. Available at http://www.mos.ru/en/press-center. Accessed 2016 Feb 24.

Moscow River (2014). *About the River. The international competition for the development of coastal areas of the Moscow River*. Available at http://themoscowriver.com/rus/about_contest.html#territory. Accessed 2016 Feb 24.

Moses, J. (2013). Russian Mayors Embattled. *Russian Analytical Digest* No. 139. Available at http://www.css.ethz.ch/content/dam/ethz/special-interest/gess/cis/center-for-securities-studies/pdfs/RAD-139.pdf. Accessed 2016 Feb 24.

Nacar, P.C. (2015). Turkish contractors undertake 70 percent of New Moscow project. *Daily Sabah*. Available at http://www.dailysabah.com/money/2015/05/26/turkish-contractors-undertake-70-percent-of-new-moscow-project. Accessed 2016 Feb 24.

Obrazkova, M. (2014). New reforms aim to make regions more independent. *Russia Beyond the Headlines.* Available at http://rbth.com/politics/2014/06/18/new_reforms_aim_to_make_regions_more_independent_37517.html. Accessed 2016 Feb 24.

Parilla, J., Trujillo, J.L., Berube, A. and Ran, T. (2015). *Global Metromonitor 2014: An uncertain recovery.* Washington D.C.: The Brookings Institution. Available at http://www.brookings.edu/~/media/Research/Files/Reports/2015/01/22-global-metro-monitor/bmpp_GMM_final.pdf?la=en. Accessed 2016 Feb 15.

Railway Gazette (2016). Moscow metro opens 200th station. *Railway Gazette.* Available at http://www.railwaygazette.com/news/news/europe/single-view/view/moscow-metro-opens-200th-station.html. Accessed 2016 Feb 24.

Russian Federation Federal Statistics Services (2015). *Demography.* Available at http://www.gks.ru/wps/wcm/connect/rosstat_main/rosstat/ru/statistics/population/demography/#. Accessed 2016 Jan 20.

Samarina, N. (2015). 'Portals' for the Moscow River. *The Moscow Times.* Available at http://www.themoscowtimes.com/realestate/quarterly/article/523779.html.   Accessed 2016 Feb 24.

Sberbank (2016). *About us.* Available at http://www.sberbank.com/ru/about. Accessed 2016 Feb 24.

Serdyukova, V. (2014). Image vs. Reality: 7 reasons to invest in Moscow. Global Real Estate Experts. Available at http://blog.mipimworld.com/2014/01/image-vs-reality-7-reasons-to-invest-in-moscow/#.VARqhLywIh0. Accessed 2016 Feb 24.

Sharkov, D. (2016). Russia caps hotel prices for world cup 2018. *Newsweek.* Available at http://europe.newsweek.com/russia-caps-hotel-prices-world-cup-2018-426639?rm=eu.   Accessed 2016 Feb 24.

Shustikov, V. (2016). Russia's Skolkovo Center Prints Organ, Transplants Into Mouse. Skolkovo. Available at http://sk.ru/news/b/press/archive/2016/02/10/russia_2700_s-skolkovo-center-prints-organ-transplants-into-mouse.aspx. Accessed 2016 Feb 24.

Stratfor (2014). Russia's Growing Regional Debts Threaten Stability. Stratfor Analysis. Available at https://www.stratfor.com/analysis/russias-growing-regional-debts-threaten-stability.   Accessed 2016 Feb 24.

TASS (2015). Sobyanin signed the Moscow budget for 2016. TASS. Available at http://tass.ru/moskva/2520493. Accessed 2016 Feb 24.

The Kremlin (2015). Working meeting with Moscow Mayor Sergei Sobyanin. Events. Available at http://en.kremlin.ru/events/president/news/50558. Accessed 2016 Feb 24.

The Moscow Times (2014). Luzhniki Stadium Renovation to Cost $537 Million. *The Moscow Times.* Available at http://www.themoscowtimes.com/business/article/luzhniki-renovation-to-cost-537-million/504202.html. Accessed 2016 Feb 24.

Transparency International (2016). *Corruption by country and territory.* Available at https://www.transparency.org/country/#RUS. Accessed 2016 Feb 24.

Turgel, I.D. (2008). *New local self-government reform in Russia: A step to decentralization or consolidation of vertical authority?* 16th NISPAcee Annual Conference 'Public Policy and Administration: Challenges and Synergies,' 2008. Available at http://unpan1.un.org/intradoc/groups/public/documents/nispacee/unpan045243.pdf. Accessed 2016 Feb 24.

World Bank (2014). Data by country. Available at http://data.worldbank.org/. Accessed 2016 Feb 9.

World Bank (2016). *Doing Business: Economy Rankings.* Washington D.C.: The World Bank. Available at http://www.doingbusiness.org/rankings. Accessed 2016 Feb 24.

World Economic Forum (2015). *The Global Competitiveness Report 2015–16.* Geneva: World Economic Forum. Available at http://www3.weforum.org/docs/gcr/2015-2016/Global_Competitiveness_Report_2015-2016.pdf. Accessed 2016 Jan 19.

Zubarevich, N. (2009). Regional Development and Regional Policy in Russia During Ten Years of Economic Growth. *Journal of the New Economic Association,* **1–2**: 161–174. Available at http://www.econorus.org/journal/pdf/Zubarevich_1-2.pdf. Accessed 2016 Feb 24.

Zubarevich, N. (2013). Four Russias: Human Potential and Social Differentiation of Russian Regions and Cities. In Limpan, M. and Petrov, N. (eds). *Russia 2025: Scenarios For the Russian Future.* Basingstoke: Palgrave Macmillan.

Chapter 13   Shanghai: Pragmatism in pursuit of global leadership

Chen, G. (2014). Xi Jinping's visit to Shanghai zone gives new hope to economic reform. *South China Morning Post.* Available at http://www.scmp.com/business/economy/article/1519496/ xi-jinpings-visit-shanghai-zone-gives-new-hope-economic-reform. Accessed 2016 Feb 17.

Chen, X. (2009). *Shanghai Rising: State Power and Local Transformations in a Global Megacity.* Minneapolis, MN: University of Minnesota Press.

Chen, X. (2014). Steering, Speeding, Scaling: China's Model of Urban Growth and Its Implications for Cities of the Global South. In Parnell, S. and Oldfield, S. (eds). *The Routledge Handbook on Cities of the Global South.* London and New York: Routledge.

Chen, X. (2015). China's Key Cities: From Local Places to Global Players. *The European Financial Review.* Available at http://www.europeanfinancialreview.com/?p=4980. Accessed 2016 Feb 16.

Chubarova, I. and Brooker, D. (2013). Multiple pathways to global city formation: A functional approach and review of recent evidence in China. *Cities*, **35**: 181–189.

Du, D. and Huang, L. (2014). *Urbanisation in China: Regional development and co-operation among cities.* UrbaChina working paper series No 3/July 2014. Available at https://hal. archives-ouvertes.fr/file/index/docid/1023259/filename/Urbachina_Working_paper_no3_ July_2014.pdf. Accessed 2016 Feb 17.

EIU (2012). *Hot Spots: Benchmarking Global City Competitiveness.* London: The Economist. Available at http://www.economistinsights.com/sites/default/files/downloads/Hot%20Spots. pdf. Accessed 2016 Jan 19.

FTZ Shanghai (2014). *Shanghai spells out policy plans for trade.* Press release. Available at http://www.ftz-shanghai.com/Advantage/trade_plans.html. Accessed 2016 Feb 17.

Hogan Lovells (2014). *New Rules Provide a Framework for Shanghai Free Trade Zone to Open the Doors on Value Added Telecommunications Services: A Cause for Optimism?* Available at http://www.hoganlovells.com/files/Publication/006f33a8-7c77-4b58-a25a-ddf67cb40c7b/ Presentation/PublicationAttachment/c8469e64-d72c-4f11-8dda-ef9866ea39aa/1092042v2- Client_Alert_-_TMT_-_New_Rules_Provide_a_Framework_for_Shanghai_FTZ-SHAL.pdf. Accessed 2016 Feb 17.

Hu, Y. (2014). A Step Forward for Chinese Local Government Debt. *China Watch.* Peterson Institute for International Economics. Available at http://blogs.piie.com/china/?p=3951. Accessed 2016 Feb 17.

Kamal-Chaoui, L., Leman, E. and Rufei, Z. (2009). *Urban Trends and Policy in China.* Paris: OECD. Available at www.oecd.org/china/42607972.pdf. Accessed 2016 Feb 17.

King & Wood Mallesons (2013). *Making sense of the Shanghai Free Trade Zone.* Available at http://www.kwm.com/en/au/knowledge/insights/making-sense-of-the-shanghai-free-trade- zone-20131001. Accessed 2016 Feb 17.

Lelyveld, M. (2014). Shanghai Blasted Over Stalled Free Trade Zone Reforms. *Radio Free Asia.* Available at http://www.rfa.org/english/commentaries/energy_watch/zone-07072014113051. html. Accessed 2016 Feb 17.

Logan, J. (ed.) (2002). *The New Chinese City: Globalization and Market Reform.* Oxford: Blackwell.

MacPherson, K.L. (1990). Designing China's urban future: The Greater Shanghai Plan, 1927– 1937. *Planning Perspectives*, **5**(1): 39–62.

MacPherson, K.L. (2002). Shanghai History: Back to the Future. *Harvard Asia Pacific Review* Spring **2002**: 37–40. Available at http://web.mit.edu/lipoff/www/hapr/spring02_wto/shanghai. pdf. Accessed 2016 Feb 19.

National Bureau of Statistics of China (2015). *China Statistical Yearbook of 2014.* Available at http://www.stats.gov.cn/tjsj/ndsj/2014/indexeh.htm. Accessed 2016 Jan 19.

Nijman, J. (2007). Place-particularity and 'deep analogies': A comparative essay on Miami's rise as a world city. *Urban Geography*, **28**(1): 92–107.

Parilla, J., Trujillo, J.L., Berube, A. and Ran, T. (2015). *Global Metromonitor 2014: An uncertain recovery.* Washington D.C.: The Brookings Institution. Available at http://www.brookings. edu/~/media/Research/Files/Reports/2015/01/22-global-metro-monitor/bmpp_GMM_final. pdf?la=en. Accessed 2016 Feb 15.

Ruwitch, J. and Blanchard, B. (2015). China probes Shanghai vice mayor for suspected graft. Reuters. Available at http://uk.reuters.com/article/uk-china-corruption-idUKKCN0SZ0QN20151111. Accessed 2016 Feb 17.

Shanghai Daily (date unknown). Shanghai leaders meet Shenzhen government delegation. *Shanghai Daily.* Available at http://www.shanghaidaily.com/metro/the-vip-gallery/Shanghai-leaders-meet-Shenzhen-government-delegation/shdaily.shtml. Accessed 2016 Feb 17.

Shanghai Municipal Government (2001). *The Master Urban Planning of Shanghai (1999–2020).* Available at http://www.encyclopedia.com/article-1G2-3291900016/master-city-plan-shanghai. html. Accessed 2016 Feb 17.

Shanghai Municipal Government (2011). *Shanghai economic and social development twelfth five-year plan.* Shanghai: Shanghai Municipal Government. Available at [in Chinese] http://www.shanghai.gov.cn/shanghai/node2314/node25307/node25455/. Accessed 2016 Feb 17.

Shanghai Municipal Government (2014). *Xi urges city to be bold in free trade zone.* Press release. Available at http://www.shanghai.gov.cn/shanghai/node27118/node27818/u22ai75275.html. Accessed 2016 Feb 17.

The Wall Street Journal (2014). China Aims to Shed Light on Local Debt. *The Wall Street Journal.* Available at http://www.wsj.com/articles/china-aims-to-shed-light-on-local-debt-1409661160. Accessed 2016 Feb 17.

Thun, E. (2006). *Changing Lanes in China: Foreign Direct Investment, Local Governments, and Auto Sector Development.* Cambridge: Cambridge University Press.

Tian, W. and Ying, W. (2013). Shanghai seeking better returns from government assets. *China Daily USA.* Available at http://usa.chinadaily.com.cn/epaper/2013-12/18/content_17182539. htm. Accessed 2016 Feb 17.

Timberlake, M., Wei, Y.D., Ma, X. and Hao, J. (2014). Global cities with Chinese characteristics. *Cities,* **41**(B): 162–170.

Tompson, W. (2015). *OECD Urban Policy Reviews: China 2015.* Presentation at Centre for Cities, March 31, 2013. Available at www.centreforcities.org/multimedia/event-catch-up-what-does-the-future-hold-for-chinas-cities/. Accessed 2016 May 24.

Wei, Y.D. and Leung, C.K. (2005). Development Zones, Foreign Investment, and Global City Formation in Shanghai. *Growth and Change,* **36**(1): 16–40.

World Bank (2014). *Data by country.* Available at http://data.worldbank.org/. Accessed 2016 Feb 9.

World Economic Forum (2015). *The Global Competitiveness Report 2015–16.* Geneva: World Economic Forum. Available at http://www3.weforum.org/docs/gcr/2015-2016/Global_Competitiveness_Report_2015-2016.pdf. Accessed 2016 Jan 19.

Wu, F. (2003). Globalization, Place Promotion and Urban Development in Shanghai. *Journal of Urban Affairs,* **25**(1): 55–78.

Wu, F. and Zhang, F. (2013). *The city and innovation: Building biotech in Shanghai.* Presentation for the Regional Studies Association Winter Conference: Mobilising Regions: Territorial Strategies for Growth, 22nd Nov 2013, London. Available at http://www.regionalstudies.org/uploads/The_city_and_Innovation_Building_Biotech_in_Shanghai. pdf. Accessed 2016 Feb 17.

Yeung, K. and Mak, C. (2013). From Qianhai to Shanghai – resurgence of regional incentives? *International Tax Review.* Available at http://www.internationaltaxreview.com/Article/3284745/From-Qianhai-to-Shanghairesurgence-of-regional-incentives.html. Accessed 2016 Feb 17.

Yeung, Y.M (1996). *Shanghai: Transformation and Modernization Under China's Open Policy.* Hong Kong: The Chinese University Press, p. 145.

Zhang, L. (2012). Economic migration and urban citizenship in China. *Population and Development Review,* **38**(3): 503–533.

Zhang, L.Y. (2014). Dynamics and Constraints of State-led Global City Formation in Emerging Economies: The Case of Shanghai. *Urban Studies,* **51**(6): 1162–1178.

Zhao, L. (2014). *Hukou reform in Shanghai and Guangdong: An update.* EAI Background Brief No. 943. Available at http://www.eai.nus.edu.sg/publications/files/BB943.pdf. Accessed 2016 Feb 17.

Chapter 14 Singapore: The opportunities and obstacles of city-statehood

Bin, T.S. (2013). *Long Term Land Use in Planning in Singapore*. Singapore: Lee Kuan Yew School of Public Policy. Available at http://lkyspp.nus.edu.sg/wp-content/uploads/2013/12/LKYSPP-Case-Study_-Landuse-Case.pdf. Accessed 2016 Feb 29.

Centre for Liveable Cities (2016). *About us*. Available at http://www.clc.gov.sg/AboutUs/Aboutclc.htm. Accessed 2016 Feb 29.

Centre for Liveable Cities and Civil Service College Singapore (2014). *Liveable and Sustainable Cities: A Framework*. Available at http://www.clc.gov.sg/documents/books/CLC_CSCLiveable&SustainableCities.pdf. Accessed 2016 Feb 29.

Centre for Liveable Cities and Shell (2014). *New Lenses on Future Cities: A new lens scenarios supplement*. Available at http://s05.static-shell.com/content/dam/shell-new/local/country/sgp/downloads/pdf/new-lenses-on-future-cities.pdf. Accessed 2016 Feb 29.

Chan, F. (2014). Challenges facing Singapore's economy. *The Straits Times*. Available at http://news.asiaone.com/news/singapore/challenges-facing-singapores-economy. Accessed 2016 Feb 29.

Cheah, B. (2013). Discussing a Sustainable Singaporean Future. *The Independent.* Available at http://theindependent.sg/discussing-a-sustainable-singaporean-future/. Accessed 2016 Feb 29.

Chen, D., Maksimovic, C. and Voulvoulis, N. (2011). Institutional capacity and policy options for integrated urban water management: A Singapore case study. *Water Policy*, **13**: 53–68.

EIU (2012). *Hot Spots: Benchmarking Global City Competitiveness*. London: The Economist. Available at http://www.economistinsights.com/sites/default/files/downloads/Hot%20Spots.pdf. Accessed 2016 Jan 19.

Huff, W.G. (1995). The Developmental State, Government and Singapore's Economic Development since 1960. *World Development*, **23**: 8.

Jones, D. (2015). Infrastructure management in Singapore: Privatization and government control. *Asian Education and Development Studies*, **4**(3): 299–311.

Long, S. (2015). The Singapore exception. *The Economist.* Available at http://www.economist.com/news/special-report/21657606-continue-flourish-its-second-half-century-south-east-asias-miracle-city-state. Accessed 2016 Feb 29.

Low, L. (2001). The Singapore Developmental State in the new economy and polity. *The Pacific Review*, **14**(3): 411–441.

Mahbubani, K. (2015). The City State of Singapore braces itself for challenges to come. *The Financial Times.* Available at http://www.ft.com/cms/s/0/a14b617a-d148-11e4-86c8-00144feab7de.html#axzz3xtU8Ou7y. Accessed 2016 Feb 29.

Mauzy, D. and Milne, R.S. (2002). *Singapore politics under the People's Action Party*. Routledge: London.

National Research Foundation (2016). *National Innovation Challenges*. Available at http://www.nrf.gov.sg/about-nrf/programmes/national-innovation-challenges. Accessed 2016 Feb 29.

OECD (2011). Singapore: Rapid improvement followed by strong performance. In *Lessons from PISA for the United States*. Paris: OECD. Available at http://www.oecd-ilibrary.org/education/lessons-from-pisa-for-the-united-states/singapore-rapid-improvement-followed-by-strong-performance_9789264096660-8-en. Accessed 2016 Feb 29.

OpenGov (2014a). Singapore government takes joined-up approach to tackle climate change. Available at http://www.opengovasia.com/articles/4553-singapore-government-takes-joined-up-approach-to-tackle-climate-change. Accessed 2016 Feb 29.

OpenGov (2014b). Tackling a 'wicked problem': Inside Singapore's one government approach to climate change. Available at http://www.opengovasia.com/articles/4205-tackling-a-wicked-problem-inside-singapores-one-government-approach-to-climate-change. Accessed 2016 Feb 29.

Parilla, J., Trujillo, J.L., Berube, A. and Ran, T. (2015). *Global Metromonitor 2014: An uncertain recovery*. Washington D.C.: The Brookings Institution. Available at http://www.brookings.edu/~/media/Research/Files/Reports/2015/01/22-global-metro-monitor/bmpp_GMM_final.pdf?la=en. Accessed 2016 Feb 15.

People's Action Party (2014). Staying ahead of social challenges. *People's Action Party: News.* Available at http://news.pap.org.sg/news-and-commentaries/commentaries/staying-ahead-social-challenges. Accessed 2016 Feb 29.

Quah, J. (2013). Ensuring good governance in Singapore. *International Journal of Public Sector Management*, **26**(5): 401–420.

Shen, R. (2015). All roads lead to Singapore: Asians study Lee Kuan Yew's mantra. Reuters. Available at http://www.reuters.com/article/us-singapore-lee-asia-idUSKBN0MJ15320150323. Accessed 2016 Feb 29.

Singapore Business Federation (2016). *Position paper for a vibrant Singapore.* http://www.sbf.org.sg/images/pdf/2016/Position_Paper_for_a_Vibrant_Singapore.pdf. Accessed 2016 Feb 29.

Transparency International (2016). *Corruption by country/territory.* Available at http://www.transparency.org/country/#SGP. Accessed 2016 Feb 29.

Wee, L. (2001). Divorce before Marriage in the Singapore–Malaysia Relationship: The invariance principle at work. *Discourse Society*, **12**: 535.

World Bank (2014). *Worldwide Governance Indicators.* Available at http://info.worldbank.org/governance/wgi/index.aspx#reports. Accessed 2016 Feb 29.

World Economic Forum (2015). *The Global Competitiveness Report 2015–16.* Geneva: World Economic Forum. Available at http://www3.weforum.org/docs/gcr/2015-2016/Global_Competitiveness_Report_2015-2016.pdf. Accessed 2016 Jan 19.

Chapter 15   Adjusting to an age of world cities

Andrews, J. (2016). City leaders demand more financial support on climate change. *Cities Today.* Available at http://cities-today.com/city-leaders-demand-more-financial-support-on-climate-change/. Accessed 2016 Mar 14.

Arretche, M. (2013). Governance and Finance in Two Brazilian Metropolitan Areas. In Slack, E. and Chattopadhyay, R. (eds). *Finance and Governance of Metropolitan Areas in Federal Countries.* Oxford: Oxford University Press, Pp. 49–76.

Bessis, H. (2016). Is the new 'Greater Paris' authority too weak to get things done?. *City Metric.* Available at http://www.citymetric.com/politics/new-greater-paris-authority-too-weak-get-things-done-1894. Accessed 2016 Mar 14.

Blais, P. (2010). *Perverse Cities: Hidden Subsidies, Wonky Policy, and Urban Sprawl.* Vancouver: UBC Press.

Bremner, C. (2010). *Euromonitor International's Top City Destination Ranking.* Euromonitor. Available at http://blog.euromonitor.com/2010/01/euromonitor-internationals-top-city-destination-ranking.html. Accessed 2016 Jan 21.

Bremner, C. (2015). *Top 100 City Destinations Ranking.* Euromonitor. Available at http://blog.euromonitor.com/2015/01/top-100-city-destinations-ranking.html. Accessed 2016 Jan 21.

Census and Statistics Department Hong Kong Special Administrative Region (2012). *Demographic Trends in Hong Kong 1981–2011.* Available at http://www.statistics.gov.hk/pub/B1120017032012XXXXB0100.pdf. Accessed 2016 Jan 21.

Census and Statistics Department, The Government of the Hong Kong Special Administrative Region (2015). *Hong Kong Population Projections 2015–2064.* Available at http://www.censtatd.gov.hk/hkstat/sub/sp190.jsp?productCode=B1120015. Accessed 2016 Jan 20.

Centre for Liveable Cities and Civil Service College Singapore (2014). *Liveable and Sustainable Cities: A Framework.* Available at http://www.clc.gov.sg/documents/books/CLC_CSCLiveable&SustainableCities.pdf. Accessed 2016 Feb 29.

City of Toronto (2016). Toronto 2016 Budget. City Budget. Available at http://www1.toronto.ca/wps/portal/contentonly?vgnextoid=e560f459354b0510VgnVCM10000071d60f89RCRD. Accessed 2016 Mar 14.

Crawford, M. (2012). Innovation in Canada: Bright Ideas, Bright Future. *Area Development.* Available at www.areadevelopment.com/Canada-Investment-Guide/Location-Canada-2012/how-Canadian-government-supports-innovation-rd-36342822.shtml. Accessed 2016 Mar 14.

de Blasio, B. (2014). *The City of New York Executive Budget: Fiscal Year 2015.* The City of New York. Available at www.nyc.gov/html/omb/downloads/pdf/sum5_14.pdf. Accessed 2016 Mar 14.

de Blasio, B. (2016). *The City of New York Preliminary Budget Fiscal Year 2017*. The City of New York. Available at http://www.nyc.gov/html/omb/downloads/pdf/sum1_16.pdf. Accessed 2016 Mar 14.

Department of Planning New York City (date unknown). *2000 Census Summary*. Available at http://www.nyc.gov/html/dcp/html/census/pop2000.shtml. Accessed 2016 Jan 21.

Department of Planning New York City (2015). *Current Population Estimates*. Available at http://www.nyc.gov/html/dcp/html/census/popcur.shtml. Accessed 2016 Jan 21.

Department of Statistics Singapore (2015). *Population Trends 2015*. Available at https://www.singstat.gov.sg/docs/default-source/default-document-library/publications/publications_and_papers/population_and_population_structure/population2015.pdf. Accessed 2016 Jan 20.

Escola de Governo (2014). É urgente renegociar a dívida de São Paulo. Available at www.escoladegoverno.org.br/artigos/1984-qe-urgente-renegociar-a-divida-de-sao-pauloq. Accessed 2016 Mar 14.

Financial Services Development Council (2014). *Annual report 2013/14*. Available at http://www.fsdc.org.hk/sites/default/files/Annual%20Report-TC%20%26%20E.pdf. Accessed 2016 Feb 19.

GLA (2015). *Second Wider South East Summit*, 11 December 2015, 14:00 Chamber, City Hall, London: Notes. Available at https://www.london.gov.uk/sites/default/files/wider_south_east_2nd_summit_-_final_notes.pdf. Accessed 2016 Mar 14.

GLA Data Store (2015). *2014 Round Population Projections*. Available at http://data.london.gov.uk/dataset/2014-round-population-projections. Accessed 2016 Jan 20.

Hedrick-Wong, Y. and Choong, D. (2014). *MasterCard 2012 Global Destination Cities Index*. Available at http://newsroom.mastercard.com/wp-content/uploads/2014/07/Mastercard_GDCI_2014_Letter_Final_70814.pdf. Accessed 2016 Jan 21.

Hedrick-Wong, Y. and Choong, D. (2015). *MasterCard 2015 Global Destination Cities Index: Tracking global growth 2009–15*. Available at https://newsroom.mastercard.com/wp-content/uploads/2015/06/MasterCard-GDCI-2015-Final-Report1.pdf. Accessed 2016 Jan 21.

Huff, W.G. (1995). The Developmental State, Government and Singapore's Economic Development Since 1960. *World Development*, **23**(8): 1421–1438.

IBGE (2015). *Estimativas da populacao residente no Brasil e unidades da federacao com data de referencia em 1 de Julho de 2015*. Available at ftp://ftp.ibge.gov.br/Estimativas_de_Populacao/Estimativas_2015/estimativa_dou_2015_20150915.pdf. Accessed 2016 Jan 19.

Île-de-France Regional Council (2011). *Île-de-France world region*. Available at www.iledefrance.fr/sites/default/files/exe-regionmonde_va_web.pdf. Accessed 2016 Mar 14.

Île-de-France Regional Council (2014). *Le Budget*. Available at http://www.iledefrance.fr/conseil-regional/budget-2015. Accessed 2016 Mar 14.

INSEE (2016). *Estimation de la population au 1er Janvier par région, département, sexe et âge de 1975 à 2015*. Available at http://www.insee.fr/fr/themes/detail.asp?reg_id=99&ref_id=estim-pop. Accessed 2016 Jan 20.

Istrate, E. and Nadeau, C.A. (2012). *Global Metro Monitor 2012: Slowdown, recovery and interdependence*. Washington D.C.: The Brookings Institution. Available at http://www.brookings.edu/~/media/research/files/reports/2012/11/30-global-metro-monitor/30-global-monitor.pdf. Accessed 2016 Feb 15.

Kan, S. (2016). Higher Education Reform: A Tale of Unintended Consequences. Nippon Communications Foundation. Available at http://www.nippon.com/en/in-depth/a05101/. Accessed 2016 Mar 14.

Kazakov, V. (2014). New Government of Canada funding supports brain health research at U of T Medicine. *U of T News*. Available at www.news.utoronto.ca/new-government-canada-funding-supports-brain-health-research-u-t-medicine. Accessed 2016 Mar 14.

Low, L. (2001). The Singapore Developmental State in the New Economy and Polity. *The Pacific Review*, **14**(3): 411–441.

Mairie de Paris (2015). *Le Budget Primitif 2015: Rapport budgétaire*. Available at http://budgetprimitif2015.paris.fr/pdf/2015/chiffres_cles.pdf. Accessed 2016 Mar 14.

Mauzy, D. and Milne, R.S. (2002). *Singapore Politics Under the People's Action Party*. Routledge: London.

National Bureau of Statistics of China (2015). *China Statistical Yearbook of 2014*. Available at http://www.stats.gov.cn/tjsj/ndsj/2014/indexeh.htm. Accessed 2016 Jan 19.

OECD Stat. (2014). *Metropolitan areas.* Available at https://stats.oecd.org/Index.aspx?DataSetCode=CITIES. Accessed 2016 Jan 19.

Ontario Ministry of Finance (2014). *Ontario Population Projections Fall 2014.* Based on the 2011 census. Available at http://www.fin.gov.on.ca/en/economy/demographics/projections/projections2013-2041.pdf. Accessed 2016 Jan 19.

Parilla, J., Trujillo, J.L., Berube, A. and Ran, T. (2015). *Global Metromonitor 2014: An uncertain recovery.* Washington D.C.: The Brookings Institution. Available at http://www.brookings.edu/~/media/Research/Files/Reports/2015/01/22-global-metro-monitor/bmpp_GMM_final.pdf?la=en. Accessed 2016 Feb 15.

Phadke, M. (2014). MMRDA used only 40% of FY 2013–14 budget. *Indian Express.* Available at http://indianexpress.com/article/cities/mumbai/mmrda-used-only-40-of-fy-2013-14-budget/#sthash.9RTDvYFf.dpuf. Accessed 2016 Mar 14.

Pinoncely, V. (2015). Learning from China: The positive role of planning. *RTPI Blog.* Available at http://www.rtpi.org.uk/briefing-room/rtpi-blog/learning-from-china-the-positive-role-of-planning/. Accessed 2016 Mar 14.

PwC (2015). *2015/16 Hong Kong Budget: Highlights.* Available at http://www.pwchk.com/home/eng/budget2015_highlights.html. Accessed 2016 Mar 14.

Russian Federation Federal Statistics Services (2015). *Demography.* Available at http://www.gks.ru/wps/wcm/connect/rosstat_main/rosstat/ru/statistics/population/demography/#. Accessed 2016 Jan 20.

Russian Federation Federal Statistics Services (2016). *Evaluation of the resident population of Moscow January 1, 2015.* Available at http://moscow.gks.ru/wps/wcm/connect/rosstat_ts/moscow/ru/statistics/population/. Accessed 2016 Jan 20.

Seoul Metropolitan Government (2015). *Seoul Statistical Tables: The population projections.* Available at http://english.seoul.go.kr/get-to-know-us/statistics-of-seoul/seoul-statistics-by-category/. Accessed 2016 Jan 20.

Soble, J. (2015). A Sprawl of Ghost Homes in Aging Tokyo Suburbs. *New York Times.* Available at www.nytimes.com/2015/08/24/world/a-sprawl-of-abandoned-homes-in-tokyo-suburbs.html. Accessed 2016 May 24.

Societé du Grand Paris (2016). Consultation des Reponses. Available at https://www.societedugrandparis.fr/question-reponse/je-salue-le-projet-du-grand-paris-express-quel-est-le-montant-estime-de-cet-investissement-et-quelles-seront-les-sources-de-financement-de-ce-projet-quelles-repercussions-en-terme-dendettement. Accessed 2016 Mar 12.

South China Morning Post (2014). Shanghai free-trade zone still has much to prove. *South China Morning Post.* Available at www.scmp.com/comment/insight-opinion/article/1608453/shanghai-free-trade-zone-still-has-much-prove+&cd=6&hl=en&ct=clnk&gl=uk. Accessed 2016 Mar 14.

Tokyo Metropolitan Government (2016). *Tokyo's population (estimated).* Available at http://www.toukei.metro.tokyo.jp/jsuikei/js-index.htm. Accessed 2016 Jan 19.

University of Toronto (2013). *Economic Impact Report.* Available at http://universityrelations.utoronto.ca/gicr/files/2013/07/economic-impact-2013.pdf. Accessed 2016 Mar 14.

Wan, Z., Zhang, Y., Wang, X. and Chen, J. (2014). Policy and politics behind Shanghai's Free Trade Zone Program. *Journal of Transport Geography,* **34**: 1–6. Available at www.sciencedirect.com/science/article/pii/S0966692313002135. Accessed 2016 Mar 14.

Woetzel, J., Ram, S., Mischke, J., Garemo, N. and Sankhe, S. (2014). *A blueprint for addressing the global affordable housing challenge.* McKinsey Global Institute. Available at http://www.mckinsey.com/global-themes/urbanization/tackling-the-worlds-affordable-housing-challenge. Accessed 2016 Mar 14.

Zeng, X. (2014). Federal funding cuts to science felt in university research labs. *Toronto Observer.* Available at http://torontoobserver.ca/2014/03/19/federal-funding-cuts-to-science-felt-in-university-research-labs/. Accessed 2016 Mar 14.

Chapter 16   Unintended consequences: Making world cities work for nations

Acs, Z., Bosma, N. and Sterberg, R. (2008). *The entrepreneurial advantage of world cities: Evidence from Global Entrepreneurship Monitor Data.* SCALES Initiative. Available at http://ondernemerschap.panteia.nl/pdf-ez/h200810.pdf. Accessed 2016 Mar 16.

Bonislawski, A. (2016). Reimagining India's Big Cities with Smart Development. Blueprint. Available at https://blueprint.cbre.com/reimagining-indias-big-cities-with-smart-development/. Accessed 2016 Feb 9.

Chacko, E. (2007). From brain drain to brain gain: Reverse migration to Bangalore and Hyderabad, India's globalizing high tech cities. *GeoJournal*, **68**(2): 131–140.

Champion, T. (2013). *The 'escalator region' hypothesis two decades on: A review and critique.* Presentation at Centre for Population Change, University of Southampton, 2 May 2013. Available at http://www.cpc.ac.uk/resources/audio/Tony%20Champion%20ER%20Updated%20Powerpoint.ppt. Accessed 2016 Mar 16.

Champion T., Coombes, M. and Gordon, I. (2013). *How far do England's second-order cities emulate London as human-capital 'escalators'?* Spatial Economics Research Centre Discussion Paper 132. Available at http://www.cpc.ac.uk/resources/audio/How_far_do_Englands_second_order_cities_emulate_London_as_human_capital_escalators.pdf. Accessed 2016 Mar 16.

China Economic Review (2013). Closing the wealth gap is a battle between China's cities. *China Economic Review.* Available at www.chinaeconomicreview.com/China-in-the-red-part-4-wealth-gap-Bijie-pensions-hukou-debt. Accessed 2016 Mar 16.

Core Cities (2015). *Prospectus.* Available at http://www.corecities.com/sites/default/files/images/publications/84819%20Core%20Cities%20CSR%20Prospectus_aw_v4%20final%20to%20print.pdf. Accessed 2016 Mar 16.

Coyle, D. and Rosewell, B. (2014). *Investing in city regions: How does London interact with the UK system of cities and what are the implications of this relationship?* Enlightenment Economics and Volterra. Available at https://www.gov.uk/government/uploads/system/uploads/attachment_data/file/429129/london-and-UK-system-of-cities.pdf. Accessed 2016 Mar 16.

Duke, C., Etzkowitz, H., Kitagawa, F. and Rhee, B.S. (2006). *Supporting the contribution of Higher Education Institutions to Regional Development. Peer Review Report: Busan, Republic of Korea.* OECD: Paris. Available at http://www.oecd.org/korea/36175268.pdf. Accessed 2016 Mar 16.

Fielding, A.J. (1992). Migration and social mobility: South East England as an 'escalator' region. *Regional Studies*, **26**: 1–15.

Fielding, T. (2014a). *Population Mobility and Regional Development.* Working Paper No 74. University of Sussex: Sussex Centre for Migration Research. Available at https://www.sussex.ac.uk/webteam/gateway/file.php?name=mwp74.pdf&site=252. Accessed 2016 Mar 16.

Fielding, T. (2014b). Taiwan's (extra)ordinary migrations. In Chiu, K., Fell, D. and Ping, L. (eds). *Migration to and from Taiwan.* Routledge: London.

Florida, R. (2015). The Distinct Personality of Entrepreneurial Cities. *City Lab.* Available at http://www.citylab.com/tech/2015/08/the-personality-of-entrepreneurial-cities/399677/. Accessed 2016 Mar 16.

Gardiner, B., Martin, R. Sunley, P. and Tyler, P. (2013). *Spatially Unbalanced Growth in the British Economy.* Presentation to Local Economic Growth: Recession, Resilience and Recovery, 11–12 July 2013, McGrath Centre, St Catharine's College, Cambridge. Available at http://www.geog.cam.ac.uk/research/projects/cger/conference/2tyler.pdf. Accessed 2016 Mar 16.

Gittus, S. (2015). Que change la loi NOTRe pour les collectivités territoriales?. *Le Monde.* Available at http://www.lemonde.fr/les-decodeurs/visuel/2015/05/28/que-change-la-loi-notre-pour-les-collectivites-territoriales_4642897_4355770.html#lS7XFAhgJLtWgf2U.99. Accessed 2015 Jan 29.

IMF (2016). *World Economic and Financial Surveys: World Economic Outlook Database.* Available at http://www.imf.org/external/pubs/ft/weo/2015/02/weodata/index.aspx. Accessed 2016 Jan 21.

Im, S. (2015). Mayors of large cities say 'we should establish three different levels of city, along with other measures, to expand our autonomy'. *Yeonhap News.* Available at http://www.yonhapnews.co.kr/bulletin/2015/04/16/0200000000AKR20150416166400053.HTML. Accessed 2016 Mar 16.

IPSOS-MORI (2013). *Ipsos' Top Cities: The largest ever global study on the best city to do business in, live and visit.* Available at https://www.ipsos-mori.com/Assets/Docs/Events/Ipsos-Top-Cities-September-2013.pdf. Accessed 2016 Mar 16.

Ji-Yoon, K. (2015). GDP in Gyeonggi surpasses Seoul. *Korea Daily.* Available at http://www.koreadailyus.com/gdp-in-gyeonggi-surpasses-seoul/. Accessed 2016 Mar 16.

Jordà, Ò., Schularick, M. and Taylor, A. (2015). Betting the house: Monetary policy, mortgage booms and housing prices. *Vox.* Available at http://www.voxeu.org/article/monetary-policy-and-housing-prices-lessons-140-years-data. Accessed 2016 Mar 16.

Kenneya, M., Breznitzc, D. and Murphree, M. (2012). Coming back home after the sun rises: Returnee entrepreneurs and growth of high tech industries. *Research Policy (online).* Available at http://innovation.ucdavis.edu/people/publications/kenney-m.-breznitz-d.- murphree-m.-2012-coming-back-home-after-the-sun-rises. Accessed 2016 Mar 16.

Kim, H.J. (2015). Investment, greenbelt rules to ease up. *Korean Joongang Daily.* Available at http://koreajoongangdaily.joins.com/news/article/article.aspx?aid=3003893&cloc=joongang daily%7Chome%7Cnewslist1. Accessed 2016 Mar 16.

Kim, J.H., Doh, S. and Kim, S.N. (2015). College and Job Location Choice Behavior and Spatial Wage Differences of the College Graduates in Korea. *The Korean Journal of Local Government Studies*, **18**(4): 369–391.

Knowledge at Wharton (2016). Will India Overcome Challenges to Build Smart Cities?. Available at http://knowledge.wharton.upenn.edu/article/will-india-build-its-smart-cities/. Accessed 2016 Mar 16.

Legislative Council Panel on Commerce and Industry (2016). Enhancing the Co-operation Relations between Hong Kong and the Mainland – Retention of a Directorate Post in the Constitutional and Mainland Affairs Bureau. Available at http://www.legco.gov.hk/yr15-16/english/panels/ci/papers/ci20151215cb1-279-3-e.pdf. Accessed 2016 Feb 19.

Leung, C.Y. (2016). The 2016 Policy Address. Available at http://www.policyaddress.gov.hk/2016/eng/pdf/PA2016.pdf. Accessed 2016 Feb 21.

London Councils (2014). Chair of London Councils re-elected. Available at www.londoncouncils.gov.uk/news/current/pressdetail.htm?pk=1795. Accessed 2016 Mar 16.

Martin, R., Gardiner, B. and Tyler, P. (2014). *The evolving economic performance of UK cities: City growth patterns 1981–2011.* Future of cities: working paper. Foresight, Government Office for Science. Available at https://www.gov.uk/government/uploads/system/uploads/attachment_data/file/358326/14-803-evolving-economic-performance-of-cities.pdf. Accessed 2016 Mar 16.

Martin, R., Pike, A., Tyler, P. and Gardiner, B. (2014). *Spatially rebalancing the UK Economy: The need for a new policy model.* Regional Studies Association. Available at http://www.regionalstudies.org/uploads/documents/SRTUKE_v16_PRINT.pdf. Accessed 2016 Mar 16.

Massey, D. (2007). *World City.* Cambridge: Polity Press.

Nair, S. (2015). India's concerns at Habitat III. *The Indian Express.* Available at http://indianexpress.com/article/india/india-news-india/indias-concerns-at-habitat-iii/. Accessed 2016 Feb 9.

Nathan, M. and Lee, N. (2013). Cultural diversity, innovation and entrepreneurship: Firm-level evidence from London. *Economic Geography*, **89**(4): 367–394.

Newbold, B. (2015). Going Up? Canada's metropolitan areas and their role as escalators or elevators. *Canadian Studies in Population*, **42**(3–4): 49–62.

Paradis, C. (2014). Opening Remarks to the Consider Canada City Alliance Event. Speeches. Government of Canada. Available at http://news.gc.ca/web/article-en.do?nid=731909. Accessed 2016 Mar 16.

Parilla, J., Trujillo, J.L., Berube, A. and Ran, T. (2015). *Global Metromonitor 2014: An uncertain recovery.* Washington D.C.: The Brookings Institution. Available at http://www.brookings.edu/~/media/Research/Files/Reports/2015/01/22-global-metro-monitor/bmpp_GMM_final.pdf?la=en. Accessed 2016 Feb 15.

Ram, A. (2016). Tourism outside London at highest level since financial crisis. *The Financial Times.* Available at http://www.ft.com/cms/s/0/69a84ba2-d714-11e5-8887-98e7feb46f27.html?siteedition=uk#axzz42trGVyAa. Accessed 2016 Mar 16.

Rand, J. (2015). Understanding FDI spillover mechanisms. The Brookings Institution. Available at http://www.brookings.edu/blogs/africa-in-focus/posts/2015/11/19-understand-fdi-spillover-mechanisms-rand. Accessed 2016 Mar 16.

Saffron (2015). *The World City Business Brand Barometer: Revealing which cities get the business brand they deserve.* Available at http://media.designersfriend.co.uk/saffron_brand_consultants/media/documents/Saffron_brand_barometer_V10.pdf. Accessed 2016 Mar 16.

Shearer, R., Ng, J., Berube, A. and Friedhoff, A. (2016). *Metro Monitor 2016: Tackling growth, prosperity and inclusion in the 100 largest US Metropolitan Areas.* The Brookings Institution. Available at http://www.brookings.edu/~/media/research/files/interactives/2016/metro-monitor/metromonitor.pdf. Accessed 2016 Mar 16.

Sobel, R., Dutta, N. and Roy, S. (2010). *Does Cultural Diversity Increase The Rate Of Entrepreneurship?* Department of Economics, West Virginia University Working Paper 10–12. Available at http://www.be.wvu.edu/phd_economics/pdf/10-12.pdf. Accessed 2016 Mar 16.

Spicer, Z. (2015). What will Trudeau's urban agenda look like?. *Policy Options.* Available at http://policyoptions.irpp.org/2015/10/30/will-trudeaus-urban-agenda-look-like/. Accessed 2016 Feb 12.

The White House (2015). *Administration Announces New 'Smart Cities' Initiative to Help Communities Tackle Local Challenges and Improve City Services.* Press release. Available at https://www.whitehouse.gov/the-press-office/2015/09/14/fact-sheet-administration-announces-new-smart-cities-initiative-help. Accessed 2016 Mar 16.

Tompson, W. (2015). *OECD Urban Policy Reviews: China 2015.* Presentation at Sciences Po, Campus de Reims, March 2015. Available at http://www.slideshare.net/CentreforCities/city-horizons-what-does-the-future-hold-for-chinas-cities. Accessed 2016 Feb 15.

Index

World Cities and Nation States, First Edition. Greg Clark and Tim Moonen.
© 2017 John Wiley & Sons, Ltd. Published 2017 by John Wiley & Sons, Ltd.